"Books about CBT can sometimes appear formulaic, giving standard accounts of typical, successful therapies. In this book the editors have given the authors scope to craft more varied narratives of couple therapy that capture the essence of working with a variety of problems. By doing so the contributors bring alive ways of working with couples whose experience is often left out of usual training manuals, such as neurodiversity, sexual minority relationships and cross cultural issues. A chapter on separation recognises that a successful outcome of couple therapy may actually be to de-couple. This will be an invaluable resource for any therapists working within the behavioural couple therapy framework."

Dr Stirling Moorey, *MD, Retired Consultant Psychiatrist in CBT*

Case Studies in Cognitive Behavioural Couple Therapy

This book gives readers a rich and detailed understanding of what it is like to work with a diverse range of couple presentations from a CBT perspective.

The book starts by outlining the principle conceptual insights and therapeutic strategies of two different approaches to CBT Couple Therapy, Contextually Enhanced Cognitive Behavioural Couple Therapy and Integrative Behavioural Couple Therapy. In part two, authors working in a wide range of clinical settings describe how they have drawn upon and applied CBT Couple therapy across a variety of issues including: couple distress, sexual issues, infidelity, inter-partner violence, transition to parenthood, separation issues, personality disorders, and more. Each chapter provides discussions of strategies for assessment and formulation and includes examples of dialogue from fictionalised case studies as well as therapist tips.

Case Studies in Cognitive Behavioural Couple Therapy will be required reading for both beginning and experienced couple therapists who wish to draw upon the wide range of evidence-based strategies available in Cognitive Behavioural Couple therapy.

Michael Worrell, PhD, is Consultant Clinical Psychologist at Central and North West London NHS Foundation Trust. Michael has for over a decade been involved in the delivery of training in CBCT for NHS Talking Therapies services. Michael also works with couples in private practice in London. Michael is the author of '*Cognitive Behavioural Couple Therapy: Distinctive Features*' published by Routledge in 2015.

Dr Marion Cuddy, DClinPsy, is a clinical psychologist at South London and Maudsley NHS Foundation Trust. She specialises in individual and couple-based CBT for adults experiencing common mental health problems. She has been involved in the training and supervision of therapists for many years and has contributed to a number of publications on couple therapy.

Case Studies in Cognitive Behavioural Couple Therapy

Couple Narratives

Edited by
Michael Worrell and Marion Cuddy

Routledge
Taylor & Francis Group

NEW YORK AND LONDON

Designed cover image: © Alamy

First published 2025
by Routledge
605 Third Avenue, New York, NY 10158

and by Routledge
4 Park Square, Milton Park, Abingdon, Oxon OX14 4RN

Routledge is an imprint of the Taylor & Francis Group, an informa business

Library of Congress Cataloging-in-Publication Data
A catalog record for this title has been requested

ISBN: 9780367456344 (hbk)
ISBN: 9780367456337 (pbk)
ISBN: 9781003024439 (ebk)

DOI: 10.4324/9781003024439

Typeset in Times New Roman
by Taylor & Francis Books

MW: To Anna, always. And to my sons Tomas and Daniel.

MC: To Matt, Colm, and Zoe, who bring meaning and enjoyment to my life and help me keep things in perspective.

Contents

Illustrations

Figures

Tables

Contributors

Michael Worrell, PhD, is Consultant Clinical Psychologist at Central and North West London NHS Foundation Trust and visiting professor at Regent's University London. He is a BABCP accredited therapist, supervisor, and trainer and an Associate Fellow of the British Psychological Society. Michael has for over a decade been involved in the design, delivery, and empirical evaluation of training in CBCT for NHS Talking Therapies services in England. Michael also works with couples in private practice in London. Michael is the author of '*Cognitive Behavioural Couple Therapy: Distinctive Features*' published by Routledge in 2015 and co-author of '*Treating Relationship Distress and Psychopathology in Couples: a cognitive-behavioural approach*' published by Routledge in 2020.

Dr Marion Cuddy is a clinical psychologist working in a primary care psychological therapy service at South London and Maudsley NHS Foundation Trust. She specialises in individual and couple-based CBT for adults experiencing common mental health problems such as anxiety and depression or living with a long-term physical health condition. She is involved in the training and supervision of CBT and couple therapists at King's College London and Royal Holloway University of London. She has delivered workshops and presentations on a variety of aspects of cognitive behavioural couple therapy for post-graduate training programmes and CBT organisations both in the UK and in France, and at international conferences. She has authored and co-authored several book chapters and journal articles on couple therapy. Marion is currently Chair of the Couples Special Interest Group in the British Association for Behavioural and Cognitive Psychotherapies (BABCP).

Andre Geel is Lead Psychologist for Addictions and a Consultant Clinical Psychologist in Substance Misuse in CNWL NHS Trust in London. He has worked in the NHS for some 34 years in a variety of areas including primary care, mental health, community, and early intervention psychology. He has a special interest in family and couples therapy, is a supervisor and lecturer on a variety of Doctoral Clinical Psychology programmes, has contributed to a number of NICE Guidelines, and has several publications in the field. He also works independently as a Chartered Clinical Psychologist.

Dr David Hambrook, DClinPsy, is a Principal Clinical Psychologist currently working in a Primary Care psychological therapies team based at the Maudsley Hospital in London, UK. Here he leads a team of psychologists and psychological therapists delivering evidence-based interventions for adults experiencing common mental health problems. In the UK, Dr Hambrook is registered with the Health and Care Professions Council as a Clinical Psychologist, and is accredited as a Cognitive Behavioural Psychotherapist with the British Association for Behavioural and Cognitive Psychotherapies. Dr Hambrook has completed post-graduate training in cognitive behavioural therapy, behavioural couple therapy and brief psychodynamic therapy. His areas of clinical interest lie in the treatment of common mental health problems (e.g., mood and anxiety disorders) using individual, group and couple therapy, and in the training and supervision of other psychologists and psychological therapists. Dr Hambrook has a special interest in couple therapy and in the mental health of individuals who identify as sexual and gender minorities (LGBTQ+). He has authored and co-authored a number of peer-reviewed journal articles and book chapters, including articles related to LGBTQ+ mental health.

Clare Kenyon is a Clinical Psychologist and Senior Team Leader in Talking Therapies Southwark (in the South London & Maudsley NHS Trust). She is trained in CBCT, CBT and EMDR and has a special interest in trauma. She has been practising therapy in the NHS for 30 years.

Dr Dan Kolubinski is a couples therapist with two decades of experience working with relationships in various degrees of distress. He holds a master's degree in counselling psychology with specialisations in Cognitive Behavioural Therapy and Child and Family Therapy, as well as a Ph.D. in Psychology. As the founder of Reconnect UK, he provides intensive therapy retreats for couples in East Anglia, addressing various relationship difficulties and runs workshops and training for therapists. At London South Bank University (LSBU), Dr Kolubinski serves as a Senior Lecturer in the Division of Psychology. Leveraging his practical expertise, he lectures about topics involving mental health, clinical skills, and relationships on undergraduate and postgraduate courses.

Dr Natasha Liu-Thwaites is a Consultant Psychiatrist who studied medicine at the University of Bristol, before going on to do her psychiatry training at the South London and Maudsley (SLaM) NHS Foundation Trust. She obtained her Certificate of Completion of Training in Medical Psychotherapy, and she also carried out special interest sessions in neurodevelopmental disorders throughout her specialty training. During her training Dr Liu-Thwaites completed a PGDip in Cognitive Behavioural Therapies at the Institute of Psychiatry, Psychology and Neuroscience (IoPPN), King's College London. She is accredited with the British Association for Behavioural and Cognitive Psychotherapies (BABCP) as a CBT therapist. She currently works in the Maudsley National Adult ADHD and ASD Service, where she is involved in the diagnostic assessment and management of ADHD and ASD in adults. She also supervises SLaM Psychiatry Core Trainees for their CBT cases. Dr Liu-Thwaites' particular interests include CBT adapted for ASD and ADHD, and Cognitive Behavioural Couples Therapy.

Leslie Rossouw is a Chartered Counselling Psychologist specialising in Cognitive Behavioural Therapy for individuals and couples. She is BABCP accredited, as well as a member of the HCPC and the BPS. Leslie has a thriving private practice where she offers treatment to individuals and couples in London, as well as supervision to qualified clinicians and students on post graduate courses in CBT and CBCT. Leslie has many years of experience in a range of settings including adult mental health services in primary and secondary care in the NHS as well as private practice, both in London and in South Africa.

Dakshina Rajapakse is a BABCP accredited cognitive behavioural therapist and supervisor, who has also trained in EMDR and cognitive behavioural couples therapy. She has extensive experience of working in Talking Therapies services as a psychological wellbeing practitioner, high intensity therapist and senior clinician. Dakshina currently practises in Colombo, Sri Lanka.

Dr Anupama Rammohan is a Consultant Clinical Psychologist, BABCP accredited cognitive behaviour therapist and cognitive behavioural couples therapy practitioner and supervisor. She has many years' experience of managing large NHS talking therapies services as well as clinical experience with a wide range of complex mental health problems. She works clinically with couples and supervises CBCT trainees. She currently heads Talking Therapies services in Barnet and Enfield (London).

Dr Satwant Singh is a Nurse Consultant in Cognitive Behaviour Therapy and was a Professional and Strategic Lead for common mental health conditions in a large National Health Trust. Satwant is a Fellow of the British Association for Behavioural and Cognitive psychotherapies has completed training in CBCT and is also a trained supervisor for couple therapists. Satwant has facilitated the London Hoarding Treatment Group, the first and only national treatment group for hoarding disorder. He has co-authored the self-help book 'Overcoming Hoarding Disorder' published in 2015.

Dr Rita Woo is a Consultant Clinical Psychologist and Programme Director of the Postgraduate Diploma in CBT, Central and North West London NHS Foundation Trust and Royal Holloway, University of London. She has extensive experience in working with individuals presenting with complex and debilitating mental health difficulties, including psychosis and chronic and recurring mood and anxiety disorders. She has presented papers on training and supervision in CBT national and internationally, and currently works as a supervisor, trainer, and clinically with couples.

Katy Wood is a CBT, CBCT and EMDR therapist with a background in integrative counselling and additional systemic training. She was a Relate counsellor for 10 years and subsequently worked in a systemic counselling service at Roehampton University and a CBT based condition management service within an employment charity. She joined an NHS IAPT service in Sutton in 2009 as a CBT therapist and moved to NHS Kingston iCope in 2013, where she worked as a Senior Psychological Therapist until 2023. Alongside her roles as a CBT therapist and supervisor, Katy was also a Cognitive Behavioural Couple Therapist for 10 years in the NHS. Additionally, from 2017, she provided CBCT individual and group supervision to couple therapists from three NHS services and was previously a committee member for the BABCP Couples SIG. She now works for Nuffield Health as well as doing some private CBCT supervision.

Foreword

This casebook on couple therapy from a behavioural/cognitive behavioural perspective hits the mark in many notable and laudatory ways. The authors of the chapters are couple therapists who practice couple therapy in the real world in the UK. They know the theory and the research behind these interventions, and this volume is a first-hand account of what they actually do and how they think and feel when they are in the room with a specific couple. They work in a variety of settings ranging from private practice to governmental agencies, and they demonstrate the flexibility that is needed to provide thoughtful and effective care adapted within the context of those settings. Some of the authors are full time clinicians, typically providing interventions not only for couples but for individuals and/or families as well. Other chapter authors, in addition to being therapists, also are trainers, supervisors, workshop leaders, and authors in the field of couple therapy. Thus, the authors provide a wonderful account of how well trained and experienced clinicians implement empirically supported interventions for couples in daily practice. As the editors note, "*Again, our aim here ... is rather an attempt to give readers an in-depth descriptive understanding of what it is like to work with couples from a CBT perspective.*" (p. 11) "The primary question and challenge we presented to our contributors was thus "what is it like for you to practice as a couple therapist, using your favoured approach (es)." We asked our authors to be creative and to include segments of dialogue to bring the therapy alive for the reader and to provide some glimpse into the lived challenges and possibilities of working with couples." (p. 12)

The authors not only demonstrate how the style of various clinicians come into play while working with couples; in addition, the variety of clinical issues chosen by the editors for inclusion in the book is vast and reflects the complexity of couples' lives. The case studies begin where this branch of the couple therapy field began – how to use cognitive behavioural principles to help couples who are experiencing relationship distress. As the field has continued to evolve, theorists, researchers, and clinicians have become keenly aware that there is a myriad of issues that must be considered in couples' lives to provide optimal treatment. In addition to broad based relationship distress, couples often struggle with specific aspects of their relationship such as sexual difficulties, infidelity, and intimate partner violence. Likewise, there are challenges at different points in the couple's relationship that are important such as the transition to parenthood or helping couples navigate the painful and complex issues involved in separation and ending relationships. Chapters on each of these topics greatly increase the breadth of issues addressed in the book.

Couples' relationships are defined not only by the couple as a unit and what they experience dyadically; their relationships also involve the two individuals and their individual well-being and challenges. The editors have chosen wisely and broadly in asking various authors to address such issues, including the complexities that result from one or both partners experiencing various individual psychological difficulties, including depression, hoarding, personality disorders, post-traumatic stress disorder, neurodiversity, and substance misuse and addictions, as well as long term conditions and medical complications. Whereas these individual challenges can exist within the context of a happy, satisfying relationship, often both relationship distress and individual difficulties co-exist. The authors provide accounts of how they integrate a focus on both the relationship and the individuals in such instances, addressing the nuances of treatment including how they sequence and prioritize a focus on these multiple concerns.

Consistent with the editors' emphasis on the importance of the couple's social and physical environment in understanding the couple's concern, the book includes thoughtful chapters on working with sexual minority couples and the complexities that arise from culture and language. The editors note that there are many other couples who are marginalized and discriminated against, and the current chapters are provided as examples and a framework for how to attend to a wide variety of contextual factors that might be central in a couple's life.

The above discussion points to the *who* (the case study authors) and the *what* (the substantive topics of the various chapters). Equally or perhaps even more important is the *how*, how the editors and chapter authors go about engaging the reader in this journey. I believe it is this *how* that in part makes this book unique and so valuable. The editors have structured the overall book consistent with how they conduct couple therapy. They begin with a broad framework and some psychoeducation, including a thoughtful and brief history of the field, how behavioural approaches to working with couples have evolved and its place within the broader couples field. They then provide separate chapters on both contextual cognitive behavioural couple therapy and integrative behavioural couple therapy, the two major behavioural frameworks adopted by the authors in the various case study chapters. Both of these approaches to couple therapy are principle-based and individualized according to the needs of a specific couple, rather than providing a lock-stepped manualized approach to intervention. Clearly, the editors have created that same environment for the authors of the case studies. There is a clear framework that each case study follows (more on this below), and within this broad framework, each chapter author is encouraged to present how they as a unique clinician work with couples, and that uniqueness is respected by the editors. I anticipate that the editors themselves might have addressed some of these cases differently, but the goal of the book was not to subscribe to some universal application of specific interventions but instead to allow each clinician to speak for themselves. And just like effective couple therapy, the book does not merely stop after a specific case study; it must come to a meaningful, integrated close. The editors accomplish that for the book by reflecting on the challenges, dilemmas, and rewards from working with couples within a cognitive behavioural framework. In reading this final chapter, it is clear that the editors live in this couple therapy world; they speak from experience and from the heart. They know what it is like to conduct couple therapy, and they share their many insights and struggles with the reader.

This principle-based approach is reflected within each case study as well, both in the substantive discussion of the particular case as well as how the editors have asked the authors to structure the chapters. The various case studies begin with a brief and informative discussion of the primary topic in the chapter (e.g., depression, sexual minority couples), including important empirical and clinical aspects that sets the stage in guiding the reader through the discussion of how the clinician worked with a specific couple. Then the couple is introduced, including each partner's background and pertinent portions of their relationship history and current concerns, followed by the author's conceptualization of the case and the subsequent treatment. Here and throughout the chapter, the authors provide their own reflections about the couple, the therapy, the clinician's own reaction to the couple, and, importantly, their reactions and feelings about themselves as clinicians while working with this couple. They are refreshingly honest about their reactions to specific partners and the couple, along with their uncertainties about how to proceed at various points in the therapy, particularly when everything does not go as planned. At the end of each case study is a section on Therapist Tips, which includes what the clinician thinks you should know and attend to when working with similar couples. Also quite valuable is a brief list of additional suggested readings, separate from the reference list. Practicing clinicians who read this book will feel supported and understood in the recognition that, indeed, while rewarding, working with couples can be demanding and things do not always proceed as planned nor can be wrapped up on a nice bow.

Pulling all of this together, what might be the takeaways from this unique and valuable book on couple therapy presented in the format of case studies from a cognitive behavioural perspective? Overall, it is an excellent volume with deep insights into the world of couple therapy as it is practiced in the real world. For therapists who are recently venturing into this realm of clinical endeavour for the first time, this book lays out what you can likely expect to experience, written in a lively, easily accessible manner without jargon and with a blend of confidence and humility. For experienced couple therapists, you will likely have many head nods and affirmations, along with many instances of "I didn't know that; I hadn't thought of that; what a valuable way to think about those issues; I've learned something valuable here." And whereas the authors and editors are all practicing in the UK at the time of this writing, other than spellings, a few acronyms, and delightful idioms from the UK which will only serve to broaden the reader's worldly knowledge, this book will have universal appeal to couple therapists around the world. While respecting the uniqueness of each couple, there are universalities among couples as well, and couple therapy follows that flexible, adaptive approach while capitalizing on this universality. The editors have done an outstanding job of creating the context for the various case study authors to demonstrate this dialectic, reflecting this universality of couples and couple therapy while respecting and engaging the uniqueness of each couple and each couple therapist. Reading and absorbing this volume is a worthwhile journey, enjoy it!

Don Baucom, PhD.
Distinguished Professor of Psychology and Neuroscience
University of North Carolina- Chapel Hill, USA

Acknowledgements

There are a number of people without whom this book would not have been possible. First and foremost, our contributors, who have been extremely generous with their time and expertise. They have shown great patience in tolerating our sometimes sporadic response to drafts and feedback and we have both enjoyed and learned from our many discussions with them about the contents of their chapters. Thank you all!

We are also grateful for the guidance and feedback that we received from experts and more seasoned authors in the field including Professor Don Baucom, Professor Andrew Christensen, Dr Stirling Moorey, and Dr Anna Streeruwitz. A number of our contributors, including ourselves, would also like to thank Professor Baucom for years of wonderful supervision with just the right blend of expert knowledge, support, and optimism.

The staff at Taylor and Francis have been immensely helpful and we would like to thank Grace McDonnell and Sarah Hafeez for their support and flexibility.

Although the case studies in this book are fictional, in preparing them we have drawn on our experiences with many couples over the years. It has been a privilege to work with those individuals and couples, who have been open with us about their difficulties and worked with us to understand and address them, and from whom we have learned so much.

Finally, we would like to thank our partners and families for their ongoing encouragement and support, particularly during the feverish final weeks when we were quite intensely and exclusively focused on the manuscript!

Part One

Major Frameworks for Practice

Chapter 1

Introduction – The Tradition of Behavioural Approaches to Couple Therapy

Marion Cuddy and Michael Worrell

Relationships are fascinating! And not just to psychologists and psychotherapists – for centuries and even millennia, writers and philosophers, artists and musicians have explored themes around relationships in their work. Romantic love, family relationships, infidelity, loss, and other relational themes are central to great works of literature, from ancient European mythology right through to modern works of fiction. Countless songs and pieces of music have been inspired by relationships and their challenges. Representations of couples, families and sexuality are common in both Western and non-Western visual arts. In daily life, people often place a high value on their relationships, and this occurs across cultures, though of course with significant variations among a number of relationship domains.

So why are relationships of such an interest to us, and why do we continue to find them so challenging? In England, over 40% of marriages end in divorce (ONS, 2022), and similar rates of divorce are reported in the US (e.g. Kreider & Ellis, 2011). Reports of relationship distress are not uncommon even in couples that stay together (Sserwanja & Marjoribanks, 2016).

Before we begin: a note about language

Couple-based interventions began as 'marital' therapy at a time when there were quite fixed societal views about what constitutes a relationship, it's legal status and gender-based roles and responsibilities within it. Over the years, terms employed have included various permutations of 'marriage guidance', 'couple therapy' and 'relationship counselling'. Choice of words has evolved over the years in line with socio-economic changes. A significant proportion of couples accessing therapy in the 2020s are not actually married, and there is a greater awareness of diversity in relationships, particularly along dimensions such as culture, sexual orientation and sexual identity. In this context the term 'marital therapy' has become much less relevant.

For simplicity, in this book unless we are referring to the name of a specific model, we will use the terms 'couple therapy' or 'couple-based intervention' to refer the range of interventions that aim to support committed partners to

DOI: 10.4324/9781003024439-2

address their relationship distress and/or individual or contextual issues that interact with the relationship.

Couple therapy: a brief history

The evolution of couple therapy has been heavily influenced by contemporaneous developments in the fields of individual psychology and psychotherapy, as well as broader societal changes. Gurman and Fraenkel (2002) examined the development of couple therapy as a discipline in the US, where much of the work in this field originates. They identified 4 overlapping phases in its history. The first phase, which they called *atheoretical marriage counselling*, began in the early 20th century and consisted largely of didactic psycho-education and practical advice giving. This was usually delivered by someone whose main profession was not psychotherapy, such as a religious leader, obstetrician, or social worker. Partners were usually seen separately, and the emphasis was on preventing and resolving common problems rather than on treating relationship distress.

During the 1930s, psychodynamic models of therapy were expanded to work with couples and this led to the second phase, *psychoanalytic experimentation*. Therapy was largely delivered by medical practitioners with further training in psychoanalysis. Initially, this took the form of 'concurrent therapy' with partners being treated separately but by the same psychoanalyst (Mittelman, 1948). As the discipline developed, therapists experimented with different ways of treating relationship problems, for example offering conjoint sessions, or offering both partners therapy with different analysts who would then liaise with each other (Greene, 1965). It is interesting to note that in this modality the therapist was seen as the central agent of change, rather than bringing about change through influencing the couple's relationship. In fact, even though conjoint sessions became more commonplace in the 1960s, the emphasis was still very much on 'treating the two individuals' in the relationship, and the focus was on the patient-therapist transference rather than on the partner-partner transference (Sager, 1967).

In the early 1960s, psychodynamic models of couple therapy and traditional 'marriage counselling' fell out of favour as models of systemic and family therapy were developed. There was an increasing realisation that theoretical frameworks focusing only on the individual, whatever their orientation, had significant limitations, and systemic approaches became widespread. Family/systemic therapy was a brand-new field – it was categorically not an extension of the existing models of couple therapy. The focus was very much on the family system, and the role of the couple/marital relationship within this was one of many considerations. Some authors go as far as to suggest that during this period earlier models of couple therapy were 'absorbed' or 'engulfed' by family therapy, and indeed Gurman refers to this 3rd phase as *family therapy incorporation*.

The period between 1975–1985 is widely considered to be the 'golden age' of family therapy (Nichols & Schwartz, 1998). During this time there were key developments both in ideas and clinical practice that continue to influence the field today. Some of those that seem particularly relevant to couple therapy include the 'marital quid pro quo' (Jackson, 1965), the idea that within couples there is an unwritten set of rules that partners live by to ensure that they are equals within the relationship. Jackson also suggested that one of the main functions of couple therapy was to help partners to become aware of their problematic rules and to help them to develop new, more adaptive ones, and emphasised the importance of behavioural change, as well as insight in therapy. These concepts heavily influenced early models of behavioural couple therapy (Jacobson & Margolin, 1979).

Another influential author, Jay Haley, emphasised the role of power and control in relationship difficulties (Haley, 1963). He believed these concepts were relevant to overt struggles, for example when the difficulty was directly related to a conflict in the couple relationship (e.g. one partner's need for greater autonomy) and also to more subtle problems, for example if the difficulty was around a particular symptom, which he saw as serving the function of 'equalising' the relationship (e.g. an anxious partner's reassurance seeking behaviour). Haley was a strong proponent of *family homeostasis* (Jackson, 1959), the idea that conflicts or symptoms often serve a function to maintain equilibrium in the couple or family, so that any attempt by one person in the system to introduce a change would be met with resistance from the other(s).

Gurman and Fraenkel's fourth phase of couple therapy: *refinement, extension, diversification, and integration*, began in the mid-1980s and still feels current today. It began around the time of the publication in 1986 of the Clinical Handbook of Couple Therapy, edited by Neil Jacobson and Alan Gurman. This phase is characterised by the advancement of empirically supported models of treatment, which continue to evolve and diversify in order to be relevant to particular presentations or populations. Gurman and Fraenkel consider three principal modalities of couple therapy to be key players in the field: insight-oriented marital therapy (IOMT; Snyder, 2002), emotion focused couple therapy (EFCT; Greenberg & Johnson, 1986) and of course behavioural couple therapy (BCT; Jacobson & Margolin, 1979).

It is beyond the scope of this book to delve into the evolution of IOMT and EFCT, but the process through which we have arrived at 'modern' cognitive behavioural couple interventions merits attention. Interestingly, of all the approaches to working with couples and families, BCT is the one most rigorously grounded in research findings and it continues to be the most extensively evaluated framework to this day.

Evolution of the behavioural couple therapies

'Traditional' behavioural couple therapy (TBCT) is based on behavioural psychology and social learning theory and the starting point of TBCT is often considered to be Stuart's paper on operant-interpersonal conditioning (Stuart, 1969). Around this time, researchers were trying to apply principles of operant conditioning to interpersonal relationships. Operant conditioning would suggest that people form relationships because they find their partner and the relationship to be rewarding, or to use behavioural terminology, *reinforcing*. For a 'happy' relationship to be maintained, there need to be more reinforcing interactions than aversive ones. (Indeed, Gottman and Levenson (1999) later estimated the ratio of positive to negative interactions required to be at least 5:1.) Reinforcers are specific to each couple and may be quite idiosyncratic. For example, some people will find a passion for sport in their partners appealing, but others will not. Reinforcers do not necessarily need to be healthy or positive – a shared interest in drug use may be one of the factors that a couple find reinforcing for their relationship.

So, what did these principles suggest with regard to interventions for distressed couples? Early versions of TBCT focused heavily on *behaviour exchange*, an idea not too distant from Jackson's marital quid pro quo mentioned above. At its simplest, a behaviour exchange intervention would involve each partner identifying aspects of their partner's behaviour that they would like them to change, and the couple making a joint commitment to 'exchange' some of these. Although the idea of behaviour exchange was appealing, it rapidly became apparent that interpersonal behaviours were too complex for this approach and also raised some ethical concerns around the transactional nature of the intervention.

Rather than abandoning the behaviour exchange idea completely, couple therapists turned to functional analyses of relationship behaviours to understand them better. Functional analysis involves defining a particular behaviour in operational terms and examining its antecedents, consequences, and the context in which it occurs in order to determine its function, or what maintains it. Functional analysis can be quite complex in a dynamic interpersonal setting such as a conversation, as an action can be both a consequence of and an antecedent for the other person's behaviour. Nevertheless, this method enables therapists and couples to develop a more accurate formulation of relationship behaviours and patterns of interactions that can inform their treatment planning.

As well as behaviour exchange, TBCT emphasised the importance of skills-based interventions such as communication and problem-solving training. Whilst early approaches emphasised the acquisition of these skills, it rapidly became apparent that in many couples, partners already possessed adequate communication skills but were not putting them into practice for one reason or another. This strengthened the rationale for the use of functional analysis in understanding and addressing patterns of maladaptive communication.

The first book describing behavioural couple therapy was published in the late 1970s (Jacobson & Margolin, 1979). Neil Jacobson and his colleagues were active researchers and early outcome studies of TBCT were very promising, showing significant reductions on measures of relationship distress and medium to large effect sizes (e.g. Hahlweg & Markman, 1988). However, when the researchers looked at clinical significance rather than statistical significance, the results were less encouraging; only approximately one-third of distressed couples scored in the 'non-distressed' range on measures of relationship satisfaction by the end of therapy, and even among couples who benefited there were high rates of deterioration at two year follow up (Jacobson, Schmaling, & Holtzworth-Munroe, 1987). Further analysis of the data showed that couples did better if they were younger, less severely distressed, did not have individual mental health difficulties, were emotionally engaged, and did not adhere rigidly to traditional roles (Jacobson & Addis, 1993).

These findings led to the development of 'enhanced' versions of TBCT, of which the best known are Integrative Behavioural Couple Therapy (IBCT; Jacobson & Christensen, 1996) and Cognitive Behavioural Couple Therapy (CBCT; Epstein & Baucom, 2002). These models will be described in detail in Chapters 2 and 3. It is important to note that these models are not 'in competition' with each other and indeed, although they have different emphases, there is a lot of overlap between them and the proponents have collaborated on a number of occasions over the years and continue to do so (e.g. Christensen et al., 2005). Other elaborations of behavioural couple therapy which merit attention include Frank Dattilio's emphasis on family schemas (Dattilio, 2005), Guy Bodenmann's coping-oriented couple therapy (Bodenmann et al., 2008), and third-wave models of cognitive behavioural couple therapy (e.g. Harris, 2009).

Interestingly, although these augmented models have been well-researched and have consistently demonstrated efficacy in reducing relationship distress across a number of well-conducted trials, they have not shown significant superiority over TBCT. For example, a randomised controlled trial comparing IBCT and TBCT for 134 couples experiencing severe relationship distress found comparable rates of improvement post-treatment and at 2-year follow-up for both interventions (Christensen et al., 2006). Nonetheless, there is some evidence that the mechanisms of change may vary across different models; Doss and colleagues (2005) reported that in TBCT, behavioural change was associated with a reduction in relationship distress, and this tended to occur early on in therapy, whereas in IBCT improvements were more strongly related to changes in reported levels of acceptance. Baucom and colleagues (1990) found that cognitive techniques employed in CBCT do lead to change in the cognitions of partners, though they do not appear to be strongly predictive of treatment outcome. So far, it continues to be challenging to isolate the specific mechanisms of change across efficacious couple therapies including the behavioural models (Snyder, Castellani, & Whisman, 2006).

More recent and ongoing developments in the field have focused on the application of couple-based interventions to treating specific individual and couple difficulties and working with diverse populations. There is now a comprehensive body of evidence supporting couple-based interventions for the treatment of depression, when the person with depression is in a committed relationship and the relationship is thought to play a role in maintaining the depression (e.g. Bodenmann et al., 2008; Baucom et al., 2018). Couple based interventions have also been developed to treat anxiety disorders such as obsessive-compulsive disorder (Abramowitz et al., 2013) and post-traumatic stress disorder (Monson et al., 2012), and as an adjunct to individual treatment for anorexia nervosa (Bulik et al., 2011). Involving partners in psychological interventions has been shown to enhance outcomes for patients with a range of physical health conditions including cancer (Baucom et al., 2009). Behavioural couple therapy is recommended by the National Institute for Health and Care Excellence for the treatment of alcohol and substance misuse (NICE, 2011).

The application of couple-based interventions to addressing individual physical and mental health difficulties is thought by some to be one of the most important developments in couple therapy in the 21st century (Lebow & Snyder, 2022). Although the models are tailored to address particular presenting problems, they generally share some common components such as an emphasis on improving communication, enhancing partner support and addressing the problem's adverse impact on the couple relationship.

Attention has also been paid to specific couple issues such as infidelity (Snyder, Baucom, & Gordon, 2008), high levels of conflict (Fruzzetti, 2006), intimate partner violence (Epstein, Werlinich, & LaTaillade, 2015), relationship enhancement (Halford et al., 2002), and particular client groups such as low-income couples (Doss et al., 2020). There has been an increased emphasis on working with more diverse couples, such as sexual minority couples and those from ethnic minority groups (e.g. Pentel & Baucom, 2022). Finally, there have been advances in the format through which couple therapy is offered, with video appointments becoming much more widespread since the Covid-19 pandemic, and internet-based resources being used as an adjunct to therapy or as an intervention in their own right (e.g. Doss et al., 2016). These developments have significantly increased the accessibility of couple-based interventions, and some of them will be discussed in the forthcoming chapters.

Common factors in couple therapy

Although a plethora of models of couple therapy have been put forward, the principal 'schools' fall under three broad theoretical frameworks:

behavioural, systemic, and psychodynamic. These frameworks all share some common factors and authors such as Jay Lebow have written extensively about this over the years (Lebow, 2014). Lebow and Snyder (2022) noted that at an elemental level, models of couple therapy share with individual therapies an emphasis on the therapeutic alliance, on instilling hope, and consider feedback from the client(s) in determining the course of treatment. In addition to this, couple therapists across all modalities strive to develop a more relational therapeutic alliance and maintain a dyadic focus, adopt an 'active' therapist approach, and attempt to interrupt maladaptive patterns of interaction while promoting more constructive ones. Shared strategies across models include working towards greater understanding and empathy between partners, improving negotiation and conflict resolution, harnessing strengths and increasing positive interaction and recognising each partner's contribution to the relationship and its problems (Lebow, 2014).

There is of course variation in how these strategies are implemented across models, and these can be considered across at least 3 dimensions (Fraenkel, 2009):

1   Time frame – whether the emphasis is on the past, present or future.
2   Entry point for change – addressing cognitions, emotions, or behaviours.
3   Degree of directiveness from the therapist, and degree of structure.

Some other aspects of difference that warrant a mention include the duration of a course of therapy, degree of reliance on a comprehensive assessment, as recommended in IBCT (Christensen et al., 2020) as opposed being action-oriented from the start as recommended by Fraenkel (2023) in his work with 'last chance' couples, and the use of language. Differences in the use of language can be a particular barrier to common factors being recognised as such. However, sometimes the opposite happens and terms which have originated in a particular model become used more widely, such as the term 'softening' of emotion, which originated in emotion focussed couple therapy and has become widespread.

Despite there being substantial differences between models, it is important to note that there is significant overlap in what they address and how they address it. For example, although behavioural models are largely present-focused, they do consider the contribution of past experiences to the current relationship. As Lebow and Snyder (2022) put it, *wise ideas become assimilated into other models.*

Although the majority of research trials and training programmes focus on a specific approach and often measure therapist adherence to it, in clinical practice many therapists are more pluralistic in their approach, perhaps working primarily within one modality but drawing on ideas and strategies from different theoretical frameworks to deliver an intervention that is tailored to a particular couple's needs. Some models have gone further than this and define themselves explicitly as integrative, synthesising principles and techniques from different sources into a new unified framework, such as Fraenkel's integrative palette couple therapy (Fraenkel, 2023).

Looking more specifically at behavioural approaches (particularly TBCT, CBCT, IBCT and 3rd wave models), there are several similarities and differences. As well as sharing the similarities outlined above that are common to all models, behavioural approaches focus largely on the present and future (while taking into consideration influences from the past) and treatment interventions are principle-based rather protocol-driven. Behavioural approaches start with a comprehensive assessment of the couple's difficulties, usually including individual assessment appointments with each partner. IBCT and CBCT particularly place an emphasis on formulation, looking at maintenance cycles, and although their approaches to conceptualisation are structured differently there is a great deal of overlap between them.

Traditional BCT and CBCT are often more highly structured than the other two behavioural models, with the choice and sequencing of interventions largely determined by the formulation and therapy goals rather than what the couple brings to each session. These approaches also place more emphasis on change-oriented interventions, whereas IBCT and third-wave approaches prioritise acceptance. All these models acknowledge a role for both acceptance and change-oriented interventions, but even within the change-oriented interventions there are differences, with IBCT and third-wave models promoting contingency governed change (see Chapter 3 for further explanation) rather than rule-governed change. As would be expected, CBCT addresses cognitions and cognitive processes, perhaps in a slightly more direct manner than the other models but it could be argued that all behavioural approaches include a cognitive dimension, even if they do not state this explicitly. Naturally, these models all target relational behaviour, and they also focus on emotions, though perhaps less directly in TBCT.

With regards to treatment focus, in TBCT the emphasis is on developing skills and addressing specific problematic behaviours. IBCT and third-wave approaches tend to focus on broader behavioural patterns, with IBCT in particular advocating a functional analytic approach to understanding these. CBCT makes a distinction between relational patterns of interaction at a 'macro' level and more specific 'micro' relational events and addresses both levels as required (Epstein & Baucom, 2002). There is also variation in the language and therapy terms used by the different approaches. Although there is no compelling evidence that one approach is superior to another, it is possible that a particular model may be a better 'fit' for a specific couple (or therapist).

Why case studies?

Using case studies to describe and illustrate psychotherapeutic interventions is not new. Sigmund Freud used this narrative structure to describe many of his early treatment successes and how he managed to unravel the mystery of hysteria and develop a theory of the mind (e.g. Freud & Breuer, 1895/1991). Of some interest is the fact that today Freud's case studies can be read as good literature, that is, they tell engaging stories, not unlike a good detective novel. Since that time, case studies or *series* have remained popular in the field of psychotherapy. There have even been a number of books presenting couple therapy case studies (e.g. Dattilio, 1998, Carson & Casado-Kehoe, 2011).

Presenting case studies can serve several purposes. In the psychotherapy literature, they are often used to describe a new or innovative approach to treatment (e.g. Abramowitz et al., 2013), or to illustrate the 'gold standard' for an intervention, as in the seminal work Cognitive Therapy; Basics and Beyond (Beck, 1995). At the other end of the continuum, case studies or reports are often used to assess the competency of therapists in training, requiring them to demonstrate a sound grasp of the theoretical framework they are working from as well as how they have applied this in practice.

Our aim in this book is different and is perhaps unusual in the field of the Cognitive Behaviour Therapies. We have not asked contributors to describe a 'perfect' or even necessarily a 'successful' intervention in order to showcase or validate a theory. None of the cases presented in this book should be read as providing any form of empirical support for the models advanced or embraced by the authors! Instead, we have taken more of a narrative approach, encouraging our authors to 'tell a story', to describe their experience of working with couples presenting with a variety of difficulties across different circumstances.

When inviting our authors to contribute, we provided the following by way of context:

> *Due to the ethical complexities of reporting on actual cases, we would like your case reports to represent the 'essence' of what it is like to work with a particular presentation rather than work you did with a specific couple. So, the 'case' you describe may in fact have been drawn from a range of different clinical experiences with several different couples. All of these will be heavily disguised with all potentially identifying information changed. The resulting description of a couple, the individuals concerned, their background, history and manner of presentation should constitute a creative construction on your part. This can be considered a piece of qualitative work. You are constructing a couple narrative that captures the essence of one or a series of dilemmas or challenges – you are not attempting to report accurately on any actual couple. Again, our aim here is different from a traditional case study or case series in CBT – it is not principally concerned with the issue of the effectiveness of the therapy or particular interventions but is rather an attempt to give readers an in-depth descriptive understanding of what it is like to work with couples from a CBT perspective.*

The primary question and challenge we presented to our contributors was thus "what is it like for you to practice as a couple therapist, using your favoured approach(es)?" We asked our authors to be creative and to include segments of dialogue to bring the therapy alive for the reader and to provide some glimpse into the lived challenges and possibilities of working with couples. We hope that the rich descriptions provided in the following chapters will engage the reader while at the same time offering new ideas and perspectives that they can bring to their work. All the couples described in the chapters that follow are fictional in the sense that they are based broadly on the authors' experience but do not seek to represent the therapy of one specific couple. As such, these 'fictions' should be read more as illustrations of the therapists thinking, experience, dilemmas, and enjoyment of working in the field of couple therapy and couple-based interventions.

Outline of the book

This book is divided into 3 main sections. In Chapters 1–3, we will outline what we consider to be the two principal behavioural approaches to couple therapy. (As these have all evolved from 'traditional' BCT, we have not included a separate chapter on this.) The 'main' part of the book consists of case studies addressing a wide range of issues with a variety of couples. The settings in which the therapists work are also highly varied and include government funded 'talking therapies services' and private practice settings. They are written by authors who have expertise in these areas, and we hope that the range of styles and approaches will make for a very enriching experience for the reader. Of some importance to us as editors is that we have approached authors who are not necessarily 'couple specialists' or well-known researchers in the field of couple therapy but rather see couples as well as individuals and groups as part of a varied and challenging case mix. In the final section we reflect on the experience of working with a range of couples 'integratively' and on our learning from putting together this book and engaging with our group of therapist-authors.

References

Abramowitz, J.S., Baucom, D.H., Wheaton, M.G., Boeding, S., Fabricant, L.E., Paprocki, C., & Fischer, M.S. (2013). Enhancing Exposure and Response Prevention for OCD: A Couple-Based Approach. *Behavior Modification*, 37 (2), 189–210. doi:10.1177/0145445512444596.

Baucom, D.H., Sayers S.L., & Sher, T.G. (1990). Supplementing behavioral marital therapy with cognitive restructuring and emotional expressiveness training: an outcome investigation. *Journal of Consulting and Clinical Psychology*, 58, 636–645.

Baucom, D.H., Fischer, M.S., Worrell, M., Corrie, S., Belus, J.M., Molyva, E., & Boeding, S. (2018). Couple-based intervention for depression: an effectiveness study in the National Health Service in England. *Family Process*, 57, 275–292.

Baucom, D.H., Porter, L.S., Kirby, J.S., Gremore, T.M., Wiesenthal, N, Aldridge, W., Fredman, S.J., Stanton, S.E., Scott, J.L., Halford, K.W., & Keefe, F.J. (2009). A couple-based intervention for female breast cancer. *Psycho-oncology*, 18 (3), 276–283. doi:10.1002/pon.1395. PMID: 18702064.

Beck, J. S. (1995). *Cognitive Therapy: basics and beyond*. New York: The Guilford Press.

Bodenmann, G., Plancherel, B., Beach, S.R.H., Widmer, K., Gabriel, B., Meuwly, N., Charvoz, L., Hautzinger, M., & Schramm, E. (2008). Effects of coping-oriented couples therapy on depression: A randomized clinical trial. *Journal of Consulting and Clinical Psychology*, 76 (6), 944–954.

Bulik, C.M., Baucom, D.H., Kirby, J.S., & Pisetsky, E. (2011). Uniting Couples (in the treatment of) Anorexia Nervosa (UCAN). *International Journal of Eating Disorders*, 44 (1), 19–28. doi:10.1002/eat.20790. PMID: 20063308; PMCID: PMC2889168.

Carson, D.K., & Casado-Kehoe, M. (2011). *Case studies in couples therapy: Theory-based approaches*. Routledge.

Christensen, A., Baucom, D.H., Vu, C.T.-A., & Stanton, S. (2005). Methodologically Sound, Cost-Effective Research on the Outcome of Couple Therapy. *Journal of Family Psychology*, 19(1), 6–17.

Christensen, A., Atkins, D.C., Yi, J., Baucom, D.H., & George, W.H. (2006). Couple and individual adjustment for 2 years following a randomized clinical trial comparing traditional versus integrative behavioral couple therapy. *Journal of Consulting and Clinical Psychology*, 74, 1180–1191.

Christensen, A., Doss, B.D., & Jacobson, N.S. (2020). *Integrative behavioral couple therapy: A therapist's guide to creating acceptance and change*. New York: W.W. Norton & Company.

Dattilio, F.M. (Ed.). (1998). *Case studies in couple and family therapy: Systemic and cognitive perspectives*. Guilford Press.

Dattilio, F.M. (2005). The Restructuring of Family Schemas: A Cognitive-Behavior Perspective. *Journal of Marital and Family Therapy*, 31 (1), 15–30. doi:10.1111/j.1752-0606.2005.tb01540.x.

Doss, B.D., Cicila, L.N., Georgia, E.J., Roddy, M.K., Nowlan, K.M., Benson, L.A., & Christensen, A. (2016). A randomized controlled trial of the web-based OurRelationship program: Effects on relationship and individual functioning. *Journal of Consulting and Clinical Psychology*, 84 (4), 285–296.

Doss, B. D., Knopp, K., Roddy, M.K., Rothman, K., Hatch, S.G., & Rhoades, G.K. (2020). Online programs improve relationship functioning for distressed low-income couples: Results from a nationwide randomized controlled trial. *Journal of Consulting and Clinical Psychology*, 88(4), 283–294.

Doss, B.D., Thum Y.M., Sevier M., Atkins D.C., Christensen A. (2005). Improving relationships: mechanisms of change in couple therapy. *Journal of Consulting and Clinical Psychology*, 73 (4), 624–633.

Epstein, N.B., & Baucom, D.H. (2002). *Enhanced cognitive-behavioral therapy for couples: A contextual approach*. American Psychological Association. doi:10.1037/10481-000.

Epstein, N.B., Werlinich, C.A., & LaTaillade, J.J. (2015). Couple therapy for partner aggression. In A.S. Gurman, J.L. Lebow, & D.K. Snyder (Eds.), *Clinical handbook of couple therapy* (pp. 389–411). The Guilford Press.

Fraenkel, P. (2009). The therapeutic palette: A guide to choice points in integrative couple therapy. *Clinical Social Work Journal*, 37 (3), 234–247.

Fraenkel, P. (2023). *Last Chance Couple Therapy: Bringing Relationships Back From The Brink*. W.W. Norton & Company.

Freud, S., & Breuer, J. (1895/1991) *Studies on Hysteria*. London: Penguin.

Fruzzetti, A. (2006). *The High Conflict Couple: A Dialectical Behavior Therapy Guide to Finding Peace, Intimacy, and Validation*. New Harbinger Publications.

Gottman, J.M., & Levenson, R.W. (1999). What predicts change in marital interaction over time? A study of alternative medicine. *Family Process*, 38 (2), 143–158. doi:10.1111/j.1545-5300.1999.00143.

Gurman, A.S., & Fraenkel, P. (2002). The history of couple therapy: A millennial review. *Family Process*, 41 (2), 199–260. doi:10.1111/j.1545-5300.2002.41204.x.

Greenberg, L.S., & Johnson, S.M. (1986). Emotionally focused couples therapy (pp. 253–278). In N.S. Jacobson & A.S. Gurman (eds.), *Clinical handbook of marital therapy*. New York: Guilford Press.

Greene, B.L. (ed.). (1965). *The psychotherapies of marital disharmony*. New York: The Free Press.

Hahlweg, K., & Markman, H. J. (1988). Effectiveness of behavioral marital therapy: Empirical status of behavioral techniques in preventing and alleviating marital distress. *Journal of Consulting and Clinical Psychology*, 56 (3), 440–447.

Haley, J. (1963). Marriage therapy. *Archives of General Psychiatry*, 8: 213–234.

Halford, W.K., Markman, H.J., Stanley, S., & Kline, G.H. (2002). Relationship enhancement. In D.H. Sprenkle (ed.), *Effectiveness research in marriage and family therapy* (pp. 191–222). American Association for Marriage and Family Therapy.

Harris, R. (2009). *ACT with love: Stop struggling, reconcile differences, and strengthen your relationship with acceptance and commitment therapy*. New Harbinger Publications.

Jackson, D.D. (1959). Family interaction, family homeostasis and some implications for conjoint family psychotherapy (pp. 122–141). In J. Masserman (ed.), *Individual and family dynamics*. New York: Grune & Stratton.

Jackson, D.D. (1965). Family rules: The marital quid pro quo. *Archives of General Psychiatry* 12: 589–594.

Jacobson, N.S., & Addis, M.E. (1993). Research on couples and couples therapy: What do we know? Where are we going? *Journal of Consulting and Clinical Psychology*, 61, 85–93.

Jacobson, N.S., Schmaling, K.B., & Holtzworth-Munroe, A. (1987). Component analysis of behavioral marital therapy: 2-year follow-up and prediction of relapse. *Journal of Marital and Family Therapy*, 13, 187–195.

Jacobson, N.S., & Christensen, A. (1996). *Integrative behavioral couple therapy*. New York: W.W. Norton.

Jacobson, N.S. & Gurman, A.S. (eds.). (1986). *Clinical handbook of marital therapy*. New York: Guilford Press.

Jacobson, N.S., & Margolin, G. (1979). *Marital therapy: Strategies based on social learning and behavior exchange principles*. New York: Brunner/Mazel.

Kreider, R.M., & Ellis, R. (2011). *Number, timing, and duration of marriages and divorces: 2009* (Current Population Reports, P70–125). Washington, DC: U.S. Census Bureau.

Lebow, J. (2014). Common factors. In J. Lebow, *Couple and family therapy: An integrative map of the territory* (pp. 113–128). American Psychological Association.

Lebow, J., & Snyder, D. K. (2022). Couple therapy in the 2020s: Current status and emerging developments. *Family Process*, 61, 1359–1385. doi:10.1111/famp.12824.

Mittelman, B. (1948). The concurrent analysis of married couples. *Psychiatric Quarterly*, 17, 182–197.

Monson, C.M., Fredman, S.J., Macdonald, A., Pukay-Martin, N.D., Resick, P.A., & Schnurr, P.P. (2012). Effect of cognitive-behavioral couple therapy for PTSD: A randomized controlled trial. *JAMA*, 308, 700–709. doi:10.1001/jama.2012.9307.

National Institute for Health and Care Excellence (2011). *Alcohol-use disorders: diagnosis, assessment and management of harmful drinking and alcohol dependence.* CG115. Available at: https://www.nice.org.uk/guidance/cg115 (Accessed 24 January 2024).

Nichols, M.P., & Schwartz, R.C. (1998). *Family therapy: Concepts and methods.* Boston: Allyn & Bacon.

Office for National Statistics (ONS), released 2 November 2022, ONS website, statistical bulletin, *Divorces in England and Wales: 2021*.

Pentel, K.Z., & Baucom, D.H. (2022). A clinical framework for sexual minority couple therapy. *Couple and Family Psychology: Research and Practice*, 11 (2), 177–191.

Sager, C.J. (1967). The conjoint session in marriage therapy. *The American Journal of Psychoanalysis*, 27 (2), 139–146. doi:10.1007/BF01873048.

Satir, V.M. (1967). *Conjoint Family Therapy*. Palo Alto, CA: Science and Behaviour Books.

Snyder, D.K. (2002). Integrating insight-oriented techniques into couple therapy. In J. H. Harvey & A. Wenzel (eds.), *A clinician's guide to maintaining and enhancing close relationships* (pp. 259–275). Lawrence Erlbaum Associates Publishers.

Snyder, D.K., Baucom, D.H., & Gordon, K.C. (2008). An Integrative Approach to Treating Infidelity. *The Family Journal*, 16 (4), 300–307.

Snyder, D.K., Castellani, A.M. and Whisman, M.A. (2006) Current status and future directions in couple therapy. *Annual Review of Psychology*, 57, 317–344.

Sserwanja, I. & Marjoribanks, D. (2016) *Relationship Distress Monitor: estimating levels of adult couple relationship distress across the UK*. Accessed at https://www.relate.org.uk/sites/default/files/relationship_distress_monitor_0.pdf.

Stuart, R.B. (1969). Operant-interpersonal treatment for marital discord. *Journal of Consulting and Clinical Psychology*, 33 (6), 675–682. doi:10.1037/h0028475.

Chapter 2

Cognitive Behavioural Couple Therapy

Michael Worrell

This chapter introduces cognitive behavioural couple therapy (CBCT), a contemporary, principle-based model that, like integrative behavioural couple therapy (presented in the next chapter), represents an evolution of traditional behavioural couple therapy. Additionally, CBCT incorporates an enhanced 'contextual' perspective on the nature of couple relationships and couple distress. This chapter introduces the basic principles of the model and discusses how these provide a framework for assessment and treatment planning. Some of the characteristic and frequently used interventions of CBCT are also described. As many of the case studies that feature in part 2 of this book are based primarily upon, or draw upon and integrate CBCT, an understanding of the basics of this model is useful in preparation for what follows. For more comprehensive presentations of this model see Epstein and Baucom (2002) and Baucom et al. (2020).

The evolution of CBCT

As Baucom et al. (2020) have described, contemporary CBCT has arisen from a confluence of three major influences: 1. Traditional Behavioural Couple Therapy (or BCT), 2. Individual cognitive behaviour therapy (CBT) and 3. An ecological or contextual perspective. The model continues to evolve, and its contemporary practice is also influenced by advances in relationship science and neuropsychological research, as well as a deepened engagement with multicultural research and considerations of difference, diversity, and intersectionality (see Sullivan and Lawrence, 2016). Empirical evidence indicates that CBCT is an efficacious treatment for a wide range of couple presentations (Baucom et al., 2020).

Behavioural Couple Therapy (BCT)

The original version of BCT was based upon the application of basic principles of learning, initially applied to the behaviour of individuals and then expanded to provide a behavioural understanding of couple interaction. At

DOI: 10.4324/9781003024439-3

this most basic level, BCT proposed that distressed relationships could be distinguished from happier or more functional ones by the frequency, intensity, and range of positive versus negative behaviours that are exchanged between the partners. This perspective was soon expanded by incorporation of principles from Social Learning Theory (Bandura) to explore the various ways in which partners shaped, reinforced, and punished each other's behaviours in either helpful or unhelpful ways. The model also proposed that distressed couples also often demonstrated deficits in skills for communication and problem solving and devised methods for directly addressing such skill deficits.

Individual Cognitive Behavioural Therapy (CBT)

As will be seen below, CBCT shares many features with contemporary versions of individual CBT, including a reliance on establishing a collaborative therapeutic relationship, clarity regarding goals and procedures, clear assessment and measurement of progress and outcome, and the development of a shared formulation to explain the onset and maintenance of distress. Conceptually, CBCT incorporates CBT's proposition that an individual's overt behaviours and emotions are significantly mediated by the way they interpret the meaning of events. As well as incorporating this fundamental cognitive hypothesis, CBCT researchers have identified and expanded the range of forms of cognitive content and process that are specifically related to couple functioning and distress. Some important differences between CBCT and individual CBT do present themselves, however. Firstly, at a theoretical level CBCT embraces a more 'egalitarian' relationship between the relative influence of cognitions versus emotions and behaviours. Some contemporary versions of individual CBT tend to highlight the 'primacy' of cognition and see changes in behaviour as a route to cognitive change and changes in emotion as principally the outcome of shifts in cognitive process or content. By contrast, CBCT regards cognitions, emotions, and behaviours as more equal in their impact and importance. This is particularly so regarding the role of emotions, as CBCT has incorporated insights and strategies from emotion-focussed therapy (Johnson, 2015) for working directly with emotion. Procedurally, there are some specific challenges that arise from seeing couples that make the more typical rational-logical manner of challenging cognitions in CBT less workable. Specifically, while it is the case that many of the typical cognitive distortions that are identified by CBT are clearly in evidence in distressed relationships, the fact that these forms of distorted cognition are often about the partner, who is also present in the room at the time, means that more indirect and experientially based strategies for working with cognitions are required.

An ecological-contextual perspective

CBCT is based upon an ecological-contextual perspective that has some affinities with systemic models of psychotherapy. This perspective emphasises that people live within broader systems that have a reciprocal influence upon each other (Baucom et al., 2020). These units, or systems, include 1. Each partner as an individual, with their own unique learning history, personality, and needs, 2. The couple as a unit that forms a distinct identity or a sense of 'we-ness', and 3. The broader social/physical and cultural environment, including family, work colleagues and wider social conditions. Key to this contextual perspective is the need for couples to both maintain their boundaries or identity across time, as well as to flexibly adjust in response to changes and demands from the environment. They need to adapt to normative developmental stages such as moving in together, having children, managing the transition to the 'empty nest' and retirement as well as adjusting to the development of health conditions and other challenges. In addition, the CBCT model suggests that cognitions, emotions, and behaviours must be understood in terms of their reciprocal interactions across these three domains. Consistent with this, CBCT does not identify a single or primary source of dysfunction (such as distorted cognitions), but rather points to a range of factors and their interactions that may be of importance for a specific couple in a specific context. This conceptualisation is represented diagrammatically below:

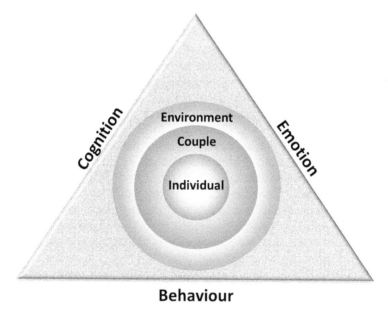

Figure 2.1 The CBCT Model of Relationship Functioning (from Baucom, Fischer, Corrie, Worrell & Boeding, 2020, P 13)

The contextual stance also includes a perspective on the nature of 'functional' couple relationships and of couple distress and dysfunction. From a CBCT perspective, a functional couple relationship is one that contributes to the health and wellbeing of both partners; where they function well as a unit; and where they can relate to the physical and social environment in an adaptive fashion. In contrast, relationship distress is often seen as being the result of the partners finding that their relationship is not meeting important needs or motivations. This frustration of important needs, desires and motives is termed 'primary distress'. In response to this frustration partners will often use ineffective or maladaptive strategies in an attempt to change the relationship so that these needs are met, such as escalation of arguments, withdrawal, etc. These strategies themselves in turn lead to further distress, referred to as 'secondary distress'. Frequently, CBCT aims to assist couples to reduce sources of secondary distress in order that sources of primary distress can be identified and addressed. This is clarified further through a discussion of the primary domains of the model: the individual, the couple, and the environment and how emotions, behaviours and cognitions interact across these domains.

The individual

While CBCT includes a systemic-contextual understanding, it equally highlights the importance of considering each of the individuals and their unique learning histories, development, personality, motivation, and needs. Additionally, current and past experiences of psychopathology, such as depression and anxiety, are important. Thus, CBCT therapists are encouraged to take a more longitudinal, developmental view and to consider aspects of individual functioning that go beyond the strictly 'clinical'. For example, types of individual *motives* are regarded as important in terms of understanding issues such as partner choice as well as sources of primary distress. Important individual motives have been divided by Epstein and Baucom (2002) into those that are individually oriented and those that are communally oriented. Individually oriented motives include the desire for a sense of autonomy and control, as well as a need for achievement. Important communally oriented motives include the need for intimacy, affiliation (the need to associate with others for example through clubs or sporting activity), as well as the need to give to others or the community as an expression of altruism. In addition, a wide range of stable, long term personality factors may be importance such as extroversion, introversion, degree of neuroticism and tendencies to live in a highly planful, detail orientated manner versus a more flexible spontaneous manner. Differences as well as similarities between the partners regarding these personality factors and motives can often be found as important sources of primary distress. Thus, an individual who is naturally more planful, organised, and introverted may be initially attracted to another who is more flexible, extroverted, and spontaneous, and find that early in the relationship this provides them with greater access to the positive aspects of these traits. Later in the relationship, these same traits may become a source of dissatisfaction and the partner is then experienced as too disorganised, flighty, unreliable, and shallow. Partners may conversely be similar in their motives and traits and attracted to each other for this reason, but where these traits are somewhat exaggerated, difficulties can also arise. Thus, two partners similar on a motive for individual achievement as well as possessing a high degree of conscientiousness and organisation may find that they value the support they provide to each other's careers but find that they have mutually planned all of their time to be focussed on individual work projects to the exclusion of time together. As a result, they find the relationship lacking in intimacy and connection. Thus, relationships that are working well may be characterised by a sense that each partner has that *"this relationship allows me to be who and how I want to be in the world"* while those that are distressed may be characterised by *"this relationship drags me down, I can't be who I want to be."*

The couple as a unit

A couple is more than just the combination of two individuals and their respective personalities and motives. Each couple forms a unique system or unit, which develops a distinct boundary between itself and the wider world. A couple considered in this way includes 'emergent properties', such that the way a couple behaves may not be entirely predictable from a knowledge of each of the individuals involved. Couples may often describe how a pattern of interaction has emerged between them over time, they may treat each other poorly (or well) in a way that is distinct to that relationship and not characteristic of their way of relating with others outside of the relationship. Couples that are doing well can be seen to have developed a distinct sense of 'we-ness' and to express that sense into specific behaviours, ways of living and dealing with the wider world that act to maintain that sense of couple identity over time (Baucom et al., 2020). The issue of relationship boundaries is one that can often be a source of couple distress. Each couple, often drawing upon both implicit and explicit beliefs they hold that are expressive of their unique family of origin and culture, need to define what forms of behaviour are 'for us only' and what types of behaviour and interaction with other people are OK and not OK. For example, while living as a 'dating couple' there may be very limited interaction with each other's family of origin. Following getting married, there may be a wide range of issues revolving around each partners beliefs and expectations regarding how the couple should relate to different family members. Thus *"do we really need to go on every holiday with your mother?"* can be a source of considerable ongoing conflict. Couples that are doing well manage to create and sustain a boundary that allows them to demarcate a sense of 'for us only' as well as allowing flexible and adaptive contact and engagement with the wider world.

Couples may at times establish boundaries that are too rigid and impermeable and where there may be a degree of detachment and disconnection with wider relationships. A partner in such a relationship may be challenged by, for example, a good friend who says: "*You know, since being in this relationship we never see you, you seem to have disappeared!*". Alternatively, a boundary that is too fluid and permeable may be established such that the partners do not maintain a sense of themselves as a unit, finding themselves frequently intruded upon by others, or alternatively becoming involved in commitments and activities as individuals in a manner that prevents the maintenance of a sense of 'we-ness'.

In addition to defining themselves as a distinct unit, each partner also needs to consider how they invest in the ongoing maintenance of the relationship. This investment can include both emotional and psychological investment expressed, for instance by a daily habit of 'checking in' with each other regarding the stresses and strains of work and family life. Additionally, partners invest instrumentally through a range of behaviours that contribute to daily life such as managing household budgets, dealing with chores, and making decisions about short and long-term plans. Perceived and actual differences in power regarding these domains can also become a source of either flourishing or dysfunction and couple distress.

The environment

In CBCT, the concept of 'the environment' is used as a broad descriptive term and covers both the physical and social environment, children, wider family members, community, and the culture(s) within which the couple lives. The couple's interaction with the wider environment is regarded as reciprocal, that is, while the couple is affected and influenced by the environment, they themselves have an impact on that environment (Baucom, et al., 2020). Additionally, the environment can also be understood in terms of the degree to which it acts as a stressor, placing demands and challenges upon each individual and the couple as a unit, as well as a potential resource. For example, a couple that relates to a wider extended family, where grandparents and others are available to provide childcare as well as advice and financial resources, experience significant advantages. Alternatively, many couples live in social environments that do not support their identity as a couple. For example, couples may experience forms of racism and discrimination that act as an ongoing chronic stressor on them both. Non cisgender couples may encounter forms of aggression and discrimination from the wider social environment that tax their ability to manage as individuals and to maintain an adaptive relationship. Couples may also experience conflict between each partner in terms of their beliefs and expectations regarding how these wider social stressors should be managed, for example, in a gay or lesbian partnership where each partner has different beliefs regarding how 'out' they should be.

In summary, CBCT takes a wide lens when attempting to understand couple functioning and distress. This includes a focus on understanding each individual involved, including long term stable personality differences and needs, the couple as a unique unit with its own emergent properties, as well as the environment in which the couple lives and moves. Additionally, CBCT explores how factors central to CBT, behaviours, cognitions, and emotions, have a wide range of reciprocal influence across these domains. Behavioural, cognitive, and emotional factors that are of importance to understanding couple relationships are discussed briefly below.

Behavioural factors

True to its roots in BCT, CBCT has maintained a strong focus on understanding and working with behavioural factors in couples. As discussed earlier, a relatively simple distinction can be made between 'positive' and 'negative' behaviours. Here positive and negative are defined primarily in terms of the consequences of the behaviour in question for relationship functioning and satisfaction. CBCT, like BCT, often includes the aim of shifting the relative balance of positive to negative behaviours in the direction of more positive and fewer negative behaviours. As negative behaviours appear to have a strong detrimental impact on the quality of a relationship, an early treatment priority is often to reduce their frequency, range, and intensity. Negative behaviours can also be seen to range on a continuum from mild, frequent, every day annoyances (*"why, oh why do you still leave the toilet seat up after all these years?"*), to more damaging patterns of criticism, judgement and contempt that act to undermine a partner's self-esteem and confidence, to more extreme forms of negative behaviours such as inter-partner violence and forms of infidelity that disrupt central standards and beliefs regarding belonging, safety, and identity.

While the distinction between positive and negative behaviours may seem obvious, what may appear less so is that fact that patterns of negative and positive behaviour can be seen as in some sense existing on separate orthogonal continua. That is, couples can be seen to exhibit a range of different patterns of both positive and negative behaviours. Thus, a particular relationship may be characterised by both a high level of positive *and* negative behaviours. Here a couple can be seen to often argue and fight, and may during these fights be very critical and verbally attacking of each other. Soon after however, they may make up passionately and express a great deal of positivity towards each other. These couples may be viewed as highly passionate and engaged. Alternatively, a couple may present to a therapist characterised by a low level of both positive and negative behaviours. These couple relationships can be experienced as 'empty' and lacking in liveliness, they are no longer arguing and fighting and have instead 'checked out'. Alternatively, a couple may be characterised by a high degree of negative behaviours and a low level of positive behaviours, a not infrequent presentation in couple therapy. The pattern of a high degree of positive behaviours and a low degree of negative behaviours is less likely to show up in a couple therapist's office (as they are instead out for a romantic dinner).

In addition to specific categories and forms of positive and negative behaviours that may characterise the individuals and the couple as a unit, CBCT researchers have also identified a range of cross-situational patterns of behaviour that are important processes to address in therapy. This includes patterns of 'negative reciprocity' where one partner's negative behaviour is responded to with a matching or escalating negative behaviour in a 'tit for tat' fashion. Additionally, during disagreements couples may exhibit characteristic patterns of 'approach' and 'withdraw' that are important to assess and work with. This can include the frequently occurring pattern of 'demand-withdraw' (Christensen, 1988). In this pattern one partner (perhaps in an attempt to get an important need meet, or to address an issue requiring a decision) approaches their partner who, for a wide range of reasons, may block or withdraw from this attempt at contact and engagement. In response to this withdrawal or blocking (what Gottman, 1994, refers to as 'stonewalling') the first partner escalates their approach behaviours which in turn results in further withdrawal and blocking. Other patterns of interaction include 'approach-approach' as well as 'withdraw-withdraw'. Thus, in addition to assessing, formulating, and working with specific forms of positive and negative behaviours, the CBCT therapist addresses these cross-situational inter-partner patterns that in turn may be expressive of central themes in the relationship, such as difficulties and differences regarding a need for intimacy, or power and control, etc.

A particularly important class of behaviours, and a frequent focus in CBCT, as well as couple therapies of many different orientations, concerns communication behaviours. One of the most frequently identified issues that brings couples to a therapist's office is difficulties in communication. CBCT makes a broad distinction between two primary forms of couple communication (Epstein and Baucom, 2002). The first is couple conversations that are directed towards creating intimacy and connection, what has been broadly termed 'sharing thought and feelings'. The function of such conversations is to help each partner feel that their inner world of experience and their central concerns are understood by their partner, thereby meeting needs for intimacy and connection, and helping couples regulate their emotional experience. The second form of couple communication is focussed upon decision making or problem solving. The function of this form of communication is to support the couple in meeting important goals and managing challenges from the environment. Adaptive couple functioning is characterised by the couple's ability to engage in both forms of conversation as the situation demands in a flexible fashion. As will be further described below, CBCT often involves working directly with the couple's skill in utilising these forms of conversation as a vehicle to both reduce secondary distress (reducing arguments) and address key sources of primary distress (allowing communication and understanding of core needs and motives and making decisions about how best to accommodate both partners' perspectives and desires in an adaptive fashion).

Cognitive factors

The broad field of CBT has been highly successful in identifying a wide range of cognitive processes and content that are related to various forms of psychological distress. Given that different forms of individual psychopathology have been found to be reciprocally influenced by relationship functioning, these cognitive factors are highly relevant to understanding of relationships (Baucom et al., 2020). In addition to cognitive factors related to psychopathology, CBCT identifies a range of cognitions and cognitive processes that are closely associated with couple distress, both in terms of factors that may lead to couple distress and its maintenance as well as those that may be a consequence of relationship distress. Below is a brief description of some of these key cognitive factors.

Selective attention

Selective attention refers to a process by which an individual attends to and interprets information in a biased fashion. Thus, an individual in a situation of relationship distress may only attend to negative behaviours of their partner while selectively in-attending to their positive behaviours. This negative selective attention is likely to be both expressive of and contribute to the maintenance of an individual's negative view of the partner and the possibilities of the relationship. Conversely, a positively skewed selective attention can be seen early on in a relationship where negative aspects of the partner (or self in relation to the partner) are brushed over and positive aspects are highlighted or even exaggerated. Selective attention may operate largely out of awareness.

Attributions

Attributions are a class of cognition principally concerned with issues of causality and responsibility. That is, individuals often seek to understand the 'why' of their own behaviour as well as the behaviour of their partner and in situations of couple distress may show a pattern of negative attributions. Thus, after selectively attending to the partner's apparent neglect of household chores, an attribution may be made that this is due to the 'fact' that the other does not care, is lazy, and is unable and unwilling to change, that is, they have not completed the household chores *because* they are lazy and uncaring. Making attributions, like selective attention, is an automatic and normal process and problems arise more when attributions are biased or rigid and thus contribute to the maintenance of relationship distress.

Assumptions, Standards, and Expectancies

Assumptions refer to an individual's beliefs regarding 'the way things are', while standards refer to their beliefs regarding 'the way things should be'. Expectancies are cognitions chiefly concerned with predictions about the future. Like the other forms of cognition mentioned above, assumptions, standards and expectancies may be strongly held, at times rigid, and distorted in a way that is associated with couple distress. Individuals may hold a wide range of assumptions that are expressive of their developmental history and cultural background. For example, assumptions may include 'men are naturally bad at expressing emotion' or 'women are naturally more gifted in dealing with children'. Many standards that individuals hold are linked to their cultural background. For example, depending upon cultural background a partner may have important standards regarding how appropriate or otherwise it is to express affection in public or in front of other family members. Couples who come from differing cultural backgrounds may find themselves in conflict in a manner that is related to such unspoken standards.

Relational Schematic Processing

Relational schematic processing is regarded as a relatively stable way of processing information about self in relation to others. As such it can also be regarded as an individual difference variable (Baucom et al., 2020). Each partner will fall somewhere on a continuum between high versus low levels of relational schematic processing. Individuals high on this cognitive aspect tend to experience events in the world primarily in terms of how these events are relevant to their relationships. That is, their tendency is to process information in terms of 'us'. For example, when an individual relatively high on this attribute is offered an exciting new job role in another part of the country, they may in the first instance have automatic thoughts and emotions related to a concern of *"how will this affect us? what will it mean for the two of us?"* Individuals low on this variable (Individual schematic processing) tend to process information in terms of 'I'. In the same example, their immediate reactions, including thoughts and emotions, may express the concern *"what will this mean for me?"* They may subsequently also consider the relational implications however this may be secondary and effortful rather than their standard, automatic way of perceiving the world. One way that

couple therapies of all orientations may 'work' is by helping people understand their position on this continuum as well as that of their partner, and
assisting in a shift towards a greater facility for relational schematic processing
where this would be helpful.

Emotional factors

CBCT has greatly enhanced the emphasis on and importance of emotions in
understanding couple relationships and has incorporated many strategies for
working directly with emotions in sessions with couples (Epstein and
Baucom, 2002). Like behaviours, emotions can be described as existing along
a number of dimensions in terms of intensity and duration, as well as positivity or negativity. Negative and positive emotions can be understood as
existing on different dimensions so that an individual or couple can, for
example, display both high degrees of positive and negative emotions or
alternatively low levels of positive emotions and high levels of negative
emotions (as well as other patterns). In addition to the dimensions of positive versus negative, individuals and couples differ in their ability to become
aware of, find language for, and communicate their emotional experience.
Furthermore, individuals and couples show great variability in their capacity
to regulate their emotions, and to soothe each other when distressed. Challenges may be presented to a couple therapist in this domain in situations
where one or both partners are to some extent neurodiverse (see Chapter 15).
Again, cultural and family of origin factors are often highly implicated in
this domain and the CBCT therapist needs to be attuned to such cultural
variation rather than explicitly or implicitly imposing demands upon the
couple to experience and express emotion in a way that is consistent with the
therapist's own culture bound beliefs.

In summary, CBCT takes a wide contextual lens to the issue of couple
relationships and distress. This includes the domains of the individual, the
couple as a unit and the environment and how behaviours, cognitions and
emotions interact across these domains. In the remainder of this chapter a
description is given of how the CBCT therapist uses this broad framework to
guide assessment, formulation, and treatment with couples in distress.

The Practice of CBCT

As mentioned earlier, CBCT is a principle-based approach rather than a
manualised treatment. Due to the complexity of couple functioning and distress, it is not workable to over specify tasks and goals on a session-by-ses-
sion basis. Instead, the CBCT therapist needs to flexibly respond to the
couple as they present, weaving in interventions that focus upon behaviours,
cognitions, and emotions across the domains of the individual, the couple
and the environment. Thus, CBCT is most appropriate for therapists who

value working flexibly and who can process complex information from multiple sources, choosing interventions that are theory and evidence-based and appropriate for the current moment of interaction with the couple. The specific relational qualities ideally embodied by the CBCT therapist are therefore important to describe ahead of technical interventions.

The therapeutic relationship and the roles of the therapist

CBCT makes a great deal of room for variations in therapists' personal styles when working with couples. Thus, a therapist who is comfortable with the use of humour, or who likes to use metaphors for example, will find that the model supports them to use their 'self' in their work. CBCT also shares many features with individual CBT and as such a highly collaborative style of engaging clients is favoured. Thus, while a great deal of 'guided discovery' psychoeducation, and discussion of communication skills may be used appropriately, the CBCT therapist is never in the position of telling couples what to think, how to behave or feel. Like individual CBT, CBCT is also empirically based. The CBCT therapist may discuss with a couple a general principle, or a finding from research in relationship science, for instance, but will then be focussed on exploring with the couple how, if at all, this principle or finding is expressed in their own unique experience. Additionally, the therapist aims to embody the qualities of flexibility and balance, balancing interventions that focus across behaviour, cognitions and emotions and the domains of the individual, the couple, and the environment. The qualities of balance and flexibility are also expressed by the endeavour to support both individuals in the couple rather than siding with one against the other, even when one partner seems to the therapist to be more naturally 'reasonable'. Key to this is the willingness and ability to validate and explore each partner's perspectives when they are in clear disagreement.

Assessment, formulation, and treatment planning

While CBCT overall favours flexibility, it also shares many structural features with standard CBT in that therapy begins with a process of assessment and formulation, and goals and therapy targets are agreed and operationalised collaboratively with the couple. Additionally, standard measures of relationship functioning and scales to measure symptoms such as depression and anxiety are commonly used as appropriate and depending upon the clinical setting in which the couple is seen (see Baucom et al., 2020 for a discussion of commonly used psychometric measures appropriate for working with couples).

The initial assessment with a couple is usually structured in a way that begins with one or two couple based sessions, followed by an individual session with each partner. This initial phase is completed through a feedback session in which the therapist describes their understanding and formulation of the couple's presenting concerns and then the discussion proceeds to an agreement on goals for the work and a description of how these might be achieved. While the therapist is highly sensitive to the goals that the couple themselves set for the work, it is important to keep in mind that CBCT does not support a meta goal of keeping the couple together. While the work will often be focussed upon improving the relationship, the overall goal of CBCT is to assist the couple in making good decisions regarding their relationship, whether this is to remain together or to part ways.

While allowing for variations of therapist style, initial assessment sessions with the couple usually involve the therapist asking each partner to speak for 10 minutes or so regarding their perspective on the difficulties and challenges the couple face. While one partner is speaking, the other is encouraged to remain silent and to listen even if they find that they substantially disagree with the description their partner is giving. Once both partners have given this initial overall description, the therapist may proceed to ask the couple to provide a history of the development of their relationship, paying particular attention to aspects such as what attracted each to the other, and how they managed various commonly occurring transitions in the life of a couple. This could include for example how they managed the transition from being a dating couple to moving in together, and whether this was done, for example, with a great deal of discussion and consideration of what this meant for them both or whether alternatively they found that they somehow managed to 'slide into' these changes without much explicit discussion. Additionally, significant events or traumas are discussed, as well as what the couple consider to be the most important and relevant precipitants to their current state of distress or dissatisfaction. Throughout this discussion the therapist notes important aspects that 'fill in the picture' regarding the various domains and principles of the CBCT model. Additionally, the therapist will note important micro level aspects, such as patterns of negative behaviour, as well as important macro level themes, such as issues around intimacy and connection, or difficulties managing wider family expectations etc.

In the individual assessment sessions the therapist ensures to establish boundaries of confidentiality, clarifying their position on what, if anything, from the individual sessions will be referenced openly in subsequent couple sessions. Different CBCT therapists may adopt different positions on this, either preferring full openness and an unwillingness to hold secrets or a more subtle position of allowing some degree of confidentiality between individual and couple sessions with an exception made for issues that would make the viability of couple therapy unlikely. This could include for instance an undisclosed affair, in which case the therapist may take the position that either the partner agrees for this information to be disclosed, or a discussion is held regarding how to bring couple therapy sessions to a close. Topics covered in the individual sessions the individual's previous relationship history, their history of mental and physical health, family of origin issues and an overall discussion of their personality and motivations in relationships. In addition to gathering relevant information, these individual sessions are often very helpful in strengthening the therapeutic relationship with each individual.

A wide range of possibilities present themselves for how to put together all the information gathered into a workable formulation or conceptualisation and the chapters that follow in this book present various ways of doing this. In general terms, while CBCT points to the complexity and range of variables and factors that may be important in understanding couple distress and functioning, when working with a specific couple it is most often the case that the work focuses on a limited range of issues and problems, and seeks to aid the couple in achieving improvements in specific domains. Thus, the formulation may focus on issues surrounding a theme of intimacy and connection, or on problems making decisions about the future, or on the inter-relationship between couple distress and one or both partners' experience of anxiety and depression. Thus, it is usually not functional to present the couple with an exhaustive analysis of all the possible factors, and instead the therapist can focus on those micro level factors (specific behaviours, etc) and macro level themes most relevant to the presenting couple.

Typical interventions

A wide range of treatment strategies are available to the CBCT therapist, and these are used flexibly and in a manner consistent with the specific goals of the couple. As mentioned earlier, a general principle is to start by assisting the couple to reduce sources of secondary distress and to reduce the frequency and intensity of negative behaviours and interactions, as well as to address any initial crises, before moving onto addressing factors related to primary distress and working to increase positive aspects of the relationship. While most of the interventions used can be seen to have an impact across behaviours, cognitions, and emotions, it is useful to specify a range of typical intervention strategies that primarily target these areas while also resulting in beneficial impacts across others.

Behavioural Interventions

Guided Behaviour Change

Interventions around behaviours can be divided into those that do not involve teaching the couple a new set of skills and those that do involve some level of skills teaching. Guided behaviour change represents a strategy that does not involve teaching news skills. In guided behaviour change the therapist uses discussion and psychoeducation to help the couple identify a range of behaviours (that currently or previously existed in their repertoire and that link to the formulation) that may have a positive impact upon their relationship. Overall, the aim of guided behaviour change is to help shift the general atmosphere in the relationship toward a more positive and more connected one. Thus, a couple may be encouraged to institute or re-establish a regular date night with the aim of improving intimacy and connection. Alternatively, each partner may be asked to experiment with engaging in at least one positive behaviour towards their partner on a daily basis and to note the impact of this both on the other and on their own mood state. In addition to targeting the overall atmosphere, guided behaviour change may be used to target specific aspects of the couple's relationship that are related to the maintenance of couple distress. For example, where an individual or both partners are struggling due to their needs for autonomy not being met, guided behaviour change (most likely used in combination with other strategies) can be used to set up experiments in allowing greater degrees of autonomy for one of both partners.

Communication skills

As discussed earlier, difficulties with communication are common in couples presenting for therapy. Working directly with a couple's communication, and achieving improvements in this domain can often serve as a vehicle for addressing a wide range of issues in the relationship. As a result, strategies to improve communication are often introduced early in therapy. Two broad categories of couple communication were described earlier: sharing thoughts and feelings and problem solving. For some couples, for a range of reasons, these communication skills have been absent in their way of relating for a considerable period or were never developed, in other words there is a skill deficit. In other couples the current poor communication is in part a result of the current level of distressed emotion, or in other words there is a performance deficit. In either case suggesting some general guidelines for these types of conversation can be very helpful. In most instances the therapist will present the guidelines in a brief conversation, emphasising that these are not rules that must be adhered to, and that the main aim is to find what will be most workable and beneficial for the specific couple. A summary of the guidelines for the sharing thoughts and feelings conversations, based upon the work of Epstein and Baucom (2002) is presented in Table 2.1.

During this type of intervention, the therapist can adopt many different roles including those of educator and coach, slowly helping the couple to shape their communication in a way that follows these guidelines but does not set them up as rigid rules that have to be followed. Where a couple is struggling or is highly conflictual, the therapist needs to be adept at skilfully and tactfully interrupting in order to help either or both partners to shape their communication, before putting the couple back on track with the intervention. The couple will often be asked to practice these types of conversation between sessions and to report back on difficulties or successes encountered in doing so.

Table 2.1 Guidelines for the sharing thoughts and feelings intervention

General Guideline

• Ensure to be clear about what role you are currently in during the conversation and swap roles with collaboration and agreement when appropriate.

Speaker Guidelines

Share your thoughts and feelings directly with your partner in a way that you feel they are most likely to be able to hear and understand.

- Talk about your experience subjectively, as your own experience rather than as an absolute truth.
- Ensure to describe your emotions and feelings.
- Make your statements specific rather than over general.
- Speak in paragraphs – avoid either minimising your statements or providing too much information and detail for the listener to follow.
- When sharing negative emotions and thoughts, ensure to also share any positive feelings you may have as well.
- Express yourself with tact and timing.

Listener Guidelines

Try to focus upon your partners experience with an effort of trying to understand what things are like *for them*.

- Think about the situation being described from your partner's perspective and avoid adding your own opinion or interpreting what they are saying.
- Adopt an open body posture and try to give eye contact as appropriate to express a willingness to listen.
- Focus on accepting what your partner is saying with the understanding that acceptance is not the same as agreement.
- When your partner finishes speaking summarise the main things you understood, their main feelings and thoughts, without doing this in a 'parrot fashion'.

Things to avoid!

- Interrupting.
- Expressing your own opinion while listening or summarising.
- Expressing judgement or criticism.
- Interpreting what has been said in a way that takes things away from what your partner actually said.
- Jumping to solving a problem even if one does exist.

Emotional Interventions

As will be clear from the above description, the domain of emotional experience is an explicit focus of the sharing thoughts and feelings intervention, and it often allows the therapist to work directly with each partner's emotional experience during the session. For some couples there can be difficulties with emotional regulation that require additional intervention, and many of these can be drawn from the broad range of strategies available within CBT. Thus, where a partner struggles to identify emotions or appears to experience a restricted range of emotions, the therapist can helpfully provide brief psychoeducation about emotions and use a range of body-focused questions to help an individual identify and find words for their emotional experience and to communicate this in new ways. This might, for instance, involve the use of metaphors, images, or narratives as a way of 'turning up the volume' on emotional experience.

Alternatively, one or both partners may struggle with dysregulated emotions and find it difficult to soothe themselves and calm down during or between couple therapy sessions. In such cases the therapist may again use brief psychoeducation around this issue and invite the partners to experiment with emotional regulation strategies such as 'time out' during discussions, mindfulness exercises, distraction techniques, thought records etc. Where a partner presents with long-term difficulties with emotional regulation, strategies drawn from Dialectical Behaviour Therapy may also be integrated into the treatment to help each partner more effectively validate their own and each other's emotions and learn strategies for self-regulation (See Fruzetti, 2006).

Cognitive Interventions

In addition to working directly with emotions and behaviours, the CBCT model weaves in interventions that clarify and help the partners to make changes in important cognitions related to their distress. Most often this is not done in the usual individually focussed method of adopting a rational-logical stance towards the evidential basis of automatic thoughts. Having one's automatic thoughts challenged in front of one's partner (as these thoughts are often about the partner) will in most instances meet with significant blocking! Instead, the therapist adopts a broad stance of guided discovery and attempts to work with the couple so that new experiences are encountered both during and between sessions that can be reflected upon in a way that will challenge unhelpful cognitions. For example, a not infrequent automatic thought may be *"my partner is unwilling and unable to listen to me!"*. Where partners are successfully engaged in sharing thoughts and feelings interventions, direct experiential evidence of their partner's willingness to listen to them is provided and can be reflected upon in a way that is helpful.

The CBCT therapist will be alert to cross-situational themes which often have an important cognitive component. One such issue is relationship standards, defined as beliefs that each partner holds about how the relationship should be. Once the couple has made some progress with sharing thoughts and feelings, this framework can be used to help identify and negotiate changes in these standards. Thus, for example, when a standard such as "*we should spend all of our free time together*" is identified, and where there may be some conflict between the partners about this (such as when the other partner holds the alternative standard "*free time should be for individual pursuits and personal goals*"), each partner will be asked to spend some time describing why their standard is important to them, how this relates to important needs and values they hold and what positives and negatives they see would follow in the event that they both agree to run the relationship in a manner consistent with the standard. This work at clarifying the underlying meaning of the standard, and its link to deeply held personality factors, motives, and needs, can provide a more workable framework for then experimenting with changes to the standard that may more effectively embody both partner's needs. Where such a compromise is not possible, this work can then usefully explore what ongoing differences in standards in the domain in question may mean for each partner and the future viability of the relationship.

Treatment planning and sequencing

CBCT is a flexible approach that does not set specific session numbers that need to be followed. Frequently treatment duration may be in the region of 20 sessions, followed by a series of follow up or booster sessions. The sequence of specific interventions used is guided by the formulation and the manner in which the couple enters therapy in the first instance. So for example, where the couple is highly emotionally dysregulated and engaging in a lot of negative behaviours, the therapist will prioritise interventions focussed on reducing negative behaviours and improving emotional regulation. Where a couple enters therapy in a more disconnected and shut down fashion and where there is an absence of arguing, the therapist may prioritise increasing positive behaviours in an effort to reintroduce more liveliness and connection into the relationship.

Adaptations

The discussion above has focussed primarily upon the issue of relationship distress. However, CBCT has also been adapted and modified to focus on work with couples where one or both partners presents with psychopathology such as depression (see Baucom et al., 2020), where the couple are struggling with the presence of a long-term health condition (see Baucom et al., 2012 and Fischer et al., 2016), where there is inter-partner violence present (Epstein et al., 2023), or where there is a current or past issue of infidelity or interpersonal trauma (Baucom et al., 2009). Many of the chapters that follow discuss these types of adaptations.

Suggestions for Further Reading

Baucom, D.H., Fischer, M.S., Corrie, S., Worrell, M., & Boeding, S. (2020). *Treating relationship distress and psychopathology in couples: a cognitive behavioural approach.* London: Routledge.

Worrell, M. (2015). *Cognitive Behavioural Couple Therapy: distinctive features.* London: Routledge.

References

Baucom, D.H., Porter, L.S., Kirby, J.S., Hudepohl, J. (2012). Couple-based interventions for medical problems. *Behaviour Therapy*, 43, 6–76.

Baucom, D.H., Fischer, M.S., Corrie, S., Worrell, M., & Boeding, S. (2020). *Treating relationship distress and psychopathology in couples: a cognitive behavioural approach.* London: Routledge.

Baucom, D.H., Snyder, D.K., & Gordon, K.C. (2009). *Helping couples get past the affair: A clinician's guide.* New York: Guilford Press.

Christensen, A. (1988). Dysfunctional interaction patterns in couples. In P. Noller & M.A. Fitzpatrick (Eds.), *Perspectives on marital interaction* (pp. 31–52). Multilingual Matters.

Epstein, N., B., LaTaillade, J.J. & Werlinich, C.A. (2023). Couple Therapy for Partner Aggression. In J.L. Lebow & D.K. Snyder (Eds.). *Clinical Handbook of Couple Therapy*. (6th Edition, pp. 391–412). New York: Guilford.

Fischer, M.S., Baucom, D.H., Cohen, M.J. (2016). Cognitive-behavioral couple therapies: Review of the evidence for the treatment of relationship distress, psychopathology, and chronic health conditions. *Family Process*, 55, 423–442.

Fruzzetti, A.E. (2006). *The High Conflict Couple: A dialectical behavior therapy guide to finding peace, intimacy, and validation.* Oakland: New Harbinger.

Gottman, J.M. (1994). *What predicts divorce? The relationship between marital processes and marital outcomes.* Hillsdale, NJ: Lawrence Erlbaum Associates.

Johnson, S.M. (2015). Emotionally focused couple therapy. In A.S. Gurman, J.L. Lebow, & D.K. Snyder (Eds.), *Clinical handbook of couple therapy* (5th ed., pp. 97–128). New York: Guilford.

Sullivan, K.T., & Lawrence, E. Eds. (2016). *The Oxford Handbook of Relationship Science and Couple Interventions.* Oxford: Oxford University Press.

Chapter 3

Integrative Behavioural Couple Therapy

Marion Cuddy

Introduction

Integrative behavioural couple therapy (IBCT) emphasises the need for both acceptance and change in alleviating relationship distress. It evolved from 'traditional' behavioural marital therapy (e.g. Jacobson & Margolin, 1979). In the 1980s Neil Jacobson and Andrew Christensen conducted a number of outcome studies of behavioural couple therapy (BCT) and noted that approaches which focused on guided behaviour change and communication training, although bringing about a rapid and marked reduction in relationship distress for many, were not effective for all couples. For example, a study by Jacobson and colleagues found clinically significant improvements in relationship functioning in only 50% of couples following BCT. Furthermore, even couples for whom BCT seemed effective showed high rates of relapse at 2-year follow-up (Jacobson et al., 1987).

The researchers identified a number of factors that seemed to predict poorer outcomes for BCT. These included lower levels of commitment to the relationship, older age, lower levels of emotional engagement, lack of shared goals for the relationship, and a fifth factor they summarised as 'traditionality'. This fifth factor is essentially a view that each partner should follow 'traditional' culturally defined gender-specific roles in areas such as career, home management and emotional maintenance of the couple/family, as opposed to seeing each other as 'peers' who share these tasks collaboratively. Jacobson and Christensen noted that these factors appear to be related to a couple's ability and willingness to collaborate, accommodate to the other partner's needs/preferences, and compromise within the relationship. This provided a rationale for adding interventions aimed at fostering acceptance within the relationship in their model of couple therapy. The concept of 'acceptance' in this context will be defined further below, but these interventions essentially shifted the focus to the partners' cognitive-emotional responses to one another (Christensen et al., 2020).

DOI: 10.4324/9781003024439-4

Theoretical basis of IBCT

IBCT has evolved from the same principles of behavioural and social learning theory that underpin traditional BCT, but it takes a number of additional factors into account. These include:

1   an emphasis on contingency-based rather than rule-governed change;
2   a greater focus on the context and the recipient, as well as the agent of a relationship interaction;
3   perhaps most notably, a shift to promoting acceptance as well as change in the relationship.

Contingency-based vs rule-governed change

Many attempts to change behaviour and/or improve health are *rule governed* (Skinner, 1966). For example, there are guidelines regarding diet and exercise, such as eating 5 portions of fruit or vegetables a day, and a person may strive to follow these 'rules' in order to adopt a healthy lifestyle. Changing eating habits is very difficult for some, and even if they succeed there is often little in the way of immediate reinforcement, as the benefits to health are likely to become apparent in the medium to longer term. This can make the behaviour hard to maintain. Therefore, an alternative way to bring about a desired change can be to create a new positive experience, which is in itself rewarding but also leads to the desired benefit. For example, rather than setting a target for a highly sedentary person to run 3 times a week to improve their fitness, they might be encouraged to try out different types of physical activity, until they find one that is enjoyable for them.

The same principle can be applied to relationships. Rule-governed change can feel less genuine, more forced and therefore harder to implement and maintain in a relationship context. Asking one's partner about their day each evening because this has been agreed as a therapy homework task will 'feel different' to a spontaneous enquiry about how the partner is doing. Furthermore, a change brought about in this manner may be seen as a temporary 'task' rather than a positive and sustainable change (although of course, the hope would be that if this new behaviour is reinforced, it will start to feel more natural and start to occur more spontaneously).

Another limitation of 'rules' is that for many couples, goals are focused more on emotional changes, such as feeling more positive towards the partner, and these are less amenable to rule-governed change. It is simply not possible to agree to feel enthusiastic about one's relationship 3 times a week! In this situation, it is much more helpful to nurture the desired change by creating new experiences for the couple that may bring to the fore the positive attributes or the partner or relationship and use these to facilitate positive emotional changes.

Finally, change brought about through manipulating contingencies is likely to be longer lasting than rule governed change. People get tired of following rules or forget to do so; a shift in behaviour that in itself is experienced as positive is more likely to be maintained.

Context of the relationship and focus on the recipient

Although traditional BCT does not ignore contextual factors affecting the relationship, IBCT focuses more explicitly on these, as described in the formulation section below. In addition, greater attention is paid to the *recipient*, as well as the *agent* of a behavioural interaction. This is because in practice, the response to a 'problem' or negative behaviour can become as problematic as the problem itself (Dimidjian et al., 2008). For example, consider Sally, who is a 'worrier' and seeks frequent reassurance from her partner Jack. If Jack provides reassurance whenever asked, Sally may feel soothed and see him as very supportive. However, this reassurance could serve as a maintaining factor for her worry. In addition, over time Jack may become fed up with Sally's constant requests for reassurance and start to respond with irritation or even hostility. This would both exacerbate Sally's anxiety and create distress in their couple relationship. Therefore, it is important to take into consideration the behaviour of both the 'initial instigator' and of the 'responder' when understanding and addressing a couple's problematic interaction.

Acceptance

Jacobson and Christensen (1996) have noted that the majority of couple distress seems to arise from relatively minor issues which relate to the individuals' vulnerabilities, rather than major transgressions in the relationship. Nevertheless, almost every relationship encounters some 'unsolvable problems'. These are usually related to key differences between partners in domains such personality, preferences, and cultural backgrounds. These differences can result in the partners feeling 'at odds' with each other or make it hard for both of their needs to be met, particularly if it is difficult to find a compromise, for example if they have different needs for closeness versus autonomy, or if they disagree on whether to have a child or not. Unsolvable problems can also include challenges the couple face that cannot be completely overcome, such as the diagnosis of a long-term health condition.

Under these circumstances, working towards some degree of acceptance rather than striving for change can be the best approach. Successful couples are able bring a 'spirit of compromise' to their differences and disagreements. Indeed, this type of response can actually facilitate subsequent change, because when partners let go of their attempts to bring the other around to their own view of the situation they can become much more open to considering different perspectives.

Acceptance has been defined along a number of parameters by IBCT theorists. James Cordova (2001) defines acceptance as behaviour occurring in the context of an aversive stimulus, which functions to maintain contact rather than to avoid or escape it. In practical couple terms, this is behaviour that serves to keep the connection between the partners in the context of a conflict or disagreement. Along similar lines, Christensen and colleagues (2020) view partners' maladaptive strategies to cope with their differences as attempts to escape from emotionally painful situations. These strategies are reinforced through immediate emotional relief, but actually maintain and exacerbate the conflict in the longer term. Emotional acceptance is the decision to stop trying to 'escape' from these situations, in order to interrupt this vicious cycle of negative interaction.

For example, Priya is anxious about her husband Dev's interactions with other women when he goes away on work trips. When he comes home after a trip, she is often upset and questions him intensely about who was there, who he spoke to, and what they discussed. Dev doesn't like to see Priya upset, so he tends to underreport the contact he had with other women as he knows this will make her feel better. Although this strategy leads to an immediate reduction in both of their anxiety, in the long term it maintains the problem as Priya is likely to continue to seek reassurance and Dev to keep withholding information. The strategy may even exacerbate the problem, particularly if Priya suspects that Dev is not telling the truth and therefore escalates her attempts to get reassurance, or if Dev starts to find his more confident female work colleagues attractive. Working towards 'acceptance' would involve helping the couple to recognise this pattern of interaction as an understandable, but ultimately unhelpful strategy they have developed as a result of each partner trying to reduce their negative emotional experience, and acknowledging and addressing the underlying factors that contribute to their anxiety, such as trust and being able to tolerate negative emotions.

Acceptance occurs along a continuum, with genuinely embracing one's partner's differences at one end, and grudgingly just-about tolerating them at the other. An individual may come to see their partner's lack of interest in home decor as an opportunity to follow their own tastes and preferences rather than as a lack of commitment to the relationship, or they may learn to 'put up with' the partner's lack of interest and reluctantly accept most of the responsibility for decorating their flat. The degree of acceptance may fluctuate at times and is likely to be influenced by other contextual factors in the relationship.

Formulation in IBCT

Two approaches to IBCT formulation are outlined below – formulation around a theme and the more recently developed DEEP analysis. Both formulations are based on a functional analysis of the couple's difficulties (see

Chapter 1) but offer slightly different ways of structuring the information gathered during assessment and discussing this with the couple. The DEEP formulation is essentially an elaboration of the formulation around a theme, as will be illustrated below. The decision regarding which to use is based on what seems to fit best for a particular couple and the therapist's personal choice.

Formulation around a theme

In their 1996 book *Acceptance and Change in Couple Therapy,* Jacobson and Christensen proposed using a key *theme* of difference/conflict affecting the couple's relationship as a basis for the formulation (Jacobson & Christensen, 1996). They outlined a number of common themes reported by distressed couples: closeness-distance, control and responsibility, conventionality/unconventionality, the Artist and the Scientist, and 'You don't love me, yes I do. It is YOU that doesn't love me'. The authors emphasised that it is not the 'difference' itself that causes distress, but rather the *polarisation process* that results from each partner's view that the other is in the wrong, and their unhelpful and ever-increasing attempts to bring the partner around to their own way of seeing the situation. This results in a *mutual trap* in which both individuals feel frustrated, misunderstood, and hopeless about their ability to resolve the conflict.

Let's take Susan and Esme as an example. Susan comes from a close-knit family in a small town. She grew up with very positive experiences of doing things 'as a family' , and she believes that she and Esme should spend most of their time together. Esme, on the other hand, values autonomy. Although she is committed to her relationship with Susan, she still wants to keep a degree of independence, for example setting time aside to pursue her own hobbies, and occasionally meeting friends without her partner. This difference in preference for independence is not problematic in itself if Susan and Esme acknowledge it and try to find a common ground. However, if Susan interprets Esme's desire to do some things without her as a rejection, and/or if Esme feels stifled by Susan's need for closeness, they could easily develop a maladaptive pattern of interaction around this *closeness-distance* theme. Susan might start to feel insecure when Esme makes individual plans, and complain or attempt to prevent this from happening. Esme might respond by being more secretive about her intentions, or by accusing Susan of being clingy. Eventually, this could lead to arguments and mistrust and result in them both feeling distressed and unhappy in the relationship.

DEEP analysis

The DEEP analysis (Table 3.1) allows for greater specification of the core issues or themes. It offers a somewhat more structured approach and was developed when IBCT was adapted to be accessible as a web-based, guided self-help intervention for couples (Doss et al., 2013). The partners are asked to identify one or two core conflictual issues or themes that they would like to address, and the DEEP analysis is used to develop a shared understanding of how and why these themes contribute to their relationship distress.

In most relationships, there will be many differences (D) between the partners. Differences can occur in a number of areas, including personality and temperament, interests, emotional expressiveness, coping style and preferences for intimacy/connection in the relationship. Cultural factors may also contribute to differences, particularly if the partners are from dissimilar backgrounds.

Differences between partners can be an asset to their relationship, or at least have advantages as well as inconveniences. An example might be if both partners differ with regard to their hobbies or interests, as is the case for Aoife and Sam. Aoife is a keen amateur musician and plays in a band, while Sam is passionate about cooking. Sam looks after their children every Thursday evening so that Aoife can go to band practice, and occasionally both enjoy going to music gigs together. In turn, Aoife supports Sam's interest in baking, making sure they have opportunities to do this on a regular basis and benefiting from the delicious results. As long as Sam and Aoife do not become excessively preoccupied with their individual pursuits and balance them with joint activities and family commitments, these differences enrich their lives together. In a DEEP analysis, however, the differences of interest are primarily those that contribute to the partners' distress, often because they affect the partners' needs in the relationship being met or relate to their emotional sensitivities, such as the differences between Susan and Esme described above.

Emotional sensitivities (E) refer to the emotional vulnerabilities of each partner and their response when these are triggered. Most individuals have some areas of 'sensitivity' when it comes to interpersonal relationships, which are shaped through a combination of genetic predisposition, social learning and lived experience. A comment that is intended as a throwaway remark by one partner could be experienced as very critical by the other if it touches on a sensitive area. There is also significant individual variation in how people experience and express emotions. Emotional responses and displays of emotional distress may vary hugely between partners, which can pave the way for misunderstandings and misinterpretations.

Table 3.1 The DEEP analysis

D Differences between partners
E Emotional sensitivities
E External stressors/circumstances
P Pattern of interaction

The range of emotional sensitivities is broad, but some common ones include sensitivity to criticism/negative feedback, fear of abandonment, strong need for validation, concerns about attractiveness to others and sensitivity to feeling controlled. Sensitivities can also occur in relation to gender, culture and socio-economic status. Partners can bring sensitivities to the relationship from prior experiences, but sensitivities can also develop within a relationship, often as a result of the partners' attempt to 'manage' a difference between them. For example, returning to the couple described above, Esme may become hypervigilant for comments from Susan that suggest she is trying to limit her independence and react strongly to these.

External stressors and circumstances (E) relate to a multitude of factors outside the relationship that can place demands on one or both partners and have an impact on their relationship. These include employment issues, finances, housing, health, problems with extended family or social relationships, and the challenges of parenting. Sometimes these stressors affect the relationship by bringing into focus existing differences or sensitivities. External circumstances can present as a 'mixed bag' of positives and negatives. An obvious example might be having a child, which can bring much joy and fulfilment to the couple whilst simultaneously adding to their financial burden and limiting the time and energy they can devote to each other.

The couple's 'pattern of interaction' (P) can be thought of as both partners' attempts to resolve the challenges in their relationship brought about by their differences, sensitivities, and circumstances. In relation to the formulation around a theme described above, a problematic pattern of interaction contributes to the 'polarisation process', and the partners' emotional reactions to that pattern are the 'mutual trap' they find themselves in.

Many couples navigate these aspects of their relationship through mostly healthy and constructive communication. However, when this is not possible, for example due to lack of motivation, not having the required skills or communication being negatively affected by psychopathology, the pattern of communication can become very maladaptive, often exacerbating the existing difficulties.

Patterns of interaction can become unhelpful in different ways. A partner can become critical or contemptuous of the other, for example belittling an area of emotional sensitivity. They may step up their demands if they feel their needs are not being met, or they may adopt a defensive stance, not acknowledging responsibility for any of the difficulties. Alternatively, a partner may attempt to withdraw from the interaction, avoid the other person or attempt to placate them.

These strategies can be effective in the short-term, eliciting a desired response or reducing a negative emotional experience, but they are often counterproductive in the long term, and in some circumstances, they can develop into relational 'safety behaviours'. Returning again to Susan and Esme, if Susan feels anxious about Esme's commitment to the relationship, she may try to set limits on Esme's independence. Esme may initially comply, thus soothing her anxiety. However, relationships by definition are not one-sided, and Esme may start to resent this curtailment of her freedom and start to pull away, or make remarks about Susan's 'clinginess'.

If a couple is unable to engage in a sustainable way of navigating their differences they can develop a very unhelpful 'dance' around them. Christensen (1988) has documented some common maladaptive patterns of interaction in couples. The one most widely referenced is the 'demand-withdraw' pattern, where when Partner A places a 'demand' on the relationship Partner B withdraws. Partner A then escalates their demand, only to be met by further disengagement from Partner B. This pattern can manifest in different ways, for example Partner B finding Partner A's attempts to discuss a problem aversive and therefore avoiding or shutting down any attempts to address it, or Partner B finding Partner A's frequent need for reassurance overwhelming and thus withholding this completely. Other maladaptive patterns of interaction include mutual attack, where both partners adopt critical or hostile patterns of communication and conversations tend to escalate into arguments, and mutual avoidance (withdraw-withdraw), where the partners avoid conflict and disagreement, often resulting in difficulty addressing problems, hidden resentments, and the loss of intimacy in the relationship.

Intervention

IBCT emphasises acceptance-focused interventions such as empathic joining, unified detachment, and tolerance building as a first line of treatment (discussed further below), though more 'traditional' BCT interventions such as guided behaviour change and communication skills training are also used where appropriate. Empathic joining and unified detachment in particular focus not on what each partner could/should do to improve the relationship, but rather on facilitating the expression of relevant thoughts and feelings in order to promote understanding, empathy, and acceptance of their differences.

IBCT differentiates 'surface' emotions, which are openly expressed and visible to the partner (and usually the person expressing them), from 'hidden' emotions, which are often more complicated and not immediately apparent, sometimes to either party. In addition, many people find it easier to express 'hard' emotions such as anger and frustration than 'soft' ones that show an element of vulnerability, such as sadness, disappointment or worry. The expression of 'hard' emotions with little 'soft' emotional disclosure is likely to elicit a defensive or hostile response, rather than to promote empathy and can contribute significantly to the polarisation process. Thus, empathic joining and unified detachment focus particularly on eliciting the hidden, softer emotions. These interventions are described in more detail below.

Empathic joining

Empathic joining allows the partners to express the distress they experience around their conflict without the blame or accusation that leads to a problematic pattern of interaction. Problems are viewed as potential 'vehicles for intimacy' (Jacobson & Christensen, 1996). This approach aims to promote a different experience of problems for the couple – one that helps them to connect with each other rather than driving them apart. When differences seem irreconcilable, empathic joining sees an opportunity for each partner to become more aware of the other's sensitivities, vulnerabilities, and emotional experience, and to understand how these are 'triggered'. This awareness can bring the partners closer emotionally, and foster the motivation to develop new and more adaptive ways of responding to their differences.

Guidelines for empathic joining

Empathic joining aims to help the partner to shift from an adversarial, polarised position to a more compassionate and caring one. Christensen and his colleagues (2020) suggest that this can be encouraged from the very start of the assessment. For example, drawing attention to and validating the emotional pain of each partner shifts the focus to the 'wound versus the arrow'. Furthermore, the conceptualisation in IBCT views the couple's conflict as arising from differences rather than deficiencies, and draws attention to each person's vulnerabilities and the mediating effects of environmental stressors. This presents the conflict as an understandable if unhelpful response to the challenges of living in a partnership.

Over the course of treatment, the therapist guides each partner to express their feelings in new and different ways in order to facilitate a more empathic response in the other. Empathic joining is a process rather than a formal technique, and in practice how it develops can vary considerably from one couple to the next. A functional analysis can be useful in deciding what approach to take. Some key principles and strategies to promote empathic joining are outlined below, but therapists will also draw on a broad range of couple therapy skills and techniques.

The first step towards empathic joining is deciding which partner to focus on. Typically, if one person is highly emotionally aroused, it makes sense to start with them. If neither is experiencing strong emotions, then their typical pattern of interaction can be used to guide the decision. Starting with the partner who is likely to find it easiest to reveal their thoughts and feelings may maximise the chances of a positive first experience.

The next step is to help the 'speaker' to move away from a position of blaming the partner towards disclosing their own emotional experience. Attention is drawn to the individual's feelings or reactions rather than what the other partner has said or done. This can be done directly, by asking guiding questions. At times individuals struggle to recognise or express emotions and it may be helpful to make tentative hypotheses about their hidden emotional experience, in order to facilitate disclosure and to validate their experience e.g. *"Nathan, it must have been pretty frightening for you when Susan developed pneumonia"*.

It is important to take the individual's current emotional experience as a starting point. Even if it seems obvious that there is hurt underneath the anger that someone is expressing, it can be invalidating not to acknowledge the anger itself. Acknowledging and validating the emotions expressed can open up opportunities to explore associated hidden emotions.

When individuals have a tendency to avoid or minimise emotional expression, the therapist may find it helpful to focus in on or intensify hidden emotions, for example through the use of more emotive language or by drawing attention to other experiences in which similar emotions were felt. For a comprehensive discussion of working with restricted or minimised emotions in a couple context, the reader is directed to Epstein and Baucom (2002).

Disclosure of soft emotions or vulnerabilities can sometimes elicit an unexpected response from the partner. This can be disconcerting for the therapist, particularly if the disclosure has felt like an important step in the right direction. Nevertheless, partners cannot be forced into showing understanding or empathy for each other and it is important to consider both of their experiences. It can be easier for therapists to feel empathy as they are not emotionally involved and have not suffered as a result of the conflict. For example, if Leila feels very angry and unsupported because Steve has withdrawn from his parenting responsibilities, it may be difficult for her to respond empathically when he discloses that insecurity about himself as a father has contributed to his withdrawal. In situations like this, a functional analytic approach (see Chapter 1) can help the therapist to understand both partners' experiences and make sense of their responses. The therapist's empathic and validating response can be serve as a model for the partners as they work towards empathic joining. It is important not to try to rush the process and to remember that for some couples, the journey may be slow and somewhat bumpy.

Unified detachment

Unified detachment is sometimes described as 'dyadic mindfulness' in that it encourages both partners to look at their conflict together and without evaluating or judging it. It aims to help the couple to develop a non-judgmental, externalised and shared perspective of their conflict, so that they see the problem as an 'it' rather than 'me' or 'you'. Like empathic joining, it is a process rather than a technique, but it involves a more intellectual analysis of the conflict and is less emotion-focused. Although emotions and emotional reactions are sometimes discussed, this is done 'from a distance'.

Guidelines to promote unified detachment

Discussions to promote unified detachment usually begin by identifying a difficult or challenging interaction which has occurred or is likely to present itself. Triggers for each partner's reaction are explored, and the contribution of differences, current stressors and individual sensitivities are discussed. Specific conflicts are sometimes linked to broader issues and themes in the couple's relationship. The discussion is facilitated in a manner that avoids apportioning blame, and partners are encouraged to explore other perspectives.

For example, Ben and Jasmin had an argument because Ben had used up the last of the bread when he came home after a late shift at work, leaving none for Jasmin's breakfast the next morning. Jasmin thought this was very selfish on Ben's part, whilst Ben countered that she had other options for breakfast and that she was overreacting. At a surface level, they both felt that this was a very 'petty' argument and felt even more aggrieved towards each other because of this.

Their therapist helped them to explore the circumstances in which the argument took place. Ben and Jasmin recalled that they had both been feeling tired and on edge on the morning of the argument as they had been kept awake during the night by noise from next door. They noted that as Jasmin took responsibility for planning and doing most of the grocery shopping, she was more aware than Ben of what items were 'running low'. Ben recognised that he could take a more active role in this domain. Jasmin reflected that this type of occurrence activated sensitivities from a previous relationship about her needs not being considered. She was able to see that there were other plausible interpretations of Ben's actions, and to acknowledge that he was generally a considerate and thoughtful partner. This discussion, which highlighted the role of different viewpoints, emotional sensitivities, and external stressors, helped the couple to reframe the incident as an unfortunate event that they could problem solve together instead of thinking it reflected flaws in either of their characters.

A problematic interaction may start at different time points for each person. Sometimes minor resentments are held back and build up until a 'final straw' results in a response that feels excessive to the recipient. It is important to go back to the partners' thoughts, feeling, intentions and behaviours at the earliest stage of the interaction rather than focusing on the 'climax' of the conflict. By developing a sort of 'timeline' of key points in the problematic interaction and eliciting each partner's thoughts and feelings at these key points, the therapist adds some context to what happened. This can help both partners make sense of how each of their responses came about and help to reduce blame. However, the therapist must ensure that this does not turn into a discussion of 'who did what', which would be counterproductive.

As well as drawing on the couple therapist's broad repertoire of skills and techniques, a number of more specific techniques can be used to promote unified detachment. These include strategies to encourage the partners to step back and reflect on the incident, such as making ratings of the intensity of the argument, their level of distress, and comparing the incident with other similar incidents which had a different outcome. Drawing attention to differences between what one person intended to convey and what the partner interpreted can help to identify important misinterpretations, and in some circumstances indicate that the couple may benefit from more structured communication skills training. A more comprehensive account of unified detachment and how it can be promoted can be found in Christensen and colleagues (2020).

Additional considerations around empathic joining and unified detachment

Both empathic joining and unified detachment could be considered forms of dyadic exposure therapy. In a similar manner to people with anxiety disorders, distressed couples sometimes either avoid discussing emotionally sensitive topics because they have developed negative expectations of doing so and anticipate having a negative or distressing experience. Empathic joining and unified detachment allow partners to approach these sensitive areas in a manner that both leads to less negative emotional arousal and yields a better outcome. Having a more positive emotional experience can reduce 'fear' around subsequent similar discussions as well as altering negative expectations about the partner and the interaction.

These interventions facilitate the contingency shaped change that is so valued in IBCT, as the learning they bring about can lead to the partners responding differently during their interactions, without being explicitly instructed to do so by the therapist. In fact, in IBCT the therapist would typically refrain from immediately following up an intervention to promote empathic joining or unified detachment with a behavioural experiment or other behavioural change strategy, but rather wait to see what impact their new perspectives will have on their interaction in a naturalistic way.

Although empathic joining and unified detachment have different objectives, they can be used in combination during treatment. For example, if the partners are still distressed and in conflict about a recent incident during a therapy session, the therapist may focus first on empathic joining in order to validate each person's experience and soften emotional expression, and then shift towards unified detachment to help the couple develop a shared and more detached perspective on the issue. Sometimes one approach can segue into the other, for example following a discussion around empathic joining, one of both partners may spontaneously 'step back' and reflect on the process through which their interaction escalates in a more mindful manner.

Tolerance building strategies

Tolerance building interventions are typically used after empathic joining and unified detachment, where a difference or conflict between partners is continuing to cause distress even after they have worked on developing a more empathic, shared understanding of it. Tolerance building aims to interrupt negative patterns of interaction by more explicitly helping partners to let go of their attempts to change one another.

Interventions to promote tolerance require the couple to have a good understanding of their conflict and pattern of interaction around it, which is usually facilitated by empathic joining and/or unified detachment. Rehearsing or faking the negative interaction, promoting self-care and benefit-finding are the most frequently used strategies to promote tolerance in IBCT.

Rehearsing/faking negative behaviour

Couples can be asked to role play an interaction around a conflict during a therapy session. Role playing a sensitive issue while calm, rather than when provoked, gives the couple the opportunity to experience the conflict without the emotional arousal usually involved and thus facilitates the development of new perspectives on the issue. It also provides a chance to rehearse their interactions around a common conflict and 'try out' different ways of responding that lead to better outcomes for them. Some couples are able to bring humour to this role play, which can defuse negative emotions and promote acceptance.

Faking negative behaviour at home is often done as a homework task after rehearsing the problematic interaction in session. As above, the purpose is to enact the behaviour without the high levels of emotional arousal usually associated with it, giving the partners the opportunity to develop new ways of experiencing and responding to it, this time in a more naturalistic setting.

Self-care and benefit-finding

In some relationships, differences and/or difficulties in meeting each other's needs can lead to ongoing conflict. A common example is when one partner wants more autonomy than the other – the *closeness-distance* theme. In these circumstances, interventions to promote self-care can be used to reduce the stress caused by the conflict. These interventions need to be introduced sensitively, often as a 'supplement' rather than a 'replacement' for the response desired from the partner.

Examples of self-care strategies include finding other ways of meeting one's needs, seeking (appropriate) support outside the relationship, and developing assertiveness. Often these are strategies that would not be 'first choice', and it is important to consider the impact they will have on the other partner. At times, benefit finding can also be used to reframe the impact of a situation and reduce the stress associated with it. For example, Marjorie and Carlos had frequent arguments because Carlos felt that all the planning for their weekends and holidays was left to him, which he interpreted as a sign that Marjorie was not invested in their relationship. Their therapist helped him to reframe this as a situation that was to his benefit, in that he got to decide what they would do. Carlos was also able to view Marjorie's laid back attitude towards the weekend as self-care for herself; after a busy working week managing a team, she wanted to let go of responsibilities as much as possible and was more than happy to follow his lead. Nevertheless, as Marjorie became more aware of and empathic towards Carlos' experience of the situation, she made more of an attempt to contribute towards their joint plans. In some situations, tolerance building interventions can actually lead to a reduction in the frequency or intensity of the problematic behaviour/difference as partners start to relate to it differently.

Interventions to promote intentional change

More 'traditional' behavioural couple therapy interventions such as guided behaviour change and work on communication/problem solving skills also play a role in IBCT, though they are usually not the first line of treatment. These interventions are described in more detail in Chapter 2. In IBCT, they are typically applied in a less rule-governed and more idiosyncratic manner, for example if a need to develop emotional expressiveness skills is identified in the context of a discussion to promote empathic joining. Indeed, Christensen and his colleagues (Christensen et al., 2020) emphasise the importance of understanding the context and meaning an issue has for both partners before embarking on a change focused intervention such as guided behaviour change.

Session structure

Like other behavioural couple therapies, IBCT begins with an assessment phase, which consists of an initial conjoint session followed by individual appointments with each partner, and a feedback/treatment planning session during which the couple's core issue/s and their conceptualisation within an IBCT framework are discussed and a treatment plan is agreed.

During the active treatment phase, an agenda is set collaboratively at the start of each treatment session. This is guided by the *Weekly Questionnaire* which both partners are asked to complete in advance of the session (Christensen et al., 2020). This questionnaire asks respondents to report incidents of violence of substance misuse, to identify the most positive and most difficult interactions they have had with their partner since the previous session, any issues of concern even if they had no recent incidents around those issues, as well as any upcoming events that could pose a challenge, and to prioritise these for discussion. After a brief review of the past week and the questionnaire responses, the therapist and couple decide what the main focus of the session will be. The therapist selects the most appropriate intervention (s) depending on the nature and aims of the discussion. Sufficient time is allowed at the end of the session to debrief, identify key learning points and agree homework tasks as appropriate.

Finally, during the termination phase the frequency of therapy sessions is reduced to 1–2 a month and sessions focus on reviewing progress and supporting the couple with any ongoing challenges they face.

Sequencing interventions

The couple's *collaborative set* (Jacobson & Margolin, 1979) typically determines whether therapy starts with a focus on change or acceptance. Collaborative set can be defined as the degree to which the partners share the perspective that they are both responsible for the difficulties they are experiencing, and therefore both need to work to address them. When couples enter treatment with a strong collaborative set, change-oriented strategies can be very successful from the start. However, this is not the case for the majority of couples seeking help with their relationship, and therefore interventions to promote empathy and acceptance are often the first line of treatment.

The DEEP formulation can be used to guide treatment planning, depending on what the most salient issues appear to be. In general, a focus on acceptance is preferable for difficulties relating to differences or emotional sensitivities. More structured, change-oriented interventions can be used to address maladaptive patterns of interaction. Depending on the context in which they occur, acceptance and/or change-oriented interventions can be employed for problems relating to external stressors.

Typically, empathic joining and unified detachment are prioritised at the start of therapy. Relevant change-oriented interventions can be interwoven as needed, for example if a need for communication skills training is identified. Tolerance-building strategies are also used to enhance empathic joining and unified detachment. As previously mentioned, the emphasis is very much on promoting contingency-based change, and therefore treatment focuses on facilitating new and more adaptive emotional experiences for the couple that will be naturally reinforced rather than following a strict protocol.

Suggestions for further reading

Christensen, A., Doss, B.D., & Jacobson, N.S. (2014). *Reconcilable Differences: Rebuild Your Relationship by Rediscovering the Partner You Love – without Losing Yourself*. New York: Guilford.

Christensen, A., Doss, B.D., & Jacobson, N.S. (2020). *Integrative Behavioral Couple Therapy: A Therapist's Guide to Creating Acceptance and Change.* New York: Norton.

References

Christensen, A. (1988). Dysfunctional interaction patterns in couples. In P. Noller & M.A. Fitzpatrick (Eds.), *Perspectives on marital interaction* (pp. 31–52). Multilingual Matters.

Christensen, A., Doss, B.D., & Jacobson, N.S. (2020). *Integrative Behavioral Couple Therapy: A Therapist's Guide to Creating Acceptance and Change.* New York: Norton.

Christensen, A., & Jacobson, N.S. (2000). *Reconcilable differences.* New York: Guilford.

Cordova J.V. (2001). Acceptance in behavior therapy: Understanding the process of change. *Behavioral Analysis*, 24 (2), 213–226.

Dimidjian, S., Martell, C.R., & Christensen, A. (2008). Integrative behavioral couple therapy. In A.S. Gurman (Ed.), *Clinical handbook of couple therapy* (pp. 73–103). The Guilford Press.

Doss, B., Benson, L, Georgia, E., & Christensen, A. (2013). Translation of Integrative Behavioral Couple Therapy to a web-based intervention. *Family Process*, 52, 139–153.

Epstein, N.B., & Baucom, D.H. (2002). *Enhanced cognitive-behavioral therapy for couples: A contextual approach.* American Psychological Association. doi:10.1037/10481-000.

Jacobson, N.S., & Christensen, A. (1996). *Integrative behavioral couple therapy.* New York: W.W. Norton.

Jacobson, N.S., & Margolin, G. (1979). *Marital therapy: Strategies based on social learning and behavior exchange principles.* New York: Brunner/Mazel.

Jacobson, N.S., Schmaling, K.B., & Holtzworth-Munroe, A. (1987). A component analysis of behavioral marital therapy: Two year follow-up and prediction of relapse. *Journal of Marital and Family Therapy*, 13, 187–195.

Skinner, B.F. (1966). *The behavior of organisms: An experimental analysis.* Englewood Cliffs, NJ: Prentice Hall.

Part Two

Case Studies

Chapter 4

Relationship Distress
"Our Demons Don't Play Nice Together"

Dan Kolubinski

Introduction

From a Cognitive Behavioural Couple Therapy (CBCT) perspective, couple distress is viewed as, in part, a consequence of learned patterns of interaction and communication within the relationship. Couples in distress often engage in negative cycles of interaction, where they may exhibit behaviours like criticism, avoidance, or withdrawing from conflicts and these maladaptive behaviours can erode trust and emotional intimacy. Often, this distress may be the result of differences in communication patterns or significant periods where one or both individuals find that their needs are not being met (Epstein and Baucom, 2002). CBCT aims to help couples recognise these patterns, develop better communication skills, and replace destructive behaviours with more constructive ones. Couples are encouraged to practice positive interactions and problem-solving techniques, fostering a healthier and more satisfying relationship. The theoretical foundation of this approach emphasises the malleability of behaviours and the idea that through intentional changes, couples can improve their connection and overall relationship satisfaction.

The presenting couple: Stephen and Jane

Stephen and Jane have been together for 15 years and married for 12 years. They have two sons (10, 7) and live in the suburbs of South-West London. They met in their late 20s when working for the same company. Stephen was just coming out of a previous marriage and Jane was seeing someone else at the time. Within a very short period after meeting, the two of them developed strong feelings for one another and started dating (*"It hit me like lightning!"*). Jane ended her other relationship immediately but insists that Stephen was not the catalyst. She had been unhappy for quite some time and had been planning on ending things for months.

Stephen and Jane embodied the idea that opposites attract. The first time I met them, he wore a three-piece suit (dark grey) and looked like he had

DOI: 10.4324/9781003024439-6

stepped out of a Jeeves and Wooster novel (think Gussie Fink-Nottle). His personality fit with his image, and he came across as very reserved. Jane, on the other hand, was a firebrand whose first words to me were a complaint about the music playing in the waiting room (To be fair, she wasn't wrong!). She looked as though she was dressed for a Kandinsky exhibition and her personality alone appeared to fill up two-thirds of my office.

In the first session, after getting a quick understanding of what brings a couple in, I ask questions that guide me through their history. I find that *how* a couple tells a story can sometimes provide as much information as the story itself. In this case, Jane did most of the talking, with Stephen nodding in agreement and making a few clarifying comments.

Their initial three years together represented an exciting time for both Stephen and Jane. They were advancing in their respective careers, and Stephen took a better paying position with another company while Jane was promoted to a leadership role in advertising. They were *"madly in love"* and the chemistry between them was *"incendiary"*.

This changed shortly after the birth of their first son. Jane acknowledged that she was not very maternal and never felt *"connected"* to either of her sons. She felt increasingly resentful for having to do most of the childcare when she was on maternity leave whilst Stephen continued to advance in his career. At the time, Stephen felt an increase in pressure to provide and was concerned every month when they went into their overdraft. As a result of the tension, Jane and Stephen began to feel less connected to one another within a couple of years of becoming parents.

Their interactions became very terse. Conversation revolved almost exclusively around the children and any difficult conversations would typically escalate to a point where Jane would start shouting and Stephen would withdraw, either physically or mentally. After five years of parenting, Jane reported, their sex life was *"virtually non-existent"* and she described their relationship as one of *"flatmates"*.

Theoretical framework

CBCT relies heavily on the idea of reciprocity, in that we tend to act towards our partner in the way that we think they are acting towards us. When we feel loved and cared for, we are more likely to respond with love and care. When we are met with defensiveness or criticism, we are less likely to respond with love and care and more likely to act negatively in response.

The Emotional Bank Account

Gottman and colleagues use the metaphor of the Emotional Bank Account to represent the sum total of the positive and negative interactions in a relationship, which underlies the partners' feelings of satisfaction and contentment within it (Gottman et al., 1976; Gottman, 1999). Whenever someone does or says something positive (e.g., giving attention, listening, paying a compliment, making a cup of tea), it's like putting a pound into the account. When someone does something negative (e.g., being defensive or critical, turning away from a conversation), it's like taking a pound out of the account.

What makes a relationship complicated, though, is that what one person considers to be a 'deposit' into the Emotional Bank Account is not necessarily what the other person would consider to be a deposit. As a result, a well-intentioned attempt at demonstrating care may not quite land in the way that one would hope it would. I like to suggest that the couple ends up depositing in different 'currencies' and the exchange rate is rather poor. If I buy my partner flowers, her eyes will light up and she will proudly display them on the dining room table, and our Emotional Bank Account goes up. However, if she were to buy me flowers, I would question whether she really knew me. This gender stereotype highlights what also happens for any potential deposit.

Modifying the Golden Rule

I say that these are well-intentioned attempts because they are generally coming from a good place. Most of us are familiar with the Golden Rule, "Treat other people the way that you would like to be treated," which crops up in many religions and schools of thought (Fun Fact: 500 years before Jesus is reported to have said, "Do unto others as you would have them do unto you," Confucius taught, "Do not impose on others what you do not wish for yourself." (Freedman, 2002)).

This is a cornerstone of moral and ethical human interaction and I do not have a problem with it, generally. The Golden Rule in its known form, though, is very bad relationship advice and needs to be modified slightly. To make effective deposits into the Emotional Bank Account, it is far more important to treat others the way in which *they* would like to be treated.

Sentiment Override

The way in which we view and interact with our partner, then, is dependent on the level of savings that have accrued over time and, to mix metaphors, the farther we feel from each other due to the length of time that we are 'off course'. Weiss (1980) refers to this as *Sentiment Override*. When things are positive, particularly at the start of the relationship, when we are making large deposits and have low expectations of the amount of savings, we view our partner's behaviour, characteristics and personality favourably. Most of their idiosyncrasies are seen as 'cute' or 'endearing'. After a long enough period of being just that one degree off, with a positive-to-negative ratio being less than 5 to 1, the view of our partner can change (Gottman, 1999). The relationship could still be mostly positive, but it's not quite positive enough. Suddenly, those cute, endearing idiosyncrasies become irritants, annoyances and character deficiencies. This is acknowledged fairly quickly in the assessment session with Stephen and Jane:

THERAPIST: So, what was it about Jane that drew you to her?
STEPHEN: Well, she was a real breath of fresh air, you know? She was creative and interesting and a real out-of-the-box thinker. I came from a staunch conservative upbringing, and she was a splash of colour in my rather grey life.
THERAPIST: I see. And what seems to be the issue now?
STEPHEN: Well, now she's just so flighty and irresponsible. She can't commit to anything, and she just wants to sit around and draw all day.

You can see that Stephen is essentially describing the same person. What has changed over the years is how he views Jane. This works both ways:

THERAPIST: And what about you, Jane? What first attracted you to Stephen?
JANE: Well, he was so thoughtful and responsible. He took care of me, was so stable, and I knew I could rely on him. My life has always been a bit chaotic and Stephen was my rock.
THERAPIST: That makes sense. And now?
JANE: Ugh! He's so boring. There's no passion; no spontaneity! He's more concerned about his spreadsheets than he is about me!

The sentiment override for both Stephen and Jane has resulted in aspects of their respective characters that were previously seen as positive being reappraised as negative, which is an indication of the state of their Emotional Bank Account. This does not happen overnight. The years that they have spent making few deposits into the Emotional Bank Account has led their relationship being off course by a couple of degrees. Over time, when combined with conflicts and missed opportunities for connection, it has eroded their savings and thus the care, goodwill and support that they had at the start of their relationship.

Formulation

As in individual Cognitive-Behavioural Therapy (CBT), a good CBCT formulation can help the couple to understand the process of their interactions, regardless of the content. I learned about a CBCT formulation from my Clinical Supervisor, Lee Grant, who drew inspiration from a longitudinal Beckian formulation (See Figure 4.1). It serves as a cornerstone for every couple that I see, because it succinctly shows the couple how their respective behaviours are locked in a vicious cycle. In this diagram, there are two main components: the present moment interaction and the schematic framework that hovers in the background, providing context for the reaction.

When drawing out the formulation, I usually start on the left side of the diagram at the 'Activating Event' and 'Behaviours' level and explain that when we act, we don't do so in a vacuum. There is no direct straight line between the event and what we do in response. Instead, our reaction starts with an interpretation of what is happening at the time, which then leads to an emotional and physical response, and this contributes to our behavioural response. So, what we do is based on how we feel, which is based on what we think about what is happening around us.

From there, I start to move up the page to highlight why we interpret the situation in the way that we do. This requires context. I tell the couple that this represents one's framework, which lies in the back of our minds and serves as the lens through which we view the world around us. As in individual CBT, this schematic framework typically lies dormant until activated by the situation occurring in the moment. Moving up from the Activating Event, this represents the rules, assumptions and beliefs that we hold about relationships, about ourselves and about what constitutes 'caring' or 'appropriate' behaviour and it is based on our past experiences. These past experiences can include what has happened between the couple over the course of their relationship, experiences from past relationships, or based on other relationships that they witnessed in childhood.

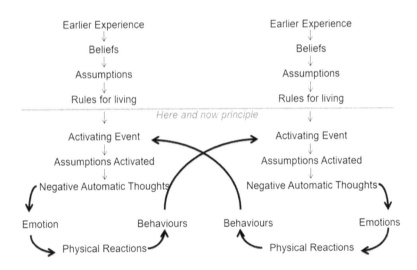

Figure 4.1 Cognitive-Behavioural Interaction of the Couple (Grant, 2011)

At this point, I reiterate the idea that what we do in the 'here and now' needs to be understood in the context of what we are feeling and thinking, which depends on our own individual framework. I then point out that what makes a relationship so complicated is that it involves two people, where the same thing is happening for the other person. They also experience an Activating Event, which sparks off their own thoughts and feelings, which also impacts their behaviour, and it does so based on their own framework, which stems from their own past experiences. I then go back to the very beginning and say *"We started this with an Activating Event that set the first person off thinking, feeling, and acting, but it is important to realise that the Activating Event is the other person's behaviour and the response then becomes the second person's Activating Event, which leads to their thoughts, feelings and behaviours, which then serves as the next Activating Event, and so on."*

Formulating Stephen and Jane

In the session following the conjoint and initial assessments, I explained the principles outlined above to the couple and we discussed how this relates to them specifically, and how the levels of savings in their Emotional Bank Account had changed over time. They both acknowledged that there had been very few deposits made in the last year or two and that the trajectory had been getting further off course since they became parents. We used the diagram below to formulate their specific relationship patterns, in order to provide a greater understanding of how their dynamic is activated and maintained (See Figure 4.2).

THERAPIST: So, let's delve deeper into this idea of the Emotional Bank Account. It's a concept where positive interactions between partners act as deposits, nurturing the relationship, while negative interactions act as withdrawals. How do you both see this concept resonating with your relationship?

STEPHEN: I think it makes sense. Lately, it feels like we've been withdrawing more than depositing. With the stress of parenthood, our focus shifted, and we haven't felt connected.

JANE: Yeah, we used to be much better at making deposits, but with everything that we need to do, we got caught up and lost track of us.

THERAPIST: That's understandable. Life transitions, like becoming parents, can be challenging. It's natural for priorities to shift, but it's essential to be aware of the impact it has on your relationship. How have you noticed this affecting your interactions and feelings towards each other?

STEPHEN: I've felt more distant, like we're co-parents rather than partners. I miss feeling emotionally connected.

JANE: I agree. There's been less laughter and more tension between us. I miss the closeness we used to have.

THERAPIST: Recognising that is a crucial step. What actions or changes do you think might help rebuild these emotional deposits?

STEPHEN: Maybe setting aside specific time for us, even if it's just a few minutes each day, to talk or reconnect without distractions.

JANE: And being more appreciative of each other, acknowledging the efforts we're both putting in.

THERAPIST: Those are excellent starting points. It's about consciously investing in your relationship. Remember, even small deposits count. How does that sound to both of you?

Stephen and Jane had spent years locked in a demand-withdraw pattern, where Jane would push forward on a conversation in a way that set off Stephen's alarm bells and these conversations often escalated when Jane sensed that Stephen was pulling away or shutting down. Jane identified that she starts to feel anxious and panicky when she senses Stephen withdrawing from her, because her parents had avoided conflict for years and she saw how that led to resentment and bitterness on both of their parts. As a result, she developed a belief that ignoring problems would lead to more problems and that any unaddressed issues would fester. She dove into conflict confidently in many areas of her life; viewing it as a 'life skill'. Her fear of having a relationship like her parents' became activated every time Stephen became sullen or disengaged in a conversation, and she responded to those uncomfortable feelings by speaking louder and insisting that they talk about things right away.

Stephen, on the other hand, was very familiar with conflict growing up. His parents had fought regularly when he was growing up and they currently live in a rather loveless marriage. These experiences led Stephen to believe that conflict in a relationship is bad and must be avoided at all costs. He learned early in life to keep his head down and his mouth shut. When Jane starts to press an issue, his anxiety starts to rise and he withdraws. He pulls away from her, physically and emotionally, by either leaving the room or by going silent and staring off into space, which, of course, brings us back to what set Jane off in the first place.

By highlighting this back-and-forth pattern with the couple early in therapy, they both started to realise how little they were aware of each other's vulnerabilities. Rather than seeing them as deficits, they started to understand that their behaviour was guided by similar emotions that stem from their different upbringings. They also shared a basic fear of losing the relationship but sought different solutions to this fear of loss. In a sense, their apparent problems are in fact the attempted solution. This was summarised beautifully in a session when Stephen looked at Jane and said with a smile, *"Our demons don't play nice together."*

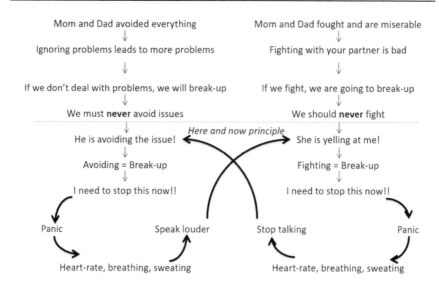

Figure 4.2 The CBCT Formulation in Action

Course of therapy

There are three fundamental pillars that a typical course of CBCT will address (Fals-Stewart & Lam, 2010), that I like to refer to as The Three C's of *Caring, Communication and Conflict Management*. As you will see in the case of Stephen and Jane, these pillars are addressed in turn. However, CBCT tends to be principle-based rather than protocol-driven (see Chapter 2) and it is far more important to develop an idiosyncratic treatment plan that addresses the couple's needs in a manner that is most appropriate. Generally, when I am meeting with a couple for weekly/fortnightly sessions, I tend to start with interventions based around increasing caring behaviours. This will then set the tone for the homework that they will be asked to do in the initial weeks.

The *Caring* aspect of treatment roughly represents increasing the deposits into the Emotional Bank Account. In even the healthiest of relationship we tend to make assumptions about what our partners consider to be positive behaviours. When the bank balance starts to decline, though, the accuracy of those assumptions might also dwindle, as will the motivation to make those deposits.

Communication in CBCT represents the different skills that are required to have conversations that involve sharing thoughts and feelings, as well as those involved in problem-solving or decision making. A clear distinction is required between those two different types of conversations since they are both legitimate ways of offering support and demonstrating care. Unfortunately, couples are not always very good at discerning between the two.

Lastly, *Conflict* is inevitable in most relationships. However, there is variation in the quantity and quality of conflict across relationships, and the aim of CBCT is to reduce the frequency, duration and intensity of conflict. For some couples, improving their communication skills will help to decrease or even prevent conflict. For others, guidelines on when and how to have the more challenging conversations and what to do to de-escalate these once emotions and tensions start to increase might be required.

Caring

The initial treatment sessions are dedicated to improving the levels of deposits into the Emotional Bank Account. The aim is to get the couple out of their 'default' behavioural dynamic and have them make effortful demonstrations of caring. Being very directive in the beginning about what this involves can be important, because for some couples it has been months, if not years, since they did anything resembling a caring act.

During the session after the assessment, when they both have a firm understanding of how their Emotional Bank Account has changed over time, I assign the first homework assignment: *Catch your partner doing something nice.* This simple exercise has two components to it. Firstly, both partners are responsible for doing 2–3 things every day that would constitute a very clear demonstration of caring. These do not have to be grand gestures, but they do have to require effort and be well-intended. Secondly, and more importantly, they are to make a record of the caring behaviours that their partner does in between sessions. Not only does this alter their behaviour in a more positive direction, but it also attempts to undercut their selective attentional biases that have built up.

When I met with Stephen and Jane in the following session, we compared notes to see what each had noticed the other person do. Stephen had a long list of things that he noticed Jane do, particularly around the efforts that she made around the house. We discussed how he was grateful for the way she interacted with the children, which, despite her difficult transition to motherhood, was generally very positive. He also stated that he noticed her paying him compliments. He acknowledged that this was less important to him *"but you told us to notice it, so I wrote it down."*

Jane, on the other hand, said she found it very difficult to see anything positive that Stephen had done. As she consulted the list that she had created, she dismissed many of his behaviours by saying *"but that's just something that you do, isn't it?"* or *"It's not showing me that he cares when he makes the dinner. Just like when he says that I spend time with the children. How is that showing him that I care? I don't do it for him; I do it because it needs doing."*

Both Stephen and Jane's reactions in the early days of therapy are typical of many couples. Given the current state of their Emotional Bank Accounts, they are both in negative sentiment override and it is a challenge to overcome the skew in their perspectives that has developed over the years. There is also a clear difference between how they both express and receive caring. Where Stephen clearly sees *instrumental behaviours*, such as housework and taking care of the children, as his default method of showing care and concern, Jane is motivated more by *expressive behaviours* (e.g., paying compliments or saying "I love you"; see Epstein and Baucom, 2002). It was no wonder, then, that the deposits into the Emotional Bank Account were not being made. They were both depositing in their own respective currencies. I reframed this to them, and they both identified that it had been a long time since either of them felt particularly cared for in this relationship.

During this session we played a game of Mr & Mrs (or The Newlywed Game for our North American readers). I gave them both a list of potential caring behaviours that include such things as: 'praising me;' 'showing that sex was enjoyable;' 'cooking my favourite meal;' etc. I asked them both to go through the list of behaviours and identify what they would consider to be their 'top five' preferences (i.e., 'If my partner did this behaviour, I would feel loved/cared for'). Once done, I asked them to identify the behaviours that they thought their partner just identified as their top five. With a possible ten points up for grabs, I am consistently astonished at how few couples can score above three.

Through this exercise, Jane and Stephen started to learn, for the first time, how they respectively defined caring behaviours and we stood back from the individual behaviours on the list to look for themes surrounding their top five lists. Many couples at this point will ask me about my thoughts on the book, The Five Languages of Love (Chapman, 1995). Chapman identified five different ways that couples will demonstrate caring to one another (Quality Time, Physical Touch, Acts of Service, Words of Affirmation, Receiving Gifts). My official take on The Five Love Languages is that I am not aware of any research that has gone into generating an evidence-base for these five themes. However, it does make for a great conversation starter to get the couple thinking about the differences in how they both show and receive caring. With a better understanding of how they both give and *receive* caring, Stephen and Jane were directed to start depositing into the Emotional Bank Account using each other's currencies rather than their own and this became the central homework for the following few weeks.

Communication

Considering that communication is a such an integral part of human inter-action, we are notoriously bad at it. As discussed in Chapter 2, CBCT aims to develop two different sets of skills to get the couple communicating more effectively. Firstly, we need to make a distinction between conversations aimed at understanding how our partner is thinking or feeling in a given situation and those conversations based around problem-solving (Epstein & Baucom, 2002). The former can be described as conversations that help the couple to fill in missing aspects of the formulation diagram in Figure 4.1. The end goal is about understanding. In problem-solving conversations, however, the aim is to generate a practical solution or to make a decision.

We often find that couples are not very good at deciding which conversation they are having, which is a significant part of the problem. There is a common misconception that women tend to want 'thoughts and feelings' conversations and men prefer to have 'problem-solving' conversations. However, this has not been my experience. Instead, it is far more likely that the person *with* the problem will want their partner to listen and understand the thoughts and feelings, but the partner who is trying to *provide support* is likely to feel more comfortable with offering problem-solving. So, who gets to choose? The answer is not that simple. The official line is that it is the one *looking* for the support who gets to decide, but we must avoid long periods of rumination and navel-gazing. At some point, if there is in fact an identifiable problem, it will need to be addressed.

Sharing thoughts and feelings

Conversations around thoughts and feelings involve a set of skills for both speaking and listening (see Chapter 2 for a description). These are not meant to be conversations about who or what is right, but rather about gaining an understanding of each partner's respective opinions, beliefs and emotions. I encourage the listener to *listen in order to understand*, rather than *listen in order to respond*. Very often, as one person is speaking, the other is thinking about their next statement or identifying holes in the speaker's message. Instead, the listener is expected to shelve their own opinions and solely reflect back what is being said without evaluation or opinion.

As we start practicing these roles, it is very common to uncover one of the worst habits that we have in the English language: the conflation of 'I think' and 'I feel'. We distinguish between the two very often in individual CBT sessions, but this has a different element when working with couples. As we started to get into this conversation, for example, Jane stated, "*I feel like you don't listen to me.*" Now, there are two significant problems with this statement, which, if left unattended, could lead to the couple escalating very quickly. Firstly, if someone starts a sentence with "*I feel*", that is generally a signal saying that they do not wish to be challenged or corrected. The hope is that the other person will validate that feeling and accept it. So, what happens when "*I feel*" is followed by an opinion (i.e., "*you're not listening to me*")? Chances are, the partner will become defensive, which is exactly what Stephen did when he responded,

STEPHEN: But I do listen to you.

JANE: Yeah, but I feel like you don't!

STEPHEN: Well, what am I supposed to do with that?! I am listening.

Stephen was not able to validate Jane's feeling, not because he wasn't listening, but because it wasn't a feeling. It was an opinion, and one with which Stephen disagreed, even if it was the impression that he was conveying, or Jane was receiving based on the state of their Emotional Bank Account. The second problem with conflating thoughts and feelings is that once Jane said the words *"I feel,"* she lost the ability to convey what she was actually feeling; in this case: hurt, sad and lonely. Feelings tend to be single words and *"I feel"* needs to be reserved solely for the expression of emotion, which is the real point that Jane needed to make.

I asked Jane to rephrase the statement using the formula *"When you do x, I feel y, because of z."* This helps to bring the conversation back to her and her emotions instead of Stephen and his behaviour. Although his behaviour may be the starting point of that sentence, the aim is to focus on the impact of that behaviour, rather than the correctness of it and to highlight the context for those feelings. Using this formula Jane looked at Stephen and said, *"When you withdraw from me when I think we need to talk about something, it makes me feel sad and hurt."* When asked why it made her feel that way, I probed into her past experiences until she revealed that it was, *"because it reminds me of how my parents avoided their problems and I don't want to end up like them."* Immediately, his demeanour changed. It required some further prompting on my part, but he was able to see that he was a variable in this equation and that there was a difference between the message he was intending to convey through his body language (i.e., *"This conversation is making me uncomfortable"*) and the message that was received by Jane (i.e., *"Our marriage is not very important to me."*). It was not that he was doing something wrong, but rather that he was triggering a fear in Jane that they needed to manage together.

In some instances, particularly when a person struggles to speak directly about their emotions or cannot find the appropriate word, *"I feel"* can be followed by a metaphor. When describing how Jane's behaviour makes him feel when she forces an issue on him, Stephen mentioned, *"I feel like I am about to be hit by a tidal wave."* Of course, although it is not an emotion, per se, this is not an opinion either, since it is not meant to be taken literally. Instead, it paints an emotional picture of his inner experiences that is roughly equivalent to saying the words 'stressed' or 'overwhelmed'.

Problem-solving

When the couple has a good grasp of what it means to listen to understand, rather than listen to respond, I start to include conversations that may require a solution or decision. These conversations can go off the rails for a couple of reasons. First, the couple are not clear in what the problem is; so, I ask them to define the issue behaviourally. For Jane and Stephen, they often get into an argument when getting ready to go on holiday, so they wanted to discuss who does what on the day of departure.

Second, the couple might not have a good grasp of the underlying issues and attempt to solve the problem prematurely. This requires a *Sharing Thoughts and Feelings* conversation about the underlying principle of what a solution would require. Why is it important to each of them? What is at stake? What would it mean if they were to get it wrong? Are there any non-negotiable elements? Using the skills learned from earlier conversations, Stephen and Jane were able to identify some of the key elements that made 'departure day' a rather unpleasant experience for both. These principles act as the foundation on which any successful solution will be built.

Through the initial conversation, Stephen highlighted that he felt 'pressured' by always having to drive the family when they went on holiday, because he felt responsible for ensuring that they were able to "*maximise the amount of time away*" and he wanted to get out the door as quickly as possible. Jane, on the other hand, felt frustrated, because she was responsible for getting the kids ready in the morning so that they could get out the door at Stephen's desired time. This is after she had already spent the previous day or two packing for herself and the kids; whereas Stephen only packed for himself. She acknowledged that this had led to her feeling resentful of Stephen over the last couple of years, which meant that she was less willing to "*behave according to your timetable.*" Jane had increasingly become noticeably 'moodier' on the day of departure, which, understandably, had a significant impact on their relationship.

The couple were then equipped to start generating possible solutions. I asked them to consider solutions that took both of their points of view into account; thus, allowing them to stand up for each other's interests in addition to considering their own. Looking out for each other's interests increases the sense of connection in the relationship and increases the sense of ownership over the solution. Knowing that a solution meets their fundamental needs on an issue makes it more likely that they will both carry out their respective parts of the agreement. In Jane and Stephen's case, they were able to recognise that any solution had to have two requirements at its heart. First, Stephen needed Jane to know how important it was for him to make an early start on a road trip. He was happy to do all of the driving but had often felt 'drained' at the end of a long day on the road, so any solution required an early start to the day. Jane understood that quickly. She knew that Stephen could be irritable when tired and she wanted to find a solution that would keep him from feel drained. However, she felt frustrated at having to do the 'heavy lifting' of preparing for the trip. Any solution, therefore, also had to include Stephen's input and effort prior to setting out on the road. Stephen was a little defensive at first but understood quickly that if Jane was going stand up for his needs, he also had to reciprocate and meet her needs. Together, they were able to come up with a plan that met both needs. I suggested that they agree to a trial period, so they did not have to make long-term decisions, but instead to see how the next trip went and revisit the conversation for the following trip.

For some problems, it is important to note that there may not be a solution that a couple can agree on. Often these occur when the underlying principles are in conflict and cannot coexist, where if one person gets their needs met, the other one cannot, such as when couples disagree on where to live geographically. In these instances, acceptance-based strategies (such as those discussed in Chapter 3) might be needed.

Conflict Management

The relationship meeting

Once the couple has a firm grounding in the different communication skills, we discuss how these can be applied to the more challenging, emotionally provoking conversations. I first like to point out that relationship conflict tends to have a paradox embedded inside of it. Whilst on the surface, conflict tends to make each individual feel disconnected from the other; prompting feelings of sadness and hurt, the main reason that these conflicts happen in the first place is because they both care about the topic and the relationship. They are both desperate to be heard, which can stop them both from hearing the other person. When both people take a position of *"not hearing you until you hear me"*, nothing changes.

To help facilitate these conversations, I recommend that couples hold a regular relationship meeting, preferably weekly or fortnightly in the beginning. Most people intuitively understand what I mean when I talk about setting up a 'date night' – time dedicated to investing in the friendship-side of the relationship; to enjoy each other's company and enjoy quality time. For many, this is a significant deposit into the Emotional Bank Account. The relationship meeting is the equivalent time spent dedicated to the business-side of the relationship. It is an opportunity for the couple to discuss what has gone well, what has not gone well, to consciously practice speaking and listening to either understand or problem-solve.

There are several reasons why having a dedicated time for these conversations can be useful. First, it provides a space where both individuals can go into a conversation knowing that they will need to practice their communication skills to hear and be heard about something that really matters to each of them. Second, it gets them to think about their difficulties with a team mindset. Knowing that the conversation is coming allows each of them to reflect on what is important to them and what they want the other person to know or understand so that the ethos is *"us against the world/mis-communication"* rather than *"us against each other."* In Integrative Behavioural Couple Therapy (see Chapter 3), this process is referred to as Unified Detachment. Lastly, Jane acknowledged that she tended to bring up an issue as and when she felt emotional. For her, being in a relationship meant *"being honest with my feelings as and when I feel upset."* However, knowing that Stephen was open to truly listening to her concerns on a Monday night relationship meeting meant that Jane was able to compartmentalise her thoughts and feelings for a time that would be more productive for them both. Interestingly, many people find that by postponing the difficult conversation by a couple of days to a relationship meeting, the issue that seemed so important at the time loses much of its urgency. By taking the raw emotion out of the conversation, they are able to move into the conversation that they are meant to have.

Stop and timeout

With all of the best intentions in the world, our emotions can still get the better of us in the moment. Relationship meetings, and triggering times in between, can be hard to navigate because our sensitivities can often get the better of us, bringing about uncomfortable emotions and all the physiological changes that come with an active fight-or-flight response. I mentioned earlier that Jane and Stephen would get into a demand-withdraw pattern during their arguments. Physically, the two of them were in a similar state of high arousal, but their emotional and behavioural reactions were very different. When in such a state, it would be very difficult for either of them to express their needs and opinions with tact and care. Nor could they hear each other out and fully understand what the other was trying to convey.

   In such a state, it is necessary for the couple to pause the conversation to self-soothe and regroup. For some, that could mean a five-minute stretch to get some air or a cup of tea. To interrupt a typical demand-withdraw pattern, both partners need to see this break as a game of trust. If feeling overwhelmed, the person who tends to withdraw needs to know that by asking for a moment to self-soothe, the 'demander' will not continue to pursue but will instead give time and space. On the other hand, the person who tends to demand needs to know that the 'withdrawer' is not going to walk away from the conversation, full stop. To help with that, I recommend that the person who requests the break *has to be* the one who reengages the conversation. By doing so, they are showing that, for the sake of the relationship, the conversation is worth having, which can be a massive deposit into the Emotional Bank Account. However, they are doing so on the condition that they are physically and emotionally ready to do so.

   Often, these breaks need to be longer than just a few minutes. When in a state of physical arousal, it might be necessary to take upwards of 30 minutes to self-soothe sufficiently to continue. In these cases, I recommend that the couple devise a signal to take an extended break, a timeout. Unsurprisingly, Stephen telling Jane to "*calm down*" had never led to a successful conversation. Instead, when either of them noticed that the tension was rising, they were to say, in as lovingly a way as possible, "*I need a timeout*". Putting the emphasis on themselves in those moments, even when it is the other person who really needs to "*calm down*", allowed them to avoid the accusation/defensiveness that came with pointing out that the other person was the problem.

Once the signal has been given, both people agree to pause the conversation and return at a designated time. I usually recommend 30 minutes to give them time to physically de-escalate, through deep breathing and imagery exercises, and to prepare themselves cognitively themselves for a productive conversation. This includes asking themselves why this particular conversation is so important to them and what they need the other person to hear. Jane struggled with this concept initially. She acknowledged that she would often go into her "*neutral corner*" and start dwelling on why *she* was the correct one and why *Stephen* was wrong. This is a common mistake for most couples, and it is important for them to go into the timeout as a team or they will not come out as one.

Bringing it all together

The final session is an opportunity to review the material learned throughout the sessions, develop a relapse prevention plan and answer any final questions that the couple may have. We review the material from our sessions that has been helpful. By this point, Jane and Stephen had taken the concepts of the Emotional Bank Account and reciprocity to heart. They were more willing to hear each other out, knowing that their communication difficulties were both a cause and an effect of the tendency to listen in order to respond, rather than to listen in order to understand. At this point, Jane and Stephen had held two relationship meetings, which had gone well. They were dedicated to continuing them into the coming months and they had even had a successful timeout that week.

Lastly, we put a follow-up session in the diary. Typically, I aim for anywhere between 1 to 3-months' time. This gives the couple enough time to entrench some of the new behaviour and to get things wrong so that they can either course-correct themselves or provide us with something to process in follow-up. Of course, where necessary, this appointment can be moved up if they need further support.

Follow-up session

I met with Stephen and Jane for a 3-month follow-up session. The aims of the session were: to review the material that we had discussed over the course of the therapy; to discuss how they had successfully applied the principles learned and to identify where they might have struggled and why.

Stephen and Jane had applied much of what we had discussed in our sessions. Stephen had gone through great lengths at work to attain a better work/life balance. They told me about their 'Magic Monday Meetings', which they had faithfully held every week since their therapy.

Challenges

Stephen and Jane often struggled to implement the timeout strategy. They could both see the value in it, but they found it hard to recognise the warning signs that tensions were rising. As we discussed the experience in greater detail, it was clear that Jane had a hard time trusting that Stephen would return to the conversation after a timeout, and so she tended to block his escapes and dismiss his calls for a stop or a timeout. Exploring this further, Jane acknowledged that her lack of trust came from years of avoidance on Stephen's part and she had to make a concerted effort to notice her default reaction and choose a different way of responding. Jane acknowledged that assuming that things would always be as they always had been limited Stephen's ability to demonstrate a willingness to change.

Therapist reflections

Working with Stephen and Jane presented an exciting challenge. The contrasting personalities and coping mechanisms they had developed from their respective family backgrounds significantly influenced their communication styles and conflict resolution approaches. Jane was so willing to express her feelings openly, and this provided insight into her thoughts and emotions. Her ability to identify patterns in her behaviour and connect them to her upbringing allowed for potential breakthroughs. However, keeping those thoughts and feelings contained in a way that wouldn't trigger a defensive reaction in Stephen was difficult at times.

Similarly, Stephen's tendency to withdraw when faced with conflict posed a challenge. His deeply ingrained belief that conflict is detrimental and should be avoided hindered the therapeutic progress at the start of treatment. Encouraging Stephen to confront his avoidance behaviour and recognise its roots required delicate handling, given how entrenched it was. Managing the couple's vastly different communication styles, and ensuring both felt heard and validated, proved to be an ongoing challenge in therapy. In the end, we were able to balance Jane's urgency to address issues immediately with Stephen's inclination to withdraw, which fostered effective communication and gradual conflict resolution.

Therapist tips

- Do not be afraid to interrupt! If you notice that the conversation is falling back into old patterns, stop it immediately, and provide some brief instruction or clarification.
- Keep the conversations more dyadic than didactic. Psychoeducation is an important part of CBCT, but it is more important to make the information relevant to the couple in session by allowing the partners to talk to one another.
- Do not be the Speaker of the House. Couples will often want to talk to each other through you. Thank them for not wanting to seem rude by excluding you and direct their attention to the partner.
- The CBCT practitioner must remain flexible to the needs of the couple and treatment can go in many different directions. This is a guide to how one couple might be treated in one specific way, but there is no reason to think that this is the only way that this couple's treatment could have unfolded.

Suggestions for further Reading

Epstein, N.B., & Baucom, D.H. (2002). *Enhanced cognitive-behavioral therapy for couples: A contextual approach.* American Psychological Association.

References

Chapman, G. (1995). *The five languages of love.* Northfield.

Epstein, N.B., & Baucom, D.H. (2002). *Enhanced cognitive-behavioral therapy for couples: A contextual approach.* American Psychological Association.

Fals-Stewart, W., & Lam, W.K.K. (2010). Marital Dysfunction. In J.C. Thomas & M. Hersen (eds). *Handbook of clinical psychology competencies.* Springer.

Freedman, R. (2002). *Confucius: The golden rule.* Scholastic Inc.

Gottman, J.M., Notarious, C., Markman, H., Bank, S., & Yoppi, B. (1976). Behaviour exchange theory and marital decision making. *Journal of Personality and Social Psychology*, 34 (1), 14–23.

Gottman, J. M. (1999). *Marriage clinic: A scientifically based marital therapy.* WW Norton & Company.

Grant, L. (2011). Conceptualisation of Couples in Therapy. In: *BABCP 39th Annual Conference.* Guildford, University of Surrey.

Weiss, R.L. (1980). Strategic behavioral marital therapy: Toward a model for assessment and intervention. In J.P. Vincent (ed.), *Advances in family intervention, assessment and theory.* (Vol. 1, pp. 229–271). JAI Press.

Chapter 5

Intimate Partner Violence and Transition to Parenthood

Katy Wood

Maria felt some relief when her health visitor suggested a referral to her local NHS psychological service for support. Both Maria and David had become exhausted by the dual demands of work and parenting, and neither had much sense of supportive teamwork. The couple loved their 15-month-old daughter Sophie and she was a much wanted child, but there was a jarring discrepancy between how they imagined this would be and the lived reality of just how hard it often seemed.

The couple would become polarised in repetitive conflicts, with Maria feeling unsupported and ignored, whilst David felt rejected and incompetent. Recently, frustrations had escalated into physical aggression, leading to increased concerns about the pushing, slapping and hitting, which was low-level but distressing. It was clear things couldn't continue this way and they didn't want to bring their daughter up in an atmosphere of tension and conflict.

The pull to work with couples

Why would anyone want to work with all this conflict? What kind of a person chooses to involve themselves in other people's disputes? Well … I have been drawn towards both the puzzle-solving and the expanded human perspectives of couple work. It is enriching to explore more multi-dimensional views, to try and make sense of the meanings, feelings, and needs which lie beneath the often one-dimensional or superficial presentations of conflict. In working to uncover some of these, we may gain a privileged access to the individual and shared hopes and fears which could help us point towards a better future for the couple. Of course, the route can be bumpy and we may inevitably experience frustrations, confusion or roadblocks along the way, but the territory overall remains absorbing. Good supervision provides essential ballast and a recalibration towards key priorities.

The impact of relationships generally is so fundamental to our experience of life. With regard to couple relationships specifically, those of us who live with a partner will know how significantly our wellbeing is affected by the

DOI: 10.4324/9781003024439-7

strengths and challenges of our daily interactions. My interest in working with couples is therefore broadly twofold: it is often rewarding and moving (despite the difficulties) to be invited into this very personal area of life, observing the live moment-by-moment processes of communication and helping couples to make more mutually satisfying choices. At the same time, it also enriches my appreciation of my own relationship and reminds me to reflect on how helpful or otherwise my behaviours and attitudes are in nourishing our life together.

In preparing you to think with me about Maria and David, I first introduce the two broad themes of partner aggression and, separately (though linked in the case of this couple), issues around the transition to parenthood. My hope is that this will help to clarify ethical and assessment considerations where physical aggression has occurred, as well as presenting a brief overview of some of the possible challenges experienced by couples facing new parenthood together. I then provide a brief theoretical framework for couple therapy in these contexts, before returning to Maria and David for a more detailed look at their specific struggles and dilemmas.

Themes, debates, and boundaries: safety first

The issue of whether it is safe or appropriate to work with couples where there has been physical aggression has sometimes been a matter of controversy. At times there have been apparently contradictory conclusions and ethical debates, although all sides value the safety of adults and children, individual wellbeing and healthy relationships.

Domestic violence and abuse (DVA) are serious concerns which can have a damaging impact on mental and physical health, as well as social and economic wellbeing. In considering intimate partner violence, the importance of differentiating between various types of aggression and violence has been recognised. Kelly & Johnson (2008) have suggested four main categories: coercive controlling violence; violent resistance; situational couple violence; and separation-instigated violence.

Coercive controlling violence, where the violence is 'asymmetric' in terms of gender (i.e. perpetrated largely by men), is more likely to be reported by studies from women's refuges, court-mandated treatment programmes, police reports and A&E departments. For example, clients attending IDVA (Independent Domestic Violence Advisors) services will in 95% of cases be women (SafeLives 2019a). Women tend to experience the most severe forms of DVA, which can also be life-threatening. An ONS report indicated that 76% of victims of domestic homicides in England and Wales were female (ONS 2021 p.7). The domestic violence terms VAW (violence against women) and GBV (gender-based violence) also reflect these realities. However, men also suffer from domestic abuse, though it is usually less severe. The impact of gender expectations may nonetheless make it harder for some men to disclose due to feelings of shame and embarrassment (SafeLives 2019b). Within lesbian and gay relationships, barriers to accessing help and support may include fears of contributing to heterosexism (Harden et al. 2022). When considering the context of male violence against women, Moore et al. (2010) explore the ways that men may struggle with unrealistic gender role norms, leading some of them to seek a sense of power and control through aggressive behaviours.

Lower-level situational couple violence (where use of hospitals, police and refuges is less likely) is associated with greater gender 'symmetry'. It is more often reported in large-scale survey research using community or national samples, as well as some clinic samples. These issues of differentiation regarding types of abuse and gender prevalence are discussed further by Epstein et al. (2015, pp389–390), and Salis & O'Leary (2016, pp96–106).

Couple therapy is not safe or ethical in situations of coercive controlling violence, severe physical violence and battering, or when victims are currently in danger from their partner, fear the perpetrator or have suffered injury. These forms of DVA are commonly linked with additional psychological aggression and pervasive patterns of coercive control, which may include sexual or financial abuse as well as harassment and stalking, or other jealous and controlling behaviours. In these cases, referrals should be made to the relevant services for domestic abuse, safeguarding or perpetrator intervention. Additionally, untreated substance misuse issues are a risk factor for domestic violence and therefore another exclusion criterion for couple therapy, with the exception of couple-based interventions that focus specifically on the addiction (see Chapter 16).

The issue on the other side of the ethical debate is that, given the prevalence of lower-level situational couple violence (which does not have an underlying power dynamic of coercive control) and the availability of safe and effective couple therapy (e.g. Epstein et al., 2015; Salis & O'Leary 2016; Jacobson & Christensen, 1996), this intervention should be considered to help reduce partner aggression and improve relationships.

When it's not all 'a bundle of joy': couples and the transition to parenthood

The experiences of individuals and couples related to conception, pregnancy, childbirth, and parenting may include many joys and rewards which also have some potential to strengthen relationships (Delicate et al., 2018). Following the transition to parenthood, up to a half of all couples maintain a similar level of relationship satisfaction or an increase (Kluwer, 2010). However, the challenges of adapting to the new demands of parenting are also considerable, often being associated with a decline in relationship satisfaction and an increase in conflict (e.g. Shapiro et al., 2000; Doss et al., 2009). This can be hard for couples to acknowledge or process, particularly when expectations have been idealised.

When becoming a parent, a significant number of life changes often occur all at the same time (e.g. Glade et al., 2005; Walker, 2014). Couples presenting for therapy may therefore be struggling with a wide variety of related issues. Even a much loved and wanted baby will bring many new physical, domestic and financial demands, along with some reduced freedoms and new responsibilities which are bound to take their toll on a relationship at times. Shifting identities have to accommodate new roles and expectations, as well as changed social and family relationships. Previous feelings of competence may sometimes give way to new anxieties or vulnerabilities.

Other factors affecting adjustment include the level and type of social support, the baby's temperament and partners' individual physical and psychological health (including the possibility of postnatal depression in mothers and / or fathers, e.g. Edward et al., 2015). Changes in work patterns and new pressures on the main breadwinner, stay-at-home parent or returning-to-work parent create further demands, and couples have less energy and attention available for each other. This may impact on communication, expressions of verbal and physical affection as well as sexual intimacy. Other postpartum sexual issues are also common (O'Malley et al., 2018).

New parenting creates a heightened need for couple negotiation (in a context of reduced time and energy), since there are far more decisions which now have to be made. This leaves relationships vulnerable if partners have limited problem-solving skills or more fragile emotional regulation.

Couple therapy for partner aggression

Different approaches to couple work for partner aggression share some common objectives e.g. interruption of aggressive behaviour patterns and the development of more constructive alternatives. When assessment indicates suitability for therapy and a couple show capacity to engage with the work, interventions have been shown to be safe and effective (Epstein et al., 2015 and Salis & O'Leary 2016). Many of the foundational principles of CBCT (Epstein & Baucom 2002) still apply when working with partner aggression, although there are particular emphases in certain areas. Epstein et al. (2015) provide a more detailed account of this, but the key over-riding goals are:

- To reduce risk factors which may lead to aggressive behaviour.
- To enhance protective factors that reduce the risk of aggression.

Table 5.1 summarises some of the issues broadly related to these aims and presents possible interventions. These combine with more general issues around relationship distress, which itself is a risk factor for partner aggression. Additionally, common CBCT strategies which help to increase positive behaviours, mutual support, intimacy and shared positive activities may be included in the treatment plan.

Table 5.1 Risk factors for partner aggression and possible interventions

Risk factors to reduce	Protective awareness, knowledge and strategies to develop
Learned aggressive responses to conflict	Psychoeducation e.g. about forms of aggression, their impact and consequences; risk factors; treatment rationale.
Escalation of negative behavioural interactions	De-escalation skills e.g. identifying early cues of anger arousal and using safe alternatives such as time out and self-soothing.
Poor skills in emotional regulation and the management of anger and conflict	Understanding that strong emotions mean something is important to us and learning to identify, acknowledge and manage these constructively; practising communication and problem-solving skills; stress management skills.
Unhelpful beliefs, for example which condone, justify or encourage aggression (whether psychological or physical) or increase anger through negative attributions	Commit to a non-aggressive baseline (encouraging a sense of personal responsibility for behaviour towards partner) and recognise feasible alternatives. Find other explanations for a (non-aggressive) partner's intentions and behaviour.
Problematic issues regarding gender roles, power sharing, family and / or cultural influences and the management of chronic stressors.	Exploration as needed and a reorientation towards more healthy and respectful coping, values and perspectives.
Individual psychopathology	CBCT interventions to address disorder specific issues and, where modifiable, traits such as lack of empathy.

Couple therapy to support the transition to parenthood

The points above concerning couple therapy for partner aggression overlap with common focal points in couple therapy generally. In the context of difficulties around the transition to parenthood, the left-hand box in Table 5.1 above on "*Problematic issues regarding gender roles, power sharing, family and / or cultural influences and the management of chronic stressors*" is particularly relevant.

There have been a number of specific interventions to support the transition to parenthood and couple conflict around parenting-related issues. These have been delivered by a variety of health professionals (e.g. midwives, nurses, therapists) and include psychoeducational group workshops, online or combination programmes as well as brief couple therapy interventions (e. g. Shapiro & Gottman, 2005; Doherty et al., 2006; Shapiro et al., 2015; Petch et al., 2012; DWP, 2017; Linville et al., 2017). Whilst these approaches differ in format, the shared themes can be helpful in conceptualising the needs of this client group. Insights from family therapy can also be valuable (e.g. Glade et al., 2005; Walker, 2014) and there is much common ground between different perspectives.

CBCT emphasises an adaptation model of couple functioning (Epstein & Baucom, 2002) which is well suited to the transitions involved in becoming parents. Kluwer's integrative Transition to Parenthood Model (Kluwer, 2010) offers a complementary approach, which shares the emphasis on resources and vulnerabilities which may intensify pre-existing issues. Both pre-birth and post-birth perspectives are considered, taking account of personal and situational characteristics (i.e. of the individual, couple and environment). These affect how the couple adapt positively or negatively to the events and requirements of new parenthood, thereby determining possible changes (for better or worse) or continuity in relationship quality and satisfaction.

In supporting couples to adapt to the 'new normal' of parenting, the changes and stressors can be normalised and validated. I have found it important to make space to acknowledge some of the ordinary negative feelings that may sometimes arise with new parenthood e.g. frustration; irritation; worry; exhaustion; loss (the feelings not advertised in the 'bundle of joy' paradigm!). I also notice the relief clients express when I encourage more realistic intentions to be a 'good enough parent', to connect with underlying values and find some empathic joining around shared difficulties. These approaches help to increase flexibility and resilience, as does paying attention to what they are doing well.

Strengths and resources are developed as individuals, parents and a couple. The impact of earlier and current family experiences can be reviewed both in order to increase an understanding of their influences and to encourage 'intentional parenting' vs 'default parenting' (Glade et al., 2005, p.330). In line with this idea, the Healthy Nests intervention includes a values-based discussion of how partners would want their children to describe their parents' couple relationship (Linville et al., 2017, p.348). The importance of father involvement is also often emphasised (e.g. Doherty et al., 2006; Shapiro et al., 2015) but, regardless of gender or sexuality, there is a principle of both parents learning to feel comfortable in the role of caregiver.

Meeting Maria and David

I collect Maria and David from the waiting area and notice they are sitting apart from each other in silence. The emotional distance between them is palpable and I sense a weighted tension as I invite them into the therapy room. I remind myself to breathe fully and am conscious of using my voice and manner to try and convey some measure of stability and ease. This is not to deny or jar with the obvious tensions, nor to 'play at being a therapist' (!), but rather to help them feel it's going to be alright to come in and speak to a complete stranger about such personal matters.

Maria and David are a white, British heterosexual couple. Maria is in her late 30s, smartly presented and practically competent, though she appears somewhat flat and expressionless, her face unmoving. David is slightly older, mid-40s, he has some artistic leanings and dresses more casually. His shoulders are slightly hunched and he has an air of concern, but a kind smile.

Maria's and David's individual triage notes indicated that Maria had pushed, slapped and hit David several times in the past few months. This had occurred in the evenings, when their 15 month old daughter Sophie was asleep in her bedroom. Triggers were mainly disagreements about parenting and household tasks, and Maria had expressed some remorse alongside her frustrations. She seemed nonetheless to have limited awareness of her own emotional processes and vulnerabilities or of how her behaviour could impact David, thus leading to frustrations escalating more easily. There was no physical aggression from David (although he occasionally raised his voice in anger and exasperation), and he confirmed he had not experienced any injuries or severe violence. Neither partner feared the other, there were no patterns of coercive control and no substance misuse issues. Both were keen to get help.

The couple met through an online dating app and had been together for about 2½ years, marrying within 6 months of meeting and becoming intentionally pregnant soon after. Both really wanted to start a family and settle down. They'd previously enjoyed some travelling, meeting other people and leading active lives.

When I ask the couple about their initial attraction to each other, it's the first time they look at each other, exchanging slightly surprised and embarrassed glances, and just a glimmer of a smile. David says he'd liked Maria for her independence and forthright manner, whilst Maria was drawn to David's kindness, and had found him trustworthy and reliable. Each now felt the other's positive qualities had more negatively morphed into Maria being 'bossy' and David being 'just not practical enough'. The last time they'd enjoyed being together had been on a short trip away 6 weeks previously, relieved of some of the pressures of day to day life.

Both were in full time office jobs but felt the financial squeeze of parenting and nursery costs. Maria hadn't really wanted to return to work after her year's maternity leave, and she felt resentful, guilty, and very stressed by this change. David felt it was a difficult, but necessary compromise.

THERAPIST REFLECTION: I sometimes winced internally at Maria's initial sharpness with David (sensing the sting of criticism he felt and recognising the challenge ahead to develop Maria's emotional awareness and tact), though I saw it came from a sense of depletion and frustration. I noticed I felt a certain protectiveness towards David and I wanted him to assert himself more. However, the process of formulating the couple's difficulties helped to orientate them towards a calmer discussion of their external stressors, personal differences and coping mechanisms, as well as the beginnings of some mutual understanding. This brought all three of us a little relief and hope.

Developing an initial shared formulation

The broad framework for formulation was based around combining the CBCT and transition to parenthood models mentioned above (Epstein & Baucom, 2002, p.12; Kluwer, 2010). Risk factors for partner aggression were considered under 'vulnerabilities' and also linked to the development of unhelpful reactions.

Pre-parenting stressors had been managed sufficiently through exercise, outings, greater social support, and hobbies such as David's artwork and football, but the couple's strong shared belief that 'parenting involves sacrifices' had led to over-adaptation and a withdrawal of these coping strategies. Previous limitations in communication skills and emotional expression were also now more exposed.

Sophie brought various rewards and satisfactions, but the challenges of parenting were harder for Maria and David to acknowledge to each other. David struggled with some of the increased responsibilities and Maria had resentfully taken too much on. Her domestic standards were also higher than David's and she often criticised his efforts, making denigratory comments about 'male incompetence'. This was sometimes delivered in an apparently light and jovial tone which was nonetheless evidently hurtful and dismissive. Maria's return to work had left her feeling overwhelmed both at home and at work, and she wanted more proactive support from David. Conflict subsequently escalated, culminating in Maria's physical aggression or a depressed defeat. David would try to keep the peace in a rather passive way, bottling things up until his own anger also surfaced. These ongoing patterns of attack and withdrawal were draining for both at a time when their energy levels were already low.

Current limited resources included a shared commitment to Sophie, some support from David's family (Maria's all lived much further away) and a mutual desire to improve the couple relationship. Maria commented that "*I know I shouldn't hit David, but I get so frustrated with him*". David didn't understand her frustration and said, "*I just want you to talk to me in a reasonable way*". The 'shared responsibility' angle of couple therapy is harder to emphasise when one person's behaviour is crossing the line, as in the case of physical aggression. However, distinguishing between content (i.e. what Maria was upset about) and process (using aggression to manage this) helped in strengthening Maria's commitment to a 'no-aggression contract'. It also validated her need to have more practical support from David, as well as his right to safe discussion. David could then consider what he might need to do to meet more reasonable requests from Maria. In support of these aims and the stabilisation of the relationship, the couple's broader treatment goals were:

- Stop the use of physical aggression.
- Improve communication (in order to be able to discuss difficult issues without escalation).
- Address issues around shared parenting and the related division of household tasks.

Course of Therapy

Over the course of 12 couple therapy sessions (after the usual four assessment sessions), we covered many of the key areas mentioned in Table 5.1 above, alongside concerns about shared parenting and household management. The following sections highlight a few main themes which, in practice, were often more interwoven rather than linear.

Committing to Safety First

Initial priorities focused on helping Maria and David to understand and use the practical skills needed for de-escalation and containment, so they could build confidence that the safety contract was achievable. Basic psychoeducation was included to explain the fight / flight system, the damaging impact of escalating conflict and aggression, and the negative effects for children. The couple's shared commitment to their daughter Sophie was a helpful motivating factor. We worked through a detailed safety plan. This included time-out strategies; a 'safe word'; protecting Sophie; re-engagement following time-out; and 'compartmentalising' if an issue needed to be put on hold until the next couple therapy session. Additionally, we considered self-soothing strategies such as breathing and imagery exercises (practiced in session), physical exercise options and alternative activities to encourage a general winding down and a more neutral or helpful focus.

The following dialogue gives a snapshot of early cue identification. Despite mainly involving Maria, David's presence is nonetheless important so that both witness the validation of a no-aggression agreement as well as experiencing the discussion of these issues in a calm and non-threatening way. The couple subsequently expressed some relief about this and the beginnings of some hope for change.

THERAPIST: Maria, you've been honest enough to acknowledge your feelings of loss of control leading to aggression. Would you be willing for us all to think together about what happens and what alternatives there might be?

MARIA: Well yes, but I get so frustrated with David and it just boils up inside me – I don't know how to control it.

THERAPIST: Many people who experience these difficulties also feel or believe that it's uncontrollable, but we can learn to identify early signals and take care of ourselves and the relationship in a different way. What, for you, are the first signs you notice in your body or mind?

MARIA: I haven't really thought about it before, I'm not sure.

THERAPIST: Perhaps I can ask you, David – what's the first thing you've noticed on these previous occasions just before Maria has become physically aggressive?

DAVID: It starts off with her voice getting much louder and there's a sharper edge to it.

THERAPIST: Maria, do you recognise David's description?

MARIA: Yes, it's true – that's what happens on the outside, but on the inside I think it's been building up before then.

THERAPIST: That's helpful for us to understand. Can you tell me a bit more about this 'building up'? For example, some people notice particular bodily sensations such as muscular tension in the jaw, throat, shoulders or hands; or maybe their heart starts beating faster, or the breathing becomes quicker or more shallow; others might start shouting or swearing in their own mind before anything is said out loud. Do you have a sense of what might happen with you?

MARIA: Actually, when you mentioned those examples, I realised I do get a really tight throat and then I feel my heartbeat getting stronger and faster.

THERAPIST: OK, so when you're able to pause and reflect, you can see there are other things going on beforehand. These kinds of signs can be important 'warning signals' for us.

An additional significant shift for Maria and David was reframing 'time-out' as being protective of the relationship rather than a 'stomping off'. Once in an argument, David wanted to try and complete the discussion. However, knowing that time-out included a commitment to later, calmer discussion helped him to 'press the pause button' once emotional arousal levels reached a certain point. Strategies mentioned in this section also helped to challenge beliefs about the uncontrollability of anger. Each week we checked in on whether or not there had been any further instances of physical aggression. This routine provided helpful reinforcement for the necessary ongoing commitment to a safety agreement.

Managing stress and anger

It's easy to see how the unchecked build-up of stress, alongside poor general stress management, can increase risk for escalation towards physical aggression. Our formulation had helped Maria and David to externalise some of the common stresses of parenting rather than blame each other. However, although they were making good use of the de-escalation skills, we needed to work on increasing their self-care repertoire.

The following interaction focuses on some of the parenting-related cognitions which had become an obstacle to effective stress management:

DAVID: I used to play a lot of football before Sophie was born, but obviously I can't do that anymore.

MARIA: Yes, I've told him we've got to take our parenting seriously, we can't just go out and do what we did before. I've had to stop things too. Sophie's the one that matters now.

THERAPIST: I hear your shared commitment to Sophie, and you're both right that adjustments have to be made, but I want to ask you something that may at first seem like an odd question. What are the recommendations for using an oxygen mask on an aeroplane if you have a baby with you?

(David and Maria look a bit confused and glance at each other in an "*I thought we were supposed to be doing couple therapy*" kind of way – well at least there's a moment of connection between them! Their facial expressions soften and they smile slightly as the penny drops.)

DAVID: Oh – well they say put your own mask on first, but that must be so hard to do.

MARIA: And that's in an emergency situation, so how can that help us in normal everyday life?

THERAPIST: Maybe I can turn the question back to you. How do you think it might help both of you and Sophie if you were occasionally able to take a little time to replenish yourselves?

MARIA: I might be a bit less tired and stressed but, particularly now that I'm working, I just feel so guilty if I don't spend all my extra time with her.

THERAPIST: How would you respond to Maria about that, David?

DAVID: (Turning to look at Maria) I think you're a really good Mum to Sophie, but I think you need a break sometimes – I think we both do.

We subsequently discussed the importance of good self-care and stress management for psychological wellbeing, whilst also acknowledging how challenging this could be alongside work and parenting responsibilities. We explored the 'all or nothing' perspectives which prevented any self-care, and considered some small, achievable goals. The couple agreed that each partner could choose one evening activity each week (e.g. swimming, football, art class) whilst the other looked after Sophie. They also offered occasional mini-breaks of 15–30 minutes when the other partner arrived home and took a shower or did some undisturbed reading. Reframing this self-care as a way of ultimately taking better care of Sophie, as well as protecting the couple relationship, provided a helpful motivation to sustain their new routines.

Re-evaluating negative attributions ("You just do it because...")

Misunderstandings based on negative assumptions about the other partner's intent were leaving David feeling helpless and Maria angrier and more aggressive:

DAVID: (sounding defeated) Sometimes I'm doing my best to calm Sophie down when she's crying, but Maria just starts telling me I'm doing it all wrong – she thinks I'm a useless father.

MARIA: (To David, in a clipped manner) I've never said that and I try to help you, but you just deliberately ignore me – what I say doesn't count.

DAVID: (To Maria, and looking bewildered) How can you say I 'ignore' you? I'm standing right there, aren't I, trying to help out with Sophie.

MARIA: (Sighs and raises her eyes and eyebrows in an expression of exasperation. She turns to me.) You see? This is what drives me mad. He thinks he's 'helping out', but he does the opposite of what I say. He winds me up on purpose.

DAVID: This is how it goes – I just can't win.

(His shoulders slump and his eyes look to the floor.)THERAPIST: I can see you're both upset with each other and feeling like you're being treated unfairly. There seem to be a few different points here, so let's 'rewind' and slow things down a little.

THERAPIST REFLECTION: I felt a certain tenderness towards both David and Maria in this exchange as I observed the pain of human misunderstandings or poor communication and the linked potential for rapid escalation. I acknowledged to myself the disheartening sense of division between them, whilst also having some hope that they could learn to manage this more constructively. At one level, Maria seemed to hold the power as the more confident and experienced parent. At another level however, there was a type of powerlessness in her thwarted (and often blunt) attempts to elicit more practical support from David. Whilst I empathised with his feelings of confusion and bewilderment, I nonetheless also saw Maria's frustration in wanting David to take more responsibility rather than settling for a sometimes passive and secondary role of simply 'helping out'.

We explored their attributions, considered alternative explanations and developed some basic communication skills around this: identifying and expressing some of the painful underlying feelings of hurt, disappointment, confusion and inadequacy; being specific e.g. working out what words and / or behaviours had led David to infer that Maria thought he was a 'useless father'? How did Maria conclude she was being deliberately ignored, or alternatively wound up 'on purpose'?; making requests rather than complaints. This was slow work which we had to review many times, but the couple glimpsed the possibility of doing things differently.

Influences from family history

Examining the possible impact of earlier history can be another way of externalising issues, helping the individual and partner to be aware of potential vulnerabilities and making sense of apparent over-reactions or challenges. When we discussed David's family background, he said there had been a lot of conflict between his parents (though no physical aggression) and he had determined that he would do things differently. He sometimes over-compensated by becoming too passive, wary of making his own needs known in case it provoked disagreements. Yet bottling things up tended to lead eventually to getting angrier than if he'd been able to discuss his concerns earlier. Either way it was painful for him to find himself caught up again in situations of heightened conflict despite wanting to avoid this.

Maria's parents were both away a lot for work when she was a child and they would often leave her with friends or relatives, or sometimes by herself once she reached sixteen. Practical needs were met and she became quite independently capable, but others provided little emotional attunement. Themes of feeling unsupported therefore carried a particular emotional charge, as did the guilt she felt when returning to work and leaving Sophie at nursery, despite the different circumstances.

Acknowledging the losses and challenges of parenting (alongside the pleasures and rewards): "We love Sophie, but sometimes it's really hard."

Since Maria and David met at a stage in life when they were both keen to settle down and start a family, much was invested in this and expectations were high. When the couple had begun to struggle with many of the normal stressors of early parenting such as sleep deprivation, reduced time and energy, increased domestic tasks and the sheer noise and regularity of a baby's crying in a small flat, neither wanted to discuss the downside. Maria soldiered on, giving the impression she was taking it all in her stride, whilst David felt he ought to know what to do but often felt quite overwhelmed or excluded.

Normalising some of these difficulties and developing 'sharing thoughts and feelings' skills helped the couple understand that both had suffered in their own ways and could instead be a resource for each other. We reframed support seeking as helpful adaptation rather than failure. The decision-making skills were a real eye-opener for Maria and David, and they worked hard on the practical problem-solving around how best to share domestic duties and parenting decisions. David began to feel more involved as a father and Maria felt better supported.

Discussion

Maria and David managed to make some early gains in stabilisation through good use of safety plans, time out and stopping the escalation of aggression. Therapy was able to provide some helpful containment for them and they developed a better understanding of external stressors and their impact. However, much of the subsequent work around communication was often painstakingly slow and required lots of reinforcement and review, sometimes leaving me feeling like I was wading through mud! I found an awkward discrepancy between David's and Maria's ability to use the 'sharing thoughts and feelings' skills as Maria was less psychologically minded (she fared better with the decision-making skills). I therefore explored 'how things land' in order to increase Maria's awareness and empathy and David's ability to speak up for himself, e.g. I would say "*Listen to these two different ways of saying something – how do they leave you feeling? Why might that be hurtful? Could you find a softer way of saying this? Can you explain the impact and what you'd like instead?*". This helped to build a more reflective capacity and to widen choices around communication for both Maria and David.

Maria had a general respect for health professionals, but there was a slight "*men are useless*" attitude which at times she invited me to collude with. I felt angry about this and had to manage my own internal reactions before responding with an appropriately edited 'therapist challenge'. David gradually gained the confidence to offer his own challenges as the couple developed more equal teamwork. Selective attention was reduced by fostering mutual, proactive appreciation and Maria was able to understand the impact of her own somewhat matriarchal family dynamic on her unhelpful over-generalisations about men.

It remained harder for me to build a rapport with Maria, and I had to work more consciously to empathise and show fairness. The protective pull I sometimes felt towards David meant I needed to explore my own line between setting appropriate behavioural boundaries in the session, whilst also encouraging David to be more assertive. Supervision was an important support and stabiliser for me in managing my own process with this couple.

Improving self-care and general stress and mood management were important for both Maria and David, and initially more focused on individual activity and increasing some social support. This was partly to encourage individual responsibility (rather than an expectation that *"It's mainly your job to make me feel good"*) and partly since the couple were not yet ready to enjoy shared activities, as communication first needed to improve more reliably. Later couple activities focused on going to a film or event which could be shared, but with modest demands regarding communication.

Reflections

'Stance' and therapeutic alliance

The overall principle of therapeutic alliance in CBCT is based on collaborative dialogue (with some additional elements of psychoeducation and coaching), yet the 'no aggression' contract requires a more directive position in order to maintain appropriate boundaries and prevent further physical or psychological abuse. Although Iwi & Newman (2015) focus on work with individual perpetrators, they nonetheless make some helpful distinctions in 'stance' between a collusive, accusatory, or neutral position (p.26), which could be adapted for considerations with couple work. In balancing the need to hold clients to account whilst maintaining a sufficiently neutral or collaborative stance, the perspectives of 'behaviour versus person' and 'content versus process' can also support the therapeutic alliance e.g. since boundaries had already been clarified and agreed with Maria, I could make a respectful request for her to describe the details of her slapping, pushing and hitting (and validate her openness and honesty, yet without conveying a collusive or minimising sense of *"well that's alright then"*). I then checked accuracy with David and asked for more embellishment from Maria, including her reflections on the impact for David and any disconnect with the wider relationship values she aspired to. This differs from a stance which is primarily judgmental about Maria as a person, or alternatively over-focuses on Maria's internal emotional process and frustrations at the expense of naming and owning explicit behaviours which cross important boundaries.

Time-out and avoidance

Iwi & Newman (2015, p.69) raise the issue of time out strategies sometimes being used inappropriately as various forms of avoidance e.g. avoiding discussion, valid criticism or negative feedback, responsibility, and any form of difficulty. The explicit purpose of time out interventions should therefore be made clear, with an emphasis on calming the situation and protecting the relationship prior to later constructive discussion. If one partner requests time out but the other still pursues an argument, this needs to be managed assertively without resorting to abusive strategies.

Relationship recovery strategies

Although only briefly referred to in this chapter, another aspect which often requires attention is the processing of previous aggressive events (see Epstein et al., 2015, pp401–402). In some cases this will need to be addressed prior to communication work. Tasks for the formerly aggressive partner are the development of empathy and support regarding the other partner's anxiety responses, trust issues or trauma symptoms; acknowledgment of past mistakes; taking responsibility for previous hurtful behaviours; a commitment to work on personal change and the relationship within reason. This foundation then opens up the possibility of the other partner's acceptance and reconciliation, thus reducing a desire for retaliation.

Unresolved trauma related to the experience of birth

Svanberg (2019) notes that whilst 1–4% of women experience PTSD after birth, many others suffer from traumatic symptoms, with up to 60% of women describing a 'negative birth experience'. In this context, she emphasises the importance of asking and talking about birth and its impact, including the influence on parents' mental health. Her chapter on "The Second Victim" considers the often disregarded effects on partners and the couple relationship (including potentially longer-term consequences), thus highlighting this area as an often important additional issue to address in the transition to parenthood.

Therapist tips

Partner aggression

- Individual assessment is important for checking risk factors, suitability for CBCT or the need for DVA services or other multi-agency support. This is where I'm looking for any concerning inconsistences in the narrative, signs of fear or remorse and the capacity to take responsibility. If the referral notes leave me unsure about suitability, I will arrange individual appointments prior to offering a joint assessment.
- Additional DVA measures include the CTS2 (revised Conflict Tactics Scales, Straus et al. 1996) and MMEA (Multidimensional Measure of Emotional Abuse, Murphy & Hoover 1999), which has four subscales: hostile withdrawal, domination / intimidation, denigration and restrictive engulfment.
- The 'no-aggression' contract is key and needs to be checked on regularly. This also links back to my earlier reflection on 'stance'. I take time (particularly in earlier sessions) to make some detailed enquiries about any situations where there was the potential for escalation or when impulses towards aggression were having to be actively managed. This then becomes an opportunity for

further review and problem solving, or for positive reinforcement and validation for developing skills.

- Anger management techniques are prioritised early on. It is helpful to differentiate between healthy vs destructive functions and expressions of anger, as well as clarifying when it's a primary or secondary emotion.
- Be aware of your own relationship to anger and reactions to client behaviours. e.g. avoidant tendencies may lead to missing the protective function of anger or its underlying values and it is important to be able to sit with discomfort.
- Be collaborative where possible, but more directive if needed for maintaining safe boundaries. I try to be explicit about why I'm choosing different approaches and I think this helps foster trust and a sense of security in sessions.

Transition to parenthood

- Help couples to normalise the challenges for each partner in adapting to the transition to parenthood.
- Encourage parents to consider the benefits for children of a strong couple relationship. I have found this to be a helpful motivator in making time for enjoyable couple-only activities, as well as using the parents' commitment to their children to boost the emotional investment in their couple relationship.
- Emphasise the 'oxygen mask metaphor' to reinforce the importance of self-care and couple-care for parents. This again loops back to additional benefits for children, since good general coping strategies are likely to lead to an improved emotional climate at home and therefore greater security for children.

Suggestions for further Reading

Epstein NB, Werlinich CA, and LaTaillade JJ (2015). Couple therapy for partner aggression. In: Gurman AS, Lebow LJ, and Snyder DK (eds) *Clinical Handbook of Couple Therapy* (5th edition), New York: Guilford Press, pp389–411.

Gottman J, Gottman J, and Shapiro A (2010). A new couples approach to interventions for the transition to parenthood. In: Schulz MSet al. (eds) *Strengthening Couple Relationships for Optimal Child Development: Lessons from Research and Intervention*, Washington DC: American Psychological Association, pp165–179.

Gottman J and Gottman J (2007). *And Baby Makes Three: the Six-Step Plan for Preserving Marital Intimacy and Rekindling Romance after Baby Arrives*, New York: Three Rivers Press.

Glade AC, Bean RA and Vira R (2005). A prime time for marital / relational intervention: A review of the transition to parenthood literature with treatment recommendations. *The American Journal of Family Therapy*, 33: 319–336.

Walker J (2014). *The Transition to Parenthood: choices and responsibilities.* In: Abela A and Walker J (eds) *Contemporary Issues in Family Studies: Global Perspectives on Partnerships, Parenting and Support in a Changing World*, Chichester: John Wiley & Sons, pp119–135.

Murphy CM & Eckhardt CI (2005). *Treating the Abusive Partner*, New York: Guilford Press.

Iwi K and Newman C (2015). *Engaging with Perpetrators of Domestic Violence: Practical Techniques for Early Intervention*, London: Jessica Kingsley Publishers.

References

Delicate A, Ayers S, and McMullen S (2018). A systematic review and meta-synthesis of the impact of becoming parents on the couple relationship. *Midwifery*, 61: 88–96.

Doherty WJ, Erickson MF, and LaRossa R (2006). An intervention to increase father involvement and skills with infants during the transition to parenthood. *Journal of Family Psychology*, 20 (3): 438–447.

Doss BD, Rhoades GK, Stanley SM, and Markman HJ (2009). The effect of the transition to parenthood on relationship quality: An 8-Year Prospective Study. *Journal of Personality and Social Psychology*, 96 (3): 601–619.

DWP (Department for Work and Pensions 2017). *Evaluation of perinatal pilots for delivery of relationship advice*, Research Report No 952.

Edward J, Castle D, Mills C, and Casey J (2015). An integrative review of paternal depression. *American Journal of Men's Health*, 9 (1): 26–34.

Epstein NB and Baucom DH (2002). *Enhanced Cognitive-Behavioral Therapy for Couples: A contextual approach*, Washington, DC: American Psychological Association.

Epstein NB, Werlinich CA, and LaTaillade JJ (2015). Couple therapy for partner aggression. In: Gurman AS, Lebow LJ, and Snyder DK (eds) *Clinical Handbook of Couple Therapy* (5th edition), New York: Guilford Press, pp389–411.

Glade AC, Bean RA, and Vira R (2005). A prime time for marital / relational intervention: A review of the transition to parenthood literature with treatment recommendations. *The American Journal of Family Therapy*, 33: 319–336.

Gottman J and Gottman J (2007). *And Baby Makes Three: The Six-Step Plan for Preserving Marital Intimacy and Rekindling Romance after Baby Arrives*, New York: Three Rivers Press.

Gottman J, Gottman J and Shapiro A (2010). A new couple's approach to interventions for the transition to parenthood. In: Schulz MSet al. (eds) *Strengthening Couple Relationships for Optimal Child Development: Lessons from Research and Intervention*, Washington DC: American Psychological Association, pp165–179.

Harden J, McAllister P, Spencer CM and Stith SM (2022). The dark side of the rainbow: Queer women's experiences of intimate partner violence. *Trauma, Violence & Abuse*, 23 (1): 301–313.

Iwi K and Newman C (2015). *Engaging with Perpetrators of Domestic Violence: Practical Techniques for Early Intervention*, London: Jessica Kingsley Publishers.

Jacobson NS and Christensen A (1996). *Acceptance and Change in Couple Therapy: A Therapist's Guide to Transforming Relationships*, Norton: New York.

Kelly JB and Johnson JP (2008). Differentiation among types of intimate partner violence: research update and implications for interventions. *Family Court Review*, 46 (3): 476–499.

Kluwer ES (2010). From Partnership to Parenthood: A review of marital change across the transition to parenthood. *Journal of family theory & review*, 2 (2): 105–125.

Linville D, Todahl J, Brown T, Terrell L, and Gau J (2017). Healthy Nests Transition to Parenthood Program: a Mixed-Methods Study. *Journal of Couple & Relationship Therapy*, 16 (4): 346–361.

Moore TM, Stuart GL, McNulty JK, Addis ME, Cordova JV, and Temple JR (2010). Domains of masculine gender role stress and intimate partner violence in a clinical sample of violent men. *Psychology of Violence*, 1: 68–75.

Murphy CM and Hoover SA (1999). Measuring emotional abuse in dating relationships as a multifactorial construct. *Violence and Victims*, 14 (1): 39–53.

Murphy CM & Eckhardt CI (2005). *Treating the Abusive Partner*, New York: The Guilford Press.

ONS (Office for National Statistics) Census 2021. *Domestic abuse victim characteristics, England and Wales: year ending March 2021*.

O'Malley D, Higgins A, Begley C, Daly D, and Smith V (2018). Prevalence of and risk factors associated with sexual health issues in primiparous women at 6 and 12 months postpartum; a longitudinal prospective cohort study (the MAMMI study). *BMC Pregnancy and Childbirth*, 18 (1): 196.

Petch JF, Halford WK, Creedy DK, and Gamble J (2012). A Randomized Controlled Trial of a Couple Relationship and Coparenting Program (Couple CARE for Parents) for High- and Low-Risk New Parents. *Journal of Consulting and Clinical Psychology*, 80 (4): 662–673.

Reynolds J, Houlston C, Coleman L, and Harold G (2014). *Parental Conflict: outcomes and interventions for children and families*, Bristol: Policy Press.

SafeLives (2019a). *Insights IDVA England and Wales Dataset 2018–19*, Bristol: SafeLives.

SafeLives (2019b). *Men and boys' experiences of domestic abuse*, Bristol: SafeLives.

Salis KL and O'Leary D (2016). Treatment of Partner Aggression in Intimate Relationships. In: Lawrence E and Sullivan KT (eds) *The Oxford Handbook of Relationship Science and Couple Interventions*, New York: Oxford University Press, pp96–112.

Schulz MS, Pruett MS, Kerig PK, and Parke RD (2010). *Strengthening couple relationships for optimal child development*, Washington, DC: American Psychological Association.

Shapiro AF, Gottman, JM, and Carrere, S (2000). The Baby and the Marriage: Identifying Factors that Buffer against Decline in Marital Satisfaction after the First Baby Arrives. *Journal of Family Psychology*, 14 (1): 59–70.

Shapiro AF and Gottman JM (2005). Effects on marriage of a psycho-communicative-educational intervention with couples undergoing the transition to parenthood, evaluation at 1-year post intervention. *Journal of Family Communication*, 5 (1): 1–24.

Shapiro AF and Gottman JM (2015). Short-term change in couples' conflict following a transition to parenthood intervention. *Couple and Family Psychology: Research and Practice*, 4 (4): 239–251.

Straus MA, Hamby SL, Boney-McCoy S, and Sugarman D (1996). The revised Conflict Tactics Scales (CTS2): Development and Preliminary Psychometric Data. *Journal of Family Issues*, 17 (3): 283–316.

Svanberg E (2019). *Why Birth Trauma Matters*, London: Pinter & Martin.

Walker, J (2014). The Transition to Parenthood: choices and responsibilities. In: Abela A and Walker J (eds) *Contemporary Issues in Family Studies: Global Perspectives on Partnerships, Parenting and Support in a Changing World*, Chichester: John Wiley & Sons, pp119–135.

Chapter 6

Working with Sexual Issues

Michael Worrell

Sex, money, the in-laws, and household chores are the bread and butter of many couple therapies. Often, therapists who are new to couple therapy will become anxious, squeamish, and avoidant when encountering the difficulties and dilemmas expressed in a couple's sexual relationship. Experiencing anxiety and uncertainty in finding a way to talk about sexuality and the erotic in couple therapy is reasonable. Especially if the type of conversation and exploration one is aiming for is not restricted to the level of concrete descriptions of behaviours and body parts! Having some basic framework when exploring this aspect of a couple's relationship can be very helpful.

In this chapter I describe work with a couple, Stephen and Claire, that sought to place the various anxieties and concerns that arose in their sexual relationship within the wider context of their relationship and individual histories, following the basic principles of CBCT. This form of therapy would not really be seen as an instance of 'sex therapy' where issues such as low sexual desire, pain during intercourse, premature or delayed ejaculation may be addressed within a more or less medicalised or behavioural framework. While there is certainly a valid place and a need for interventions that fall within the 'sex therapy' domain, including medical interventions, there also remains a wide array of issues and difficulties in sexual relating that can be helpfully addressed from a more relational, contextual perspective. Some basic knowledge about sexual functioning and the various forms of sexual difficulties that can be encountered, and how these may be affected by such issues as depression, anxiety, medication, acute and long-term medical conditions as well as life stages such as transition to parenthood, can all be extremely helpful for the couple therapist who does not purport to be an expert in sex therapy (see Metz, Epstein and McCarthy, 2018 and Hall and Watter, 2023).

In this work I like to consider the erotic aspect of a couple's relationship as an 'existential given', as a basic aspect of what it is to be in the world as an embodied human being (Worrell, 2023). All individuals respond to the given of sexuality in some fashion or other, even if this response is one of avoidance or denial. The way in which individuals and partners respond to the

DOI: 10.4324/9781003024439-8

dimension of sexuality, is also expressive of their wider way of being in the world. In this way, dilemmas and concerns about relating sexually are likely to also be expressive of wider concerns about self-in-relation. Thus, 'fixing a sexual issue', in any straightforward behavioural or medicalised fashion, without a wider exploration of the couple's relational context, the meaning of the sexual issue and the meaning of its resolution or modification, seems to me at best incomplete and potentially ill-advised.

Stephen and Claire – "a sexless relationship?"

Stephen sits slumped in front of me during his individual assessment session. He presents as dishevelled, agitated, and distracted. His eyes are downcast and there is an air of angry resignation about him. I know from our first couple session that he has struggled with issues of depression in the past, as well as anxiety and generalised worry. He states though that over the past few years he has not experienced these issues with mood and that a previous episode of CBT was very helpful to him. He states that he found the 'tasks, lists and techniques' to be very useful and that he still occasionally fills out a brief 'thought record' when he is struggling with an issue.

STEPHEN: Well listen, I know in our first session we talked about how we fight a lot. We fight, sometimes shouting at each other and then we just avoid talking to each other, sometimes for a whole day… I mean I really do love her. But what we didn't say, what I think she just won't say when you see her, is that the issue is sex. That's the real issue. If she does mention it she will say that I am a maniac, that I want sex all the time, that I try to convince her that if we just had more sex we would be happier. Well guess what? I would definitely be more happy…much more happy! I mean I read something the other day, a self-help book, but it really scared me as it basically told me that I am in a sexless relationship and a sexless relationship won't work…I mean sometimes we only have sex twice a week! But lately, the past few months, it's been not at all! And when it does happen it's so restricted…I mean there are loads of things that I want to do with Claire but she just says no. It's frustrating. We used to have lots of sex and now it's just run dry…I am really worried!

The following day, I see Claire for her individual session. Well dressed in a somewhat corporate fashion, she sits uneasily on the edge of the seat, not fully allowing herself to relax. She seems to avoid eye contact and speaks quietly and quickly.

CLAIRE: So the main issue is sex. He wants sex all the time. He's basically a bit of a maniac when it comes to sex, and he gets worse all the time. Just nagging me and sulking when it doesn't happen. I mean we usually have sex twice a week and sometimes more! But this is not enough for him...I should be 'on tap'! It's ridiculous. And he talks about it all the time. ALL THE TIME! I mean it's not as if we don't talk about sex is it? He has even tried setting up a schedule of when we will have sex. Basically, a star chart! I am on a star chart for having sex. A good girl if I do and a bad girl if I don't.

The most commonly reported dilemma in couple therapy is the temptation to side with one partner against the other (Epstein and Baucom, 2002). It is not always easy to manage to achieve the recommended level of even-handed balance that is needed. While I felt that I had managed to be adequately open towards Stephen's complaint, as well as genuinely interested in what this may be about for him, I couldn't help but be 'turned off' (!) by the *way* in which he spoke about these concerns. Behind this concreteness, however, I could sense how anxious he was about his relationship with Claire and about himself and what it may mean for him (and about him) to be in a sexless relationship. It seemed to me that his apparent pride about being freely able to use 'anatomically correct' language covered up this more vulnerable and anxious side. I wondered however about the level of coercion and possible abuse of power that may be present in the relationship and wanted to ensure that I would not somehow fall into a potential trap of agreeing that 'the problem' consisted in Claire's lack of interest in sex.

Some context

Stephen and Claire sought private couple therapy with me following a recommendation from a previous couple that Stephen knew. Both agreed that they wanted to achieve some resolution of their difficulties in relations to sex. Claire, despite her obvious distress at Stephen's pressuring of her, also stated that she did want to improve that aspect of their relationship, but she wanted him to approach her differently, in a less demanding, softer, and more romantic fashion. Both partners could identify with the typical 'demand-withdraw' pattern and how this might be something that they both needed to take a part in resolving. For his part however, Stephen was clear that he remained highly anxious that if he became less demanding that Claire would withdraw even more and that their relationship would become a sexless one and would end. Over a series of couple sessions, more details of their relationship were clarified that eventually allowed some contextualising of the sexual concern.

Stephen and Claire, a white British couple in their early 30s, met through mutual work colleagues at a conference. They had been together for the past 6 years and had lived together in a comfortable flat for the past 3 years. They had no children and stated that they did not feel ready to consider this. Both worked in secure and financially rewarding roles in the IT security industry.

They worked in different companies but in similar roles and they both valued the support that they could provide to each other in dealing with the stressors of their highly technical jobs that occasionally required them both to work very long hours. They felt that people outside of these roles would struggle to understand and would be unlikely to support the needed lifestyle adjustments. When things were good, they felt that they were a 'great team' and enjoyed exciting adventure focused holidays several times a year.

As part of the initial assessment, I had asked each to talk about what they had initially found attractive in the other, and what prompted them each to want to pursue the relationship. Claire responded to this invitation with somewhat uncharacteristic assertion, wanting to go first and to be given time to give a full description:

CLAIRE: I felt immediately and strongly attracted to Stephen, and yes...Stephen...sexually attracted as well! But what I liked was his stability, his sanity, and his reliability. Unlike other men I had known, he didn't want to go out partying and drinking and taking drugs the whole time. He wanted to make something of himself, and he was interested in me and my career. You have no idea how rare this is! Most men just talk about themselves and are just incredibly narcissistic and selfish. Stephen isn't or at least wasn't like this! I just liked the fact that he was so solid. He seemed to know who he was or at least who he wanted to be.

THERAPIST: So you really were attracted to his solidity, his clarity. Sounds like you felt you could really rely on and trust this man?

CLAIRE: yes exactly!

THERAPIST: What's that like to hear Stephen?

STEPHEN: yeah...solid...solid, dull, predictable, and boring! And is it narcissistic or selfish to want to have sexual needs met? I don't know, I know she likes those things about me. Being solid and reliable. But there must be more, no?

THERAPIST: So you have an ambivalent reaction to hearing this, Stephen? On the one hand you hear the positives, but these also feel limiting?

STEPHEN: Yes! Limiting is correct...I want more in this relationship, I want more for us!

THERAPIST: Ok, we certainly need to explore that. What 'more' means for you. For now, could you tell me a bit about what attracted you to Claire? What drew you to her? You seem clear that the 'more' you speak of is a 'more' with Claire'...so what drew you to her initially?

STEPHEN: Well obviously...I mean look at her... she's totally hot isn't she! I just really fancied her immediately. But it's not just physical attraction. She's deep and intelligent and caring. She thinks deeply about life and is interested in everything. She's read loads and knows things I just never heard of. So our early dates were just great. I just thought her engaging and special. I still do... but I know she gets depressed...(addressing

Claire directly): you do get depressed! I know it because I have been depressed before...I got help! You always have had periods where you felt insecure and just terrible about yourself. I just think we have to address that. You haven't had therapy like me and I think if you did and you were less depressed you would be more in touch with wanting sex again!

THERAPIST: Ok Stephen let me interrupt as you are going on to other issues that we do need to look at but maybe let's do that more thoroughly and with Claire's collaboration? What you are saying is that you found Claire very attractive both physically and emotionally from the beginning, your learnt things from her and found her engaging and exciting to be with. What's that like to hear Clair?

CLAIRE: well...he has said before if I go for CBT for depression maybe I will want more sex...I find it incredible... unbelievable really...we need to fix Claire, so Stephen gets more sex!

One of the most frustrating aspects of the work with Stephen and Claire, from my perspective, was the pattern illustrated above. While Stephen seemed more than capable of communicating something in a soft, caring fashion, he so often followed this up with a criticism or demand of Claire that she should 'try harder'. Claire would in most instances respond to this perceived demand to fix herself with a negative in return. While both partners appeared to respond well to efforts at pointing this out, and wondering about its function and consequence, the pattern itself was remarkable in its persistence.

Initial Formulation

The range of factors that may be important in understanding a couple's difficulties can be highly varied. Nevertheless, an attempt at an initial formulation can be useful in gaining agreement on some initial tasks and goals for the work. Equally important is that this formulation should not be so authoritative and final that no new information or surprises might arise that affect the way therapy proceeds. Following the principles of CBCT the following seemed of relevance early in our work:

Individual Factors: Claire was in fact experiencing depressed mood and in her individual session had described a long-term pattern of repeated episodes of depression that lasted several months in most instances. She had had periods of taking antidepressant medication which she described as being of some help but had never had psychological therapy. She described herself as perfectionistic and highly self-critical with a strong need for achievement and to feel that her efforts were noticed and valued by others and to be seen as coping and effective. When depressed she viewed herself as "*worthless and out of control*". Claire was very hesitant when describing her family of origin and her childhood years, saying only that things had been 'chaotic', that her parents, who were never formally married had lived what would today be described as polyamory. Additionally, she stated that there were other family members, such as aunts and uncles, living in the house and that there were frequent arguments and lots of drinking and drug use. She felt that her parents largely neglected her and her younger sister, apparently not caring about her school attendance and achievement. Things improved for her, she stated, once she moved away from home to attend university. She maintains very little contact with her parents and wider family. Claire stated that she had many *"short term meaningless"* relationships with men at university and after university. She felt that some of these had been with highly unsuitable men who were shallow and *"only interested in fun"*. Several had had issues with alcohol and drug use.

Stephen also described a history of problems with depression and anxiety. As mentioned above, he had found CBT very helpful and was not depressed at the time of the couple therapy. Like Claire, he described a strong achievement motivation. Unlike Claire, he described his family or origin as being *"conservative, dull, money focused, uncultured and uninteresting"* Nevertheless he stated that his parents were supportive of him and his older sister, had expected them both to do well and to work hard. As will be illustrated below, Stephen presented with a somewhat rigid cognitive style, liking structure and order. He experienced difficulties when describing his emotional experience, finding it much easier to focus on behaviour. My sense was that he found it difficult to find words and images to describe his emotional life. Stephen stated that he had had two girlfriends prior to his relationship with Claire. Each had lasted a period of approximately two years and on each occasion, he had ended the relationship. He felt that on both occasions the relationships had 'fizzled out'.

Couple Interaction Factors: As described above, the couple entered therapy with significant 'secondary distress' that is, there was frequent arguing, low level sniping and negativity and a clear pattern of demand-withdraw in their communication. They described finding it difficult to really listen to each other, despite feeling that early in their relationship this had been a very strong positive for them, that they had been able to understand each other in some depth. For a period of some six months prior to entering therapy, their frequency of shared social and leisure activity had decreased, they spent less time with each other engaging in enjoyable activities and they had ceased to have conversations about planning positive things for their future together. As Stephen resentfully and angrily noted, their frequency of sexual intimacy had drastically declined.

Environmental Factors: In many ways their environment provided them with a wide range of resources. They had a good flat that they loved spending time in and had access to a wide range of social and leisure activities. The most significant environmental factor was their respective jobs. They both worked very long hours in jobs that made a strong demand on their intellectual capacity in a social environment that was notably critical, perfectionistic, and unforgiving. They both stated that losing their jobs, by either being fired or made redundant, was not an unforeseen or surprising occurrence. They had so far *"been fortunate"*.

Working with depression

As noted, Claire was experiencing significant problems with depressed mood. It was important that this was addressed but in a way that avoided this meaning that *"Claire is the problem"*. Claire described a history of experiencing periods of low mood that could last several months, characterised by very severe critical and perfectionistic thinking, avoidance of socialising, poor sleep, appetite, and indeed low libido. In an individual session with her, we agreed that spending some time in couple sessions addressing this would be important. These sessions, that lasted a period of three months, utilised many of the standard CBCT interventions for depression described in chapter 10 of this book. This included working with Stephen and Claire utilising the guidelines for 'sharing thoughts and feelings' as well as problem solving and behavioural activation. Stephen showed himself to be very willing and able to listen empathically to Claire's experience of depression as well as sharing some of his own feelings of helplessness and anxiety that her withdrawal provoked for him. Key to this was gaining agreement from Stephen to put aside, for a period of time, the issue of their sexual relationship. Despite his reluctance and anxiety that this would mean they are having a *"sexless relationship doomed to failure"*, Stephen agreed to this and as a result the pattern of 'demand-withdraw' was reduced. Claire remained concerned, however, that Stephen was, underneath it all, resentful of this change and just biding his time before presenting her with his sexual demands. Nevertheless, Claire's mood steadily improved, as did their communication, to the extent that the question of sex, could now be put on the table.

Working with the physical relationship

When addressing a couple's sexual relationship, it can be helpful to begin by placing this within a widened context of their ways of relating to each other physically. Some brief psychoeducation (based on Epstein and Baucom, 2002) that clarifies various forms of physically relating and their function, can be helpful. An offer of a hug or placing a hand on the back of a neck can have different intentions and consequences. These include:

1   Giving comfort. One function of physically relating to another is to provide a degree of comfort when the other is in a negative psychological state. That is, the physical expression of a hug may function to reduce the intensity of the other's negative psychological state.

2   Showing affection. In contrast to providing comfort, a physical gesture such as a hug may be intended to induce a positive psychological state. Providing affection is intended to induce a positive emotional state in contrast to reducing a negative one. A hug therefore can either have the function of reducing a negative emotional state or inducing a positive one. A great deal depends however on each individuals' natural preferences and needs for giving and receiving both comfort and affection.

3   Relating sexually. Relating sexually includes a wide range of behaviours that can have many different functions including self-expression, drive reduction, playfulness, joy, and indeed occasionally, but not usually (in terms of frequency) reproduction! Again, people's needs, preferences desires, anxieties and concerns in this domain can be hugely variable.

After having clarified this basic framework, the therapist can invite each partner to talk about their needs and preferences in the domains of comfort and affection prior to moving onto a discussion of sexual relating. One common pattern, that can be discussed, is where sexual relating has become problematic or anxiety provoking and the couple or one partner responds by also avoiding either giving and/or receiving comfort and affection. Stephen and Claire responded very positively to the discussion of this framework for thinking about their physical relationship. Claire acknowledged that she had been avoiding any form of physical relating with Stephen due to her anxiety, which was well founded, that it would be perceived by Stephen as 'a green light' for sexual relating.

CLAIRE: I know I have been avoiding. Sometimes I literally duck and dive in order to avoid you hugging me, Stephen. I feel bad about it as know you are a very physical person. But in less that 2 seconds one of your hugs can turn into something like a grope and I will need some sort of jiu-jitsu move to free myself!

STEPHEN: That's just horrible though! Am I so repulsive?

CLAIRE: No! it's not that you are repulsive of course not! But why can't it just stay as affection sometimes? I want more of that in fact not less! If I felt that it would be ok for you to give affection and for it not to automatically lead to the bedroom then I feel I would welcome it more and would also start being more affectionate myself!

THERAPIST: How would that be for you Stephen? I mean for you to experiment with that? To really up the frequency of showing affection and comfort but with a clear expectation that this does not need to lead to sex?

STEPHEN: Of course I will try that; I will try anything! But will it lead to us having more sex eventually? I think I have tried this before; I have tried being less demanding and it hasn't worked. And surely, it's like in the work we did on depression? Don't we have to push ourselves to relate sexually rather than just waiting for it to happen magically at some point?

CLAIRE: But you see that's the problem right there! You are saying "I will only be more affectionate if it means I will get sex!" So, the affection is a manipulation of me! A control tactic!

THERAPIST: Ok let's pause a bit. Claire, I think that's important what you are saying. We really do want the increase in affection to be for the purpose of increasing affection, not as a prelude to sex only. Increasing the affection in your relationship may help you feel more connected, more intimate and will also likely help with mood. I think you both really do value affection for its own sake. I know Stephen you are anxious about the sexual aspect, and we do need to address that. And there is something to what you are saying about at some point needing to challenge yourselves to move forward. But there is a question of timing and tact...

Stephen and Claire agreed to work to increase the frequency of giving and receiving comfort and affection. To support this, I asked each of them to focus primarily on their own role as initiators of affection and comfort rather than tracking whether or not the other was behaving in a more affectionate manner or offering comfort. This can be helpful in reducing the tendency for each to adopt a *"you first"* or an *"I won't until you do!"* position.

After some weeks Claire indicated that she felt ready and willing to more directly address their sexual relationship. It was some relief to Stephen to hear from her that she remained sexually attracted to him but that she needed him to change his way of approaching her. She wanted him to approach her in a more romantic, more emotionally soft manner.

CLAIRE: Look Stephen, I know you keep saying we have to be blunt, we have to be explicit. Your idea is we should talk clearly about what we want in the bedroom and not shy away as otherwise it won't happen.

STEPHEN: (Interrupting). Exactly! That's what we need to do! Can't we just be clear about it? I want more sex! I want you to go down on me and I want to go down on you... I want to be able to put my head between your legs and to...

CLAIRE: Stephen! Stop! Why do you have to make it sound like a porn film?

STEPHEN: I'm not! I'm just being clear! Why can't we just be clear?

THERAPIST: Stephen, can we pause just a second? I think Claire is trying to tell you something important. What I hear Claire saying, on more than one occasion, is that it's important to her the way you talk about this. I hear you saying that you really want to be able to talk clearly and directly. And I agree it's important to be able to talk clearly, but what do you hear Claire saying to you about this? What is she asking of you?

STEPHEN: To be softer and more romantic. I know. But soft and romantic hasn't worked.

THERAPIST: And what's your experience of being really concrete and direct? Does that seem to work from your perspective?

STEPHEN: No, it's not working. But then I don't know what to do.

THERAPIST: OK so finding some new way of talking about this. Some way of talking that allows you to be clear but doesn't alienate or distress Claire…

CLAIRE: Look I'm not a prude. I can talk about things. But please just stop talking like you are a porn actor! Be my partner not a sex maniac!

To my considerable relief Stephen appeared to take this information in. I think it was the directness of Claire's statement rather than anything I said. Her last statement was said with considerable force and with direct eye contact and an upright open posture. Claire seemed like quite a different person when she said this, not requiring a clever male therapist to defend her.

Over the subsequent six weeks, Claire and Stephen worked on slowly re-starting their sexual relationship. Claire founds it helpful to compare approaching this as similar to how any other object associated with anxiety could be addressed, that is, by a process of slow repeated exposure. Claire needed to feel from Stephen that her desire to go slowly and that her need for him to approach her in a more romantic manner was respected and valued. For his part Stephen was mostly relieved that Claire had finally agreed to a *"more direct approach"*. And still, there were setbacks, most often related to the persistence of Stephen's style of talking in an overly concrete manner. To counter this I started to adopt a somewhat counterintuitive response for a couple therapist, more usually prone to emphasising the value of open communication:

THERAPIST: So how have things progressed for you both in the sexual domain…again, as I've said before, I don't need the details of specific behaviour, I'm more interested in your sense of how things are.

STEPHEN: Its way better…I mean we have had sex. It was good. We used several different positions…I even was able to approach from behind and…

Therapist – Sticking a finger in each ear, looking at the ceiling and loudly humming a well-known 'punk' song.
Claire – Laughing and looking directly at Stephen.

STEPHEN: Ah yes…OK. There I go again…

THERAPIST: Yes! Sorry to act weird. But when you talk like that, I just get anxious! What do you think it's like for Claire to sit here with two men and have that sort of conversation?

STEPHEN: Ok…yes, it's a bit cringe worthy for her. Let me skip the details then. Things are better, I think. I feel closer to Claire and less anxious about us.

CLAIRE: I do too. AND! I still worry when you talk like you did just then. Maybe I will start singing punk songs too!

Freedom and Certainty

Stephen and Claire took a six week break from therapy, feeling that their relationship was more on track and that they could continue to use the communication skills plus collaborating around behavioural changes both in their sexual relationship and more generally. Claire however contacted me by email requesting an urgent couple session as things had now 'fallen apart'. During this session Claire tearfully explained that in addition to continuing to push for greater sexual experimentation in the relationship, Stephen was now pushing for her to agree to take recreational drugs with him (which he had never before taken) as well as wanting to go out with her to "*take drugs with others and party*". Stephen agreed that this was in fact what he wanted, he wanted their relationship to feel more exciting and adventurous. During this session I asked each to attempt to stay with the guidelines for listening well to each other and to try and describe what was happening for each of them and what they felt this meant.

CLAIRE: It's like I really don't know him anymore. He wants to be more experimental, to take drugs and do lots of sexual things that he hasn't done before.

STEPHEN: And why not? It's not like you haven't done these exact same things in previous relationships. You have done these things with other boyfriends. Why not with me?

THERAPIST: Stephen, can I slow you down a bit there? I'm concerned that Claire will just hear your last statement as a demand on her. What's this about for you? Can you let Claire know a little more what's happening for you? This does sound like quite a big change for you – wanting to take drugs and so forth. What's this about? Claire, I can see this is really distressing for you, but would you be willing to hear a little more from Stephen about what's going on for him? And I will want you to do that same shortly and for Stephen to do his best to give you space and understand your perspective.

STEPHEN: Well, it's not that new. I really just want to experiment a bit with making our life more interesting. Claire has told me a lot about her past relationships. She's had a pretty wild time of it. I really haven't. I've only had two previous relationships and they were not at all wild. I do feel jealous of her past in that regard. Why must I be the predictable solid boring partner she has after having her wild years. What about my wild years?

THERAPIST: Sounds to me like you are talking about wanting more freedom...to have your relationship with Claire to be less predictable, you want excitement. Claire, what is it you are hearing Stephen say?

CLAIRE: I think I get it. He wants a lot of excitement, he wants to party, to have sex and be irresponsible. Freedom, sure, it sounds like chaos to me, and I don't want to go there!

STEPHEN: It's not chaos! I'm not talking about quitting our jobs and going to India! I just want more, I don't know... I just want more!

THERAPIST: Claire, this sounds really difficult for you to hear, and it looks like you are finding it really upsetting. Can you let Stephen know a little more about what this means to you?

CLAIRE: I should never have told you about those other boyfriends. You think it was wild and fun. Maybe some of it was but some of it wasn't. I didn't really know myself back then and what I wanted, what I needed. I felt used and like I didn't respect myself as I should have. But how could I? With parents like mine! You should know that by now as I have told you? I hated the chaos at home when they were with all their different partners. I didn't know who was with who or what was going on. I don't want or need that in my life and if that's what you want then I can't stay with you. I want to be with the strong stable Stephen that I fell in love with!

THERAPIST: What are you hearing Stephen?

STEPHEN: Well, I know some of this. I get it that your childhood was not great. That your parents were crazy. They took drugs and didn't look after you properly. And me now saying that I want to take drugs and party makes you scared that it will be like that. I don't think it has to be like that though.

In subsequent sessions Claire spoke more about her experience of her parents' relationship and their relationship with her and her sense of constant insecurity and unpredictability that her home environment provoked. It became clearer how a great deal of the attraction to Stephen was related to a sense of his warm stability and predictability that for her was anything but boring. It allowed a sense of security and belonging. His new desire for greater freedom and experimentation felt like an overwhelming threat to this. If they were to go in the direction he seemed to be suggesting, she felt "*I would not know who I, you, or we are anymore!*". For his part Stephen clarified how his increasing success at work seemed to bring with it a paradoxically greater dissatisfaction with himself and what he had allowed himself to experience in his life. He felt that due to his need to achieve he had 'missed out' on something. He felt that he had failed to allow himself a time to "*just let go and enjoy life*". He wanted desperately to do this with Claire and for her to also let go and was convinced this would be an effective ongoing antidepressant.

I was often left wondering about Stephen's experience and what it meant for him to engage sexually with Claire and especially what it was like for him when this was not happening. At times I found myself feeling critical and rejecting of his demanding and 'anatomically correct' approach to this aspect of their relationship. In individual sessions with him I encouraged him to describe his experience of frustration and what it was like for him. He was clear that during these times he did not masturbate or use pornography and nor did he consider being unfaithful. Also, he stated strongly that it was not that he expected that Claire *should* and *must* meet all his sexual needs or that he was somehow entitled to have these needs met, but it was that he wanted her to be motivated to engage him sexually and for him to feel wanted. In subsequent couple sessions, using the communication guidelines, he was able, with support, to describe aspects of his experience that Claire could more readily hear.

THERAPIST: Stephen, can you say more about what this is like for you? You have been clear that you feel frustrated. What else is there for you?

STEPHEN: (looking directly at Claire). I guess I feel lonely. I mean when we do have sex it's not just about getting some relief, I also want to feel close, and to feel like you really do desire me. Is that wrong to feel that?

THERAPIST: Claire what are you hearing?

CLAIRE: (responding direct to Stephen) That you also want to feel close and to feel desired by me. I understand that. I do too! But I don't want to feel like I am just an object or that I *have* to give you what you want!

STEPHEN: But I don't think you are an object! And it's not that I think you have to! I would just like to feel that you want to!

THERAPIST: You raise a really important issue, Claire. This notion of being an object, being objectified. I am wondering, it's difficult isn't it…there is a sense where if you have having sex with each other, there is often an aspect of objectification happening…desiring the other physically. Is that not so? But it's not only that, there is also a desire to be seen and validated. Finding a way to talk about these aspects without it becoming only one aspect seems challenging.

Stephen agreed to put his demands for 'experimentation' on hold while we explored further what this was about for both of them and what the consequences of change might be for them both. One way of framing this dilemma (consistent with IBCT described in Chapter 3), that seemed to fit for them was that of a tension between 'freedom and excitement' on the one hand and 'predictability and security' on the other. I suggested to them that this theme can often be the source of many difficulties in couple relationships and that part of this is that partners can become polarised (Christensen, Doss, & Jacobson, 2020), and apparently fixed in one of these positions in a way that does not fully represent what is important for them. Stephen took up this theme enthusiastically:

STEPHEN: Well, I guess we are polarised then aren't we. It's true. I am all about freedom and excitement. That's what I want. And Claire is all about security. I know it's important for her, and I am not giving it. But what can I do – it's true, I want the freedom.

THERAPIST: Ok that much is clear...and yet let me ask you, both in our couple sessions and even more in our individual sessions, you have always emphasised to me very strongly that the freedom you want is a freedom with Claire, it's not freedom on your own. You have also repeatedly said, during the times of your greatest sexual frustration, that while you felt really awful and limited, the one thing you never considered is cheating on Claire, or starting a new relationship... am I wrong in this?

STEPHEN: Definitely that's correct. I want to be with Claire. I want this to work with her. I can't even imagine us ending it.

THERAPIST: So as much as you are now all about freedom, your sense of certainty is that you are certain you want this to be with Claire. This is what you don't want to change?

STEPHEN: Yes...so we are stuck then. I want a freedom I cannot have.

THERAPIST: Well, let's pause that part. Claire, you have so often emphasised your need for certainty and predictability. Are you only about this?

CLAIRE: No....I'm not. I don't think Stephen is hearing me clearly. I get it he wants change. But what I am saying is that the change that will happen is that I will leave this relationship! I am not prepared to live in chaos. I can deal with the chaos and pain of losing the relationship. And it would be a big loss. But I can do that. So, no... I am not just about predictability.

Stephen appeared visibly shaken in response to Claire's statement that was delivered in a very level, matter of fact manner. Rather than stay with and explore his response to this however, I chose to pursue the issue of polarisation.

THERAPIST: So, I am wondering if it's possible that you both might not be as polarised as it can seem? While you Stephen want to move the relationship towards greater freedom, at the same time you continue to greatly value the maintenance of the relationship, its security and predictability. And Claire, while you greatly value the security and predictability the relationship has provided, you are aware of your own capacity to face and respond to change. I wonder if the task here is for you both somehow to find a way of including greater freedom but in a way that allows the sense of the security and predictability in the relationship to be maintained. This probably means avoiding the extremes of either freedom or predictability. If a relationship is only about predictability and security it becomes stifling and lifeless, but if it's all freedom and unpredictability then we really do have punk rock, which really isn't the best music around.

Thankfully, both Claire and Stephen laughed at my reference to my earlier absurd behaviour and were willing to entertain this notion of holding onto both polarities in an attempt to find a new balance that did not threaten the ongoing maintenance of the relationship itself. The concept of 'relationship expectations' from CBCT (Epstein and Baucom, 2002) provided a helpful framework to consider small experiments in greater freedom, both in their sexual relationship and in their way of engaging with the word more widely. Claire remained unwilling to consider the use of recreational drugs as this for her was too much of a reminder of a childhood that she experienced as far too unpredictable and unsafe. Stephen, for his part, could see how some of their past holidays had met his need for adventure and that the fact that they had not engaged in such holidays more recently may be related to his growing frustration. He was willing to remain with the idea of planning and experimenting with more adventurous trips and recreational activities, but that drugs and alcohol would not feature in this. Upon reflection, he noted, had he followed through with some of his ideas, he may have risked the maintenance of his job also, something he also noted he was unwilling to consider losing. Additionally, Stephen managed to slowly find a more workable way of discussing sexuality with Claire, a way that could be direct but less concrete and anatomical and that included more aspects of his experience.

At the close of our work together, which in total spanned the course of 12 months, Claire expressed an interest in finding an individual therapist to help her explore some of her early childhood experience and how this might be related to her depression and her anxieties in the relationship. As she no longer felt that Stephen was demanding that she 'fix' herself, this possibility, although anxiety provoking, also seemed more hopeful.

Therapist Tips

- There is no clear dividing line between sex therapy and therapy that addresses the sexual dimension of a couple relationship.
- Many of the issues surrounding the sexual relationship can be helpfully addressed within a broader relational perspective.
- The sexual aspect of a couple relationship is often an essential area to address, it can be very helpful for couple therapists, who are not sex therapists, to educate themselves about this domain and develop, through exposure and supervision, greater familiarity with this.
- Addressing the sexual relationship within the broader frame of the couple's physical relationship (which includes, comfort, affection, and sexual intimacy) can allow the broader psychological and emotional themes to emerge. Issues arising in the sexual relationship are often not just about sex, broader themes of freedom and control, authenticity and self-expression, identity, belonging, and acceptance are also often at stake.

Suggestions for further Reading

Hall, K.S.K., & Watter, D.N. (2023). Couple Therapy and Sexuality. In J.L. Lebow & D.K. Snyder (Eds.). *Clinical Handbook of Couple Therapy*. 6th Edition. New York: The Guilford Press.

Metz, M.E., Epstein, N.B. & McCarthy, B. (2018). *Cognitive-Behavioural Therapy for Sexual Dysfunction*. Routledge: London.

References

Christensen, A., Doss, B.D. & Jacobson, N.S. (2020). *Integrative Behavioral Couple Therapy: A Therapist's Guide to Creating Acceptance and Change*. New York: Norton.

Epstein, N.B., & Baucom, D.H. (2002). *Enhanced Cognitive-Behavioural Therapy for Couples. A Contextual Approach*. Washington DC: American Psychological Association.

Hall, K.S.K., & Watter, D.N. (2023). Couple Therapy and Sexuality. In J.L. Lebow & D.K. Snyder (Eds.). *Clinical Handbook of Couple Therapy*. 6th Edition. New York: The Guilford Press.

Metz, M.E., Epstein, N.B. & McCarthy, B. (2018). *Cognitive-Behavioural Therapy for Sexual Dysfunction*. London: Routledge.

Worrell, M. (2023). *CBT and Existential Psychology. Philosophy, Psychology and Therapy*. London: Wiley.

Chapter 7

Working with Sexual Minority Couples

David Hambrook

Introduction

Nick and Josh were walking home through the park when they spotted a group of young people playing football. They both knew immediately to stop holding hands and increase the physical distance between them to evade being noticed and harassed.

Nadia and Rachel were out for a meal to celebrate the second anniversary since their first date. They took a 'selfie' photo together to mark and remember their happy occasion. Rachel wanted to post the selfie on her social media, but Nadia asked her not to because she knew that her family would disapprove of their public display of affection.

Daniel and Tiago had been married for 18 months. They had both always wanted to have children and were excited at the prospect of starting their own family. After researching their options for adoption and surrogacy they felt anxious and deflated that their opportunities were limited, prohibitively expensive and risky.

Sexual minorities include those whose sexual identity, orientation or practices differ from the majority of the surrounding society. LGBTQ+ is an acronym primarily used in reference to individuals who identify as lesbian, gay, bisexual or the more flexible umbrella descriptor 'queer'. The '+' refers to the growing number of other non-heterosexual orientations such as pansexual and asexual. It also encompasses gender minorities such as those who identify as transgender, gender non-binary or intersex individuals. This chapter is primarily concerned with couple therapy in the context of people who identify with a non-heterosexual sexual identity as the sparse available literature about LGBTQ+ relationships tends to focus on same-sex cisgender couples, though consideration will be given to gender minorities as well.

There is some evidence that the proportion of people openly identifying as LGBTQ+ in the UK is increasing (Office for National Statistics, 2020) and so are the number of LGBTQ+ couples living together (Office for National Statistics. 2019). These increases are probably a result of changing attitudes towards

DOI: 10.4324/9781003024439-9

sexual minorities, which are fluid and vary significantly along intersecting socio-political vectors. However, even in the most liberal of communities, LGBTQ+ people still experience significant societal oppression, discrimination and stigmatisation throughout their life course. These negative experiences can have a profound impact on all aspects of their lives and relationships.

Theoretical Framework

There is substantial evidence that sexual minorities are much more likely to experience common mental health problems, such as anxiety and depression, compared to heterosexuals (e.g., Plöderl and Tremblay 2015). Minority Stress Theory (Meyer 2003; Hatzenbuehler 2009) proposes that chronic exposure to stigmatising and discriminatory social environments gives rise to unique stressors and stress processes that cause the excess rates of mental health problems amongst LGBTQ+ communities. Minority stressors exist on a continuum from distal (external) to proximal (internal), and examples might include experiences of prejudice and discrimination, negative internalised beliefs and feelings about one's identity, and unhelpful efforts to cope with the stress that stigma creates (e.g., concealing sexual orientation, substance misuse, risky sexual behaviour).

Over time, the effects of minority stressors aggregate and contribute to deleterious physical and mental health consequences for sexual minority individuals. In the context of an LGBTQ+ relationship with two people who have both been exposed to minority stressors, it is likely that the combination of each partner's cumulative stress will impact on relationship quality. Indeed, sexual minority-related stress has been linked to greater severity of conflict, poorer overall relationship quality, and less commitment among same-sex couples (e.g., Totenhagen et al. 2017).

Sexual minority couples: differences and similarities with heterosexual, cisgender couples

Dominant definitions of relationships and family have historically excluded or pathologised sexual and gender minorities. Arguably, the science and practice of couple therapy has mirrored prevailing heteronormative attitudes, thus helping to perpetuate this silencing and 'othering' (Giammattei and Green, 2015). Outcome studies evaluating the efficacy of couple therapy often do not report the sexual orientation of participants or assume participants to be heterosexual and cisgender male or female (Spengler et al., 2019). Institutions and courses training new couple therapists may also struggle to adequately prepare trainees for working with sexual and gender diversity in intimate romantic relationships (e.g., Corturillo, McGeorge and Carlson, 2016).

In recent years there have been significant strides forwards in recognising, understanding, and validating LGBTQ+ identities and relationships. Despite this, we still know much less about the intimate relationships of those in the most marginalised corners of the LGBTQ+ community (e.g., bisexuals, transgender couples, non-monogamous relationships). Much of the existing LGBTQ+ relationship literature focuses on same-sex-couples, who share many commonalities with heterosexual couples. Their day-to-day lives are often similar, but the social context in which they operate differs greatly due to the influences of the dominant heterosexual culture and traditional gender roles. Overall, it seems that 'core' relationship processes (e.g., effective communication and conflict resolution skills) that predict relationship satisfaction and stability are very similar across same- and different-sex couples (Scott, Whitton, and Buzzella 2019). Key relationship outcomes (e.g., satisfaction, love, intimacy, commitment) are also comparable across same- and different-sex couples (Balsam et al. 2008). There is evidence that LGBTQ+ relationships can be as stable as heterosexual relationships when they have access to marriage and legally recognised civil partnerships (Rosenfeld 2014).

Sexual minority couples also struggle with many of the same issues as heterosexual cisgender couples including difficulties communicating, shared finances, sexual and physical intimacy, parenting, and division of labour within the home. LGBTQ+ couples are probably more likely to seek support with these types of issues than problems specifically related to their sexual minority status. Nevertheless, there are important differences that clinicians should be aware of when working with LGBTQ+ couples. Many of these differences are a direct result of discrimination, stigmatisation, and heteronormativity.

Considerations unique to LGBTQ+ relationships

Heteronormativity and the institutionalisation of heterosexism

There is a pervasive assumption that the default model of sexual relationships in society is heterosexual, involving cisgender men and women. Heteronormativity results in heterosexism; discrimination or prejudice against LGBTQ+ people based on the belief that heterosexuality is the only 'normal' and 'natural' expression of sexuality. Heteronormativity and heterosexism result in specific forms of discrimination and abuse towards LGBTQ+ people (e.g., homophobia/biphobia/transphobia), but also in systematic 'othering' and marginalisation from broader social structures and institutions (e.g., marriage, family) that might provide support and cohesion for couples.

Reduced social support

One of the consequences of heterosexism and homophobia is that sexual minority couples often experience a lack of support and rejection from their family and communities of origin. This can make navigating important commitments and life transitions more challenging. Some LGBTQ+ couples manage to forge a 'family of choice' – a network of people providing social support and kinship but who have been chosen by the individual/couple, and whose support has the potential to mitigate the lack of support provided by family of origin.

Effects of minority stress

Discrimination: LGBTQ+ people regularly experience pervasive discrimination ranging from daily 'microaggressions' (brief, commonplace indignities that communicate hostile, derogatory, or negative connotations about sexual minority identity) to frank physical violence and hate crime. There is clear evidence that such discrimination, abuse, and prejudice has a significant negative impact on individuals (e.g., Hatzenbuehler 2011), but it also places significant stress on LGBTQ+ romantic relationships (e.g., not being able to marry in certain countries, having to keep a relationship secret due to risk of familial rejection or legal punishment, being unable to show affection in public due to fear of harassment).

Internalised stigma: LGBTQ+ people are exposed to pervasive negative messages about sexual minorities throughout their lives and can internalise these attitudes, subsequently coming to devalue their same-sex attractions, queer identities and relationships. This can lead to internal conflict and cognitive dissonance whereby one might wish to be cisgender or heterosexual while simultaneously experiencing same-sex attraction or a gender identity different to the one assigned at birth. Often internalised stigma (e.g., homophobia) operates outside of conscious awareness but can result in self-hatred, shame, difficulties establishing emotional intimacy with partners, and an increased risk of anxiety, depression, and unhelpful coping mechanisms (e.g., substance misuse, self-harm). All these factors can impact on relationship quality and stability.

Degree of 'outness': Public disclosure of one's sexual orientation and/or gender identity ('outness') can help to reduce shame, hypervigilance, and self-monitoring in social situations, and can increase opportunities for validation and support. Coming out is an ongoing process and many individuals and couples feel more confident and safe being out in some contexts than others. Higher levels of outness predict greater relationship satisfaction in sexual minority couples (Jordan and Deluty 2000). In many LGBTQ+ couples, partners will have different preferences and expectations about with whom, where and when they feel comfortable being out as an individual and as a couple. These differences might be a source of conflict and distress. Negotiating complex coming out decisions as a couple can be challenging and place an additional strain on relationships.

Parenthood

For many LGBTQ+ relationships, considering the prospect of parenthood is complicated and stressful. For some couples it may not be possible to have children through any means, which can be devastating. For others, it may be very difficult finding resources and medical professionals who can help them become parents. Artificial insemination and surrogacy can be very expensive and risky, and the adoption process in many parts of the world is complex to navigate and systemically suspicious of LGBTQ+ intended parents. When LGBTQ+ couples do become parents, the lack of legal recognition for sexual minority families in many countries/states puts both the parents and children in these families at great risk and causes significant stress. Parents raising children from prior heterosexual relationships can struggle to navigate the transition from their previous parent identity to one which is explicitly LGBTQ+. Children of LGBTQ+ parents may also be more likely to experience homophobic bullying and discrimination, causing distress for the whole family.

Relationship roles

Many heterosexual couples still organise their roles and responsibilities according to 'traditional' patriarchal gender roles (e.g., man as breadwinner, woman as nurturing parent and homemaker). LGBTQ+ couples have less access to relevant relationship templates or role-models due to widespread censoring and erasure of queer relationships in the media and educational settings for example. As such, decisions regarding the division of labour, degree of monogamy and autonomy, financial obligations to one another, and planning for the future among other issues are often more flexible and the responsibility of each couple to define and explore. This greater flexibility can confer advantages by allowing LGBTQ+ couples to determine relationship roles that best meet their unique needs, and potentially leads to a more equal relationship. However, the explicit negotiation of roles and responsibilities may require additional communication and conflict management resources.

Intersectionality

Many LGBTQ+ people will hold one or more additional minority identities, for example in relation to their age, ethnicity, race, religion, (dis)ability, and social class. Intersectionality theory (Crenshaw 1989) states that our different social identities intersect and overlap with each other, and individuals who possess multiple, intersecting minority identities will experience intersecting and magnifying layers of oppression, marginalisation, discrimination and stigma. Such individuals are therefore at even greater risk of poor mental and physical health through accentuated minority stress processes (Balsam et al. 2011). Given the established link between individual partner mental health and relationship distress, LGBTQ+ couples involving partners with intersecting minority identities are likely to be at even greater risk of relationship difficulties.

Norms within the LGBTQ+ community

Like all sub-cultures, there are norms, stereotypes, and expectations which prevail within LGBTQ+ communities, including expectations related to queer relationships. Internalised 'intra-minority stress' (Pachankis et al., 2020), or within-group pressure to conform to these hypothetical 'rules' and standards, places additional pressure on LGBTQ+ relationships and can limit the forms of relationship that one finds oneself entering into. For example, in some gay male communities there is an expectation that all gay men are promiscuous, and that long-term, satisfying, and stable monogamous relationships are not possible or desirable.

Advantages of being an LGBTQ+ couple

The factors described above paint a rather negative view of the challenges faced by LGBTQ+ relationships, but there is also evidence that sexual minority couples in community samples are at least as satisfied and happy in their relationships as heterosexual partners (Balsam et al. 2008). There may be many positive qualities associated with being in an LGBTQ+ relationship that provide protection and resilience against these challenges (e.g., post-traumatic growth and strengthening of teamwork through jointly facing and fighting oppression and discrimination, deepening the emotional bond between partners).

Evidence-base for couple therapy in LGBTQ+ couples

Little is known about whether empirically supported couple interventions like cognitive behavioural couple therapy (CBCT) (e.g., Epstein and Baucom 2002; Baucom, Epstein, Kirby, and LaTaillade 2015) are effective in helping sexual and gender minority couples. The vast majority of existing couple therapy research has either explicitly only sought to recruit heterosexual couples, or failed to report participants' sexual orientation or gender identity (Spengler et al. 2019; de Brito Silva et al., 2021; Kousteni and Anagnostopoulos 2020). Pentel et al. (2021) recently described the results from a pilot study exploring the effectiveness of a new intervention that integrated principles of Minority Stress Theory (Meyer 2003) with the empirically supported CBCT framework. This was the first culturally tailored CBCT intervention for same-sex couples to be empirically evaluated. Results of the pilot involving 11 same-sex female couples indicated that participants experienced significant decreases in relationship distress and improvements in couple coping with minority stress.

Adapting therapy to meet the needs of sexual minority couples

Guidelines have been published and endorsed by major international therapeutic regulation bodies which set out a series of standards and expectations for psychological therapists working with gender, sexuality and relationship diversity (e.g., British Psychological Society 2019). Whilst welcome, these do not provide detailed guidance on working with LGBTQ+ couples specifically.

According to Scott, Whitton, and Buzella (2019) there are several specific challenges to providing couple therapy that is culturally appropriate, acceptable, and beneficial for LGBTQ+ couples. First, because most existing relationship interventions have been developed for monogamously partnered, opposite-sex heterosexual couples, they often use heteronormative language and images, and are based on heteronormative assumptions. Some of these assumptions may not translate well to working with sexual minority couples. This can make the therapy less relevant and engaging, and at worst may alienate LGBTQ+ couples and pathologise what are normal differences in intimate relationships. Second, most evidence-based couple interventions do not aim to address unique challenges faced by LGBTQ+ couples, such as coping with discrimination, the absence of LGBTQ+ relationship role-models, or lower social support. Again, this may mean that therapy is less helpful for LGBTQ+ couples whose difficulties are in part maintained by these challenges.

In addition, culturally sensitive and adapted interventions are desired by LGBTQ+ couples (e.g., Whitton and Buzzella 2012), and sexual minority couples report negative experiences of working with some heterosexual clinicians who they perceive as lacking specific knowledge about LGBTQ+ issues and making unhelpful assumptions about them (e.g., Scott & Rhoades, 2014). Many clinicians also report receiving little to no training in working with sexual minority couples and understandably feel unprepared for this work (Green and Mitchell 2015).

In the absence of a robust evidence-based road map to follow, Scott, Whitton, and Buzzella (2019) have proposed a series of clinical considerations for adapting cognitive-behavioural couple therapies for LGBTQ+ couples, which are described below.

Removing heterosexist bias

This includes therapists and service-providers being open to reviewing all aspects of how they advertise and deliver therapy and aiming to remove heteronormative assumptions and biases where possible. One example might be the use of inclusive imagery in advertising a couple therapy service (i.e., not solely depicting images of different-sex couples while also making specific reference to LGBTQ+ relationships within advertising and marketing materials). Another includes therapists being mindful of potentially heteronormative assumptions they might make about relationship processes that might be rooted in gender inequality.

Enhancing 'core content' of CBCT

A good understanding of how core relationship processes common to all couples intersect with the unique experiences of LGBTQ+ couples and other identities can enhance the quality and cultural sensitivity of couple therapies. In general, therapists should approach relationship topics from an *affirming stance*, curious to explore experiences associated with being in a sexual minority couple and validating these, balancing knowledge of common ways that minority stressors may influence couple functioning, with an openness to learning about the couple's specific experiences. Clinicians should be careful not to attribute relationship distress and dynamics solely to the couple's LGBTQ+ status and avoid the microaggression of assuming that the couple's main concerns will necessarily be rooted in their sexual minority identities.

Within this overall approach, there are several standard CBCT interventions that might benefit from enhancement to meet the specific needs of LGBTQ+ couples. For example:

- *Relationship assumptions, expectations and standards*: it may be helpful to explore and clarify partners' beliefs around what they expect from their partner and relationship, including standards of behaviour for how their partner *should* behave or how their relationship *should* function. This can be particularly helpful when there is an obvious mismatch between different partner's expectations and standards. In such cases it can be helpful to try and negotiate a new set of realistic and flexible standards that feel agreeable to both parties. Due to the lack of LGBTQ+ relationship role models or clear social norms for what sexual minority relationships should look like, this content might be particularly helpful. Incorporating a strengths-based perspective in interventions can be helpful, highlighting how the couple have more flexibility in establishing relationship roles outside of the constraints of heteronormative, gender-based standards, whilst also acknowledging the additional effort this might require.
- *Sexual intimacy* – there are numerous differences in sexual norms and practices between heterosexual and LGBTQ+ relationships. It is important that therapists demonstrate a non-judgemental, open and curious stance in discussing topics around sexual intimacy with LGBTQ+ couples, who may be particularly sensitive to potential signs of disapproval. It can be helpful for therapists who aren't familiar with sexual norms and practices within different sub-sections of the LGBTQ+ community to educate themselves using reliable sources (e.g., Neves & Davies, 2023), whilst also offering interventions which are common in standard CBCT protocols (e.g., strategies to improve communication about sexual desires).
- *Parenting* – Given the unique challenges that LGBTQ+ couples face in parenting and becoming parents, therapists should develop a basic understanding of how local legal frameworks and policies may affect

family planning for LGBTQ+ couples. These might include financial issues, legal issues related to surrogacy and adoption, co-parenting arrangements, and challenges imposed by reduced social support. Whilst it is not necessary to be experts on these topics, some basic research is helpful, and can be supplemented by taking time to ask questions of the couple and understand their unique challenges. Clinicians can work with couples to problem-solve and approach these issues as a team.

- *LGBTQ+ specific content* – CBCT interventions may also benefit from incorporating novel content to address the specific experiences of sexual minority couples, including the impact of minority stress and oppression (Meyer, 2003). At a basic level this might include psychoeducation and normalising related to the minority stressors that couple have been exposed to and validating that these stressors will have made their lives more difficult and created challenges for their relationship. It could also include a specific focus on cognitive-behavioural strategies for managing stress as individuals (e.g., enhancing self-care, reducing avoidance and unhelpful emotion regulation strategies) and/or helping couples optimise how they work together to cope with stress (e.g., using effective communication skills, focusing on supporting one another during times of heightened stress).

Exploring the impact of internalised LGBTQ+ stigma on individuals and the relationship between partners might also be important. Psychoeducation and Socratic enquiry to help couples identify and understand the impact of internalised homophobia can be empowering and help foster compassion.

Another specific area that may need addressing is the heteronormative assumption that intimate romantic relationships will consist of two people in a monogamous pairing. Many LGBTQ+ relationships will be non-monogamous, and this model of doing relationships can lead to satisfying long-term partnerships. The success of such relationships often rests on clear expectations and effective communication about each partner's wants and needs. In relationships where non-monogamy appears to be a source of stress, it can be helpful to support the couple to clarify 'rules' and standards about which sexual partners are allowable, under what circumstances extra-dyadic sex can occur (e.g., only outside the home, never with the same partner twice), and what protections from sexually transmitted infections are required.

The presenting couple: Amy & Zarah

In Amy's initial consultation she reported feeling very stressed and low in mood because a recent application for a promotion at work had not been successful. She described feeling rejected and 'not good enough', and she believed there was an element of homophobic discrimination influencing her manager's decision not to promote her. She had been finding it difficult to sleep, feeling irritable, had withdrawn from previously enjoyed hobbies like exercise and socialising, and was generally feeling on edge most of the time. She described herself as a 'perfectionist' and said that she had very high standards both for her own performance across multiple life domains, and for others too. Amy acknowledged that these unrelenting standards were driving some of the stress she was experiencing, leading to lots of self-critical rumination and being snappy with others. Amy was concerned that her recent stress and low mood were impacting negatively on her relationship with her partner Zarah, who often bore the brunt of her irritability at home. Amy and Zarah were offered a course of CBCT as Amy's mood and anxiety difficulties were impacting negatively on their relationship, and vice versa.

Both Amy and Zarah were in their late 30s. They met 8 years prior, when Amy had been on a sabbatical from work and backpacking around Europe. At first they had lots of fun together and enjoyed the same sense of humour and thirst for adventure. After a few years living abroad, they eventually moved back to Amy's home city in the UK. They decided they did not want to get married, but had entered a civil partnership 7 years ago. They had a 3 year-old daughter, Eva, who was conceived through artificial insemination. Amy and Zarah felt that they started to run into problems about 3 years into their relationship. Amy's pre-existing perfectionism really began to escalate when she resumed her career as an architect. She would work long hours and become very stressed with deadlines, spending a lot of time paying great attention to details. At home she would also be very precise with tidying and cleaning, be constantly making 'to do' lists, and would become very stressed when Zarah's attempts to complete household tasks were not up to Amy's standards. This often led to conflict and arguments. Difficulties resolving problems and communicating ineffectively had intensified since Eva was born. Having a child and with both working full-time, they were under significant pressure as a couple. They had little social support; Zarah's parents and siblings lived abroad, and Amy's parents lived 30 miles away but had not been forthcoming with offers to help with childcare. Zarah felt isolated and had struggled to develop a strong friendship network after moving to the UK. Although Amy did have a group of good friends, she saw them infrequently because she was working so much.

Amy acknowledged that her perfectionism was a problem, but felt that it was a strategy she had developed to cope with a long-standing fear of failure and not feeling 'good enough'. She reported that her parents were very religious when she was younger and had set strict standards for her academic achievement. Amy described how she was initially very scared when she started to realise she was sexually attracted to men and women, and attributed this fear partly to the negative messages she internalised about what it means to be non-heterosexual from her family, church and her boarding school environment. Amy said that over time, she learnt that she would feel safe, liked and in control by working extremely hard and achieving. Zarah on the other hand was much less focussed on details. She worked in Theatre and was much more laid back about things needing to be done in a precise way at all times.

The fundamental differences in Amy and Zarah's personalities would clash at times of stress and could lead to heated arguments. Amy believed that she was good at communicating, but in observing them talking together it became clear that Amy could be quite critical and passive-aggressive when trying to communicate her thoughts and feelings. Zarah would tolerate this to a degree but would usually choose to disengage by withdrawing and shutting down. They both retreated into their work, whilst trying to share childcare between them throughout the week. They no longer spent any quality time together as a couple, they reported a lack of sexual or other physical intimacy and gave the impression they existed in the same home but 'like two ships passing in the night'. The main thing that kept them together was their love for Eva and desire not to let their relationship problems impact on her.

THERAPIST REFLECTION: In our early therapy sessions I noticed that I found it easier to empathise with Zarah, and that I sometimes felt like I was 'walking on eggshells' with Amy. She presented herself as very poised, stylish and well put together. Zarah on the other hand exuded a more relaxed and calm presence. Amy's perfectionistic coping mechanisms – of trying to exert tight control and being highly critical of others – were observable in her interactions with Zarah and myself. I caught myself feeling anxious before and during sessions and was concerned that I might not be 'getting it right' as a therapist, and this could lead to Amy disengaging from our work. My therapeutic response was to work harder to keep Amy onside e.g., being very careful in how I phrased my summaries and interjections. Through reflecting on this within my own clinical supervision I decided to sensitively and selectively share this experience with the couple later on in the course of therapy. Amy was able to hear this with humility, and it helped to provide a sense of validation to Zarah's experience of Amy as unfairly harsh and critical.

Formulation

Our collaborative case formulation drew on the CBCT model of relationship functioning (Baucom et al. 2020), considering the impact of environmental, couple, and individual level factors that influence problematic thoughts, feelings and behaviours of the couple. This generic CBCT model is flexible in being able to incorporate consideration of the impact of sexual minority stressors too.

Overhearing homophobic comments in her office, and then subsequently not being successful with a recent promotion application had been key triggers for the exacerbation of Amy's anxiety and low mood. When Amy became stressed and low, her pre-existing negative beliefs about herself and perfectionism were activated, leading her to be both self-critical and then depressed, but also focussed on other people needing to conform to her own high standards. We discussed how Amy's perfectionism made sense in terms of her developmental history (high standards set by parents and school, internalised homophobia), and that it could confer some advantages (allowing her to perform well in her career, being super-efficient), but also had a negative impact on her own self-esteem and relationship with Zarah when either of them inevitably fell short of Amy's unrelenting high standards. When this did happen, it could lead to hostility and a demand/withdraw or withdraw/withdraw pattern of communication, and difficulties addressing problems together as a couple. Over time this pattern of negativity and withdrawal had reduced positive feelings and led to declining intimacy.

THERAPIST REFLECTION: Amy could come across as quite intimidating when she was expressing her thoughts and feelings in a veiled way which indicated an underlying, but not directly expressed, hostility or irritation. It was clear from the start that while she had insight into her perfectionism, she also found it very difficult to inhibit a punitive, harsh response when she believed that she or someone else had not met her standards. As her therapist I was wondering what standards she might be holding me up to and trying to maintain a balance between engaging her in Socratic curiosity about her standards (and the impact that these have on her/others), whilst also being very careful to not give the impression that I was criticising her. This felt like hard work at times! Lots of normalisation, psychoeducation, and externalising the problem as 'the perfectionism' helped.

Aims of intervention

It was relatively straightforward to reach some mutually agreed goals for therapy:

- Improve their communication (less demand/withdraw, less hostility, be better able to problem-solve as a team).
- Help Amy to be less self-critical and not set such high standards for others.
- Improve support for each other and spend more quality time together and as a family.

Course of therapy

Their course of therapy spanned 14 sessions. In line with Scott, Whitton, and Buzzella's (2019) suggestions above, therapy for Amy and Zarah included several 'core' elements of CBCT which had been adapted to meet their needs as sexual minorities, but also some novel LGBTQ+ specific content which is not part of standard CBCT protocols.

Enhanced 'core content'

1. Psycho-education: This included an introduction to Minority Stress Theory (Mayer, 2003) and the impact of internalised LGBTQ+ stigma. We discussed this specifically in relation to Amy's perfectionism, her fear of failure and not being 'good enough', and the harsh self-critical thinking that drove her low mood and anxiety. We also spoke about the impact of experiencing continued discrimination and microaggressions at work and more generally. It was important to validate the impact of reduced social support for them as a family, and how this was in part due to their LGBTQ+ status. Amy's family had never fully accepted Zarah or Eva; struggling without their support (practical and emotional) or regular contact with Zarah's family was isolating. Much of this psychoeducation helped to normalise and validate their experiences.

THERAPIST REFLECTION: As an out gay therapist myself, I found it easy to empathise with some the themes discussed with Amy and Zarah e.g., the impact of internalised stigma. I was able to use this to my advantage to help build rapport and empathy with some limited self-disclosure (e.g., *"As LGBTQ+ people growing up in hostile, threatening, homophobic environments it's no wonder that we might develop certain strategies to help us feel safe and in control"*). Bringing one's own lived experience into therapy in this very controlled and limited way felt like a helpful decision on many levels (normalising, building rapport and empathy, strengthening the therapeutic alliance).

2. Communication skills training: This formed the basis of many of the earlier therapy sessions and included teaching and practising skills to share thoughts and feelings helpfully, and problem-solving/decision-making skills. It involved both psychoeducation and discussion, but also a heavy focus on skills practice within the sessions and for 'homework'. Much of this part of our work was not very different to working with heterosexual cisgender couples. One exception is that it felt important to again validate the impact of internalised homophobia and how this may have contributed to Amy's somewhat harsh and critical tone when expressing her emotions to Zarah. Both seemed to find this helpful and it encouraged empathy from Zarah.

THERAPIST: Zarah, could you now tell Amy how you felt and what you were thinking when she shouted at you and told you off for not cleaning the kitchen up after lunch?

ZARAH: Ok…well I just felt really attacked. When you started laying into me I was thinking gosh was it really that bad what I did? Can't she see that I had my hands full with Eva and I didn't have time to put the plates in the dishwasher? And also does it even really matter that much? I actually felt quite scared and on edge. The tone you used and the way you said it made me feel like I was letting you down or something, like I'd done something really awful.

THERAPIST: Amy, could you summarise what you heard from Zarah.

AMY: You said you felt like I was laying into you for no reason and over-reacting. You were thinking that I thought you had let me down and I was being too harsh.

THERAPIST: Is that right Zarah?

ZARAH: Yeah, I just felt quite shocked because you couldn't see all the other things I'd had done that day to help and zoomed in on the one thing I messed up.

THERAPIST: Amy, do you want to respond to Zarah?

AMY: Ok look I'm sorry. I know I was being mean but I was freaking out about work, and then I came home after feeling super stressed all day and the kitchen was a total bomb site. I know I was being nasty now, but sometimes it just takes over me and I get so angry. I felt really bad about it after, but then you stayed away from me for the rest of the evening.

THERAPIST: Thanks Amy. Let's pause for a second. It sounds like there is a bit of a theme emerging here. When you're feeling really stressed out and worrying about work especially, you can sometimes blow up and become quite critical of Zarah. I'm wondering if this is a similar kind of process to what's happening when you feel bad about yourself, when you think you're not meeting one of those high standards you set for yourself?

AMY: (Pause) Yeah. I guess you're right.

THERAPIST: Where do you think that harsh, critical voice comes from Amy?

AMY: It's probably all related to what we talked about before. It's got to have come from the way my parents spoke to me, and the total fear I had of not living up to what they expected of me. And school obviously.

THERAPIST: And that was their expectations about your academic perfor-mance, but also about the broader heteronormative expectations they had for your life in general?

AMY: Yes.

3. Relationship assumptions, expectations and standards: In the mid-phase of treatment we started to explore Amy and Zarah's expectations for each other and their relationship. We had already framed Amy's perfectionism as being about 'unrelenting high standards' that she held for herself and others, and alongside our couple sessions she had been doing some CBT self-help to work on developing and experimenting with more flexible rules herself. It was helpful to normalise and validate the fact that when growing up LGBTQ+ people have less access to relationship role models in their own lives and the media, and that defining their own relationship standards now could be challenging but could bring some benefits too. We developed new rules related to working as a team to solve problems, and about how they can mutually demonstrate respect for each other in their behaviour, and we designed guided behavioural change interventions to try and test-drive these new rules.

LGBTQ+ specific content

We dedicated time within our sessions to helping Amy manage her own stress in a more adaptive way. Amy was signposted to CBT self-help resources to help her understand and address her core perfectionism issues, as well working on her own self-care and work-life balance. Communication skills helped Amy and Zarah learn how to express their negative feelings in a more constructive way and start to work together to face their problems as a team. In relation to the homophobic culture in her workplace, Amy was referred to a Career Coach in our team who helped her to better understand her rights as an employee, and then to research new jobs in organisations which publicly adopted an LGBTQ+ welcoming stance. Their lack of social support from family of origin was validated and normalised, and we worked together to brainstorm how they might be able to expand their social network, including linking in with a peer support and social group for LGBTQ+ parents, and strengthening connections with their existing LGBTQ+ friends.

THERAPIST REFLECTION: I knew little about support for LGBTQ+ parents before working with this couple but was happy to discover, though my own research, that there are a number of UK-based LGBTQ+ parent networks who offer a range of different services and advice. It was helpful to be able to add this information to a 'LGBTQ+ signposting document' to share with other sexual minority patients and couples accessing our service.

Discussion & Reflections

Although not always easy, it felt very rewarding to work with Amy and Zarah. Amy's engrained perfectionism and sometimes passive-aggressive communication style could impact negatively on the therapeutic alliance. As a therapist I felt the need to work hard to keep Amy 'on board' and not to appear that I was taking sides with Zarah. I also felt an internal pressure of my own to do my absolute best as a therapist to help this couple, as some of the themes emerging in the work resonated with my own experience as a sexual minority. Though I believe I managed this well overall, it was a challenge. I wondered if at times there was a parallel process in operation, whereby I found myself expecting very high (higher than usual!) standards for my own performance as a therapist. I found it useful to try and model 'imperfection' at times, though this felt risky. It helped me to empathise with the efforts that Amy was putting in to try and work on addressing her own perfection.

LGBTQ+ stigma and prejudice can be expressed in both obvious and more subtle forms. Some couples may find it difficult to recognise and label these stressors in their lives. Other couples don't realise the impact of these stressors until one or both partners begin to experience psychological or physical health symptoms. Therapists should adopt a curious attitude in asking about the presence of minority stress, without imposing their own pre-defined ideas on the couple.

Overall both Amy and Zarah reported that they found therapy helpful and their self-reported scores on outcome measures of relationship satisfaction and perceived criticism also improved from the time of their assessment. Although the work was sometimes challenging, it helped that both Amy and Zarah were committed to improving their relationship and did well to complete most of the homework assignments considering how busy their lives were. Amy did make some positive progress in starting to address problematic perfectionism, but she needed a bit more help than I was able to provide within a course of couple therapy. After their CBCT sessions ended, Amy went on to access some individual CBT to continue working on addressing her unrelenting high standards.

Working with Amy and Zarah was, overall, very rewarding. I felt proud to be able to help a fellow LGBTQ+ couple who were struggling, in part, because of the minority stress they had been exposed to as individuals and a couple. Being a gay therapist myself I think did provide a small advantage, in that I had some lived experience of minority stress to be able to relate to and was familiar with some of the literature in this field. However, by no means was it 'essential' in this case that I shared a sexual minority identity with the couple. Unless a couple specifically requests a LGBTQ+ therapist, it is perfectly possible for a cisgender heterosexual therapist to be a good enough therapist for sexual minority couples. A key factor influencing the success of this is likely to be the willingness of the therapist to step out of their frame of reference, adopt an affirmative stance throughout, be vigilant for heteronormative language and assumptions, and do some basic research to understand LGBTQ+ relationships and the challenges they face.

As noted above, the evidence-base for CBCT and other relationship interventions in sexual minority populations is still very sparse. We currently know even less about transgender/non-binary, bisexual and non-monogamous relationships than we do about same-sex cisgender relationships. There are likely to be additional minority stressors and specific challenges faced by the transgender and gender non-binary community and these will inevitably trickle down into their relationships. Clearly more research is needed to help us understand whether existing approaches and protocols, adapted to try and address some of the specific needs of LGBTQ+ couples, are both effective and acceptable for sexual minorities.

Therapist tips

- It is not necessary to 'start from scratch' when working with sexual minority couples in CBCT. The standard approach to assessment, formulation, and intervention should be used, but it will be helpful to enhance these with some specific focus on minority stress processes.
- It may be important to add some specific 'modules' that attend to unique LGBTQ+ issues (e.g., dealing with internalised homophobia, discrimination, LGBTQ+ parenting, outness as a couple, lack of relationship role-models etc.).
- It is not necessary to be LGBTQ+ yourself to work effectively with sexual minority couples. However, you do have to be willing and able to provide a queer affirmative atmosphere, to do some basic research about LGBTQ+ relationships, and to be open about what you don't know with patients. Genuine curiosity and willingness to learn from LGBTQ+ couples will go a long way.
- Be mindful about your own therapist assumptions and potentially heteronormative biases. At the same time, it also important not to make assumptions that there will necessarily be differences in fundamental/universal aspects of relationship functioning. Furthermore, even amongst LGBTQ+ couples there will be a lot of within-group heterogeneity.
- Try to remove heteronormative images and language in your service marketing and supplementary therapy materials. Actively encourage and welcome couple referrals from the LGBTQ+ community.

Suggestions for further reading

Bigner, J. J., and Wetchler, J. L. (2015) *Handbook of LGBT-Affirmative Couple and Family Therapy.* Abingdon: Routledge. This is a really helpful all-round introduction to the field of couple therapy for LGBTQ+ relationships. Some helpful chapters dedicated to issues specific to different groups.

Rostosky, S. S., and Riggle, E. D. B. (2015) *Happy Together. Thriving as a Same-Sex Couple in Your Family, Workplace, and Community.* Washington, DC: American Psychological Association. This is a very easy to read and accessible self-help book written for LGBTQ+ couples wanting to enhance their relationship.

Neves, S., and Davies, D. (2023a) *Erotically Queer: A Pink Therapy Guide for Practitioners.* London: Routledge.

Neves, S., and Davies, D. (2023b) *Relationally Queer: A Pink Therapy Guide for Practitioners*. London: Routledge. These two companion books provide an excellent and inclusive introduction to thinking therapeutically about queer sex and relationships.

References

Balsam, K. F., Beauchaine, T. P., Rothblum, E. D., and Solomon, S. E. (2008) "Three-year follow-up of same-sex couples who had civil unions in Vermont, same-sex couples not in civil unions, and heterosexual married couples". *Developmental Psychology*, 44 (1), pp. 102–116.

Baucom, D. H., Epstein, N., Kirby, J. S., and LaTaillade, J. J. (2015) "Cognitive behavioral couple therapy", in Gurman, A. S., Lebow, J., and Snyder, D. K. (eds.) *Clinical handbook of couple therapy* (5th ed.). New York: Guilford, pp. 23–60.

Baucom, D. H., Fischer, M. S., Corrie, S., Worrell, M., and Boeding, S. E. (2020) *Treating relationship distress and psychopathology in couples. A cognitive-behavioural approach*. Oxon: Routledge.

British Psychological Society. (2019) *Guidelines for psychologists working with gender, sexuality and relationship diversity*. Leicester: British Psychological Society.

Corturillo, E. M., McGeorge, C. R., and Carlson, T. S. (2016) "How Prepared Are They? Exploring Couple and Family Therapy Faculty Members" Training Experiences in Lesbian, Gay, and Bisexual Affirmative Therapy". *Journal of Feminist Family Therapy*, 28 (2–3), pp. 55–75.

Crenshaw, K. (1989) "Demarginalizing the Intersection of Race and Sex: A Black Feminist Critique of Antidiscrimination Doctrine, Feminist Theory and Antiracist Politics". *University of Chicago Legal Forum*, 140, pp. 139–167.

de Brito Silva, B., Soares de Almeida-Segundo, D., de Miranda Ramos, M., Bredemeier, J., and Cerqueira-Santos, E. (2022) "Couple and Family Therapies and Interventions with Lesbian, Gay and Bisexual Individuals: A Systematic Review". *Journal of Couple & Relationship Therapy*, 21 (1), pp. 52–79.

Epstein, N. B., and Baucom, D. H. (2002) *Enhanced cognitive-behavioral therapy for couples: A contextual approach*. Washington, DC: American Psychological Association.

Giammattei, S. V., and Green, R. J. (2015) "LGBTQ Couple and Family Therapy. History and Future Directions", in Bigner, J. J., and Wetchler, J. L. (eds.), *Handbook of LGBT-Affirmative Couple and Family Therapy*. Abingdon: Routledge, pp. 1–22.

Green, R. J., and Mitchell, V. (2015) "Gay, lesbian, and bisexual issues in couple therapy". in A. S. Gurman, J. L. Lebow, and D. K. Snyder (eds.), *Clinical handbook of couple therapy*. The Guilford Press, 5th ed., pp. 489–511.

Hatzenbuehler, M. L. (2009) "How does sexual minority stigma "get under the skin"? A psychological mediation framework". *Psychological Bulletin*, 135, pp. 707–730.

Hatzenbuehler, M. L. (2011) "The social environment and suicide attempts in lesbian, gay, and bisexual youth". *Pediatrics*, 127, pp. 896–903.

Jordan, K. M., and Deluty, R. H. (2000) "Social support, coming out, and relationship satisfaction in lesbian couples". *Journal of Lesbian Studies*, 4 (1), pp. 145–164.

Kousteni, I., and Anagnostopoulos, F. (2020) "Same-Sex Couples' Psychological Interventions: A Systematic Review". *Journal of Couple & Relationship Therapy*, 19 (2), pp. 136–174.

Meyer, I. H. (2003) "Prejudice, social stress, and mental health in lesbian, gay, and bisexual populations: Conceptual issues and research evidence". *Psychological Bulletin*, 129, pp. 674–697.

Neves, S., and Davies, D. (2023) *Erotically Queer: A Pink Therapy Guide for Practitioners*. London: Routledge.

Office for National Statistics (2019) "Statistical Bulletin. Families and households in the UK: 2018 Trends in living arrangements including families (with and without dependent children), people living alone and people in shared accommodation, broken down by size and type of household". Released 7th August 2019. Accessed at: https://www.ons.gov.uk/peoplepopulationandcommunity/birthsdeathsandmarriages/families/bulletins/familiesandhouseholds/2018.

Office for National Statistics (2020) "Sexual orientation, UK: 2020 Experimental Statistics on sexual orientation in the UK in 2020 by region, sex, age, marital or legal partnership status, ethnic group and socio-economic classification, using data from the Annual Population Survey (APS)". Released 25th May 2022. Accessed at: https://www.ons.gov.uk/peoplepopulationandcommunity/culturalidentity/sexuality/bulletins/sexualidentityuk/2020#:~:text=The%20proportion%20of%20men%20in,2.8%25%20over%20the%20same%20period.

Pachankis, J. E., Clark, K. A., Burton, C. L., Hughto, J. M. W., Bränström, R., and Keene, D. E. (2020) "Sex, status, competition, and exclusion: Intraminority stress from within the gay community and gay and bisexual men's mental health". *Journal of Personality and Social Psychology*, 119 (3), pp. 713–740.

Pentel, K. Z., Baucom, D. H., Weber, D. M., Wojda, A. K., Carrino, E. A. (2021) "Cognitive-behavioral couple therapy for same-sex female couples: A pilot study". *Family Process*, 60 (4), pp. 1083–1097.

Plöderl, M., and Tremblay, P. (2015) "Mental health of sexual minorities. A systematic review". *International Review of Psychiatry*, 27, pp. 367–385.

Rosenfeld, M. J. (2014) "Couple longevity in the era of same-sex marriage in the United States". *Journal of Marriage and Family*, 76, pp. 905–918.

Scott, S. B., and Rhoades, G. K. (2014) "Relationship education for lesbian couples: Perceived barriers and content considerations". *Journal of Couple and Relationship Therapy*, 13 (4), pp. 339–364.

Scott, S. B., and Whitton, S. W., and Buzzella, B. A. (2019) "Providing Relationship Interventions to Same-Sex Couples: Clinical Considerations, Program Adaptations, and Continuing Education". *Cognitive and Behavioral Practice*, 26, pp. 270–284.

Spengler, E. S., DeVore, E. N., Spengler, P. M., and Lee, N. A. (2019) "What does 'couple' mean in couple therapy outcome research? A systematic review of the implicit and explicit, inclusion and exclusion of gender and sexual minority individuals and identities". *Journal of Marital and Family Therapy*, 6 (2), pp. 240–255.

Totenhagen, C. J., Randall, A. K., Cooper, A. N., Tao, C., and Walsh, J. J. (2017) "Stress Spillover and Crossover in Same-Sex Couples: Concurrent and Lagged Daily Effects". *Journal of GLBT Family Studies*, 13 (3), pp. 236–256.

Whitton, S. W., and Buzzella, B. A. (2012) "Using relationship education programs with same-sex couples: A preliminary evaluation of program utility and needed modifications". *Marriage & Family Review*, 48 (7), pp. 667–688.

Chapter 8

Long Term Health Conditions

Marion Cuddy

Introduction

Catherine was referred to her local psychological therapy service by her GP. She had been diagnosed with rheumatoid arthritis (RA) 18 months previously and was experiencing fluctuating levels of pain and fatigue. She complained that her symptoms and their unpredictability were very life-limiting, and she was feeling demoralised and anxious about her future.

From her very first appointment, it was clear that Catherine was a highly competent person and used to being in charge of her life. She reported that her diagnosis had caused her to lose her identity and she was no longer able to do many of the things that had been important in her life. She said she was not sure psychological therapy would help her, but she was willing to 'give it a go'. Catherine's health problem was affecting her relationship with her husband Guy as well as her individual wellbeing, so a couple-based intervention was suggested. Guy was also somewhat sceptical about the potential benefits of therapy. It was clear from the start that careful consideration would have to be given to engagement with these clients.

Many couples will have to face the diagnosis of a significant medical problem over the course of their relationship. Being diagnosed with an illness, particularly a serious or long-term condition (LTC), affects the lives of both the person diagnosed and their partner, and necessitates a process of adjustment within the relationship, as well as individually. For example, roles and responsibilities may need to change, physical symptoms may restrict the couple's activities, and there can be financial consequences due to inability to work. Partners may need to support the person affected in making and adhering to decisions concerning treatment or lifestyle changes and may be called on to provide additional practical and emotional support. Couples may need to re-evaluate their goals and plans for the future.

Individuals with a LTC have a significantly increased risk of depression compared to individuals who are in good physical health (e.g. Bhattarai et al., 2013). Furthermore, being in a *distressed* relationship can have an adverse

DOI: 10.4324/9781003024439-10

effect on both physical and mental health. (e.g. Orth-Gomer et al., 2000). Several studies have reported reduced quality of life and increased risk of psychological distress among caregiving partners of individuals with LTC, and conditions where there is a high level if disability such as chronic pain can be particularly demanding on partners (e.g. Suso-Ribera et al., 2020). Couples sometimes describe the illness as an 'uninvited guest' or unwanted 3rd person in the relationship. Some report that they have difficulty 'drawing a boundary' around the illness so that it does not infiltrate all aspects of their lives.

How couples respond to illness

Many couples deal quite well with the changes imposed by a chronic health condition, but others do not. The factors that predict a couple's adjustment to living with a LTC are unclear. Some data suggests that gender can play a role, with couples in whom the male partner is ill faring better than those in which the female partner has the LTC (Glantz et al., 2009). The life cycle stage during which the illness develops may also be important, with an illness occurring later in life more likely to be seen as a normal part of the lifespan, whereas one that occurs 'out of sequence' may be harder to adjust to, particularly if it impedes important developmental goals such as having a family or career aspirations.

A partner can play a significant role in helping a patient to make treatment decisions and health behaviour changes, and/or in providing emotional and practical support. For instance, one of the strongest predictors of long-term smoking cessation is whether one's partner is also a smoker (Palmer, Baucom & McBride, 2000). However, misconceptions about the LTC or its symptoms can lead to partners offering the 'wrong' kind of support, for example encouraging rest and colluding with avoidance behaviours in patients with chronic pain.

Quality of communication seems to play an important role. As mentioned above, roles and responsibilities may need to change, and this may happen in an overt or covert manner, for both emotional/interactional roles and practical ones. Partners sometimes engage in 'protective buffering' and avoid sharing their thoughts and fears about the LTC because they do not want to upset their loved one. Although this is an understandable response, there is some evidence that it is leads to poorer emotional wellbeing and less optimal relationship functioning (e.g. Perndorfer et al., 2019). In a study of adjustment to breast cancer, women reported that one of the most important factors for them was emotional support from their partners with regard to issues such as changes in body image or fear of death (Neuling & Winefield, 1988).

How each partner copes, to what extent he/she accepts the LTC, and the degree of alignment between each partner's response to the illness can help or hinder the adjustment process. For example, if a husband copes with his diagnosis by withdrawing emotionally, perhaps with the intention of not burdening his wife with his worries and concerns, this may increase the wife's perception of being isolated and create conflict in the relationship.

Individuals and couples sometimes report a shift in values, priorities, or world view following a diagnosis of serious illness. This has been termed 'posttraumatic growth' or 'benefit finding' (Tedeshi & Calhoun, 2004). For example, they may develop a greater appreciation of the 'here and now' and the daily pleasures accessible to them. They may take stock of their relationship, find new ways of relating to their partner and increasing satisfaction with the relationship, or there may be individual changes in values. Both individual and couple-based psychological interventions for people with LTC can include an element of benefit finding where appropriate in order to help those affected to find meaning in their illness. It is also important to acknowledge the sense of loss experienced by the person with the health condition and/or their partner and to allow them to grieve (Ruddy & McDaniel, 2023). Losses can be felt in a number of domains including lifestyle, physical and sexual intimacy, financial security and of course where the illness reduces the person's life expectancy.

Theoretical framework

Living with a LTC necessitates an ongoing process of adjustment as the condition and its management evolve. Adjustment is a dynamic process, requiring a degree of cognitive adaptation to accommodate the change in circumstances as well as a flexible balance of change and acceptance on the part of both partners.

The literature on stress and coping is very relevant to work in this field. The distinction between problem-focused and emotion-focused coping made by Lazarus & Folkman's (1984) is useful and these concepts map quite well onto change and acceptance strategies respectively. Balance is a key principle here – change (e.g. in lifestyle) may be essential, but an exclusive focus on change will not help the individual (or couple) to cope emotionally. Similarly, insufficient acceptance of the 'new normal' is likely to lead to greater distress and/or conflict, but too much acceptance can lead to 'giving up'.

Stirling Moorey has suggested a third dimension of 'life-oriented' coping, which refers to living in the present moment and 'compartmentalising' the stressor to an adaptive degree (S. Moorey, personal communication, 2019). Again, the principle of balance applies, with too much emphasis on the present being akin to denial, whilst too little can result in excessive preoccupation with the illness.

Both the CBCT and IBCT frameworks described in Chapters 2 and 3 of this book can be used to conceptualise and address a couple's adaptation to changes in health. The couple's specific issues can determine which model has the best 'fit'. For example, IBCT interventions promoting acceptance could be relevant to encourage partners to face their challenges in a more unified manner, whereas CBCT interventions lend themselves well to facilitating the cognitive changes required for healthy adjustment.

Don Baucom and colleagues have proposed 5 broad domains that couple-based interventions around LTC should consider (Baucom et al., 2012). These are principles rather than a strict protocol, and treatment can focus on different areas depending on the couple's needs. Although the main emphasis is usually on helping the partner with the LTC, the wellbeing of the other partner and of the relationship are also taken into account.

1   Providing psycho-education about the illness and ensuring that the partners have a shared understanding of the condition, as well as its recommended management.
2   Facilitating 'sharing thoughts and feelings' conversations about the illness and broader concerns, and therefore enhancing emotional support within the relationship.
3   Facilitating decision-making conversations around treatment, lifestyle changes and other decisions that need to be made in the context of the LTC.
4   Addressing relationship issues that arise from the LTC, such as adapting to changes in roles/responsibilities, coping with reduced finances, or changes in the couple's physical or sexual relationship as a result of the LTC.
5   Addressing broader relationship issues unrelated to the LTC if required.

The presenting couple: Catherine and Guy

Catherine and Guy are in their late 50s. They are both clever, hard-working, strong-willed people. They have led busy and successful careers, raised a daughter together, and had been looking forward to travelling during their retirement. They report that the onset of Catherine's health problems has *"pulled the rug out from under them"*. It has interfered with their daily lives, curtailed their hopes and plans for the future, and the efficient problem-solving strategies they have previously relied on to manage their trials and tribulations are no longer working. They have a tendency to talk over each other, and their frustration with the situation is evident.

THERAPIST REFLECTION: I felt quite anxious during the first few meetings with Catherine and Guy. On the one hand, I really wanted to 'engage' them, to make them feel heard and to give them some hope that therapy could help. However, their tendency to express frustration and interrupt each other meant that I had to direct the session quite a bit. I really tried to stay 'balanced' and the fact that they were both quite forceful probably made this easier – neither was going to leave the session without expressing their point of view!

The couple met at university. They both recall being attracted by the other's intelligence and drive to succeed in life. They dated for several years before marrying and report that their life has been hectic but satisfying until now. They agree that they have never had to face anything this stressful. They have some shared interests, such as exercising and traveling, but have also maintained quite a lot of independent activities, which they both value. They are not a very emotionally expressive or 'touchy feely' couple but have clearly been a highly competent team.

The partners have responded very differently to Catherine's diagnosis; whereas she has withdrawn from many areas of her life, Guy believes she is 'giving up' too easily and thinks she should push herself more. He expresses this a little harshly but goes on to say that he worries her life is not very rewarding. Catherine reports feeling resentful and abandoned when Guy meets friends or their daughter without her. These are new feelings for them both, which are quite uncomfortable and have led to some hostile and tense interactions.

Catherine worries a lot about her health and finds it hard to 'switch off' from this. She feels alone with her illness and says it makes her feel like a burden on the family. She would like more support from Guy and said that he helped more when she was initially diagnosed but things have gone back to 'normal' now. Whenever she tries to discuss her concerns about her health, he tells her she is worrying too much.

Catherine is the eldest of 5 children. Both of her parents worked while she was growing up and she was often required to care for her younger siblings. This has left her with a strong sense of duty and responsibility. She still has a close relationship with her family of origin, who see her as the 'strong and stable' older sister.

Guy acknowledges that he thinks Catherine is overly focused on her health. He becomes a little upset as he describes how he would like to support her but doesn't know how to, as he thinks she is 'giving in' too easily to her illness. Their camaraderie, physical, and sexual intimacy have all disappeared and it feels as if he has 'lost' his partner. He is not sure whether to accept this or continue fighting.

Guy grew up in quite an affluent family, the younger of two boys. Although he got along well with his parents and brother, there was not a great deal of emotional closeness between them. His family tended to connect around shared activities, and he has some lovely memories of family outings and holidays. His parents were supportive, but he felt a lot of pressure to do well at school and then later in his career.

THERAPIST REFLECTION: I felt quite sad about the polarisation between Catherine and Guy's responses and the fact that rather than 'joining forces' to cope, their different perspectives had driven a wedge between them. I could see each person's rationale for their approach, and my view was that a compromise between the two would be an optimal solution, both with regard to managing the illness and for their relationship. Their stubbornness in insisting that their approach was the right one did irritate me at times and gave me an inkling of how it must be experienced by the other partner.

Formulation

Catherine and Guy considered their main problem to be their very different approaches to dealing with Catherine's health problems. This was causing arguments between them on a regular basis, and these were often followed by periods of mutual avoidance until the tension eased.

Until recently, both had favoured a 'keep calm and carry on' attitude to challenges. This had served them very well, particularly in their careers, and the shared approach helped them to feel like a team. However, although this strategy still made sense to Guy, Catherine reported feeling that she had hit a 'brick wall' after her diagnosis. She had always seen herself as a strong and reliable person, and her new experience of needing to curtail her activity due to health problems felt like a failing to her. She preferred not to make commitments rather than risk letting others down by having to cancel plans. Guy could not understand this rationale, particularly as their busy lifestyle had been one of the things both partners found so rewarding about their lives together.

We discussed how the lack of alignment in their response to Catherine's illness and unwillingness to compromise were causing distress in the relationship and preventing them from moving forward. We looked at 'adjustment' on a continuum and considered the possibility that Catherine and Guy had 'over' and 'under-adjusted' respectively, she by limiting her plans and activities more than she needed to; he by not quite taking on board the impact of her illness. Coping styles were also discussed: both partners' strong preference for problem-focused coping was not what was needed in this context, and their lack of emotional expression created little opportunity to foster empathy and left them feeling alone and frustrated.

It was helpful for Catherine and Guy to recognise that their difficulties were not caused by fundamental differences in their values, but rather that their previously shared strategy was no longer quite fit for purpose for this next stage in their lives and needed to be reviewed.

Aims of the intervention

During the assessment, both Catherine and Guy expressed scepticism as to whether therapy would be helpful to them or not. I validated these concerns and gave some examples of how the sessions might be used. We discussed the interaction between health problems, interpersonal relationships, and wellbeing, as well as the different types of coping responses that people engage in. At the end of the assessment phase, Catherine and Guy agreed on two initial goals:

1 To improve their communication
2 To cope better with Catherine's illness as a couple

THERAPIST REFLECTION: Agreeing the goals and tasks of therapy was hard work! I firmly believed that working with Catherine and Guy as a couple could be beneficial and could see a number of different areas we could focus on. They didn't seem to have a very strong 'collaborative set' though, and their ambivalence about therapy also led me to rein in my enthusiasm. The goals we identified were not very 'smart' but they did provide some direction regarding early therapy tasks...

Course of therapy

Catherine and Guy attended 14 treatment sessions together, during which a range of ideas, tools and techniques were interwoven to address their goals and concerns. Their attendance was somewhat irregular due to Catherine's fluctuating symptoms, but they did try to attend briefer video appointments when she was feeling too unwell to attend in person in order to avoid long gaps between sessions. It is difficult to neatly categorise the interventions, as a particular conversation often touched on more than one domain. However, the tasks of therapy loosely fell under the following themes:

Psycho-education

During early sessions Catherine's diagnosis of rheumatoid arthritis, the main symptoms and their recommended management were discussed. I liaised with Catherine's rheumatology nurse, who confirmed that normal activities and gentle exercise were not contra-indicated and that in fact keeping active was recommended. This ensured that any misconceptions were dispelled and that we were all 'on the same page' regarding Catherine's health condition.

Behavioural activation (BA)

Individual BA was used to address Catherine's reduced activity and avoidance. We worked on very gradually increasing her physical activity and avoiding patterns of 'boom and bust'. She also identified some of the rewarding activities that she had stopped doing since her diagnosis and worked on reinstating some of these, adapting them where necessary to take her fluctuating pain/fatigue symptoms into account. For example, Catherine was a keen gardener but now found the upkeep of her garden too physically demanding. What she loved about gardening was the contact with nature, for example the sight and smell of her plants. Therefore, she developed a 'menu' of gardening-related activities she could engage in depending how she felt, and that would all put her in touch with nature. This menu ranged from heavy gardening work, such as trimming hedges, through more gentle tasks such as weeding, to simply taking the time to appreciate her plants and flowers in a mindful way.

BA in a couples context was also used to increased shared positive experiences between Catherine and Guy. This was quite delicate to start with, due to tension created by the discrepancy between Guy's ambitious sugges-tions (e.g. booking theatre tickets) and Catherine's more homely ideas (e.g. watching TV together). In order to achieve some 'easy wins', we identified more modest shared activities to start with, including things that could be done on a regular basis, such as having breakfast together. 'Bigger' plans were gradually worked towards, where possible using the 'menu' principle described above so that the activity could be adapted if Catherine was having a bad day.

Work on communication

During early therapy sessions, I introduced guidelines for sharing thoughts and feelings and for decision-making conversations. Catherine and Guy observed that they both had a tendency to veer away from the disclosure of vulnerable feelings. Their conversations about sensitive issues either escalated into an argument or moved rapidly into problem solving, sometimes before the 'problem' had been fully articulated and understood, leading to mis-understandings and less than optimal 'solutions'. Furthermore, their ten-dency to adopt a problem-solving approach to everything did not work for 'unsolvable problems' such as managing fluctuating ill-health.

Sharing thoughts and feelings conversations

These were the basis for a number of therapeutic interventions over the course of treatment. Initially, we used a structured conversation framework, using standard BCT communication guidelines, observing and coaching their efforts and giving them feedback on strengths and areas to be mindful of. For example, both partners found the concept of 'listening to understand' rather than 'listening to respond' quite a helpful, if challenging one.

As neither found it particularly easy to disclose emotions, this was one of the early tasks of therapy. Using a loosely structured communication frame-work, we worked on the disclosure of 'softer', more vulnerable emotions in both partners. Although this felt awkward at first, they both worked very hard and their efforts led to greater understanding and empathy, both around their different approaches to Catherine's health difficulties and more generally in the relationship.

THERAPIST: Guy, you mentioned that Catherine worries too much about her health, and this frustrates you. Can you tell Catherine a bit more about this, what it's like for you and how it makes you feel?

GUY: Yeah, your arthritis seems to be the main thing you think and talk about. I know it's upsetting for you but we have to get on with life as well as we can. (getting aroused) Moping about it won't help and it seems to me like you're giving in.

THERAPIST: It sounds like watching Catherine do what you see as 'moping' really upsets you Guy. Can you say more about why it bothers you?

GUY: It just seems like such a waste, you know? We had all these plans for the next few years, and now because of this shitty arthritis it looks like we won't be able to do most of them. That's upsetting in itself, but when I see Catherine worrying and she doesn't want to do anything at all, I feel like I've lost her completely. It makes me really sad – and angry to think that she's given up. I think we could still have some good times together, and the way she lets her arthritis take over our lives sort of feels like a rejection.

THERAPIST: Catherine, can you tell us what you've just heard Guy say?

CATHERINE: You're saying you think my worrying is a waste of time and that I've given up. I don't agree with that. You also said that you feel shut out and rejected when I worry about my health, and I hadn't thought about that before. I wish things would improve, that we could start 'living' properly again – that's what I'm holding out for but then I get upset when I have a flare up or something, I start thinking there's no hope and that brings me down, and I suppose I wallow in it a bit. I hadn't realised how this was affecting you and I'm sorry, it wasn't my intention.

Problem solving/decision-making conversations

Catherine and Guy's greater openness in their communication sometimes highlighted decisions that needed to be made or problems that needed to be addressed. The decision-making guidelines helped them to approach these in a systematic way. As they had both previously enjoyed a good deal of autonomy in their relationship and were accustomed to making many decisions independently, they also found it useful to differentiate individual versus couple decisions.

Cognitive work

One of the more challenging problems addressed over the course of therapy was the lack of alignment between the partners' approaches to dealing with

Catherine's illness. Catherine favoured a more cautious, risk-averse approach, whereas Guy's preference was to carry on as normal and revise plans only when necessary. The partners seemed quite polarised on this matter, each convinced that their approach was best. After a decision-making conversation failed to lead to any form of compromise, we agreed it would be useful to explore this issue at a more cognitive level. We started by eliciting each partner's beliefs about their preferred strategy:

THERAPIST: I can see that you each feel strongly about the approach you've chosen, and unfortunately as they are not really compatible this is causing some friction. There are undoubtedly pros and cons to each, and it would be good for us to look at these but first, I think we really need to understand each of your perspectives more fully. Catherine, let's start with you. Can you tell us a bit more about why it's so important to you not to cancel plans?

CATHERINE: I think it comes down to wanting to be reliable. I hate wasting money and letting people down. I never know how I'm going to feel from one day to the next and the thought of having something in the diary that I might need to cancel really stresses me out. I'd rather not make plans and if I feel good on a given day I'll do something spontaneously.

GUY: But that never happens...

CATHERINE: That's not fair. You know I'm fed up and would like to do more but the pain has been really bad these last couple of months.

THERAPIST: (interrupting) Let's stay with how Catherine feels about cancelling plans if that's ok. So Catherine, it sounds like being reliable and seeing plans through is really important to you. I know this might seem like an obvious question, but what bothers you most about the possibility that you might need to cancel?

CATHERINE: I'm not quite sure. I think it's the waste – of money, or other people's time. It just seems wrong to waste either of those things. I worry people will think badly of me if I do.

THERAPIST: It sounds like we've touched on some important beliefs or values here – is there a sense that it will reflect badly on you if you have to cancel something, and that people will think badly of you if you do?

CATHERINE: Yes – other people and me as well. I've always prided myself on being reliable and also on not taking things for granted. I don't want to turn into one of those 'flakey' people you can't count on, who makes lots of plans they can't follow through on. I don't think my friends and family would like that, but I wouldn't like myself much either.

Once we had elicited Catherine and Guy's beliefs around this issue, we considered the pros and cons of each approach by asking each partner to think about the advantages of the other's point of view:

THERAPIST: Catherine, can you see any benefits in doing things Guy's way, that is trying to carry on as normal so avoid 'giving in' to your illness?

CATHERINE: I suppose so. I mean, if we kept planning things then I probably would end up doing more, at least on the days I feel up to it.

Once pros and cons of each belief/approach have been discussed, areas of commonality were identified, such as an aspiration on both sides not to let the arthritis 'win out' and to have more experiences together. Catherine and Guy were able to build on these shared priorities through decision-making conversations. They also set up behavioural experiments to test beliefs that seemed unhelpful or extreme, for example regarding the probability of having to cancel plans.

Compartmentalisation

Both partners acknowledged that Catherine's health problems seeped into all areas of their lives to a degree that felt excessive. Guy was able to 'shut out' unwanted thoughts about this issue quite successfully, but this seemed like quasi-denial to Catherine, and she felt unsupported by him as a result. As the person experiencing ill health, she found it more difficult to compart-mentalise her concerns, and when she felt 'shut down' by Guy this often increased her anxiety and distress, leading to a demand-withdraw pattern of interaction between them.

I normalised the discrepancy in the partners' level of preoccupation with the LTC and helped them to understand it within the broader formulation of their relationship. We did some guided self-help around worry, for example helping Catherine to use 'scheduled worry time' and 'present moment focus' strategies to compartmentalise her worry (for more information on cognitive models of worry and generalized anxiety disorder see for example Hirsch et al., 2019). Catherine's health posed a number of 'current problems', but many of these were not amenable to problem solving in a traditional sense. Therefore, it was useful for her to distinguish between current problems that needed addressing, problems that were not solvable (e.g. because she had done all she could to address them for the moment), and hypothetical concerns.

Some of this work Catherine did by herself, but Guy was very involved in helping her to put worry-time into practice. They agreed that every evening, she could talk to him for up to 30 minutes about her health concerns and during this time he would listen attentively. Knowing that she would have the opportunity to discuss what was on her mind helped Catherine to 'park' her worries when they occurred at other points in the day and made her feel more supported, whilst having an agreement that the discussion would be time-limited reassured Guy that it would be contained.

Re-evaluating life goals

To some degree, engaging in the behavioural activation and compartmentalisation tasks described above helped Catherine and Guy to reflect on their priorities and goals. One of the additional ways in which Catherine and Guy were encouraged to reconsider their values was whilst developing the blueprint in the second last session:

THERAPIST: Let's think back on everything we've discussed in our sessions, and the things you've tried to do differently, such as change the way you communicate and do more meaningful activities together. Could we start to think about some goals for you for the next 6 months or so, both in terms of your relationship but also what you would like from your life more generally?

Drawing on their values and their experience in therapy, Catherine and Guy were able to identify some areas to continue working on:

1 Spending some quality time together every day to stay connected.
2 Recognising and sharing their thoughts, feelings and concerns and making time for this.
3 Continuing to have new experiences together (with the understanding that these need not always be *adventurous* or physically demanding ones) at least once a month and working towards planning a trip together as part of this.

Discussion

Catherine and Guy were not an easy couple to work with. They voiced their ambivalence from the very beginning, and I had to work hard to pique their curiosity regarding what therapy could offer. Their strong-mindedness, an asset at times, sometimes got in the way as both had a tendency to interrupt or speak over each other if they felt they needed to make a point. Balancing the sessions required a lot of direction and was not always welcomed. In addition, Catherine's health and the couple's other commitments meant that attendance was a little sporadic, making it harder to build up the necessary momentum for change.

In spite of these challenges, I was impressed by Catherine and Guy's commitment to each other, their willingness to work on their relationship and to address Catherine's health problems together. I observed positive changes in their interactions over the course of our sessions and both partners reported feeling quite pleased with the outcome of therapy. There were improvements in communication, particularly with regard to emotional expression and support. They still held somewhat different beliefs about how much they should be adjusting their lives due to Catherine's LTC, but they had worked hard to achieve some compromise in their strategy and were more empathic about each other's perspectives. They had resumed some joint activities, particularly around socialising, and Catherine had started doing some gentle exercise, which she felt good about. They both found the principles of compartmentalisation very appealing though putting these into practice remained a work in progress.

The therapeutic alliance with this couple was tricky at times. Both partners were older than me and conveyed the impression that they were used to being in charge. I had to be quite directive to encourage engagement and also to manage their interactions, and this was not always easy. The balance between validating each person's point of view and encouraging them to see things from a different perspective was a delicate one. At times, their reluctance to consider alternative perspectives to their own left me feeling frustrated but also sad for them, especially when they both seemed stuck and polarised. It was extremely helpful to discuss this couple in supervision and to consider the interaction between their beliefs and behaviours and mine.

Over the course of the sessions, I began to feel braver (i.e. less worried that they would tell me off or not come back the following week) and I was able to express some of my dilemmas and concerns more explicitly to Catherine and Guy. This helped a little and it seemed to me that after this they took more responsibility for making good use of therapy (or perhaps I just felt I had let go of some of the responsibility). Occasional use of humour about their stubbornness also helped us all to step back.

Chapter Reflections

Benefits of couple-based interventions

Although not always an obvious first choice following the diagnosis of a LTC, couple-based psychological interventions offer a number of advantages over individual therapy. Having a partner on board promotes a shared understanding of the illness and its management, and the partner can be instrumental in supporting health-behaviour changes and/or individual therapy tasks. Work on communication can help both partners to discuss their concerns more openly, counteracting protective buffering and facilitating shared decision-making. Importantly, couple-based interventions give the well partner a voice, explicitly considering their thoughts, feelings and needs and normalising uncomfortable emotions such as feelings of resentment and disappointment. Furthermore, couple-based interventions can address broader relationship distress if present, thus optimising outcome.

Impact of ill health on engagement

Working with couples in whom one partner is physically ill does present some challenges. Ill health can affect attendance, and long gaps between sessions can make it hard for therapy to gather the momentum necessary for change. To some extent the increased acceptability of video sessions has helped with engagement in this population, as couples can still be encouraged to attend a (briefer) appointment remotely during periods of ill health. Indeed, the use of tele-therapy has made couple-based interventions more accessible to many couples who for one reason or another would not be able to attend sessions in person.

Symptoms and treatment side effects can affect engagement and concentration and engagement during therapy sessions, compromising how much is taken away from the appointment. For example, engaging in an emotionally demanding conversation may be difficult for a patient who is in severe pain.

Some authors have suggested that the short-term treatment model offered by many psychological therapy services is not optimal for patients with LTC (e.g. Ruddy and McDaniel, 2008). They suggest this client group may need more support and be more willing to engage consistently when there are crises or changes in physical health status. A service with an open door policy, where people with LTC are offered long-term, low-level support but can promptly access more intensive help when needed would be more suitable, but unfortunately is rarely available in the public health service.

Therapist expertise and flexibility

The therapist does not always need to be an expert on the patient's physical health problem, but some understanding of the condition and recommended management is essential. Liaising with the physical healthcare team can be helpful, and it can be reassuring to all parties to know that the goals and tasks of therapy have been 'sanctioned'. This is particularly important for interventions aiming to increase activity as many patients believe this could be harmful and therapists are sometimes reluctant to push too hard.

Working with couples with LTC requires a degree of flexibility from the therapist, but this needs to be exercised with caution. There are often several different concerns that could be addressed, and deciding what to prioritise, especially in a brief course of treatment, can be difficult. Some interventions such as increasing activity can feel very difficult for a patient, going against their common sense or perhaps leaving them feeling exposed in front of a partner who is not particularly sympathetic. In such circumstances, the therapist must be careful not to abandon therapy tasks that could be hugely beneficial (and for which there is strong empirical evidence) too readily, whilst at the same time respecting the patient's concerns, ambivalence and anxiety. Subtle persistence and tenacity can pay off.

Therapist beliefs

The therapist needs to be aware of his/her own illness beliefs and response to the patient, as these can impact on treatment. For example, buying into the patient's hopelessness can lead to collusion with unhelpful beliefs and strategies. Working with patients with degenerative or terminal conditions can be emotionally difficult, and self-care and access to supportive supervision are important.

There is huge individual variation in people's preferred coping styles and there is no one optimised combination of problem, emotion, and life-focused coping that suits everyone. The therapist needs to understand and optimise each partner's coping response and also be aware of tension caused by differences between them, as was the case for Catherine and Guy. Some degree of denial or avoidance is common and not always bad. It can provide the couple with hope and if it does not interfere with engagement in treatment or with making plans for the future, then it can serve a protective function and it may not be in the couple's interest to address it.

Working with couples with LTC can be hugely rewarding, as visible improvements in adjustment and quality of life, as well as in the couple relationship, can be apparent during the treatment sessions. The principles and techniques presented in this chapter may also be relevant to couples facing other life transitions, such as retirement.

Therapist tips

- Developing a shared formulation is essential.
- Familiarise yourself with the condition and liaise with physical health care team if possible
- Ask the patient and partner about their illness beliefs.
- There are often a number of issues to address. Prioritise, start with some 'easy wins' but don't leave difficult tasks until the very end.
- Balance validation, change and acceptance strategies.
- Stay objective – avoid colluding with either partner's unhelpful beliefs and look for strengths.
- Be prepared for some resistance. Therapy tasks can be tough! Acknowledge this but don't give up too readily - patients won't benefit from therapy if they disengage, but they may need a bit of a 'push' at times.

Suggestions for further Reading

Baucom, D.H., Porter, L.S., Kirby, J.S., & Hudenpohl, J. (2012). Couple-based interventions for medical problems. *Behavior Therapy*, 43: 61–76.

Ruddy, N.B., & McDaniel, S.H. (2023). Couple therapy and medical issues. In J.L. Lebow & D.K. Snyder (Eds.), *Clinical handbook of couple therapy* (pp. 615–635). The Guilford Press.

References

Baucom, D.H., Porter, L.S., Kirby, J.S., & Hudenpohl, J. (2012). Couple-based interventions for medical problems. *Behavior Therapy*, 43: 61–76.

Bhattarai, N., Charlton, J., Rudisill, C., & Gulliford, M.C. (2013). Prevalence of depression and utilization of health care in single and multiple morbidity: a population-based cohort study. *Psychological Medicine* 43: 1423–1431.

Glantz, M.J., Chamberlain, M.C., Liu, Q., Hsieh, C.C., Edwards, K.R., Van Horn, A., & Recht, L. (2009). Gender disparity in the rate of partner abandonment in patients with serious medical illness. *Cancer*. 2009 Nov 15; 115(22): 5237–5242. doi:10.1002/cncr.24577. PMID: 19645027.

Lazarus R.S., & Folkman S. (1984). *Stress, Appraisal and Coping*. New York: Springer.

Hirsch, C.R., Beale, S., Grey, N., & Liness, S. (2019). Approaching Cognitive Behavior Therapy For Generalized Anxiety Disorder From A Cognitive Process Perspective. *Front Psychiatry*. 2019 Nov 4; 10: 796. doi:10.3389/fpsyt.2019.00796. PMID: 31780964; PMCID: PMC6852150.

Neuling, S.J., & Winefield, H.R. (1988). Social support and recovery after surgery for breast cancer: Frequency and correlates of supportive behaviours by family, friends and surgeon. *Social Science & Medicine*, 27(4): 385–392.

Orth-Gomer, K., Wamala, S., Horsten, M., Schenck-Gustafsson, K., Schneiderman, N. & Mittleman, M. (2000). Marital stress worsens prognosis in women with coronary heart disease. *JAMA*, 284: 3008–3014.

Palmer, C., Baucom, D.H., & McBride, C. (2000). A couple approach to smoking cessation. In K.B. Schmaling & T.G. Sher (Eds.), *The psychology of couples and illness*. Washington, DC: American Psychological Association.

Perndorfer, C., Soriano, E.C., Siegel, S.D., & Laurenceau, J.P. (2019). Everyday protective buffering predicts intimacy and fear of cancer recurrence in couples coping with early-stage breast cancer. *Psychooncology*. 2019 Feb; 28(2): 317–323. doi:10.1002/pon.4942. Epub 2018 Dec 3. PMID: 30426612; PMCID: PMC6815683.

Ruddy, N.B., & McDaniel, S.H. (2008). Couple therapy and medical issues: Working with couples facing illness. In A.S. Gurman (Ed.), *Clinical handbook of couple therapy* (pp. 618–637). The Guilford Press.

Ruddy, N.B., & McDaniel, S.H. (2023). Couple therapy and medical issues. In J.L. Lebow & D.K. Snyder (Eds.), *Clinical handbook of couple therapy* (pp. 615–635). The Guilford Press.

Suso-Ribera, C., Yakobov, E., Carriere, J.S., & García-Palacios, A. (2020). The impact of chronic pain on patients and spouses: Consequences on occupational status, distribution of household chores and care-giving burden. *European Journal of Pain*, 24(9): 1730–1740. doi:10.1002/ejp.1616.

Tedeshi, R.G., & Calhoun, L.G. (2004). *Posttraumatic Growth: Conceptual Foundation and Empirical Evidence*. Philadelphia, PA: Lawrence Erlbaum Associates.

Chapter 9

Complexities of Language and Culture

How Not to Get Lost in Translation

Anupama Rammohan and Dakshina Rajapakse

Introduction

Understanding, acknowledging, and respecting cultural diversity is essential in establishing a collaborative and trusting therapeutic relationship, regardless of whether one is treating an individual or working with couples. Therapists' sensitivity to clients' cultural viewpoints can help promote engagement and positive outcomes (Addison & Thomas, 2009). Therapists today need to add knowledge of the diverse groups they will have to work with to their repertoire of therapy skills and techniques and be able to adapt formulations and interventions where necessary. Diversity has several strands, and for the purpose of this chapter, the authors will focus on considerations for working with couples where language and cultural differences have formed part of the work in therapy. The couples described here by the authors AR and DR, both couple therapists who are themselves from different cultural and linguistic backgrounds, raise interesting therapeutic questions and challenges. For instance, how to treat a couple where both come from different backgrounds and where English is the common language, though neither speak it well? How best to convey meaning? And how much is this also contributing to conflict around communication, e.g. *"you don't understand what I'm trying to say",* with this being true in a literal sense? Lots of repetition, summarising, and reframing! For us as therapists, it meant being curious, not being afraid to ask questions to ensure we understood concepts, e.g. *"what does this mean in your language?",* or *"how does sharing thoughts and feelings in relationships feel and how is this done from your experience?"* Being therapists who are both from non-English, non-Western cultures ourselves, we felt we could understand this better, but also that we should not be complacent that we were indeed 'experts' on matters of diversity and should maintain a curious and enquiring stance towards the couples we present below.

Cross cultural perceptions of mental illness and its treatment

Stigma associated with mental illness has been well documented across cultures. For example, mental illness can be perceived as a form of punishment

DOI: 10.4324/9781003024439-11

for breaching moral, social or religious codes, as a sign of weakness, or as a result of adverse events or misfortune. This can affect attitudes to help seeking, in particular uptake of psychological therapies. In non-Western cultures, there can be less of an emphasis on 'talking' as a form of treatment, and a difficulty comprehending the collaborative approach required by cognitive behavioural therapies. For example, it can be challenging to establish a collaborative relationship with a patient who says "*you are the expert - you need to advise me*". This need for or expectation of more direction and instruction in therapy can impact on communication with the therapist and the therapeutic relationship in individual therapy (Bhui & Morgan, 2007). Additionally, in couples work one has to be mindful of how cultural differences impact on the couple's view of the progress of treatment and their engagement in therapy tasks such as sharing thoughts and feelings or problem solving. If the partners are from a different cultural background to the context in which they are being treated, or indeed both from different backgrounds to each other, this creates an additional layer that needs to be understood and considered in the formulation and treatment.

Case example I

Mary, 51, and Imran, 34, were assessed for couple therapy after Mary was referred by her GP for psychological treatment of recurrent depression. At her initial assessment Mary identified that difficulties in her relationship with her husband Imran were a significant factor in maintaining her low mood. She requested couple therapy and Imran reluctantly agreed to attend a couple therapy assessment.

At the first session, Mary entered the room ahead of Imran, and pulled her chair close to the therapist (AR). She presented as being very agitated, and keen to get her point of view across, repeatedly stating "*Doctor, you don't know how difficult things are for me, and he makes so many problems for me*" and "*I had to drag him here, he says we have no problems, and it is all in my head*". She presented as trying very hard to get the therapist 'onside', with remarks such as "*you are a woman, you understand we are emotional; men don't understand*". She was hard to interrupt but also very engaged in the session.

Imran appeared hesitant and reluctant, often avoiding eye contact with the therapist. He presented as upset by his wife's distress and wanting to help, but he also seemed helpless. His English was less fluent than his wife's and the therapist had to work hard to ensure that he was not 'forgotten' by turning to him to repeat questions.

In the initial session, Mary and Imran were argumentative, speaking over each other and presenting as being at 'cross purposes'. Imran reiterated to the therapist that he did not feel they had a problem, and that he did not think they should 'waste NHS time'. Mary on the other hand was vocal in stating that she did not feel understood by Imran, that it was causing her immense distress and that it was important that Imran 'see' how bad things were for her. She repeatedly stated that Imran 'did not listen' to her. For his part, Imran said that Mary did not understand that he was trying to help and support her. Mary reported that she often felt worried about their 17-year age difference and the fact that they had no children, which was something very important in both their cultures. She worried that Imran could *"leave me for someone else and get married again"*. Imran reported he felt he had to 'keep proving' himself and that this made him feel angry and upset. He thought the fact that he worked hard 7 days a week to 'provide' for them, and always picked up and dropped Mary to work for her shifts as a keyworker was 'proof' he cared.

The couple also cited some 'cultural' differences which came up in their arguments, with Mary saying that she tried hard to accommodate Imran's cultural and religious practices, such as observing a fast for Ramadan, but felt Imran did not show similar respect for her culture and family in Malaysia. Neither spoke English as their first language, but given their different backgrounds, had to use this language to communicate with each other. Their levels of proficiency with this varied, with Mary having a better ability to use English. When asked to describe the difficulties within their relationship, they tended to speak over each other, with Mary often appearing to 'drown out' Imran.

MARY: I feel so upset, I cry and cry. He does not listen to me, he thinks this is all a big drama. He says it is all ok, why are you simply making such a big thing out of small things. I can't talk, he just does not listen, and then it is like he slams the door in my face. When I feel sad I just lie down, I cannot do anything. And then he says why are you just lying there, get up and do something otherwise you will feel more upset. He does not understand.

THERAPIST: Imran, I wonder if you could describe what happens to you when Mary is upset, and how you respond to her and try to help?

IMRAN: I work long hours yeah? I go at 7 in the morning, I come back late. I am tired. I just want some peace and quiet. I know she has bad days. But as I come in the door, she starts off crying and making so much tension in the house. I have no time to think. Then anything I say is wrong, she starts shouting, she threatens to do things, says she will take tablets, and I just want to get out of the house again. Sometimes I just say this is too much, I will go out and come back when you stop shouting.

THERAPIST: And what happens then?

IMRAN: She cries some more! What can I do? Nothing I do is helpful.

Mary reported feeling 'shut out' by Imran when she tried to communicate how upset she felt. An example below:

MARY: I feel low, I'm very depressed. I look for comfort, you understand? I need him to tell me everything is ok, but he says nothing, nothing, nothing. I don't feel like doing anything and I get more sad.

IMRAN: What does she want me to do? I work early morning to late evening, I come home for some peace. She jumps on me as soon as I am in the door yeah? She does not allow me space to breathe. Then she shouts at me and says I am not understanding that she will take tablets, and that she wants to die. How do I feel then? I just keep quiet because I don't want to hear all this.

The interaction above illustrates how Mary felt shut out by Imran when she wanted to be comforted, while Imran, anxious about triggering an argument, tended to remain silent or to withdraw. This appeared to trigger Mary even further, leading to the very arguments both partners were trying to avoid, which often culminated in Mary threatening to take an overdose of tablets, at times standing in front of him with the box of her antidepressant medication. This made Imran want to walk away and shut down further, with Mary feeling even more invalidated and upset and escalating her verbalisations of distress, thereby creating a vicious cycle in their relationship, and an unhelpful 'demand-withdraw' style of interaction (Epstein and Baucom, 2002).

It was also evident that Mary and Imran both worked long hours in demanding jobs, which was physically and emotionally draining and left them with little time for each other. Part of the motivation for this was that both partners were financially providing for relatives in their countries of origin.

The therapist's focus in the initial stages of therapy was to gather information, formulate difficulties and develop a treatment plan, while also attempting to explore the couple's understanding of their difficulties and their best hopes as a couple within their relationship. The assessment also included asking questions about their respective cultural contexts, their experience of immigrating to the UK and adapting to a new culture, learning a new language, loss of existing social and familial networks, and whether new ones had been established. The impact of all these factors on their relationship and their individual wellbeing was explored, and a section of the assessment is presented below to highlight this:

MARY: I feel that he takes things the wrong way. I feel bad. I am just explaining things to him, and he does not let me open my mouth. He wants to shut me up. I want him to listen to me, I don't shout. He shouts and he exaggerates the things I say because he does not understand. So, I need to explain again. This makes me tired, and like I don't want to do anything, and I feel bad in my head. I feel like I am not worth anything. Then I just lie down and don't want to do anything.

IMRAN: If she texts me nicely and not accuse me of things…I can't reply in work time, and she cannot understand that. If I don't reply, then she says I don't have any time for her. Then she does all this and says I don't care. I am working so long…get everything for her…I drop her to work early morning and pick her up however late because she is tired and I don't want her taking the bus. After all this she is saying that I don't care for her.

MARY: He does not understand how bad I feel. I am taking medication; I would not be taking medication if I felt normal.

IMRAN: I don't understand why. She is getting up, going to work, everything…normal. What is the big problem?

MARY: (getting upset and raising her voice) So, you think I am doing a big drama, that I have no problem?

THERAPIST: (intervenes) Lets pause here a minute Mary. It sounds like you feel that Imran does not understand how you feel, and that you struggle with your mood at times. Is that right?

(Mary nods.)

THERAPIST: And Imran, you were saying that you wonder what the problem is, and why Mary takes medication, as she seems 'normal' to you. Is this how it seems to you?

IMRAN: Yes, she looks fine! She is chatting, talking to friends, then suddenly she gets upset with me and she starts crying. She tells me she feels rubbish, and I feel bad. I don't understand that one minute she is happy and then she tells me she has some illness. What illness?

THERAPIST: So, you see Mary happy one moment, and that she seems fine to you, and her feeling upset, when she tells you she feels bad about herself, that you don't know what this is about. Is that right?

IMRAN: (nods) I know she takes tablets, and I think this is for sleep.

At this point it was clear that an understanding of depression and its symptoms, and of how it could affect their relationship, particularly communication and expression of needs, was essential (see also Chapter 10). Mary was expressing her needs for affection, support and validation in a way that was unhelpful, by demanding immediate reassurance, or threatening to harm herself. Imran tended to respond with anger, or by shutting her out, which led to her feeling uncared for and thus increased her distress further. Furthermore, Imran also appeared to not recognise that Mary was experiencing depression, as she appeared outwardly 'fine' and getting on with life as far as work and social activities with friends were concerned.

The therapist spent time in the initial stages of therapy providing psychoeducation about depression. Given the language barriers for them both, this had to be done gradually to ensure that they were both able to understand the information. This initial stage was also used to formulate the difficulties in their relationship and share this understanding with the couple. For instance, Mary had experienced previous episodes of depression, which were related to a difficult earlier marriage where her husband had been emotionally abusive and frequently criticised and belittled her, and eventually walked out of the relationship with no explanation. This made her anxious about being a 'good enough' wife and led her to frequently seek affirmation that she was. Failing to obtain this was a sign to her that she was 'failing' as a partner. Her difficulties communicating this to Imran had triggered low mood. Imran's difficulty initially in understanding depression as an illness, and attributing Mary's behaviour as 'dramatisation' made him angry and upset and led him to feel that he was being 'disrespected' as a husband, despite what he saw as his best efforts to be a 'good man'. This led to him shouting and raising his voice, which Mary responded to by becoming increasingly distressed and resorting to behaviours such as threatening to take an overdose. As a first step, the couple were asked to not engage in these negative behaviours as a way to de-escalate conflict in the relationship.

THERAPIST: Imran and Mary, I have listened to your description of the difficulties in your relationship, and how this upsets and distresses you both. From what I am hearing, you both respond to this in different ways. Mary, you would like Imran to be available for you immediately and offer support when you are feeling bad. Not getting this from him makes you feel like he is not listening, that he does not love you or care about you and you say this to him. Imran, this makes you upset as you feel that you do show your love for Mary in numerous ways, such as dropping her to work and picking her up. This makes you angry and you express this by shouting. Is this what usually happens?

MARY: Every time. He shouts, he has a big voice, he can shout louder than me.

THERAPIST: (interrupts) Mary I hear you, but let me finish my summary of what seems to be going on for you both and then you can tell me if I have understood you correctly. Is that ok?

(Mary nods.)

THERAPIST: Imran, when you shout, this makes Mary feel even more upset, and as she gets increasing upset, she may do things like cry, or tell you she does not want to live anymore and that she will take her tablets. How does that make you feel?

IMRAN: I don't like this. I get more angry, I get upset, I feel hot inside. It is like whatever I do I can't make her happy.

THERAPIST: So, this means you are both upset and when you are both feeling like this, you can express this in ways that are not helpful. Shouting, for example or threatening to take an overdose. This makes you more upset and angry at each other. Are you able to listen to each other when you are in these situations?

IMRAN AND MARY: No…

THERAPIST: So, the first thing we are going to do, is to try to make some changes to how you both respond to each other when you are upset and distressed. There are things it appears that you both do, that are just not helpful, and you have both said so. There are also things that are just not safe, such as saying you will hurt yourself in some way, and actually do things to harm yourself. So, Mary, you have said how upset and distressed you feel and how you want Imran to respond to you. As a first step it is important we work on helping you communicate that in a way that is helpful and can be responded to, rather than saying you will harm yourself by taking tablets. It is important that you not try to hurt yourself and I want an assurance that you are not going to take tablets or threaten to do so. I will ask Imran to also stop shouting at you and we can think of what other things you can do instead, but threatening to take overdoses must stop, as you are both here to work on your relationship, and these threats will not help you work towards your goals as a couple, So, let us start by thinking about what other things you could do to help yourself when you feel very upset and overwhelmed? Does that sound ok?

The therapist then used contracting with Mary to ensure that she only took her medication as prescribed, and that she would also not keep additional medication such as painkillers easily accessible. She agreed to keep them in a cabinet that was not easily reachable as part of this contract. Imran agreed to use strategies such as leaving the room when he felt his anger increasing (and telling Mary he needed some time out), and then returning to the conversation when he felt calmer. The couple also jointly explored ways of talking about their difficulties and agreed that they were better able to do so when they were outside their flat, such as when out for a walk. They worked on scheduling some time for this within their week, though it was challenging given their busy work schedules.

There was a real difficulty for them at times communicating certain feelings to each other due to their different levels of understanding of English. Mary's English was better as she had been in the UK for 30 years, in comparison to 10 for Imran. The therapist was very aware that they were both expressing their distress in a secondary language, and that this might feel removed from the reality of their experience. The therapist took time to check out their level of understanding, attempted to use simple language as far as possible and frequent summaries. Both Mary and Imran acknowledged the impact of communicating through their second language and how this could escalate conflicts between them as they struggled to make themselves understood by the other. As part of a shared exercise to spend more time together and increase positivity, they came up with a plan to watch more English language entertainment programmes together, as previously Imran would listen to Bollywood based programmes and Mary would watch her soaps separately.

Imran and Mary began to schedule some joint activities together in addition to the above, such as going for a walk and cooking their evening meal together. Mary still struggled with her desire for immediate reassurance and validation from Imran, she but had stopped threatening to take overdoses and this helped Imran feel less angry. He also accompanied her for a medication review appointment with her GP. He found this helpful, alongside the psychoeducation provided in therapy, to improve his understanding of depression and its treatment. Mary also reported feeling happier and more understood. Imran had started sending her a text message everyday, just to say *"how are you? You all right?"* and she expressed how happy she felt to receive this and that she felt reassured of his affection for her.

MARY: He sends me a message, short one just to ask are you all right. I feel happy, it lifts my mood. I feel he loves me. It is a small thing, and why could he not do it before?

THERAPIST: It is good to hear this Mary, can I ask you to speak to Imran directly and also let us focus on changes he has made and what is working well for you now?

MARY: (to Imran) You sent me a text yesterday and also all of this week. I felt happy, that you are thinking of me.

IMRAN: (smiling shyly) It is all right. It is small thing, sometimes I forget.

At the end of couples therapy, both Mary and Imran reported experiencing fewer arguments, reduced conflict and said that they were communicating better. Although Mary's mood had improved somewhat, she acknowledged that she required further individual therapy to address depression as well as some other underlying difficulties and she accepted a referral for individual CBT within the service.

Case example 2

Kurt and Lara are in their early 40s. When they initially presented in the therapy room, I was struck by how different they both were in their personalities and ways of communicating with each other. Interestingly this was also what had led them to seek couples therapy as they reported feeling disconnected from each other. It is important to mention that Kurt is of Eastern European background and works in the military, where he is used to order and having set systems in place. Lara on the other hand is of South American origin and is enthusiastic, spontaneous, and bubbly, with a laid-back attitude. She is used to a slower pace of life. I also observed differences in their mannerisms as they sat in front of me. Kurt's expressions were more serious, with minimal hand gestures, whereas Lara smiled often and was very animated. I could feel myself warming more towards Lara because of this and I was mindful from the start of not being biased towards Kurt. Kurt and Lara's common language is English, but this is not their mother tongue. They both agreed that this too has an impact on how well they are able to express things, particularly for Lara whose English language skills are more limited than Kurt's.

Their communication difficulties soon became apparent in the sessions, and I could see where the frustrations were coming from. It became clear that Kurt comes from a cultural background that values independence and 'low-context' communication, where things need to be explicitly stated and there is no room for interpretation. Lara on the other hand is from a culture that values interdependence and 'high-context' communication, where communication focuses on underlying context, meaning and tone and not just on words. Kurt would often expect Lara to be precise in her communication with him, whilst Lara expected Kurt to be able to read between the lines. Kurt and Lara's relationship had also progressed very quickly, as they had moved in together three months after they met and had a baby soon after. It was interesting to hear Kurt saying he was initially attracted to the way Lara spoke. Equally, Lara reported that she initially found Kurt easy to talk to, responsive and predictable, which she liked. We had a moment of shared laughter as we reflected on the fact that the qualities that attracted them to one another at first had now become a source of conflict in their relationship. Without a doubt this also made me reflect on some of my own experiences with relationships.

Kurt and Lara both reported feeling that their relationship was going through an ongoing period of adjustment, particularly for Kurt due to his set standards and rules relating to how their home should be. They mentioned a lack of quality time together, as Kurt was often tired when he came home, and Lara was tired from looking after the baby. Lara also reported finding it stressful to go out with Kurt due to his high standards regarding getting ready on time, which was sometimes difficult to do now that they had a baby. As a result, she would tend to avoid going out with him, which then added to his frustration and to their relationship distress.

They reported a demand-withdraw pattern of communication where Lara would shut down and avoid Kurt during a disagreement, which would increase his frustration. At times during these interactions he would say quite hurtful things in order to get a reaction from her. Lara mentioned that these comments had upset her and contributed to her withdrawing further from the relationship and feeling low in mood.

I saw Kurt and Lara for 16 sessions, during which we mainly worked on improving their communication patterns, negotiating relationship standards, and increasing couple level activities. It was particularly useful to formulate how their differing personalities and cultural backgrounds impacted on their relationship. However, I was mindful of not wanting to add to their hopelessness by creating a bleak overview of their current situation as they became aware of their differences.

We used a sharing thoughts and feelings exercise (see Chapter 2) as a platform to begin to discuss openly how they both felt within the relationship. Kurt spoke about his feelings of frustration regarding Lara not being able to understand the importance of his standards, and Lara was able to share how she felt regarding the pressure to 'get things right' all the time. She also expressed how unhappy she sometimes felt, which came as a surprise to Kurt. We also explored the impact of Kurt's hurtful words on Lara's mood and their overall relationship, and it was important for me as the therapist to set boundaries around acceptable and unacceptable behaviours.

THERAPIST: Okay, Lara can I ask you to tell Kurt what it's like for you when he speaks to you like that, help him to understand what that's like for you.

LARA: It's horrible to hear that from the person you love and care about, it's the same when you told me the wedding was a mistake, when you shouted at me that you hate me. It's making me scared (crying), I feel offended…humiliated.

THERAPIST: Kurt, what's Lara saying to you?

KURT: Well…you are horrified about my behaviour, and it makes you very (long pause) yeah… this is what you said…

THERAPIST: Kurt, did you pick up anything about how it's making Lara feel? What it's like for her?

KURT: (looking away) Obviously she doesn't like it and it makes her feel very bad.

THERAPIST: What is it like for you Kurt to say those words to Lara?

KURT: It's easy, the reason why it's happening is easy, it's because she doesn't speak when I am talking to her. When there is a problem, I ask you a question and you refuse to speak to me for 50 minutes and the only way to make her react on what I am saying or asking is this…then you start reacting again and it's humiliating and it's not nice, but you don't speak to me…

LARA: But you don't have the right to speak to me like that, if you think you do then we have to end this relationship.

THERAPIST: Kurt, what did you hear in particular about what Lara is saying around the appropriateness of some of the things you might say to her?

KURT: You're saying it's not appropriate to talk to you like this.

THERAPIST: And what do you think? Do you think it's appropriate?

KURT: It's the same thing I said before, she's ignoring me and then I say things to get a reaction, she makes me get that way.

THERAPIST: I suppose if I could intervene…when it comes to couple relationships there might be things happening from both parties that create a problem, it might not be just one person or the other. There are also certain ways of being that are appropriate within a relationship and certain things that are not appropriate. Verbal abuse or physical abuse of any kind is inappropriate Kurt. So, if either of you are doing this then I am going to say it's not appropriate. There might be certain things, for instance thoughts or feelings or experiences that are affecting Lara's behaviour and leading her to withdraw. I can see this is frustrating for you when it happens, and she stops responding to you. This then triggers you to say things to Lara so you can get a reaction from her. However, we need to think about how appropriate that behaviour is…and I am going to say it's not appropriate because it is verbal abuse when you are putting someone down. I totally get your frustration, the anger, if Lara is not talking to you and you really want that reaction from her, I get that, but let's try to think about how we can manage this situation so you both can communicate effectively with one another and you don't get to that point of saying something hurtful so you can get a reaction from Lara, because what that's doing is it's damaging your relationship even further. Does that make sense? (Kurt nods). What do you both think about what I have just said? If I can start with you Kurt?

KURT: In general, it makes me feel positive that we can change something but I think I have to live with my frustration because Lara won't change.

THERAPIST: Okay…what do you think specifically about what I have said Kurt?

KURT: That the behaviour is not appropriate…something I should not do because it has a short term reaction but in the long term it's more damaging and it's something you just don't do no matter what.

This was quite an important moment in our therapy and for their relationship, as Kurt stopped making hurtful comments during their arguments following this session and their relationship distress improved significantly. We explored some of the factors contributing to their demand-withdraw pattern. As well as noting that Lara tended to withdraw as a coping strategy when feeling overwhelmed, and that her withdrawal left Kurt feeling uncomfortable and frustrated, which he coped with by escalating his attempts to re-engage with her, we also identified some differences in how they approached conflicts. It appeared that Kurt had a preference for addressing concerns and reaching an action plan straight away, whereas Lara preferred to take some time to think about things, and to consider options by herself before discussing the issue together with Kurt. Following some work on problem solving, we decided that if either of them had a concern they would like to address, they would both agree on a mutually convenient time to address the issue.

It was also important to help Kurt and Lara to explore and deepen their understanding of the way they approach problems in their relationship by exploring their cultural differences. The goal was not so much to change the way in which they communicated, but more to promote acceptance of this understandable difference. We did this through reflecting on what had attracted them to each other in the first place, which was very much to do with differences in their personalities and cultural backgrounds. We also spoke about how these differences could feel positive and negative, but in the end how they are a part of our identities that cannot necessarily be changed, even if we wanted to change them. As sessions progressed, this acceptance led them to move towards a middle ground in dealing with their differences.

In addition, we looked at self-care strategies, such as having time apart for cooling down when their interactions became heated. This was essential given their problematic style of interaction and verbal abuse. Self-care for this couple included doing more things they enjoyed, both individually and as a couple. We re-introduced some behaviours they had previously enjoyed together as a way of increasing pleasure and increasing their ability to tolerate challenging experiences and manage conflict. I expected this to be a difficult one for them both, considering Kurt's need for precision regarding timing, but it was rewarding to see them both increasingly able to negotiate their standards and reach a common ground. At times I found it challenging to maintain a balanced perspective, rather than seeing their difficulties as being primarily around Kurt's military background and his unrealistic standards. I was also mindful of how my own cultural beliefs around relationships were being activated, particularly when at one point they were both contemplating whether to end their marriage. It was important to recognise and reflect on what was coming up for me as a therapist when working with this couple.

Treatment Principles and Strategies

We recommend adopting a respectfully curious stance in therapy, asking and 'checking out' with the couple rather than making assumptions. A common misperception is to attribute certain unhelpful or negative behaviours to 'cultural' rather than 'personal' factors, which can lead to personal and relationship issues being missed and not addressed in therapy. While therapists need to ensure they are sensitive to culture and take steps to inform themselves about a couple's cultural background, at the same time they need to be able to adequately assess the function of a couple or individual's behaviour and to question or challenge this when it is not adaptive. Even when a behaviour may be in some sense culturally consistent, it is important to explore the consequences of this behaviour for each partner and the couple as a unit.

The assessment, formulation, and treatment planning stages need to emphasise positive aspects of the relationship and find out what brought the couple together, despite their differences. In the case of Mary and Imran, they both shared common values about maintaining close bonds with extended family. They understood each other's need to provide financial assistance to family members back in their countries of origin and supported each other with this. Hsu (2001) suggests the therapist can act as a 'Cultural Broker', encouraging flexibility and appreciation of differences and what they bring to the relationship as well as finding common ground. The therapist might in addition suggest homework that includes steps to learn more about each other's cultures and participate in cultural rituals or practices.

Challenges

Difficulties in communication can be a major issue. Communication difficulties can arise both with the therapist, who may be from a different culture, as well as between the two partners if both are from different backgrounds. Language plays an important part here, particularly if more subtle aspects such as nuances and meanings behind certain words or phrases are not understood or not translatable, causing further problems and misunderstandings (Hsu, 2001).

Different cultures also have very different ways of expressing emotions, communicating in relationships, and solving problems. Many therapy models assume that talking about emotions, communicating feelings directly, and problem solving are an essential part of the treatment, and a goal for all couples. It is important here for therapists to recognise that not all cultures value speaking openly about problems, particularly about feelings and emotions, and that this value may be more reflective of individualist Western cultures. The therapist has to tread carefully to promote adaptive behavioural change, without suggesting behaviour that is not congruent with cultural beliefs and values. Therapists should therefore be flexible in their approach, asking questions and 'checking out' with the couple whether the principles, strategies and tasks suggested are in line with their values.

Conclusions

It would be fair to say that all couples go through periods of adjustment, change and difficulty, if not open conflict. Relationship difficulties can stem from a variety of sources, including differences in personal values, communication styles, overall worldview and expectations of each other and the relationship. Cultural differences between partners, or differences between the couple's background and their host culture can exacerbate some of these challenges.

Therapist Tips

- We do not propose major changes to core cognitive behavioural couple interventions and techniques. It is important to stay 'on model' and avoid linguistic and cultural diversity issues becoming a cause of therapist 'drift' and dilution of the core model.
- Understanding, awareness and acknowledgement of differences, and adoption of a 'curious' stance are key to exploring diversity and how it affects a couple's interaction and their relationship. Ask questions and check things out!
- Incorporate cultural differences into formulation and treatment plans and be mindful of introducing tasks and concepts that do not fit in with the couples' cultural beliefs and values.
- Reflect on your own cultural background and assumptions as a therapist and how this also impacts on the work you are carrying out.

Suggestions for further Reading

Rastogi, M., & Thomas, V. (2009). *Multicultural Couple Therapy.* London: Sage.

References

Addison, S., & Thomas, V. (2009). Power, privilege, and oppression: White therapists working with minority couples. In M. Rastogi & V. Thomas (Eds.), *Multicultural Couple Therapy* (pp. 9–27). London: Sage.

Bhui, K., & Morgan, N. (2007). Effective psychotherapy in a racially and culturally diverse society. *Advances in Psychiatric Treatment*, 13, 187–193.

Epstein, N.B., & Baucom, D.H. (2002). *Enhanced cognitive-behavioral therapy for couples: A contextual approach.* American Psychological Association.

Hsu, J. (2001). Marital Therapy for Intercultural Couples. In *Culture and Psychotherapy: A Guide to Clinical Practice* (pp. 225–242). Tseng, W.-S. & Streltzer, J. (Eds.), Washington DC: APA.

Chapter 10

Depression

Leslie Rossouw

Depression is the most widely researched mental health issue in the context of relationship distress. Half of couples where one partner is depressed will experience relationship distress, and conversely, relationship distress is a predictor of depression (Baucom et al., 2007). The bi-directional link between relationship distress and depression has been widely documented (e.g. Baucom, Whisman & Paprocki, 2012). With prevalence rates of over 15% in the UK (ONS, 2022), most couple therapists can expect to see couples presenting with difficulties around depression within their working career. It is therefore of paramount importance for any couple therapist to understand depression and the key principles that will guide treatment. This chapter delves into the dilemmas that low self-worth and suicidality bring into the couple therapy space. We meet Sylvia and her partner John, who are both experiencing depression. The couple struggle with the burden of their distress and seem to be trapped – too withdrawn to take the first step, and too hopeless to try. We will explore the therapeutic experience for both the couple and the therapist – should the therapist resign herself to their hopelessness, or could there be hope for repair and new beginnings?

Theoretical Framework

When thinking of depression, the seminal work of Beck (1967) comes to mind, alongside other key authors such as Christine Padesky and Christopher Martell (e.g. Greenberger & Padesky, 2016; Martell et al., 2013). Beck proposes that cognitive, emotional, and behavioural factors all contribute to a deeper understanding of the origin and maintenance of depression. However, some unique challenges exist for the therapist working in a couple context. Where in individual therapy we would simply engage our clients directly in learning and applying various CBT strategies to help them, there is an additional layer to consider in couple work – maintaining a couple-based understanding of the problem and facilitating a dyadic process to not only engage each client directly, but also to facilitate their couple interactions to help build these skills.

DOI: 10.4324/9781003024439-12

THERAPIST REFLECTIONS: In this complex and multi-layered view of depression and relationship distress lies my personal interest and enjoyment of working with couples. Where, in individual therapy, the context of the individual lies outside our reach, here we have it with us in the room! Who is to say who is right or wrong? Instead, we can see the interactional nature of mental health (chicken or egg?) and this gives us more scope in terms of how we can help a couple.

The experience of major depressive disorder (depression) is characterised by the DSM-V as the persistent presence (for more than two weeks) of at least 5 of the following symptoms: depressed mood, anhedonia, weight loss or weight gain and loss of appetite or increases in appetite, a slowing down of thought and behaviour, fatigue or loss of energy, feelings of being worthless or excessive and inappropriate guilt, loss of concentration or indecisiveness, and suicidal ideation or suicide attempts and plans (APA, 2013). Depression can be severely debilitating and distressing for any individual experiencing it. It is therefore also very understandable that the presence of depression in a relationship (in one or both partners) can severely impact relationship functioning and relationship satisfaction for both partners. Sylvia and John found themselves trapped in an unhappy relationship which maintained their depression, while the depression hindered their efforts (or more to the point their drive) to address their relationship distress.

It is easy to understand why depression can be so devastating to a relationship, once you connect with all the key relationship areas which can be affected. Depression can affect communication, a key factor for relationship success (Baucom et al., 2007). Couple conversations can become more charged and defensive. Depression can change how we interact with each other in a relationship. Partners of depressed individuals may start to shield depressed partners from responsibilities or activities which they know the partner will find difficult (a concept described as 'accommodation' by Baucom et al., 2020), thereby unintentionally lowering the depressed individual's sense of self-efficacy and maintaining the depression. Couples may lose out on shared positive interactions and activities and see an increase in negative and hostile behaviours towards each other. Through these behaviours, roles in the relationship change. We also know that distressed couples' interactions with each other often follow demand – withdraw cycles (Baucom et al., 2011; Donato et al., 2014). The increasing distance between them only serves to maintain the communication difficulties, lack of closeness and time spent together, and increase in arguments and fractured interactions.

The efficacy of couple therapy to relieve depression and relationship distress is widely documented (e.g. Lebow et al., 2011). This chapter uses a cognitive behavioural couple therapy (CBCT) framework to facilitate an understanding of what was happening to Sylvia and John, and address their difficulties (e.g. Baucom et al., 2020). Key to the model is the understanding that each individual has their own set of thoughts, feelings and behaviours, which occur in a relational context, thus influencing the partner's thoughts, feelings, and behaviours. In this way, seeing each main focus point (cognitions, emotions or behaviours) as an entry point into the couple's interactions (and therefore distress), the therapist can use different strategies to bring about awareness, understanding, and change.

Key interventions for depression in this model include individual and couple-based behavioural activation, guided behaviour change, communication training, cognitive restructuring, and managing suicidality. Work on communication is often recommended early on in therapy and as Baucom and colleagues (2020) have noted *"conversations between partners are one of the most important contexts within which specific interaction patterns occur and which serve as a basis of intervention"* (p57).

A note on risk

Some degree of suicidality is not unusual in depression and there are some considerations for assessing (and managing) risk in the context of couple therapy. Discussing suicidal thoughts or intent in front of a partner may feel difficult, leading individuals to underreport or shield a partner from what they are truly feeling. Even if this is not happening, therapists need to be aware of how assessing and monitoring risk may impact the balance of a therapeutic relationship with a couple. The early individual assessment sessions are a good opportunity to fully assess for risk. However, if an individual presents with very high levels of risk to themselves, couple therapy may be contra-indicated, with the individual's safety being prioritised first before resuming couple therapy.

Meeting the couple

When I first met Sylvia and John in the waiting room and called them in for their appointment, Sylvia got up from her chair with great effort, and walked slowly towards me with the use of a cane, with John's arm protectively around her waist. Her expression was anxious but also keen to engage me with a smile. John remained quite stoic and strong beside her, ushering her into the room with a respectful nod my way. Sylvia looked creative in her colourful and slightly bohemian flowy dress, while John wore chinos and a white work shirt, scuffed brown shoes, and had a pen in his shirt pocket. My sense was that he looked like this most days!

I already knew that Sylvia was the one who first sought help from our service after her GP had diagnosed her with depression. The service suggested couple therapy instead of individual therapy, as relationship distress seemed to be a key factor in maintaining her low mood. John was here to support Sylvia, but interestingly he also presented with symptoms of depression based on the set of measures he completed before the session, though he made no reference to this at all. Sylvia presented as visibly depressed and tearful, slow in speech and timid in her responses, with quick unsure glances towards John whenever she said anything, as if she was nervous about how he might react. John presented as somewhat detached and logical, with a strong focus on problem solving and a certain confidence about how he viewed things. He wasn't without care for Sylvia, but he was keen to see the emotions settle for sure.

John and Sylvia have been married for 12 years. John (aged 52) has an adult son (aged 32) born out of an intense and tumultuous relationship John had as a young adult. The mother of the child had deserted him when John was only 20, leaving him with full responsibility for his son. It brings tears to his eyes (which he quickly wipes away before regaining composure) talking of that time, how hard it was to grow up so fast, but how he 'did what he had to do' to be a good father and make a living for them. He got on with life, worked hard, and dedicated the rest of his time to his son. By age 40 John was established in his career, and his son was independent, but John never managed to step beyond this to think about finding new love, until he met Sylvia. Colourful and vibrant, Sylvia represented everything that John didn't have. Full of fun, playfulness, and creativity, she was a breath of fresh air in his responsible and dutiful way of living.

Sylvia and John described being attracted to each other from the moment they met. Sylvia remembers being drawn to John's calm and composed manner. He was dapper and handsome and strong and competent. He was easy to be around and lifted her spirits with his competent caring. She loved to see his relationship with his adult son and felt excited at the prospect of having children of her own. John had a senior role in a marketing firm by now, and Sylvia respected his self-made climb to success. John remembers being drawn to Sylvia by her energy and warmth, and he liked that she was so accepting and appreciative of his care. Sylvia worked as a nurse in a special needs department, and was well respected in her place of work. She was close to her mother and sister and regularly saw them. John liked this as it spoke of values like loyalty and care which he shared with her. John liked her independence and felt that she didn't 'need too much of him'. He liked the freedom this gave him, together with the benefit of now having a loving partner to turn to.

Sylvia and John married within a year of meeting, both describing that they 'knew what they wanted'. They went on to have two children, and to a large extent their early years together gave them a level of support and intimacy that left both feeling fulfilled. However, sadly life brought up stressors and changes which the couple found hard to navigate. Sylvia suffered a stroke three years ago, which left her with a reduced capacity to work, severe headaches, and mobility difficulties. In addition, she struggled with health anxiety in the ensuing months, fearing another stroke. At home, John 'did what he had to' and took on more responsibility to make sure the family and Sylvia were ok. Just as they were coming out of this crisis, Sylvia's mother sadly died, leaving her bereft, and causing a significant gap in their support network.

THERAPIST REFLECTIONS: I was already aware at this early stage that I was drawn towards supporting (and maybe even defending) Sylvia. I felt so sad for all the loss she had to endure and felt slightly baffled by John's logical (did I think it was too harsh?) view of what was going on.... but quickly corrected myself to acknowledge the couple in fact had experienced so much loss. Even here, in that first meeting in a too-tiny office, I found it difficult to get beyond John's competent exterior, and I was worried about how I might remain balanced in my dyadic approach to the couple. Could I find enough compassion for him too?

Presenting problems

Since her stroke and her mother's death, Sylvia had increasingly been struggling with depression. Her self-esteem was low, and she felt anxious in the relationship. For his part, John reported feeling stressed due to the increased demands on him within the home. By the time I met them, the couple described very low levels of relationship satisfaction and feeling that a lot of the things that had initially drawn them to each other were now lost. They often got tangled up in heated arguments, which at their worst, could escalate into scenarios that would make Sylvia suicidal, and leave them reeling for days. Sylvia was in a lonely place, not doing much, not seeing many people, and seemed stuck in a depressive loop. They wanted help to understand what was happening to them, and strategies to help them cope with Sylvia's depression. They wanted to learn to communicate better, to see if they could repair their relationship.

The couple was desperate and needed change. The assessment process gave us the chance to unpack their life stories, learn about their strengths and struggles, and build a good therapeutic relationship (it took harder work to engage John!). This set the scene to develop a formulation that could guide our work together.

Making sense of what was happening to the couple

From an IBCT perspective (see Chapter 3) we understood that the couple had become polarised around their differences, to a point where they found themselves in a mutual trap. Closeness and distance were a simple theme that helped us see their dance in an interactional framework – she stepped closer, while he stepped back (or stayed immobile), or they would both just withdraw and step back, too anxious that an interaction would trigger another fight. We noted how this polarisation process could escalate all the way through to suicidality on Sylvia's side and stonewalling on John's.

It was also helpful to use a CBCT framework (see Chapter 2) to consider how individual, couple, and environmental factors contributed to their polarisation and distress, and how these factors coloured in the various behavioural, cognitive and emotional factors at play in keeping the problem going.

Sylvia's depression was connected to her sense of having lost so much recently through her own illness and her mother's death. She struggled to come to terms with her reduced capacity and missed her mother's compassion and guidance. She lost her sense of self-worth and of what she brought to the relationship. Her earlier zest and energy for life gave way to withdrawal and rumination, and the fatigue and headaches she continued to experience only made it harder to cope. Without her mother's support, she felt very stuck, with no idea how to get up and out the door. Sylvia found herself in an impossible situation now, as she knew John valued her independence and the fact that she did not ask too much from him, but she didn't know where else to go for support. Whenever she asked for help, he seemed cold and uninterested, and she feared that she was irritating him. This gave Sylvia a sense that she did not matter anymore and she and grew increasingly more insecure around him. Her depression gradually worsened as she withdrew from family life, leaving most of the responsibilities and decisions to John. She spent hours ruminating and sleeping, stopped socialising, and found herself struggling even with small menial tasks at home.

John's stoic approach to life and his reliance on rational thought and to-do lists to 'get him through' difficult times showed up here in full force. In the face of Sylvia's depression, John did exactly what he knew how to do – stayed rational, focused on what to do, and tried to 'keep the boat afloat'. He believed that not giving emotion more space than absolutely necessary was helping Sylvia, and this was part of his attempt to deescalate, and in fact, anchor the situation. When his attempts not to engage with emotions were met with distress, anger, and contempt, John was at a loss for what to do apart from pushing harder. He also started to become depressed in the face of the ever-increasing powerlessness he experienced. John's preference for practical problem solving over emotionally soothing conversations (which Sylvia yearned for) made her feel alone and unsupported. John stepped in to support Sylvia as best he could, but increasingly felt overwhelmed and alone in their partnership. This grew into resentment towards her – why didn't she just get on with it? Why did she leave everything to him? He found himself lonely, resentful, and deeply afraid of losing her. He feared that history would repeat itself to leave him alone with it all.

With less support and fewer resources, the partners' normal coping strategies were stripped bare, and the things they loved about each other were no longer readily apparent. At times, attributes that had initially attracted them to each other became sources of distress. For example, John's routine and careful provision became triggers for Sylvia to feel criticised ("*he thinks I am not good enough*") and Sylvia's attempts to be spontaneous and creative made him think she was not pulling her weight ("*she thinks this is nothing, she's making light of this*"). Her attempts to share her difficult emotions with him left him feeling overwhelmed, and led to highly explosive arguments which further damaged their relationship.

As a couple they ceased to have meaningful and fun times together, and as a family John did more and more with the children to leave Sylvia to rest (as well as out of anger). This all took place shortly after they bought their 'dream home' – a big renovation project which they had intended to do together. With the shift in their relationship, the renovation project paused, and living in their unfinished home became unbearable. They were living separate lives now and felt confused and hopeless about the future. Neither of them felt able to continue in this way.

THERAPIST REFLECTIONS: I was extremely concerned about the severity of their arguments. They described how these had become increasingly destructive, and neither of them could quite explain why. In the sessions they often escalated very quickly, and it took some assertiveness and clear ground rules from me to contain this at first. I was alarmed by how this did not fit with the couple that sat in front of me – they looked so calm and collected, it was difficult to imagine them in such a state of disarray. It helped me understand that it was really important to help this couple talk about how they were feeling in a safe space.

Aims of therapy

The couple hoped that therapy could support them in the following ways:

- To reduce (or hopefully stop) destructive arguments and to develop new coping strategies for when things escalate.
- To improve their communication.
- To address their depression (at first it was just Sylvia's depression, but this changed during therapy).
- To help them reconnect and feel like a team.
- To manage risk.

Sylvia and John felt that should they be able to achieve these things, they might find a way back, or in fact a way forward to an even better place in their relationship. It would mean that both of them could reconnect with what was meaningful in their lives and return to a sense of a safe haven (albeit an altered version of their early relationship) at home.

THERAPIST REFLECTIONS: Setting goals with the couple felt very therapeutic already as it gave the couple the opportunity to start thinking about what they wanted while standing 'outside' the arguments. Sylvia's depression symptoms actually started to improve at this early stage. The DIY home improvement project became a metaphor for rebuilding their relationship as they were intending to rebuild their home. We were ready to embark on the journey of therapy.

Course of therapy

Sylvia and John attended 18 weekly treatment sessions together, including 4 assessment sessions. Some of the key interventions used are discussed in more detail below.

Psychoeducation

It felt important to let both partners spend time talking about their experience of their relationship and depression. As we did this, I used the opportunity to weave psychoeducation into the sessions rather than having a directive approach where we 'educated' them on how depression might impact a relationship. I listened carefully to their descriptions of how they personally experienced things and often responded with comments aimed at building insight, while also validating their experiences and feelings.

SYLVIA: I felt so useless over the weekend, and as usual, John had to get on and get the kids ready for their day. I am so useless!

(Crying)

THERAPIST: Gosh, that sounds really painful the way you are talking to yourself there. Were those thoughts present when you struggled on Saturday?

SYLVIA: Yes... yes, it was. I just stayed in my bed crying the whole morning. I didn't know what to do and I didn't want him to know I was struggling so much because I know he doesn't like that...

THERAPIST: It sounds like you were experiencing something that lots of people struggle with. It's really common in depression to get stuck in these difficult places with lots of self-critical thoughts swarming around and just feeling yourself emotionally plummeting further. Do you think I am understanding you?

SYLVIA: Yes, the depression felt out of my control. I am so stuck there...

THERAPIST: (after asking John to reflect back to Sylvia what he heard her expressing) Did you have a sense of what her depression was like for Sylvia on Saturday?

JOHN: I had no idea. I guess I was just stuck with the resentment of having to get the kids ready again.

THERAPIST: And now that you do?

JOHN: My heart breaks for her (therapist gently prompting him to talk to her directly) My heart breaks for you sweetheart. I am so sorry, I didn't know you felt so alone with this.

THERAPIST: So if we can just pause there, it sounds like we are really getting in touch with what it is like to live with depression. Do you think it's important to get better at understanding depression and how it might impact things for you both?

Communication training

We spoke about guidelines for good communication and unpacked what their difficulties in communication had been. The couple acknowledged they were uncomfortable with sharing more vulnerable (or 'softer') thoughts and feelings. They found it normalising to consider communication as requiring a set of skills that can be learnt rather than an innate failure or weakness. Communication training started from the first treatment session and was probably the key ingredient to their success. After initially discussing the basic theory behind communication and outlining the ground rules (e.g. speaker – listener guidelines), we started to address their communication directly. This required active therapist involvement to start with. I would guide them (*"John, before you respond, could you first tell Sylvia what it is you heard her say?"*), or prompt them (*"Say it to him Sylvia, not to me" or "John, I am noticing you are talking about your anger now, can I encourage you to tell Sylvia more about the softer feelings behind the anger?"*), or stop and redirect them (*"Can I just stop you there… it seems you just started escalating again… is this what it looks like at home? Why don't we try again, but this time I want you, Sylvia, to really try and listen to what John is trying to say and first just focus on letting him know what you hear…"*). As their communication improved, I was able to step back and be less directive.

THERAPIST REFLECTIONS: One of my favourite interventions with couples remains sharing thoughts and feelings exercises. I usually aim to slow the couple right down, to enable them to connect emotionally and really feel each other, and in those moments couples become a little bit more unstuck every time! I felt that one of our key breakthroughs in therapy took place quite early on, when we did a sharing thoughts and feelings exercise around a recent argument. John was for the first time able to hear and connect with the idea of how insecure and frightened Sylvia became during their arguments, in particular around fears of his leaving her. On realising this, John started crying in the session, admitting that the thought of Sylvia's distress made him feel immense remorse. It brought a massive change to their interactions, as it helped John under-stand how much she needed reassurance and gentleness in those moments, and it gave him new insight into why in those moments empathy and closeness were so important, and inversely, why his rational, 'cold' stance made things worse. Later in this same session, when it was John's turn to share thoughts and feelings, Sylvia was able to recognise that it was fear that made John turn towards his rational / logical stance, and she too started understanding that when John becomes 'cold' he is actually highly anxious and feeling overwhelmed.

Through practice and repetition, and lots of in-session opportunities to talk in-depth around different topics, therapy allowed them to have more successful conversations, and over time they felt more confident to try this at home. Sylvia learnt how to talk to John without overwhelming him, and John learnt that he could listen to Sylvia's feelings, and that once he did, Sylvia would settle. Their conversations became more constructive and much less likely to escalate.

Reducing reactivity which led to out of control arguments

We used the Grant (2011) interactional cycle to gain insight into the factors that contributed to these arguments and why they kept escalating so quickly (see Chapter 4 for a detailed description of this model). We focused on making links – when Sylvia thought *"he doesn't care about me"*, it made her feel angry, but also terrified, and so she reacted by escalating her behaviour, almost to try to get a reaction. The more John withdrew, the more dramatic she became. When John saw this escalation, he thought *"she's out of control, I need to stop this"* which made him feel anxious, and so he resorted to his preferred coping strategy – using logic and pushing feelings away.

THERAPIST REFLECTION: We often spoke of their 'dance'. She would step closer, and he would step back. We tried to think of a dance that they would rather have, one with enough space for both, a slower dance with more pausing points, and this allowed them to spiral less and less over time. Even so, their occasional setbacks were helpful as each of these led to new insights into what was happening between them.

Risk management

It was clear from very early on that the couple needed support around risk – firstly in that Sylvia had regular thoughts of self-harm at the time she came to therapy, and secondly because they described a distressing cycle around her suicidality. This cycle was usually triggered by an argument, during which John would become more logical and colder, while Sylvia felt increas-ingly desperate for not getting emotional warmth from her husband. This would lead to her becoming severely distressed and threatening to kill herself. Through communication training, where we enhanced John's ability to stay emotionally present and in active listening mode with Sylvia, while teaching her to express her needs in less overwhelming ways, we started to see a reduced frequency of these escalations. We also agreed on a code word ('hippopotamus') which either could use if they felt their dance was entering into dangerous territory and they needed to de-escalate, or take a period of time-out before resuming their conversation.

THERAPIST REFLECTIONS: I had a lot of difficulty not going straight into individual therapy mode here with Sylvia. Whilst a risk contract was in place, I wanted to do thought records and individual therapy work with her around risk. I learnt that these couple-based interventions were enough to calm the storm. However, in some circumstances it may not be possible to adequately assess and manage risk within a couple context and additional individual support may be necessary.

Behavioural Activation (BA)

It was important to start working on behavioural activation with the couple right from the start. We introduced individual BA with Sylvia (self-care, creating a routine, re-introducing things she liked doing, re-engaging with responsibilities around the home, etc.) and this provided a platform to explore John's accommodating behaviours which were helping to maintain her inactivity. We also focused on couple-based BA, for example doing more things together as a couple and as a family, starting to work on their house, and setting time aside for therapy homework such as having meaningful conversations. We discussed their expectations to make it feel safe for them to try these activities while they were still wary of setbacks.

Guided behaviour change

Further to activity scheduling, we discussed how, since they had withdrawn from each other due to their depression, John and Sylvia had stopped various caring behaviours towards each other. The couple agreed that their time together was often spent skirting around the edges to avoid trigger points, instead of drawing close. We explored what sort of behaviours each of them felt would make a difference to the other's wellbeing (being careful not to let partners fall into a "*I want more of this and less of that*" prescription), guiding them to come up with ideas of what they might want to do for the other. In this way, the couple slowly re-engaged in positive, caring behaviours towards each other.

At various points in the therapy process I also encouraged Sylvia and John to 'test things out' by setting up behavioural experiments. This was relevant both to Sylvia individually and to them as a couple. For example, we encouraged Sylvia to tackle tasks at home that she would normally avoid, and then see what the outcome was and learn from it (e.g. *"I was able to do more housework before getting tired than what I thought I could"*). We also applied this approach to them as a couple, experimenting with ways in which they could alter their behaviour towards each other or new ways for them to spend time together. By creating a 'try-it-and-see' attitude in their relationship, it felt a bit easier to make changes, as there was now more space for 'trying' with the understanding that not everything would turn out as expected, but that the point was to try.

De-pathologising differences

John's careful and organised style had originally felt kind and supportive to Sylvia, but now she saw it as controlling and cold. Sylvia's playfulness and impulsiveness had originally felt exciting and a welcome break from the normal routine to John, but now he viewed it as irresponsible and inconsiderate. It can be the case that couples in distress will start viewing their partner's differences in more negative ways, and this can make behaviour change towards each other difficult (Baucom et al., 2020). Some sessions were therefore spent exploring and working through these differences, to help Sylvia and John find compromises where they could, develop more acceptance of each other's quirks, and even remember the positives these differences brought to their relationship at times (Jacobson & Christensen, 1996).

Cognitive restructuring

Broadly speaking, cognitive work was probably present in most therapy sessions. We used it to build awareness, deepen insight, and eventually change some unhelpful thinking patterns that had developed over time. Many unhelpful cognitive processes trapped the couple in their distress. For example, John was low on Relational Schematic Processing (see Chapter 2) and did not have a strong ability to think in relational terms, whereas Sylvia probably did this too keenly. Both John and Sylvia selectively overfocused on certain elements of the other's behaviour, while very much not noticing other things (selective attention). When reflecting on difficult interactions, both described distorted or unhelpful cognitions (such as the attributions they were making about each other's behaviour) which contributed to their distress. Lastly, both of them (as all of us) held assumptions and standards which impacted their experience of their relationship. Working with the couple to first highlight these cognitions and cognitive processes, then discussing these beliefs in more detail, and finally attempt to bring about change in some of them, contributed to their relationship and their depression shifting to a better place.

It was extremely helpful for the couple to unpack, review, and update some of the beliefs, rules and assumptions that had led to marital discord. We cautiously used thought records to encourage them to reflect on their own thoughts and feelings during trigger situations. For example, while they were using a 'time out' strategy, they would each complete a thought record individually to help them to step back from the situation and understand what had contributed to the escalation, before returning to the conversation at a later time. We hoped that a better understanding could safeguard them against the same escalation as before.

THERAPIST REFLECTIONS: I felt it was appropriate to use individual thought records in this context, but we had some clear ground rules around not needing to share these records with each other as they were merely tools to get each partner to a point where communication was again possible and felt safer. If the couple started using these written records as weapons against each other, this would have been contra-indicated and very quickly discontinued in the therapy!

Other 'standard' CBT strategies were helpful to support cognitive restructuring. For example, where I noticed unhelpful rules or assumptions they held, I explored these with the couple to help them become more aware of their beliefs, the impact these had on the relationship, and to consider whether they might need to be addressed in therapy.

JOHN: Well, she's clearly just leaving everything to me as she's not bothered to step up. She's so focused on her own sadness, that she has forgotten about her family. She doesn't care about us anymore...

SYLVIA: That's not true! I care very much about my family! I just think it's better if I am out of the way... you are so distant anyway, it's very clear that you don't want me there...

THERAPIST: That's striking how different your views are of what is going on here. Shall we unpack that a bit more? John, you said that you believe that when Sylvia withdraws, she does this because she doesn't care about you, is that right?

JOHN: Yes, I guess so, but now that you put it that way, it sounds a bit harsh.

THERAPIST: Mmm, that's interesting. And Sylvia, you withdraw because you believe that they don't really want you there, is that right?

SYLVIA: Yes, I mean, I am not really fun to have around... I am so useless now...

THERAPIST: That sounds really painful for you Sylvia. Do you guys think it might be good to unpack these beliefs a bit more to see if they are indeed helpful and true?

(couple agrees)

THERAPIST: John, do you want to check out with Sylvia to see what's really going on for her when she disappears?

JOHN: Um, okay... Sylvia, when you disappear like that, to me it feels like you dump everything on me and just leave me to it. What's going on when you disappear like that?

SYLVIA: (crying) I feel so guilty. I didn't realise that you would have felt like that. I thought you preferred me just getting out of your way... When I disappear like that, I guess I do so because I feel absolutely useless, in the way, and you just look so distant. I don't know how to talk about this, because I just think we'll end up arguing again, so I just leave quietly. I can't just sit there... I never meant to just dump you in it, John. I thought I was making it easier for you. And of course, I need the rest as well, because I just feel so down. I don't want the kids... or you... to see me like that.

THERAPIST: John, can you tell Sylvia what you understood about what she is thinking and feeling?

JOHN: (after some discussion and prompting) You feel so bad about yourself Sylvia, it must be horrible... You think I want you to leave, which can't be further from the truth. We love having you around ...

THERAPIST: And I wonder if this gives you a different view of what it means when Sylvia disappears – do you still believe she is intending to dump everything on you?

Helping the couple generate more curiosity about the other and encouraging them to ask questions before jumping to conclusions was very helpful to them. Quite often the themes that led to discord were recurring, and once we had unpacked the theme in session, we could draw up a 'blueprint' that they could use at home whenever it came up. For example, we agreed that the next time Sylvia felt that she should leave the room, she would first tell John how she felt, and they could then have a constructive conversation about it and decide together on the best course of action.

Working with emotions

Over the course of treatment, we worked on both targeting the intensity of emotional expression (Sylvia over-expressed, John under-expressed), and on targeting the couple's emotional responsiveness to one another (as neither was initially able to respond with sufficient 'thereness' or presence to the other).

THERAPIST REFLECTIONS: To me, the 'glue' of couple therapy is the therapist's ability to engage and enhance communication between the two individuals. In every session, there would be parts where, once we had discussed or noticed something, I would shift gears and bring them back to simple sharing thoughts and feelings exercises. This was highly relevant to the work on emotions. John for example would often just focus on one feeling (usually irritation or anger) and needed prompting to go deeper to the softer feelings of sadness or loneliness. Sylvia had a tendency to become very emotional very quickly, which scared John, and so for her gentle prompting to stay with one feeling at a time and give John time to process things helped her to come back to a level where John could once more hear her.

Discussion

Sylvia and John initially presented as severely distressed, and their arguments were alarming. I was, to start with, not very hopeful for the couple, and found myself thinking that therapy would be 'too little, too late'. I was perhaps as surprised as they were to see them improve so rapidly once we had the arguments under control. It challenged me to think of my own beliefs as a therapist, how working with particular couples impacts me, and how this can adversely affect therapy. I was reminded that even severe presentations can respond well to therapy if key underlying beliefs which are maintaining the distress are unlocked. It instilled a lot of hope in me about working with couples. We had a few other things in our favour – Sylvia and John's commitment and engagement (to the therapy process and to each other) made a massive difference to the outcome of the therapy, and they brought with them an array of other strengths.

Sylvia and John were very happy about the outcome of their sessions. Both reported significant improvements in their mood, and they told me that friends and family commented on how well they seemed. They mentioned how touching it was when their daughter told them she was glad they came to see me, because it made them happy again. They were able to navigate their conversations more safely and increased their activities meaningfully. Sylvia found ways of reclaiming her life through her increased activity and pacing, no longer felt useless and reported that she was no longer having suicidal thoughts. They were well on their way to finishing the work on their house. Hope now replaced the despair they had felt when we first met.

I had to work hard with this couple to maintain a balanced couple stance throughout therapy. Being female myself, and identifying more with the things Sylvia said, I had to be mindful not to let my own assumptions and beliefs get in the way. This process became easier as I got to know the couple better, and as I grew to understand the slightly more hidden emotional side of John. Jacobson and Christensen (1996) rightly talk about the importance of cultivating acceptance in a relationship as a way to improve empathy and closeness. This is also true for the therapist – as we attempt to listen and learn from the couple, we too become more accepting of them! Baucom et al. (2020) helpfully point out that the role of the couple therapist is not to focus only on the partners themselves, but also on the interaction between the two. This greatly helps in keeping a balanced neutral stance.

Chapter reflections

Therapy focus: Relationship distress or Depression?

The interplay between depression and relationship distress is evident in the work with a couple. You find yourself fluctuating between talking about an issue that relates to unhappiness in the relationship and then again working directly on depression. Therapists need to be flexible enough to go with the ebb and flow of a session, while keeping in mind what it is that they want to achieve overall.

The benefit of couple-based interventions

Sylvia's initial individual CBT sessions were filled with reflections about her relationship with John, and it quickly became clear that her experience of her relationship was significantly contributing to her depression. It was therefore agreed that a couple-based intervention would be more suited to her needs. John was happy to attend on the presumption that he was there to support Sylvia in getting better. At our first meeting, it was striking to see that John in fact also scored in the moderate range for depression symptoms, even though he did not identify as being depressed, and even though the couple's view remained one focused on Sylvia only as the depressed partner. This became instrumental in the therapy going forward. Some work was clearly needed to help the couple understand that the depression they were experiencing was a shared problem related to their relationship, rather than an individual problem situated in Sylvia. This is a good example of a case where individual therapy might not have been ultimately helpful – even when individual CBT is helpful, it often does not address the relationship difficulties, therefore meaning recovery will be less likely, and the risk of relapse remains higher if the relationship remains distressed (Fisher et al., 2016).

Therapist skills in navigating conflict in the room

Couple therapists need to be ready to manage heightened emotions and escalating conflict in the room. The level of anger, hostility or distress expressed during sessions can be very hard to contain. Therapists need to be able to intervene and stop these escalating arguments in a non-confrontational, therapeutic manner that does not add fuel to the fire, or draw in their own personal (or even accusatory or critical) responses. For this couple, it often worked to notice with the couple what had just happened and to create a curiosity about how they had got there, using previously discussed themes and processes as anchors (e.g. *"If I can jump in there, I am noticing John that as you are becoming more withdrawn, Sylvia, you seem to be getting more agitated. This seems to be around your theme of emotional vs rational again, is that right? Is that what often happens at home as well?"* etc.).

Therapist tips

- Only move on to working on the problem once it has been clearly agreed and defined.
- Keep the focus simple. Empower a couple to understand a few key principles well than trying to incorporate too much.
- The power of 'simple' speaker – listener conversations should never be underestimated. In fact, it's often these experiences that bring around the most change.
- It is important to build empathy from early on in therapy to increase the couple's engagement in sessions and homework tasks.
- It is sometimes useful to not rein the couple in too quickly if they get argumentative. Therapists don't need to be afraid of 'letting it go' a little bit in a session, and then get the couple to stand outside of it and reflect on what went wrong. However, as mentioned above therapists should not allow conversations to escalate to the point where they are detrimental to the relationship.
- Practice difficult conversations – allow the couple to repeat exercises if it went wrong or turned out to be more complicated than they thought.

Suggestions for further Reading

Baucom, D. H., Fischer, M. S., Corrie, S., Worrell, M., & Boeding, S. (2020). *Treating relationship distress and psychopathology in couples. A cognitive behavioural approach.* Routledge.

References

American Psychiatric Association (2013). *Diagnostic and statistical manual of mental disorders: DSM-5.* 5th edn. Washington, D.C.: American Psychiatric Publishing.

Baucom, B., Eldridge, K., Jones, J., Sevier, M., Clements, M., Markman, H., Stanley, S., Sayers, S. L., Sher, T., & Christensen, A. (2007). Relative contributions of relationship distress and depression to communication patterns in couples. *Journal of Social and Clinical Psychology*, 26(6), 689–707.

Baucom, D. H., Whisman, M. A., & Paprocki, C. (2012). Couple-based interventions for psychopathology. *Journal of Family Therapy*, 34(3), 250–270. doi:10.1111/ j.1467-6427.2012.00600.x.

Baucom, B. R., Atkins, D.C., Eldridge, K., McFarland, P., Sevier, M., & Christensen, A. (2011). The language of demand / withdraw: verbal and vocal expression in dyadic interactions. *Journal of family psychology*, 25(4), 540–580.

Baucom, D. H., Fischer, M. S., Corrie, S., Worrell, M., & Boeding, S. (2020). *Treating relationship distress and psychopathology in couples. A cognitive behavioural approach.* Routledge.

Beck, A. T. (1967). *Depression: Causes and treatment.* Philadelphia: University of Pennsylvania Press.

Donato, S., Parise, M., Pagani, A. F., Bertoni, A., & Iafrate, R. (2014). Demand-Withdraw, Couple Satisfaction and Relationship Duration. *Social and Behavioural Sciences*, 140, 200–206.

Grant, L. (2011). Conceptualisation of Couples in Therapy. In: *BABCP 39th Annual Conference.* Guildford, University of Surrey.

Fischer, M. S., Baucom, D. H., Cohen, M. J. (2016). Cognitive-Behavioral Couple Therapies: Review of the Evidence for the Treatment of Relationship Distress, Psychopathology, and Chronic Health Conditions. *Family Process*, 55, 423–442.

Greenberger, D., & Padesky, C. A. (2016). *Mind over mood: change how you feel by changing the way you think.* 2nd edition. New York, NY: The Guilford Press.

Jacobson, N. S., & Christensen, A. (1996). *Integrative behavioral couple therapy.* New York: W.W. Norton.

Lebow, J. L., Chambers, A. L., Christensen, A., & Johnson, S. M. (2011). Research on the treatment of couple distress. *Journal of marital and family therapy*, 38(1), 145–168.

Li, P., & Johnson, L. N. (2018). Couples' depression and relationship satisfaction: examining the moderating effects of demand/withdraw communication patterns. *Journal of Family Therapy*, 40(Suppl 1), S63 – S85.

Martell, C., Dimidjian, S., & Herman-Dunn, R. (2013). *Behavioral Activation for Depression: a Clinician's Guide.* Guilford Press.

Office for National Statistics (2021). *Cost of living and depression in adults, Great Britain: 29 September to 23 October 2022.* Accessed at: https://www.ons.gov.uk/p eoplepopulationandcommunity/healthandsocialcare/mentalhealth/articles/costoflivi nganddepressioninadultsgreatbritain/29septemberto23october2022.

Chapter 11

Hoarding

'Souvenir': To Have and To Have Hold: The Impact of Hoarding on Relationships

Satwant Singh

Introduction

Individuals who hoard collect and save items which they perceive to have intrinsic value and purpose. They often have sentimental attachment to certain possessions, and this leads to the excessive accumulation of items and the inability to discard them. This results in an environment that is cluttered and rendered unfunctional for its intended purpose. For example, a bedroom might be used to store items to the point where the room can no longer be used as a bedroom. Often, all spaces of a home will be cluttered, so that most areas are not functional for the individuals living there.

Over the last two decades of treating individuals with hoarding issues I have found that one of the key presenting issues, apart from a cluttered environment filled with items, is the impact of the hoarding, directly or indirectly, on relationships. Relationships between partners are often strained, fraught, and filled with resentment. This couple distress can in turn make therapy with a hoarding individual that much more difficult. For the 'non-patient' partner, hoarding can be hard to understand, with the patient partner seemingly more oriented towards inanimate objects than the relationship.

Theoretical framework

The dominant cognitive behavioural model of hoarding proposes that individuals with hoarding issues form intense emotional attachments to their possessions, to the extent that they perceive their possessions to be an extension of themselves (Frost & Hartl, 1996; Frost, Hartl, Christian & William, 1995). This can lead them to love their possessions in the same way as they would love another person (Frost & Gross, 1993). The intense emotional attachment (Frost & Hartl, 1995; Frost et al., 1995) and attribution of human qualities to their possessions (Neave et al., 2015; Timpano & Shaw, 2013) can impact the dynamics of their interpersonal relationships, and in some instances the possessions displace the importance of a partner. Fromm

DOI: 10.4324/9781003024439-13

(1947) proposed that individuals with hoarding issues form attachments to objects in lieu of attachment or relationships with people. One possible reason for this is that they perceive objects to be stable, safe, and unlikely to abandon them or cause them emotional pain. This can result in relationship distress for couples and families, leading to intense emotional outbursts, disharmony and sometimes eventual breakdown of these relationships. A study by Grisham and colleagues (2018) found that individuals with hoarding issues show increased attachment-related anxiety and avoidance, as well as emotion regulation difficulties. Frost et al., (1995) report that individuals with hoarding tendencies utilise their possessions as a source of emotional comfort.

Baucom, Whisman and Paprocki (2012) suggest that an intimate partner relationship can be the most important interpersonal relationship someone develops over their lifetime. This would indicate that relationship distress caused by either individual pathology, trauma within the relationship, or conflict, can have a significant impact on a person's wellbeing. Distress within couples can be understood as 'primary' (i.e. arising from an individual's needs in the relationship not being met) or 'secondary' (developing as a result of maladaptive attempts to have these needs met) and can result in high levels of emotional turbulence. As described by Baucom and colleagues (2012), the success of a relationship and attachment to a partner across the lifespan requires adaptation and accommodation by both partners. Early on in a relationship, partners often tend to be more accepting of the other person's 'quirks' and 'habits', including for example their tendency to collect objects. In the context of hoarding disorder, this can be seen as symptom accommodation, i.e. the way in which the relationship 'makes room' for the hoarding disorder, potentially both in helpful and unhelpful ways, that may act either to challenge or maintain the disorder (Baucom et al., 2020).

Currently there is no model of couple-based CBT for hoarding disorder. However, the couple-based intervention for obsessive compulsive disorder (OCD) developed by Abramowitz and colleagues (Abramowitz et al., 2013) provides a good framework for the treatment of hoarding disorder. In this model, partners are included in all sessions to support the patient in engaging with the treatment. As well as supporting the individual with OCD to engage in exposure and response prevention, disorder-specific partner behaviours and aspects of the couple's relationship which perpetuate the disorder become the targets of treatment, e.g. accommodating the partner's checking behaviours or rituals. Couple-based CBT for OCD also focuses on improving expressive communication and problem-solving skills, in the context of both OCD and broader relationship issues. Communication is often an initial focus of therapy, in order to foster better understanding and a reduction in negative patterns of interaction. Emotional experiences contributing to, as well as resulting from the disorder are of great importance and need to be attended to (Fischer, Baucom, Hahlweg & Epstein, 2013).

The CBCT framework for OCD described above can be used to conceptualise and address the relationship distress for individuals with hoarding issues. It is important to understand how emotional and sentimental attachments to possessions play a role in providing emotional comfort for the individual and the impact this has on the relationship. Additionally, the well-established bi-directional influence between relationship functioning and individual psychopathology suggests that addressing hoarding issues within a couple focussed intervention may hold significant clinical advantages (Baucom et al., 2020).

How couples respond to hoarding issues

There has been little research in understanding the impact of hoarding issues on interpersonal relationships. In an internet survey, Tolin and colleagues (2008) identified elevated reports of child and family strain in those living with individuals with hoarding issues. A qualitative study by Wilbram, Kellett and Beail (2008) concluded that carers struggle to cope with both the environmental and interpersonal impacts of the hoarding. In a more recent study, Drury, Ajmi, Fernandez de la Cruz et al. (2014) found that relatives of those with hoarding problems reported significantly greater carer burden and accommodation of hoarding behaviours in comparison to relatives of collectors.

Despite the negative impact on their lives, partners of those with hoarding issues will often accommodate the person's hoarding behaviours in order to maintain relationship harmony, at least initially. However, over time the impact of excessive hoarding and clutter on their shared space, activities and social lives can lead to responses such as distancing from each other and living in separate quarters, thus negatively impacting the relationship. Couples face an increased risk of angry outbursts, possible violence and further deterioration in the relationship. The individual with the hoarding problem may collect, buy and save items as a means of coping with the emotional distress experienced, and these behaviours in turn increase the level of clutter and further complicate their situation.

The presenting couple: Lisbeth and Seb

Lisbeth self-referred to a monthly hoarding treatment group at the request of her husband Seb to seek help for her hoarding issues. Lisbeth has had a life-long problem of excessive saving, but until recently she was able to regulate the quantity of items she collected by regularly sorting her home out. However, 3 years ago both of her parents died within a short space of time. Lisbeth was their only child and had the sole responsibility for sorting their belongings in France. She could not bear to discard and part from her parents' belongings and had them shipped back to the London home she shares with Seb. Their home in London became heavily cluttered, leaving little space and severely impacting their comfort. This served as a trigger for their marital disharmony. The home environment became cluttered to the point where it was almost impossible to move freely, which caused major disruption and expressions of anger from Seb.

In desperation, Seb undertook an online search and found the hoarding treatment group. He gave Lisbeth the ultimatum to seek help or he would end their relationship. When Lisbeth attended her assessment, she revealed that she was seeking help mainly as a result of the marital distress caused by her hoarding. However, it was also noted that she was currently experiencing significantly depressed mood. Lisbeth's hoarding problem was perpetuated further by her distress coping mechanism of shopping. The assessment revealed three main areas of concern: Lisbeth's depression, excessive clutter and hoarding and marital distress. She was asked to invite her husband to attend the next session with the intention of discussing the option of offering them Cognitive Behavioural Couple Therapy (CBCT) to work collaboratively with both partners in dealing with the presenting concerns.

Lisbeth, a warm, kind, hardworking woman in her early 60s, was employed as a senior secretary, a job she enjoyed and excelled in. Seb was a fun-loving man with a sense of adventure. He was in his mid-60s and had retired from his job as a bank manager. They had no children, led a comfortable life, and engaged in a range of social activities individually and together. Upon his retirement Seb had travelled around Europe on his own, with Lisbeth joining him for her holidays. It was their plan to travel together when she retires.

THERAPIST REFLECTION: From the initial assessment, I felt strongly that a couple focussed intervention could be of help to both partners. As noted above, individuals with hoarding issues tend to collect and save as a means of coping with their emotions. It is important to work with their partners to reduce the level of distress within their environment and minimise the risk of escalation of their hoarding issues. I felt that it was important to work with both partners as Lisbeth reported significant relationship distress, and also it was at Seb's insistence that Lisbeth had self-referred to the hoarding group. I was uncertain as to how Seb would react to the suggestion that they both be seen together for therapy, but Lisbeth appeared hopeful that Seb would agree – she believed that despite their difficulties, they were still very much a couple. Seb attended the session with Lisbeth, which was a positive indication that they both valued their relationship and a significant point I could use to engage them in therapy.

Background

Seb met Lisbeth when he started his first job after university in the company where she worked as a trainee secretary. Lisbeth had grown up in France and had moved to London to work. They married in France after a year-long courtship. Both Lisbeth and Seb shared an interest in travelling, and early on in their life together they decided not to have children and pursue their dreams. Lisbeth always had a tendency to collect items for sentimental reasons but did so in small quantities. Seb noticed that Lisbeth collected souvenirs from their holidays, but she was a good organiser and tastefully decorated their home, so it never appeared cluttered. The hoarding really became a problem after Lisbeth's parents died, when she became depressed and was not able to sort out her parents' belongings that had been transported back from France. Around that time, she also started shopping excessively to cope with her emotional distress.

Seb had always been a supportive partner who did his best to meet Lisbeth's needs. As Lisbeth's depression got worse, she started doing less at home and disengaged from their joint activities as well as activities with her friends, and she was spending more time alone. Seb believed that Lisbeth needed time and space to deal with her loss, and in his attempt to be supportive, he reduced pressure on her and spent more time with his own social group. This resulted in Lisbeth feeling left out and disconnected from their relationship. She started to believe that she was a burden and no longer a good wife and partner to Seb. They grew emotionally distant, spending more time apart and communicating less. When they did talk it was often in a critical manner. Lisbeth started to rely more on her possessions for emotional comfort, especially those from her childhood. By gentle exploration through Socratic questioning and showing curiosity, we were able to start to develop an understanding of some of these themes over the course of the assessment.

THERAPIST REFLECTION: The assessment revealed a complex presentation and I had to consider which of the 3 areas (Lisbeth's depression, her hoarding, and the couple's relationship) should be prioritised for treatment. The hoarding issue appeared to be the main stressor in the relationship and as such it seemed to me a reasonable clinical hypothesis that achieving change here would have a beneficial impact also on couple distress and depression.

From the first joint session, it was clear that Lisbeth and Seb still loved each other. They both wanted to be able to communicate without being critical or angry and recognised that the major contributors to their difficulties were Lisbeth's depression, the hoarding issues, lack of engagement in joint activities and poor communication. In their individual assessment sessions, special attention was paid to helping each partner recognise the other's positive attributes and what connected them as a couple. Lisbeth's individual assessment appointment included careful questioning about her hoarding issues, for instance the emotional significance, attachment, function, and role the possessions held for her. The impact of her attachment to objects on her relationship with Seb was also explored.

Formulation

Together with Lisbeth and Seb, we developed a shared understanding of their difficulties. Initially, we considered their individual attributes and the values, including those that attracted them to each other in the first place. I felt I needed to be quite cautious when asking Lisbeth about the impact of her loss and subsequent depression on the relationship, and also when exploring her attachment to possessions and use of these to derive comfort and cope with her emotional distress. I felt that it was important not to make assumptions as to the reasons and to allow the individual to tell their story. Often the 'blanks' can be filled in by allowing adequate time and opportunity for individuals to share their experiences. Using guided discovery, which facilitated Lisbeth's storytelling, we made the connection between her shift to seeking solace in her possessions rather than from Seb, and the subsequent distancing from Seb. We noted how the deterioration in their communication contributed to and was maintaining their relationship distress. We were able to uncover Lisbeth's underlying beliefs of 'not being wanted' and not being a good wife and see how these led to further distancing from each other. These beliefs were also related to Lisbeth's attachment to her possessions and the increasingly important role they played in helping her cope with her depression, providing a connection to the past where she felt comforted, safe, secure and loved.

THERAPIST REFLECTION: I felt it was crucial to begin by acknowledging the significance of Lisbeth and Seb's relationship and appreciating the fact they both had attended the session together despite their difficulties. It was also an opportunity for each of them to be able to share their experiences and understanding of their issues and hear their partner's perspective. As a therapist I found them warm, caring, and there was a sense of a strong connection between them. This made me focus on helping them recognise the attributes and aspects that had attracted them to each other when they became a couple. This contributed to the CBCT formulation and also helped to instil hope and energy to work on their issues.

Aims of the intervention

Following the assessment and formulation sessions, I invited Lisbeth and Seb to discuss their goals for therapy. It was interesting to observe their interactions during this process, as they showed a high degree of consideration and accommodation for each other's needs. This was highlighted to them as a strength in their relationship. However, it also made it quite difficult and challenging to agree on priorities for therapy. They both had different priorities, and negotiating these was a useful exercise in helping them to recognise the importance of joint problem solving. Early on in therapy, it was also important to provide psychoeducation on depression (see also Chapter 10), especially to help Seb to understand the psychological and physiological symptoms and their potential impact on Lisbeth's motivation to engage in activities. Following discussion and negotiation, the goals they agreed on were:

1 To support Lisbeth to cope with her low mood, and her losses.
2 To be able to communicate about their difficulties and improve their relationship.
3 To reduce the clutter in their home.

Course of therapy

Lisbeth and Seb attended 22 sessions of therapy including the 3 assessment sessions. It was evident from their commitment to therapy that they cared deeply for each other and valued their relationship. A range of tools, techniques and exercises drawn from CBCT were used dynamically across sessions. Therapy was structured into three main phases as outlined below.

The prospect of therapy can be daunting, and having a clear structure and aims for each stage aids both the therapist and clients to manage their expectations, maintain their focus and monitor progress. It also provided both Lisbeth and Seb with the assurance that their key concerns would be attended to over the course of treatment.

Initial phase

Psychoeducation and compassion

Working with both Lisbeth and Seb to develop a deeper understanding of Lisbeth's symptoms of depression, particularly changes in her mood, behaviour and interactions with Seb since her parents had died was extremely useful in helping them to understand her current presentation. Lisbeth disclosed that she felt guilty about 'not being a good wife' and this provided an opportunity to move towards conversations focused on understanding and empathy rather than on blame. Both Lisbeth and Seb could relate to Lisbeth's depression and the impact it had on them as a couple. We discussed how to approach treatment for her depression, for example outlining the principles of behavioural activation (BA) as an important intervention to help lift her mood. Involving Seb in some joint activities gave him the opportunity to be part of her recovery process.

BA was introduced in a graded way. At the outset, the aim was for Lisbeth to increase her activity levels above and beyond going to work, and to include some pleasurable activities including re-engaging in social activities with Seb and her friends. There were some challenges in getting both partners to work together to develop a routine of activities, especially within their home due to the clutter. Therefore, initially I encouraged them both to engage in external activities such as going to the cinema, theatre, and meeting friends for social outings. Engaging in activities outside the home had the added benefit of facilitating emotional distancing and detachment for Lisbeth from her possessions, which was good preparation for addressing her hoarding issues later in therapy. We agreed that Seb would try to organise activities that they both used to enjoy together prior to the loss of her parents, and Lisbeth would also suggest activities she would like to participate in.

Communication

BA provided some good opportunities to address their communication issues, with discussions around joint activities shifting the focus away from the hoarding problem. I paid special attention to the way both Lisbeth and Seb interacted, especially the language they used and impact it had on them. At times there was a pattern of critical communication, with one partner attacking and the other withdrawing. Initially, the focus was on helping them to recognise the critical comments they made to each other, the impact of these and the reactions they themselves experienced. This highlighted the underlying resentment that Seb felt due to the restrictions he experienced in their home. During sessions, they practiced recognising and expressing their expectations of the relationship, and learned to problem solve when they held different expectations and to assert themselves without anger. Lisbeth found it difficult to assert herself due to the guilt she felt for not being the wife she used to be.

THERAPIST: It was interesting listening to you both discuss your week between yourselves. How did you feel you were both conversing?
SEB: It is the way we normally speak.
THERAPIST: Lisbeth what was it like for you having that conversation?
LISBETH: Umm I am not quite sure what you mean?
THERAPIST: Shall we listen to that bit of conversation, I will play the recording?
LISBETH AND SEB: (together) okay.

(Therapist plays a few minutes of the recording of the conversation the couple have just had.)

THERAPIST: Now having heard the conversation, what did you notice?

LISBETH: We were being very hard on each other – blaming and finding fault.

THERAPIST: What did it feel like?

SEB: I have never looked at it that way, it did not feel nice listening to it.

LISBETH: No, it didn't, it makes me feel sad listening to it now.

THERAPIST: Listening to your conversation, it came across for me there was a lot of criticism and I wonder what may be driving that. Often underlying resentments can play out in how we speak. Unfortunately, this can mean that the resentment isn't actually addressed.

THERAPIST REFLECTION: Playing back a recording of the session to the couple might seem quite confronting and so this needs to be done with tact and after having established to good therapeutic relationship with both partners to avoid this being experienced as a form of shaming. Fortunately, in this case it seemed to me to be a useful and timely intervention as it helped them both take a different perspective on their communication style and set the stage for some more explicit work on changing this aspect of their relationship.

Middle phase

The middle phase of therapy involved consolidating work done in the initial stage with the aims of improving communication, building on the strengths of the relationship, and addressing the hoarding issues.

Communication

Once both Lisbeth and Seb started engaging in more activities together and there was an improvement in Lisbeth's mood, it felt appropriate to start addressing their communication difficulties as highlighted in the initial stage. Their lack of communication affected their relationship as they no longer shared their views or discussed their difficulties or the problems each faced. Instead, they tended to internalise their feelings, resulting in limited critical communication mainly expressing their dissatisfaction with their situation. There was little in the way of emotional or social support. For example, Seb had stopped asking Lisbeth how she felt, and Lisbeth had become more insular and distant. She never spoke to Seb about her loss, and this perpetuated her depression and sense of being alone. They both felt resentful towards the other and over time developed unhealthy communicating patterns.

Lisbeth and Seb were introduced to guidelines for sharing thoughts and feelings (see Chapter 2), which they found challenging. The concept of 'empathic' listening was new to them, and they were more in the habit of reacting to key 'hot' words. Role plays within the sessions were used to practice their communication with each other and 'sharing thoughts and feelings' exercises were a key homework task.

Once communication had improved, conversations moved on to trickier topics. Both partners were reminded to be sensitive and show compassion during these conversations and to engage with listening and feedback. This was the ideal opportunity to address the impact of the hoarding, as well as facilitate Lisbeth's grieving process for the death of her parents by sharing her experience with Seb.

THERAPIST: In the same spirit and attitude, I would like you to try this exercise. I would like to focus on the clutter and hoarding issue. Lisbeth let's start with you asking Seb how he feels about the situation at home, is that ok?

LISBETH: I feel nervous about it as I know it will make him angry.

THERAPIST: I hear that you feel nervous that Seb will get angry. Seb could I ask you first of all to listen to Lisbeth, let her know what you heard before responding. Can we try it?

LISBETH: How do you feel about the situation at home?

(Seb's voice becomes strained and he breaks eye contact with Lisbeth as he replies.)

SEB: I am very unhappy as I have no home, we had a lovely home now there is no home. I have no space and I can't bear to be there.

THERAPIST: Could you describe what its actually like for you? You seemed agitated when you mentioned "I have no space and I can't bear to be there"?

SEB: It is impossible to be comfortable. I cannot walk around without hitting into a pile of things that are all over the place.

THERAPIST: Could you tell Lisbeth more about how this feels for you, this experience of not being comfortable in your own home?

SEB: It feels horrible! I can't relax… there's no space for me…it doesn't feel like 'my' home, 'our' home anymore.

THERAPIST: Lisbeth, I would like you to let Seb know what you heard.

LISBETH: I hear that you're unhappy, you have no space and it's hard to relax, it doesn't feel like your home anymore and you can't bear to be there.

THERAPIST: Seb, do you feel Lisbeth has understood how this feels for you?

SEB: Yes, I think she does.

THERAPIST: Lisbeth let's put you into the speaker role now. Can you talk directly with Seb?

LISBETH: I am sorry you feel that way, I have a problem but I don't know how to cope.

THERAPIST: Could you tell us more about what you mean by not being able to cope?

LISBETH: All the stuff is too much but it means so much to me. I just don't know how to sort it out or what to do with it. I am afraid I will lose my connection with my parents, like I would be closing a door on the past if I got rid of things. I know it sounds strange, but in a way it would feel like a betrayal.

THERAPIST: Seb, let Lisbeth know what you heard.

SEB: I hear that you are sorry, that you have a problem and you don't know how to deal with it. It is only furniture! It means a lot to you and the items connect you with your parents and getting rid of the would seem 'wrong' in some way. I just don't understand that, as I don't associate items with my parents or family.

THERAPIST: Let's keep to what was said. Lisbeth was that a good summary?

LISBETH: Yes.

THERAPIST: Just checking if it was as bad as you thought it was going to be?

LISBETH: No, but I am afraid that it might be difficult at home.

THERAPIST: Yes it might be and that's understandable. Seb what was that like for you?

SEB: It's the first time I have said it without getting angry. I felt we were talking again.

THERAPIST: Can this be part of your homework to continue this conversation at home? At this stage don't rush into deciding actions – keep the focus on understanding what the clutter and hoarding mean to Lisbeth and checking out what do both of you want to change. Share your thoughts and feelings in the same way we did it in the session today.

What I like about you – addressing selective attention and inattention

One of Lisbeth and Seb's identified goals was to improve their relationship. It was important to help them recognise their engagement in therapy as a strong indicator of the value they placed on their relationship. They were encouraged to look out for positive aspects of their partner during the week and to feedback what they had noticed in the following therapy session. Refocusing attention on the aspects that attracted each partner to the other is an excellent means of helping individuals to reengage in their relationship helping them reconnect with the feelings they previously had for each other. They also became more aware of their strengths as a couple and how they could use these to make the relationship more resilient and enhance mutual support.

Cognitive restructuring and relationship with objects

As therapy progressed, Lisbeth's beliefs about her relationship with her possessions and also her relationship with Seb were identified and addressed. Lisbeth acknowledged having a life-long tendency to hoard, which she had managed well prior to her parents' deaths. Hoarding is a complex problem and cognitive restructuring around the significance of possessions for the individual is a slow process which must be undertaken sensitively, particularly in a couple context. A direct overly challenging or too rational-logical approach will often simply be met with resistance or avoidance and so more of a guided discovery approach is required.

THERAPIST: Lisbeth, we've talked about how your attachment with your objects has got stronger since your parents died and your relationship with Seb has become strained. I think it is important for us to try to understand your relationship with your objects better. What do your possessions mean to you? Let's look at this item. What does this item mean to you?

(The therapist points towards a small carved wooden box.)

LISBETH: It belonged to my mother. She loved it and told me about where she got it from. It brings back memories and feelings of being with my mother.

THERAPIST: It sounds like this little box has a really strong connection with your mother for you. Can you tell us a bit more?

LISBETH: That's right, and keeping it makes me feel like I'm staying connected to her in some way. The thought of letting it go feels a bit like I'm betraying my mother by breaking that connection.

THERAPIST: So that's really hard, letting go of the object feels in some way like a betrayal, like letting go of the relationship with her in some way that just feels terrible. Is that right?

LISBETH: I know it sounds strange to say it out loud. But that is how I feel.

THERAPIST: It sounds like you're in a difficult position, with so many things in your home that it's causing stress for you and Seb, yet thinking of letting go of some of them feels like a betrayal to your parents. Let's just pause for a moment and consider your relationship with Seb now, what does that relationship mean to you?

LISBETH: Well he's my husband and someone I love and care for inside.

THERAPIST: Ok, he's someone you love and care for. What's it like being in this relationship?

LISBETH: Well we've grown old together, we know each other well. I can tell when he is upset or angry without even speaking. He knows me and what I like or dislike.

THERAPIST: What does that feel like?

LISBETH: It's special. I can't describe it, I don't have words for it.

THERAPIST: That's interesting. And can I ask – that feeling you have about the items you save because they have special meaning for you – how does it compare to how you feel about your relationship with Seb?

LISBETH: It is very different. Both of them are important. I love Seb and I cannot imagine my life without him. My childhood stuff means a lot to me but I didn't think about it for a long time until I had to clear out my parents' home.

THERAPIST: Letting go is really hard. Facing loss. It makes me wonder…if letting go of an object could be done in a way that does not mean one is letting go of the connection, of memory and of feelings for the relationship? I suspect it would be scary for you to try that?

LISBETH: Yes it would. I'm not sure I can. But I have to try I think. Its driving Seb crazy and wrecking our relationship. I don't want to lose that.

THERAPIST: My hope would be that Seb and you could try this together, to help you face the anxiety about letting go of objects, and experiencing that this does not mean letting go of the emotional connection you have to your parents. What's this like for you to hear Seb?

SEB: It's a relief to hear. I want to help you with this Lisbeth. I struggle to understand why it's so hard for you to let go of all this stuff. I think I understand a bit better now. And we have to do something to change this. I want to know how to help you do that!

THERAPIST: That's really great to hear Seb. I have some ideas of how you can more effectively help Lisbeth with this. To encourage and support her through a process of letting go of objects and getting though some of the anxiety that that may provoke for her. I think if you approached this as a team you will make progress.

Dealing with hoarding

Once communication between Lisbeth and Seb had improved and discussions about the significance of Lisbeth's possessions had begun, we started to introduced the idea of decluttering in order to address the hoarding issues. This was done sensitively and very gradually alongside other conversations to help Lisbeth come to terms with the loss of her parents. Initially, this was practiced during the treatment session, supporting Lisbeth to 'take the risk' of discarding an object. The process was highly emotional (distressing and anxiety provoking) for both Lisbeth and Seb, and they were encouraged to use sharing thoughts and feelings exercises to share their experiences and identify ways to mutually support one another whilst undertaking the decluttering. During this I encouraged Seb to express support for Lisbeth and his faith in her ability to face these strong negative emotions and to nevertheless carry through with the discarding of the object.

As we progressed with this work, decluttering was incorporated into Lisbeth's activity schedule, so that she focused on decluttering a specific area for a time-limited period each day and followed this by engaging in a pleasurable joint activity with Seb. We agreed on what support Lisbeth needed from Seb around the decluttering (e.g. providing emotional support, helping to discard, transport, shared decision making), particularly when she was finding it a challenge to discard an item. Seb showed himself adept at providing good emotional and practical support, now that he has understood Lisbeth's experience more.

End phase

The final phase of treatment focused on consolidating the improvements Lisbeth and Seb had made with regard to their communication, developing a plan for dealing with the ongoing hoarding issues, and preparing for setbacks.

Progress, communication, and relapse prevention

Each therapy session began with a bridge from the previous one and a homework review, thus reviewing interventions that had a positive impact on the relationship, identifying difficulties, and reinforcing the need for continued practice as part of the relapse prevention plan, especially where difficulties were encountered. We continued to explore the interplay between the partners' emotions, cognitions and behaviours, both individually and interpersonally. For example, both tended to engage in 'emotional reasoning', and they were encouraged to ask more questions rather than making assumptions or jumping to conclusions. The improvements in Lisbeth and Seb's communication skills helped them gain confidence in their ability to manage conflicts, and they were also more able to accept that conflict is a normal experience that happens in other relationships. They were encouraged to consider potential future challenges for their relationship and to continue to develop skills in problem solving and negotiation in order to address these.

Hoarding issues

Progress in addressing Lisbeth's hoarding issues was reviewed on a regular basis and it was clear that the couple would need to continue to work on this problem post-therapy. As mentioned above, a regular schedule to declutter was put in place. This provided some structure for the ongoing work and assisted with time management. The work on helping Lisbeth and Seb to negotiate, communicate and challenge the assumptions they made around the possessions and Lisbeth's need to hold on to them was vital in making progress. For example, during sessions they discussed the rationale for keeping or discarding items and this helped them to challenge some of their beliefs. Whilst working with the hoarding issues, Lisbeth was encouraged to engage with the feelings she has for Seb as they are in the present, and not related to the past as are the feelings she has about her objects. Lisbeth was encouraged to share her feelings and concerns with Seb whilst decluttering as it was an emotionally challenging activity for her. This also reinforced the importance of being open and honest with each other in their relationship. Seb was encouraged to remain in a listening role when needed and to express support for Lisbeth's ability to continue with this exposure work and decluttering. Of some importance was his willingness to refrain from directly challenging Lisbeth's thoughts in a critical or overly logical way.

Discussion

Hoarding disorder is a complex psychological condition which is difficult to address in any therapy. Hoarding issues can occur in the context of difficult relationships with partners, families and the wider interpersonal context and can exacerbate pre-existing relationship distress. This needs to be considered when assessing and planning an intervention to address the hoarding problems. It is also prudent to consider the sequencing of interventions over a course of treatment. Addressing hoarding too early in therapy could lead to disengagement if a strong therapeutic relationship has not been established. When the problem is long-standing, long-term work may be required to deal with both the clutter and the underlying mechanisms that drive the problem.

It is important to work collaboratively and to make an explicit agreement regarding whether or not hoarding will be addressed in treatment. This includes discussing what the specific goals and tasks of therapy will be. One of the major areas of focus in a couple-based intervention is communication, and ensuring the partners can communicate in a clear and constructive manner about sensitive issues is essential before the focus can move to the hoarding issue. Interventions around communication need to focus on showing mutual respect and promote a non-threatening, non-judgemental, and compassionate communication style, which allows the individuals to take the stance of curiosity to facilitate exploration and cognitive restructuring. For the non-hoarding partner, the hoarding behaviour can seem highly irrational and this can pull for critical, judgemental responses. Helping the partner to understand the experience of hoarding and the distress associated with letting go of objects is essential, as is learning effective ways to communicate support and encouragement for engaging in the exposure work.

Recent studies indicate that CBT is the intervention of choice for the treatment of hoarding. However, a meta-analysis by Tolin et al. (2015) found poor maintenance of therapy gains following the end of treatment. Given the impact of hoarding on partners and family members and the well-documented bi-directional relationship between relationship distress and psychopathology, there is clearly scope for couple-based interventions to be more widely used in the treatment of hoarding issues. Individuals often find it extremely difficult to address hoarding on their own, and engaging a partner in treatment can provide much needed support as well as offering the opportunity to address the partner's role in maintaining the problem. Helping the couple to develop a shared understanding of the problem and improving their communication, so that relationship distress can be addressed, and the non-hoarding partner can support the treatment plan to address hoarding would be likely to enhance treatment outcomes and their long term maintenance.

Reflections

The therapist should have a good understanding of hoarding disorder and the treatment protocol. Being non-judgemental and accepting the significance, value and meaning of the items collected and saved regardless of their utility is important to engage with individuals fully. It is important to remember that each presentation of hoarding is different, and an idiosyncratic formulation needs to be developed collaboratively with both partners to aid joint understanding. The therapist's own self-reflection is important to ensure their own prejudices, attitude feelings towards the clutter is not conveyed negatively in the session whilst remaining objective. Active use of guided discovery can help clients to reflect on their hoarding behaviour and the impact it has on others such as their partner. Sessions may be challenging and at times frustrating and the therapist needs to be able to manage this and promote realistic expectations for therapy. Progress is often slow, and it is important to help the couple to remain positive and to recognise gains regardless of their magnitude and focus on how they can build on these.

Therapist tips

- Clearly define the therapist's role, the nature of therapy and everyone's expectations.
- Ensure that a comprehensive assessment of the hoarding issues is undertaken, especially beliefs around the role the possessions play for the individual.
- Developing a collaborative formulation is essential to guide therapy. The formulation is dynamic and expanded with new information and observations.
- Agreeing on the goals and priorities will need skilful management as there may be conflicting priorities between partners.
- Identify the resources within the relationship.
- Be explicit about the challenges of therapy especially in dealing with the hoarding issues.
- Only attend to the hoarding issues once there is good enough communication between the partners, where they are able to express and negotiate their needs safely without feeling criticised, judged or that their views are disregarded.
- Foster good communication between both partners, both by developing their expressive and problem-solving skills and also by fostering guided discovery when dealing with hoarding to develop mutual aid, and support in dealing with challenges.

- Encourage discussion of challenges, stressful experiences, and difficulties in discarding cherished items with the aim of fostering support from the partner.
- Encourage the use of activity scheduling during the sorting and clearing process, alternating with other tasks and pleasurable activities, particularly those that improve self-care and reduce isolation.
- Celebrate the space that is reclaimed by both partners and encourage them to use the space and engage in activities that are pleasurable, for example dancing, rearranging the furniture, or decorating.

Suggestions for further Reading

Singh. S., Hooper, M., & Jones, C. (2015). *Overcoming Hoarding: A Self Help Guide Using Cognitive Behavioural Techniques.* London: Robinson Press.

References

Abramowitz, J.S, Baucom D.H., Wheaton, M.G., Boeding, S., Fabricant, L.E., Psproki, C.*et al.* (2013). Enhancing exposure and response prevention for OCD: a couple-based approach. *Behaviour Modification*, 37, 189–210.

Baucom, D.H., Whisman, M.A., & Paprocki, C. (2012). Couple-based interventions for psychopathology. *Journal of Family Therapy*, 34, 250–270.

Baucom, D. H., Fischer, M. S., Corrie, S., Worrell, M., & Boeding, S (2020). *Treating relationship distress and psychopathology in couples: a cognitive behavioural approach.* London: Routledge.

Drury, H., Ajmi, S., Fernandez de la Cruz, L., Nordsletten, A.E., & Mataix-Cols, D. (2014). Caregiver burden, family accommodation, health, and well-being in relatives of individuals with hoarding disorder. *Journal of Affective Disorders*, 159, 7–14.

Fischer, M.S., Baucom, D.H., Hahlweg, K., & Epstein, N.B. (2013). Couple Therapy. *The Wiley Handbook of Cognitive Behavioural Therapy. Chapter 30, p.* 704. London: Wiley-Blackwell.

Fromm, E. (1947). *Man for himself: An inquiry into the psychology of ethics.* New York: Rinehart.

Frost, R.O. & Gross, R.C. (1993). The hoarding of possessions. *Behaviour Research and Therapy*, 31, 367–381.

Frost, R.O. & Hartl, T. (1996). A cognitive-behavioural model of compulsive hoarding. *Behaviour Research and Therapy*, 34, 341–350.

Frost, R.O., Hartl, T., Christian, R., & William, N. (1995). The value of possessions in compulsive hoarding: Patterns of use and attachment. *Behaviour Research and Therapy*, 33, 897–902.

Grisham, J.R., Martyn, C., Kerin, F., Balwin, P.A., & Norberg, M.M. (2018). Interpersonal functioning in Hoarding Disorder: An examination of attachment styles and emotion regulation in response to interpersonal stress. *Journal of Obsessional-Compulsive and Related Disorders*, 16, 43–49.

Neave, N., Jackson, R., Saxton, T., & Honekopp, J. (2015). The influence of anthropomorphic tendencies on human hoarding behaviours. *Personality and Individual Differences*, 72, 214–219.

Tolin, D.F., Frost, R.O., Steketee, G., & Fitch, K.E. (2008). Family Burden of Compulsive Hoarding: Results of an Internet Survey. *Behaviour Research Therapy*, 46 (3), 334–344.

Tolin, D.F., Frost, R.O., Steketee, G., & Muroff, J. (2015). Cognitive Behavioural Therapy for Hoarding Disorder: A Meta-Analysis. *Depression and Anxiety*, 32 (3), 158–166.

Timpano, K.R. & Shaw A.M. (2013). Conferring humanness: The role of anthropomorphism in hoarding. *Personality and Individual Differences*, 54 (3), 383–388.

Wilbram, M., Kellett, S., & Beail, N. (2008). Compulsive hoarding: A qualitative investigation of partner and carer perspectives. *British Journal of Clinical Psychology*, 47, 59–73.

Chapter 12

Personality Disorder

"We Love and Hate Each Other with Passion"

Rita Woo

I was waiting outside the consulting room to meet Toby and Margot for the first time. Shortly a smiling, handsome, casually but well-dressed man bounded up the stairs, looked me in the eyes and greeted me enthusiastically. Despite this, there was a sense of detachment. Margot, an equally well-dressed woman followed, slowly making her way up the stairs. She had a face like thunder. She looked me up and down and nodded to acknowledge my presence. The outward contrast between the two could not have been starker. I already felt dazed by the different emotions and their intensity and was wary about starting the session, but at the same time extremely curious and excited. How could that be? I was uncertain that 'excited' truly captured what I felt, but whilst there was rage, disappointment, hurt, and cold distance, there was also a sense of determination. I was unsure whether this was mine or theirs, but there was also an energy, and with energy, there is hope.

Emotional regulation difficulties and couple therapy

'Emotional vulnerability', a sensitivity to experiencing intense emotions, and a reactivity to these without effective strategies to regulate them and re-establish an emotional equilibrium can result in unhelpful and sometimes destructive behaviours that can greatly affect an individual's quality of life (Linehan, 1993). Within the couple context, a partner's high emotional vulnerability, reactivity, and dysregulation can lead to conflict or other unhelpful patterns of interaction, and over-time the couple can become increasingly sensitive and reactive to each other. As interactional patterns become more entrenched, any constructive way of communicating and engaging the other diminishes, and increasing emotional distance, lack of intimacy, and relationship distress ensues (Fruzzetti & Payne, 2015). It was within this context that Toby & Margot reached out for couple therapy.

Toby & Margot

Following the general principles and processes suggested in CBCT (Baucom et al., 2020), I met with Toby and Margot as a couple for our first session as

DOI: 10.4324/9781003024439-14

part of my private practice. After entering the therapy room, the couple sat at opposite ends of the couch, each person squarely facing me directly. There was however a flatness that had not been so evident moments earlier. When I asked, *"Tell me, what brings you both to couple therapy at this stage in your lives?"*, both Margot and Toby stared at me. Instead of the two outwardly different presentations of their emotional worlds I had encountered outside the therapy room, in front of me were two people who seemed sad, lost, and drained. After a brief moment of silence, Toby, who had initiated the therapy appointment replied, *"I'll go first so Margot has time to calm down"*. Margot was bristling at Toby's words and I could sense her anger starting to bubble again. She looked at me as if to say, *"You're going to let him say that?"* Toby continued, *"We love each other a lot, really a lot, but have some major issues with communication and at times it has turned downright ugly. Neither one of us is a saint and we both have our own stuff but we can't go on like this. It constantly feels like we can explode anytime. We're a high-conflict couple but we really want to put in the hard work to change things and don't want our child growing up in this nasty environment"*. As Toby was speaking, I could sense Margot's restlessness and before there was any opportunity either for Toby to continue or for me to ask further questions, Margot spoke, *"That's right, it's always me that starts fights, calm down, what do you mean calm down? You make me mad, always coming across as the reasonable one that everybody likes, why don't you tell Rita what you did last night? Go on, why don't you tell her? Calm down! Why don't you tell her what you do when we argue, not so Mr Reasonable nice guy then, are we?"*

The session had only just begun and already I felt tired and like I had been hit by a train, resulting in dizziness and concussion, affecting my ability to think, process and understand the panoply of emotions erupting without warning, as well as the sudden change in atmosphere which contributed to a sense of cautiousness in asking more questions. The latter is not something I usually have difficulty with! I wondered whether this was what it might feel like for the couple on a daily basis and got a sense of the challenges ahead. Whilst there was certainly energy in the room, alongside the sense of hope that was initially present was a sense of despair. The patterns felt and observed in the first ten minutes of the initial session epitomised what was to follow.

Toby, 40, and Margot 35, stated that their relationship had been very good in the past, but currently those very good times were being increasingly replaced by 'war'. It was Margot who described the event that contributed to her anger before the session. She stated that Toby had agreed to leave work early yesterday so that he could take care of their son while she went to the gym followed by a drink with friends. She said this was the first time since their two-year old had been born that she had asked for 'time off' and felt able to do something that she had previously enjoyed. However, in the afternoon, Toby called to say that due to an urgent meeting at work he could not come home early as planned, but he had asked his mother to help instead.

At this stage, Toby chimed in and pointed out that before he could say anything else, he had received a string of profanities and so he had ended the call. In the session, he stated that he could not understand why Margot became so angry about something so minor when he had made alternative arrangements. Margot glared at him, and stated *"Do you think I'm stupid? I know about the work that you do, remember, I used to work in the same area before having YOUR child. There is nothing that comes up that is urgent, the Asian markets are fucking closed! You just single-handedly made that decision! But Rita, that's not the worst of it, he fucking goes drinking with his mates and comes home reeking of alcohol at one in the morning! I call and text him throughout the evening and he just ignores me and then turns off his phone!"* Toby added that by the time he saw the numerous messages, it was late so he had decided not to call.

When he came home, he did not want to wake the family so decided to stay downstairs and sleep on the sofa. However, he added that before long, he heard Margot come downstairs and then an argument ensued. Margot stated that when she came downstairs, Toby was looking at his mobile and at that stage described that her *"blood was boiling"* and a barrage of accusations followed, *"you're an irresponsible husband and father, you don't care about anybody else but yourself, you're selfish and inconsiderate, would you like your son to grow up like you and abandon his wife and child?"* Toby said that he could see Margot was angry and did not want to provoke her further, so he decided to go to the kitchen to get some water. However, he also felt that Margot's criticism of him was unjust. Moments later he felt a magazine fly past his ear, and he reported that at that moment he snapped. A mutual exchange of insults and accusations followed. There was so much noise that their son started to cry and the neighbours phoned them to see whether everything was ok.

Margot then went storming back upstairs and Toby remained downstairs on the sofa. Margot stated that in that moment, she *"hated Toby with a passion"* and Toby stated that Margot *"was acting like a crazy woman"*. Toby left for work in the morning without saying a word to Margot as he needed to *"get on with things"*, and Margot was left in tears. She cried in the session when recounting the incident and asked Toby *"How can you be so heartless and carry on like nothing has happened?"* On hearing this, Toby who previously seemed indifferent started to sob.

The couple had first met eight years ago when Toby was based in Asia and Margot was there for three months. They both worked in finance, and were introduced to each other by friends. Their attraction was instant, and they spent the rest of the evening in each other's company. Margot was attracted to Toby's good looks, smile, fun, and easy-going but calm nature. Toby was equally attracted by Margot's good looks, sense of humour and intelligence.

They bonded over their shared love for books, theatre, travel and 'enjoying life', and their work was also a shared topic of interest. They fell in love quickly. As time went on, Margot also appreciated Toby's decisiveness and sense of responsibility, and he, her ability to 'keep him on his toes'.

When recounting this, both wondered how they managed to focus on their demanding workloads during the dating period. Toby recalled not being able to wait until the next time they met, and when they were apart, he was constantly thinking about her. He added that he *"loved Margot with passion"* and Margot described the period as *"a heady mix of desire, alcohol and unadulterated fun"*. This was the only time in the session where Margot and Toby physically moved to sit closer to each other, and there was shared laughter and light touches. I did not have to work hard at all to elicit positive emotions and the couple's attraction to each other was palpable. In fact, once they started talking about the early stages of their relationship, it was hard for them to stop. It almost felt like this was the one part of the relationship that they needed to hold onto to make the current pain they were both feeling more bearable and perhaps worthwhile.

Listening to them retell their interactional pattern from the previous night felt like watching a drama where I was taken on a roller-coaster ride of emotions. I felt exhausted and wanted to come off that ride, probably like Toby and Margot too. I liked both of them as individuals, as well as a couple, and was hopeful that CBCT would help with their distress and reduce, although I would like to think also repair, some of the more damaging aspects of their interaction. At the end of the session, Margot stated, *"Rita, we love and hate each other with passion"*.

Margot

Margot was born in the States and is the youngest of two siblings. Her father was a hugely successful surgeon who invented some ground-breaking medical equipment, and her mother was an economist. Margot described home as being cold and her parents distant, as they were focused on work and they rarely got involved in their children's lives. She described feeling forgotten and abandoned and managed these feelings by being busy with after-school activities. She stated that she became independent at a young age but when her peers talked about their family with warmth, Margot too craved this warmth and closeness. At weekends, her parents would insist that they cancel any plans made so that they could spend time as a family, and initially Margot looked forward to these occasions where she could share her life with her parents. However, when Margot started to talk about school, her parents did not listen and sometimes interrupted her so that they could discuss the news or their work. Even dropping cutlery or arguing with her sister did not stop their parent's discussions. Instead she was often criticised for arguing, and her parents would just talk over the children and eventually shout at them or send them to their rooms. On these occasions, she felt angry and hurt but was resigned to the situation. She also felt she and her sister were an 'accessory' that made their parents' lives look perfect. When Margot described feeling upset, her parents responded with *"what's so upsetting about that? It's life so don't be so feeble and get on with it"*. When Margot was older, they expected her to participate in discussions around the dinner table and when she did not show an interest, they expressed their disappointment in her and stated, *"Who would have thought you were our daughter"*. She forced herself to read philosophy books but was actually more interested in art and fashion. She stated that she also studied hard in the hope of gaining her parents acknowledgement, but this was not forthcoming despite graduating from an Ivy League university and eventually working in a large international financial organisation. Margot did however, experience care, warmth, and kindness from an aunt.

Toby

Toby has a sister who is two years younger. His Dad was French and his mother Chinese, and he was born and grew up in France and identified as being 'Western'. Before his parents' separation when Toby was eight, there were frequent fights between his parents, which were worse when his father was under the influence of alcohol. He recalled his father leaving and saying, *"you can take the children, I don't want them"*, and he wondered whether there was something 'faulty' about him. After his father left, he stated that life was tough as the family were not well off financially and he had to grow up quickly. He recalled being bullied at school but tolerated it as he did not want to worry his mother, who saw him as *"my boy, my support"*. The bullying stopped after he could no longer tolerate it and retaliated using taekwondo. He described this as *"payback time for all the disrespect"* and said that he felt *"special and powerful"*.

Toby added that he had a loving relationship with his sister, but when she argued with him, his mother would say *"don't disrespect your brother, he's the man of the house"*. Toby stated that whilst it felt great that his mother appreciated him, he also felt that he must have done something wrong for his loving sister to argue with him. He recalled feeling guilty and described a sense of self-hatred for arguing with her and said that after arguments he would either avoid his sister or go out of his way to make amends. As he grew older, his sense of responsibility for his family grew along with his need for respect and appreciation. Toby also grew to look like his father, something his mother would continually remind him about.

Both Margot and Toby valued trust, respect, and intimacy in relationships. Autonomy and achievement were also important for them as individuals. Margot valued reliability and stability, which were partly achieved by discussion, thought, careful planning and consideration of all possibilities, and Toby valued efficiency, 'getting things done', and only problem-solving when needed, as well as respect. Whilst a part of me could understand the importance of respect in a relationship for Toby, I did wonder whether he really meant 'appreciation'. The couple denied the occurrence of domestic violence.

Meeting Margot and Toby individually enabled me to gain a more detailed picture of their personal and relational histories and backgrounds that might have shaped their individual needs and expectations in a relationship. This is part of the assessment process in CBCT (Baucom et al., 2020). In addition, it was also helpful to understand each individual's family interactions, including the factors that may have contributed to the development of emotional dysregulation, and any attempts, helpful and unhelpful, to manage this, as well as listening out for accurate and inaccurate expression of emotions and invalidating and validating responses (Fruzzetti & Payne, 2020).

Understanding the couple

The couple's difficulties were understood with consideration of factors at an individual, couple, and environmental level (Baucom et al., 2020). The role played by emotional vulnerability, heightened emotional arousal, inaccurate expression including of secondary emotions, and invalidation (Fruzzetti, 2006) in forming unhelpful patterns of interaction that do little to meet individual or the couple's needs was also considered.

Toby described Margot and himself as being a *"high-conflict couple"*, and their pattern of interaction did seem to fit this picture, where the pervasive pattern of interaction is characterised by conflict involving verbal and sometimes physical aggression, rigid beliefs about the other, together with reciprocal negativity such as blame, criticism, and lack of empathy which escalates into a cycle of attack and counterattack that becomes more entrenched over time (Anderson et al., 2011). Moreover, it was hypothesised that underlying this interaction was high emotional vulnerability and emotional dysregulation.

Margot had grown up in an environment where love and closeness might be associated with doing what others wanted, with her own needs and sense of enjoyment being ignored, her self being engulfed (Greenberg, 2016), and her emotions invalidated. So, when Toby called to say that he was not coming home as planned, Margot experienced an immediate sense of anger, as yet again no one was considering what she wanted. This gave her a sense that she did not matter, even though Toby had made alternative arrangements so that she could still carry on with her evening as planned. She saw Toby as being selfish, inconsiderate and a bad husband and father, and this rigid negative judgement of him further fuelled her anger. This was exacerbated by his avoidance of her calls and text messages. So, when he came home drunk and in her view had enjoyed his evening, she exploded with a verbal and physical attack of his character.

Toby's view of himself as a responsible man and father, and his tendency to avoid conflict, contributed to him not replying to Margot's messages and when he found himself on the receiving end of her verbal attack, his need to be respected was triggered and he felt little inclination to try to understand her hurt and disappointment, and instead felt angry that he was being treated unfairly. Given his value to only deal with things when necessary, together with his interpersonal style of shying away from conflict and distress, he tried to avoid Margot, but when the magazine came flying past his ear, he erupted and returned her anger with the same intensity.

Thus, an initial demand-withdraw interaction pattern turned into one of mutual attack and as this continued, each partner's level of emotional arousal increased, causing them not only to temporarily forget that the person that they were attacking and the person that they loved were the same, but also preventing them from listening to, empathising with, and understanding the other. The description of their interaction resonated with them and I felt sad that this couple had ended up in this situation and wanted to do my best to help them. Both were always regretful afterwards and felt guilty and ashamed for *"behaving like a monster"*. Unfortunately, the interactional patterns that the couple were engaged in heightened their vulnerability to negative emotional reactivity in future situations. There was some hope, however, as there were the rare occasions when they enjoyed a glass of wine together and Toby would share his work stress with Margot, which made her feel competent and intelligent like her old self again before she had stopped working. These moments reminded them of their previous life in Asia.

THERAPIST REFLECTION: I got the impression that this couple experienced the emotions related to conflict as being unbearable, Toby perhaps seeing himself as being less than perfect and experiencing a sense of guilt and self-hatred; and Margot perhaps seeing herself as being 'bad'. I felt anxious and questioned my skills in being able to help this couple, as well as guilty that perhaps they would do better with another therapist.

Treatment

Toby and Margot wanted to stop fighting and hurting each other and to communicate better. These goals, together with my understanding of the couple and the principles of CBCT guided our work. In addition, specific DBT strategies were used to help the couple develop emotional regulation skills (Fruzzetti, 2006; Kirby & Baucom, 2007). These included individual mindfulness and emotional regulation skills, relationship mindfulness, validation, and acceptance and closeness. Thus, the treatment aimed to address both emotional dysregulation and relationship dynamics. Some of the areas of focus addressed in treatment are described below.

Increasing positives and reducing negatives

As Toby and Margot had moments where they enjoyed each other's company, we worked towards increasing these times that were focused on individual interests that they could share with the other person. To help the couple develop relationship mindfulness, they also explored how they could hold in mind that the other person was someone they cared about and loved. While they were engaging in enjoyable activities together, they were encouraged to pay attention to what they were doing, to how each person as an individual was feeling, how the other person was reacting, and how the two of them were interacting. As Margot was doing a diploma in wine tasting, the couple also suggested that Margot could share her developing knowledge of wine with Toby, whilst also enjoying a glass, something that conjured up positive memories for both of them.

THERAPIST REFLECTION: I was initially hesitant about this idea and felt slightly anxious, but I did not know why and could not come up with questions or ways to explore this at the time, as I was swept up by their enthusiasm and energy whilst discussing this. I had also not asked in depth about their alcohol and substance use but got the impression that their drinking was not excessive. However, alcohol was something that triggered traumatic memories for the couple as I was to discover in later sessions.

Whilst I did not want to focus on Margot as I did not want her to feel blamed for the interactional patterns both of them got into, she did seem to experience intense emotions which quickly spiralled, so I wanted to increase her ability to manage these. She recognised when she was starting to "bubble" and agreed at these times to engage in activities that would trigger a different emotion. For example, this could involve being mindful of the present moment by either describing the act of cooking or any activity via the five senses, mindful colouring, smelling a fragrance and then trying to describe the top, middle and base notes, or playing with Lego. Margot noted that these activities were certainly easier to do when she first started to feel uneasy, and by the time she was focused on Toby's perceived faults, they became harder to engage in.

The results of increasing time together were mixed. Discussion about a financial article went well, as Margot rediscovered glimmers of her competent and confident self which Toby found sexy, and he enjoyed the intellectual 'sparring'. Some of the relationship mindfulness exercises ended in cahoots of laughter. Whilst this was experienced by the couple as being positive, I wondered whether it had been difficult for them to focus on themselves and the other, without the pervasive negative judgements about the other being triggered. They reported largely abandoning these tasks.

However, more unexpectedly for me, the wine related task went horribly downhill very quickly and triggered the established pattern of mutual attack, with Toby storming out of the house and checking-in to a hotel for the night. Following this, we decided to move on to communication and to explore the mutual attack and demand-withdrawal patterns in more depth.

Communication – Sharing thoughts and feelings

Whilst it was clear that high levels of emotional arousal and negative reciprocity affected the couple's ability to communicate effectively with each other, I also wondered about their ability to listen and to describe their emotional experiences accurately. There was very little in their developmental histories to suggest that they had developed these skills, and their relationship had progressed very quickly. After 3 months of dating, Toby had been relocated to another Asian country and although he had known about this before starting his relationship with Margot, he had not shared this. He asked Margot to join him and she willingly agreed and resigned from her job. She had enacted a familiar pattern of forfeiting her own needs whilst chasing closeness with Toby. The couple seemed to have experienced intense and satisfying closeness in a short period, but I felt that this intimacy was fragile with both being vulnerable to any slight perceived changes in this. Furthermore, the couple had minimal experience of discussing emotions and difficulties before living together. It was at this point in their relationship that the couple experienced an event which laid the foundations for the interactions patterns that developed and the heightened emotional sensitivity and negative reciprocity to follow.

Due to the new job, Toby was working incredibly long hours and leaving Margot in their home with little apart from household chores to occupy her. She experienced difficulties making new friends as she did not speak the local language and was not interested to learn. Toby often came home tired and reluctant to talk to Margot, and he spent most of the weekends recovering from the week or playing football with his colleagues to unwind. Resentment accumulated in Margot, who wanted to have fun with Toby during the weekends. His long work hours also meant that he was eating take-outs at the company and as he was rarely exercising, he had gained weight. The couple had also stopped having sex. One evening, Toby returned home after an impromptu night out with colleagues. This was one of the evenings where he had agreed to finish work early so that he and Margot could spend some time together. However, the team which Toby belonged to decided to meet after work as it was the head of department's birthday. On hearing this, Toby had contacted Margot wanting to invite her to join them. Unfortunately, she missed the call and did not check her phone until later on in the evening. When Toby eventually returned home, he was met by a furious Margot, and before long a heated argument ensued which culminated in Toby's belongings being broken and his clothes being cut to shreds. The below conversation took place after a previous experience of sharing thoughts and feelings.

THERAPIST: Margot, you have talked in passing about moving to a new country to be with Toby, and Toby... you don't mention it at all. What happened?

There was a sudden silence in the room and a breaking of eye contact before Margot began...

MARGOT: Toby had just started a different job and we had moved in together. At first, everything was great, we had a lovely place and I could enjoy not working. I spent the day decorating our new place, shopping, going to the gym, painting, and cooking, I felt close to Toby, we loved each other's company and I was happy that I could support him in his new role. Sometimes he was working from 8 until 9 or 10 at night, which was insane and I could see that he was stressed. As I was busy I didn't mind not seeing or being with other people, but as time went on, I was getting unhappier and more frustrated with staying at home. I didn't have friends as I didn't speak the language and felt handicapped by this, and Toby was continuing with his insane hours, leaving me alone for long stretches of the day. When he came back, he was too tired to do anything, not even eat when I had spent so much time making stuff for him. I didn't mind and it was ok, as I thought that it would get better as Toby said that once he's more settled, he can work less.

As Margot was describing the situation, I could see her shrink further into the couch and she came across as increasingly depressed. I felt compassion for her yet at the same time frustration with her helplessness about learning a new language and willingness to completely change her life for Toby. It felt as if there was tension between Toby's needs and desires versus her needs and desires without the consideration of both, as well as a tension between Toby's needs and the relationship needs. I observed a slight furrowing of the eyebrows in Toby as well as a clenching of the jaw and I wondered whether this reflected a sense of increasing irritation.

TOBY: I was doing my best for us and was really stressed, I thought you understood...
MARGOT: Hm...I could see that you were busy and stressed and I might have been living with you but we weren't really doing anything... even on weekends, you were too tired to go out and have fun and I was beginning to wonder whether it was all worth it. You were just not there and we were not having sex anymore... I cooked for you and you were eating take outs in the office and you were putting on weight...

TOBY: You were, you were, you were, all I am hearing is that I did everything wrong, I made all the mistakes, whilst you were Miss Perfect, cooking and cleaning and waiting for me to come home, it's this poor me again...

THERAPIST: Ok, let's pause for a moment, before we continue, I would like to invite you both to notice what is going on for you right now, in this very moment. Margot when you were talking about being at home, not going out at weekends, what were you feeling?

MARGOT: I see red, I'm at home during the weekdays and HE can't be bothered to spend time with me during the weekends after I move half-way around the world to be with him...

THERAPIST: Tell Toby why you moved half-way around the world to be with him...

MARGOT: I beginning to regret it now, I'm wondering what it was all for.

THERAPIST: What is it that you regret the most?

MARGOT: Fury at...

TOBY: You see, it's totally....

THERAPIST: Toby, I'm going to interrupt you there, what do you think you can do right now to help you put your feelings on pause for a bit so that we can work towards the both of you understanding each other more and show Margot that you are willing to listen although it might be difficult to?

We had discussed strategies to manage a level of arousal before. For Toby, this involved thinking about the five tenets of taekwondo, a sport that he derived considerable pleasure from and associated with more positive emotions. He would then think about how he could apply one of the five tenets in the rest of the day, and one of these tenets was self-control.

THERAPIST REFLECTION: I felt ambivalent about asking Toby to do this, which was partly driven by the need to 'do something' whilst recognising his tendency to over-regulate and then for his feelings to accumulate before finally exploding, in the same way that he had managed the bullying at school. For Toby, I hypothesised that anger and rage were triggered when there were feelings of inadequacy or insecurity. Nonetheless, I encouraged him to 'pause' with the hope of being able to elicit a softer emotion from both him and Margot and to slow the pace down. In hindsight, I think that Toby might have felt blamed and criticised.

THERAPIST: Margot, we were talking about you moving half-way round the world to be with Toby and then fury, when thinking about what you regret the most....

MARGOT: Why did you suddenly get all angry for nothing?

TOBY: Angry for nothing?! (Toby was beginning to raise his voice.) You're always like this. Yes, that's right of course you're the only one whose life changed, who had to make all the sacrifices, what about me? I was working all the time, tired and stressed and you were at home doing nothing, did you think about me? All you do is nag, nag, nag... we don't do this, we don't do that, you're so needy. I'm so tired of listening to the same old story. I just don't want to do this anymore.

Toby, whilst still looking at Margot, started to move further away from her. Margot had noticed this and she squared up to face him, at which point Toby moved even further away to the end of the sofa. He also turned his face slightly away from her and angled his body more towards me. I felt him beginning to withdraw emotionally, no longer entirely present in the session, and felt that I was losing him. Margot did too.

MARGOT: And you think I do? You think I enjoy this? You never listen, you don't even try, you're so selfish and a bad lover...

(Margot was getting more animated and her voice was getting louder.)

TOBY: You bitch, you...
THERAPIST: Ok stop (with a very firm but calm tone). Let's stop right there before you end up hurting each other more. Words said in the heat of the moment that can't be taken back, words that you both hold onto afterwards, words that actually push the other person away instead of bringing you closer. (I take a breath and pause to change the pace and to build in a miniscule break.) What do both of you notice in your body right now? Tell me, describe to me what you notice in your body.
MARGOT: My heart is going to jump out of my body, I'm seeing red, I'm clenching my fists.
TOBY: It's hard for me to say, you see Rita, we always end up here, Margot just loses it, she's just unreasonable...
THERAPIST: (interrupting Toby) I know that you are trying really hard to do your best for the relationship and get angry when you don't feel appreciated, so when that happens, what do you feel in your body?
TOBY: I'm feeling really uncomfortable, my head is about to explode.
THERAPIST: It seems that both of you are getting angrier and angrier with each other and want to get your point across but in doing so, have lost the ability to listen to each other. Toby, it's hard when you hear or feel blamed for something that you don't think is justified or fair to not to put things right (short pause). Margot for you, you're trying extra hard to feel heard and say things to get Toby's attention (short pause), but both of you trying to do that at the same time means that you end up attacking each other. Once that happens, there's a point of no return and you don't get to say what you really want the other person to understand. (I remain silent for a short while in the hope that they can reflect on what has occurred and I also use the time to gather my thoughts.) When you experienced those sensations, what was going through your mind?

Addressing unhelpful patterns of interaction

The above conversation was fairly typical of the sessions with Toby and Margot, with any attempt to discuss their needs and vulnerabilities very quickly escalating into a mutual attack pattern, which in turn contributed to their negativity about the marriage. I could sense the build up of tension between the two of them and it could go from that to an eruption in a blink of an eye, simultaneously leaving me feeling powerless to do anything about it whilst also working hard to minimise the damage and pain caused by and to them both. Whilst the pain they both felt motivated the couple to work towards what they valued in a loving and supportive relationship, at times it almost felt as if this dance they were engaged in was so entrenched that experiencing a different way of relating to each other felt too frightening. On these occasions I felt silenced by the couple, who would shout over me as if they were rebuffing my attempts to help them express other feelings apart from anger, and perhaps this was safer territory than being vulnerable. At times I also felt that Toby was trying to change the course of the conversation, perhaps to avoid any threat to the self (Janusz, Bergmann, Matusiak, & Peräkylä, 2021). Moreover, behind his need to be appreciated and respected might have been the fear of being a failure and less than perfect, and when this need was not met anger and withdrawal ensued, the latter related to his view of Margot as being 'unreasonable' and 'crazy'. This is turn increased Margot's fear of abandonment. For Margot, beneath her ineffective attempts at engaging Toby might have been her fears about being worthless, unloved, and unlovable, and afraid of being abandoned by Toby and believing him to be 'bad'. Anxiety tended to follow her anger.

With these hypotheses in my mind and the idea that emotional regulation promotes connection (Fruzzetti, 2006), I persisted with trying to reduce the hostility between the couple by trying to slow down the pace of the session every time I sensed tension, and by reflecting back their pattern of interaction of mutual attack. I soon became a part of this couple's dance. At times this was somewhat successful, and at others the mood in the session would change from hostility to despair, with Toby commenting on how difficult and boring having the same conversations repeatedly felt. It took many more sessions of sharing thoughts and feelings, encouraging Margot's use of mindfulness-based and self-soothing strategies (practising these with her in the session, as well as her practising outside the session), and helping both partners to label their emotions and notice what was occurring cognitively and physiologically, before the exploration of relationship expectations and individual beliefs, and eventually a discussion about the incident that resulted in Toby's clothes being cut to shred and his belongings being smashed could occur. Additionally, whilst at times I felt irritated with Toby by his cutting remarks and criticism about Margot and felt that I was not doing enough to protect her, I was careful not to alienate him by taking sides and tried to remain empathically attuned to his experiences, as well as paying attention to the couple's interaction.

As the sessions progressed, Margot and Toby were more able to notice changes in their emotional state and interrupt their pattern of mutual attack themselves. When they were unable to do this, I paused their conversation and invited them to reflect on what had just occurred. They seemed to experience a sense of relief and hope as they continued to develop their ability to manage the emotional intensity they sometimes experienced. This seemed to provide the momentum and courage for all three of us to broach the critical incident that had contributed to their heightened emotional sensitivity and the increasing negative reciprocity observed in their relationship when they started therapy.

THERAPIST: Tell me about what happened that night when Toby stayed out drinking and Margot, you were looking forward to spending some time with him.

MARGOT: Toby, you were always busy and that night I was so looking forward to you coming back early. I was busy getting ready and it felt like going on a date. I was so looking forward to you coming back. I didn't think to check my phone but when I did, and heard you couldn't come back early as planned, I was livid. You selfish son of a bitch...

THERAPIST: Margot, can you tell Toby a bit more about your feelings of what it meant to you to spend time with him?

MARGOT: I was excited and I wanted us to feel close but when I picked up your message and then tried to call you back, you didn't pick up or text back. I kept trying and trying and was getting angrier and angrier as you weren't picking up, you're so inconsiderate...

TOBY: All I'm hearing from you is that you didn't do this, you didn't do that, you're so selfish, you're so inconsiderate, I am always in the wrong...

THERAPIST: let's pause there for a minute, Margot I understand why you would be angry if you had spent time getting ready and were looking forward to going on a date with him only to find out that he's not coming back early as planned. Try to tell Toby what other feelings you had apart from anger.

MARGOT: I felt let down, hugely disappointed.

TOBY: That's right I'm to blame again...

THERAPIST: Toby, I know it's hard for you to hear what Margot is saying when you're feeling blamed and you think that it's unfair for her to do so. I'm wondering whether you feel unappreciated in that moment, which makes it really difficult to hear how let down and disappointed she was feeling?

TOBY: I do think it's unfair that I'm seen as being selfish and inconsiderate, I was working hard for a better life for us.

THERAPIST: I know, you're the responsible guy who looks after his family, can you tell Margot what it feels like for you when you hear that she was hurt and disappointed?

TOBY: I understand, but when you kept calling and texting, it felt like I was being nagged. It was just too much and I knew what was coming. I didn't want to hear you screaming down the phone at me like a crazy woman...

MARGOT: Crazy woman?! You call me crazy? You came back home drunk, sent me flying across the room and slapped me, and had the police knocking on our door! Tell me now, who's the crazy one?

Despite, the many sessions spent practising sharing thoughts and feelings, Margot practising self-soothing and mindfulness strategies, and my attempts at being empathic and attuned with Toby, I realised that it did not take very much for intense emotions to arise for this couple and for them to be trapped in the familiar interactional pattern of mutual attack.

After several attempts at discussing this incident, the key themes that emerged were Margot's anger when she felt that Toby was ignoring her and did not understand the hurt and her need for closeness with him; a need she tried to assuage by repeated unsuccessful attempts to contact him. As Toby's sense of failure and inadequacy kicked in, he started to feel nagged and avoided Margot's calls. This in turn contributed to her increasing anger and inflexibility in her thoughts about him being an inconsiderate and selfish person. When he returned, she exploded instead of communicating her sadness, disappointment and hurt, and instead of offering comfort, Toby launched a counter-attack of insults, which increased her anger and resulted in her shredding his clothes and breaking some of his belongings. Toby was taken aback by the intensity of Margot's anger, and responded in kind. The most distressing part for both of them was when Toby, fuelled by alcohol and consumed by rage, barged through the door and sent Margot flying across the room. The argument continued and culminated in Toby slapping Margot.

Both were scared by the intensity of their emotions and the destruction caused by these. Furthermore, Toby felt a deep sense of shame and was wrecked by guilt and self-hatred, as whilst he looked like his father, he certainly did not want to behave like him. They both made steadfast promises to each other that physical violence would never happen again and cried whilst holding the other person tightly. I was struck by Toby's departing words in one of our sessions *"Rita, we need each other"*.

Reflections

One of the things that struck me about working with Toby and Margot was how exhausted I felt after each session, and I think that there were many factors that contributed to this. Firstly, there was a huge demand on my attentional resources, as I was often battling to make sense of everything in the room whilst remaining attuned to the couple's emotions and those which were incongruent or disallowed in their narrative. Secondly, I was drawn into their emotional roller-coaster and effort was required to detach myself from this. Thirdly, I had to adopt a more active and directive stance at times in an attempt to limit the damage caused to both as a result of their interaction. All of this was with the aim of being able to help the couple develop an awareness of the unhelpful interactional patterns they routinely found themselves engaged in. The importance of supervision in this situation cannot be underestimated as well as the ability to look after oneself and one's own needs.

During sharing thoughts and feelings exercises, couples are encouraged to talk to each other so that they learn more effective and helpful ways of communicating. However, for this couple I felt that it was important for them notice and understand their own emotions and how they attacked each other. So, in the early stages of sharing thoughts and feelings, I encouraged the partners to talk to me rather than directly at each other to minimise the destructive pattern of interaction that was so easily triggered. This helped with modelling validation, listening to each other, and clarifying and communicating the softer emotions. Toby and Margot were encouraged to talk to each other when they became more skilled at interrupting their escalating pattern of interaction. I think that this was helpful in moderating the intensity of the sessions and helped with their engagement and perseverance with therapy.

I had underestimated the intransigence of the couple's mutual attack pattern of interaction and wondered whether more systematic and focussed DBT strategies might have been helpful. For example, the use of the 'Double Chain Analysis' as a way for each partner to identify specific behaviours, emotional reactions, appraisals that contributed to the eventual mutual attack. This might also have helped the couple to understand, validate and accept each other's experience (Fruzzetti & Payne, 2015), perhaps adding to the couple's relationship mindfulness skills.

Sometimes the focus on the content of the communication can be useful i.e. what they argue about, but at other times, focussing on the nature of the interaction and how this might have been influenced by each partner's individual histories might also be important. Whilst working with this couple, tensions such as abandonment and sadness vs. security and closeness, attachment and dependence vs. detachment and contempt were present. From discussions in supervision, I often wondered whether including more attachment theory and adopting a more emotionally focussed approach in line with Johnson's (2020) ideas of helping couples connect might have added a different dimension to my work with Margot and Toby.

Therapist's tips

- A good understanding of each partner's vulnerabilities and how they experience and regulate emotions is essential when formulating the reciprocal influences of emotion dysregulation and relationship dynamics.
- It might be helpful to respond to each partner's needs separately e.g. validation when responding to Margot, and gentle but persistent evaluation of Toby's beliefs about himself and the impact these have on his emotions and responses to Margot, as well as the couple's dynamics.
- Follow the affect!
- Do not be alarmed by the ebb and flow of the pace of therapy. In high-conflict couples expect quick changes in interaction patterns in the sessions and be consistent in helping the couple identify changes in any cognitions and behaviours or in emotional arousal, as well as with the application of emotional regulation strategies. Rate of change might be slow. Be ready to be there for the long haul!
- Use supervision well to explore any therapist's beliefs and schemas that will arise from the work with the couple as well as the factors behind the possible emotional exhaustion.

Suggestions for further Reading

Goldman, R.N. & Greenberg, L.S. (2010). Self-soothing and other soothing in emotion-focused therapy for couples. In A.S. Gurman (Eds.), *Clinical casebook of couple therapy* (pp. 255–280). New York: Guilford Press.

Oliver, M., Perry, S., & Cade, R. (2008). Couples therapy with borderline disordered individuals. *The Family Journal: Counselling and Therapy for Couples and Families*, 16(1), 67–72. doi:10.1177/1066480707309122.

References

Anderson, S.R., Anderson, S.A., Palmer. K.L., Mutchler, M.S., & Baker, L.K. (2011). Defining high conflict. *The American Journal of Family Therapy*, 39, 11–27. doi:10.1080/01926187.2010.530194.

Baucom, D.H, Fischer, M.S., Corrie, S., Worrell, M., & Boeding, S.E. (2020). *Treating relationship distress and psychopathology in couples: A cognitive-behavioural approach*. UK: Routledge.

Fruzzetti, A.E. (2006). *The high conflict couple: A dialectical behavior therapy guide to finding peace, intimacy & validation*. USA, Oakland, CA: New Harbinger Publications.

Fruzzetti, A.E., & Payne, L. (2015). Couple therapy and borderline personality disorder. In A.S. Gurman, J.L. Lebow, & D.K. Synder (Eds.), *Clinical handbook of couple therapy* (5th ed., pp. 606–634). New York: Guilford Press.

Fruzzetti, A.E., & Payne, L.G. (2020). Assessment of parents, couples and families in dialectical behaviour therapy. *Cognitive and Behavioural Practice*, 27, 39–49.

Greenberg, E. (2016). *Borderline, narcissistic and schizoid adaptations: The pursuit of love, admiration and safety*. New York: Greenbrooke Press.

Janusz, B., Bergmann, J.R., Matusiak, F., & Peräkylä, A. (2021). Practices of claiming control and independence in couple therapy with narcissism. *Frontiers in Psychology*, 11: 1–16. doi:10.3389/fpsyg.2020.596842.

Johnson, S.M. (2020). *The practice of emotionally focussed couple therapy: Creating connection* (3rd ed.) London: Routledge.

Kirby, J.S. & Baucom, D.H. (2007). Integrating dialectical behavior therapy and cognitive behavioral couple therapy: A couples' skills group for emotional dysregulation. *Cognitive and Behavioral Practice*, 14(4), 394–405.

Lachkar, J. (2003). *The narcissistic/borderline couple: new approaches to marital therapy* (2nd ed.). London: Routledge.

Linehan, M. (1993). *Cognitive behavioural treatment of borderline personality disorder*. New York, NY: Guilford Press.

Chapter 13

Post-Traumatic Stress Disorder

Making Sense of Trauma Together

Clare Kenyon

"I know that you've been through something really terrible but why do you have to be so unpleasant to live with?!"

Jane, usually so calm and gentle, spat out these words in the first couple session. Sam, who in his professional life was known for his energy and charisma, sat opposite her with his head hanging down, gazing at the carpet. Right now, as they embarked on couple therapy, they both felt so far from being the kind of partner that they wanted to be.

Introduction – PTSD and intimate relationships

There is a significant interaction between post-traumatic stress disorder (PTSD) symptoms and couple relationships. As with any mental health difficulty there is a bidirectional relationship between the disorder and the couple dynamic; the disorder impacting on the state of the relationship and the couple interactions, but also the quality of the relationship exacerbating or alleviating the severity and manifestation of the disorder (Pukay-Martin, Macdonald, Fredman & Monson, 2016). In addition, with PTSD there are core features of the disorder which relate to close interpersonal interactions and are particularly likely to negatively impact on the relationship. For example, in PTSD there is often a disturbance in trust, intimacy, and sexual relationships and there is likely to be some emotional numbing which can manifest as apparent withdrawal from the partner and trigger relationship distress. Also, irritability and aggression in PTSD can be particularly difficult for partners to tolerate, creating considerable 'caregiver stress' (Zayfert & DeViva 2011). Hence, just when the person with PTSD needs more support and care, their partner may feel overloaded themselves and may understandably start to withdraw.

There is strong evidence, particularly from US army Veteran data, that PTSD has a negative impact on relationships. For example, studies of Vietnam war veterans showed that those with PTSD showed more severe relationship problems than veterans without PTSD (Kulka et al., 1990) and a Canadian epidemiological study showed that a PTSD diagnosis has one of

DOI: 10.4324/9781003024439-15

the highest associations with marital distress of any mental health problem (Whisman, Seldon & Goering, 2000)

A couple relationship can potentially be used to assist with coping with and reframing trauma; for example, a strong buffering relationship can help with rebuilding trust following a trauma which has violated trust or assumptions about trust. However, if the partner is not involved in the treatment process there can be a risk, as with many anxiety disorders, that a well-meaning, sympathetic spouse can inadvertently reinforce unhelpful processes such as avoidance (referred to as 'accommodation' by Baucom, Fischer, Corrie, Worrell and Boeding, 2020).

For these reasons there is a strong argument for considering a couple treatment for PTSD. It is likely that the partner will benefit from being included in the treatment if the relationship distress can be alleviated, and with the partner involved the couple relationship can be utilised positively as a tool for change. It is also possible that inviting a significant other could encourage attendance and reduce the risk of treatment drop out.

The role of CBCT in PTSD

Cognitive Behavioural Couple Therapy (CBCT) for PTSD is not offered routinely in the UK, where the first line of treatment is almost always individual therapy. However, couple approaches have been developed and refined in the USA and Canada, and Monson and colleagues have developed a 15-session cognitive behavioural treatment model for couples which has been shown to be at least as effective as a waiting list control condition (Monson, Fredman et al., 2012), achieving an improvement in PTSD, comorbid symptoms and in relationship functioning. It has also shown promising results in an intensive weekend group format for veterans (Fredman, Macdonald, Monson et al., 2019). The main components of this model (varying in emphasis depending on the needs of the couple) are; 1. Psychoeducation about PTSD, including correction of misattributions of symptoms, 2. Communication skills training, which is useful in its own right but also specifically helpful in overcoming the emotional avoidance which commonly manifests in PTSD, 3. Explicitly overcoming avoidance (but not re-living of trauma memories), such as avoidance of intimacy and closeness, 4. Understanding and challenging maladaptive cognitions about traumatic events such as a self blame, trust, acceptance, and 5. Discussing post traumatic growth. This is broadly the model used in this case study.

Whilst couple therapy is not advocated in the NICE guidance for PTSD (NICE, 2018) in the UK, there are some clients presenting for help for PTSD where couple factors seem to be a key part of the presenting picture and where partners are eager to be involved in treatment.

The presenting couple

Jane and Sam were referred for CBCT within an NHS psychological therapy service following the completion of a partially successful course of individual trauma focused CBT for Sam. This treatment had been helpful in alleviating some of the most disruptive PTSD symptoms such as nightmares, flashbacks and severe sleep disturbance, but some symptoms remained, such as avoidance, emotional numbing and low mood. Sam had experienced a traumatic event 2 years ago; an incident where a group of young men attacked him and stole his bike. They hit him in the face with a hard object, knocking him to the ground and causing concussion. He was also humiliated while he lay on the pavement as they called him offensive names and spat on him, before leaving with his bike.

Sam explained that this incident had triggered distress related to earlier trauma in childhood, when he had been severely bullied by other boys at school. He said that he had thought that he had coped 'ok' with this bullying, until now.

Sam and Jane had been together for 15 years and married for 11, with children aged 10 and 8. Both were in full time employment in jobs with high levels of responsibility but Sam was on long term sick leave with partial pay, because of his PTSD.

During the 3-session couple assessment Jane and Sam described how their relationship had become very fraught during the period 1–2 years ago when Sam's PTSD symptoms were at their worst. At this time Sam was experiencing frequent flashbacks and nightmares and struggled to function in their family as a result. He admitted to high levels of irritability directed at both Jane and their children at this time, and Jane said that she had felt she needed to protect the children from the impact of this; not needing to protect them from physical harm, but feeling obliged to monitor and anticipate Sam's moods and to intervene quickly so that he did not lose his temper in front of the children. They both commented that Sam was now much less irritable and that there was far less conflict in their home, but Jane expressed some lingering resentment about just how much she had needed to adapt and 'tread on eggshells' around Sam. Now things were much easier day to day, but they presented as being somewhat withdrawn from each other and in Jane's case, continuing to view Sam with some caution and unease, even though he was now much more able to regulate his emotions. This was evident when observing their communication in the assessment phase.

As quoted at the start of this chapter, Jane made some strong comments about how difficult Sam had been to live with over the last 2 years. My sense, watching her, was of a calm, composed and considerate person who had reached the limits of her patience. She sat very still, holding her hands firmly together, as if literally needing to hold herself together to contain her frustration. Her jaw was slightly clenched, conveying tension. Sam, on hearing her words, exuded a sense of despair and weariness. As their therapist it was difficult to witness this exchange. Initially I felt a strong sympathy towards Sam, knowing that his PTSD symptoms would have caused such fear and misery that some irritability was understandable. In this context Jane's words seemed unkind and hurtful and I imagined how they might increase his feelings of shame and hopelessness. For couple therapists this is a familiar experience; hearing harsh critical words directed at someone who is feeling vulnerable. Deciding when to intervene in these situations can be one of the most challenging dilemmas as a therapist, balancing the need for expression of emotions with the need to limit further distress. In this case, when Jane explained further it was clear that she had tried very hard to support Sam for months, initially with considerable sympathy. Eventually it became too much. It felt important to explore the distress underlying Jane's angry statement.

THERAPIST: Jane, can you say a little bit about what felt so difficult?
JANE: It wasn't hard to support Sam at first… but then after 6 months of working full time, doing everything for the children while Sam was out of action, I got so tired. Even that I could have dealt with but then it was his anger. He'd bite my head off over the slightest thing. And even worse – he'd yell at the kids. I had to tiptoe around him and make sure that the children kept quiet and didn't argue. And no proper conversations with Sam. It just got so hard. I felt like I'd lost the man I used to love.

When asked about their style of communication the couple said that they had not tended to express their difficult emotions in great depth to each other, whilst knowing that they were loved and valued by the other. They said that they had not felt their relationship tested until the time of the trauma. They had previously worked well as a team, solved problems effectively together and had talked to each other with empathic pragmatism rather than an intense focus on feelings. Prior to the trauma there had been very little conflict, or even disagreement, which is partly why Sam's irritability and anger had been such a shock to Jane. Neither of them were particularly comfortable with expressing anger or hostility and preferred to move on from it, after finding practical solutions where possible.

During the assessment and early sessions of treatment the couple were able to identify some of their own relevant beliefs. Jane spoke about feeling that her 'job' was to protect others, including Sam where necessary and to keep the peace. She stepped into this role very naturally whilst also more recently feeling some resentment about it; she related this to her own early experiences in her family of origin where she had needed to take on a peacekeeper role when her parents were in conflict. Sam spoke about his belief that other people could not be trusted. He said that he was conscious of this belief since the traumatic event 2 years ago, but also felt that it related to his experiences in childhood. He reported having been able to manage to trust others despite the childhood trauma but now feeling that he had been right all along to have suspicions about others and should never have trusted anyone. He stated that no one could be fully trusted, including Jane. He emphasised that this was not a reflection on Jane and her value as a person, but more just a fact of life that it was foolish and risky to trust others and more sensible to rely on oneself wherever possible. Sam had initially withheld from Jane the nature of his childhood trauma and had expressed concerns to his individual therapist about how Jane (or anyone) might judge him for it or use the information against him in some way. By the time couple therapy started he had shared some of this information about his past with Jane but still held on to some of his beliefs that she could not be fully trusted. Sadly such beliefs about trust are common amongst trauma survivors, even when they are in relationships where there is no evidence of the partner being 'untrustworthy'.

Perhaps this reserved emotional stance had meant that Sam maintained some of his implicit beliefs about it being best to be cautious around intimacy and trust, and to avoid sharing his true self fully even with those he loved. This became more problematic after the trauma when Sam was overwhelmed by the PTSD symptoms but felt unable to reveal the full extent of his fear and vulnerability to Jane. This reserved approach possibly heightened his tension and irritability, leading to snapping, shouting and outbursts of frustration. The couple then moved into a position of mutual withdrawal; Sam feeling that he should 'hold back' his strong emotions when with Jane, and Jane avoiding expressing feelings around Sam (initially to avoid triggering his outbursts and later because she felt hurt and resentful and did not want to be intimate with him). This mutual withdrawal pattern maintained Sam's sense of being unable to fully trust and share his true self, and also perpetuated Jane's feelings of resentment and frustration. My sense was that in therapy they needed to be able to take some risks in sharing their feelings in order to understand each other's perspective and also to feel more understood and supported. This couple had been strongly tested by the PTSD and now needed to be more emotionally open and expressive with each other than they had ever been before. Before therapy this was not possible as resentment and distrust acted as impenetrable barriers.

The interpersonal context is also significant for this couple; at the time of Sam's trauma their 2 children were very young, which meant that Jane carried most of the responsibility for childcare as well as trying to support Sam. This made it much more difficult for the couple to manage the stress in the relationship; Jane understandably needed to focus on the needs of the children and also felt quite worn down by this, on top of her job. My impression was that if Sam's trauma had occurred before their children were born, Jane would have had more emotional resources to deploy in helping Sam and also would not have needed to minimise emotional intensity (to protect the children). Perhaps pre-children this couple would have managed and found a way through the PTSD phase without seeking couple therapy.

Summary of the Formulation and how this guided therapy

Sam and Jane were a couple who both preferred to avoid conflict in their relationship and this approach had seemed to serve them fairly well until the traumatic incident hit. Sam's underlying beliefs about it being best to be cautious around intimacy and trust meant that he struggled with showing Jane his primary distress (fear). What she witnessed more were irritable outbursts, which were distressing for her and also reduced her compassion towards Sam. This led to a pattern of mutual withdrawal which exacerbated their individual distress and encouraged further withdrawal. Their family context added to this as they both needed to limit emotional expression in various ways when their young children were present. There were few occasions for open sharing of difficult emotions and as time went by Sam and Jane chose not to make use of these and spent less and less time communicating. It was important to address both the lack of communication (by increasing and enhancing it) and also the reasons underlying the withdrawal from communication (i.e. Sam's beliefs about trusting people with his vulnerability and Jane's cumulative frustration with Sam's irritable behaviour).

Course of Treatment

Jane and Sam attended for 3 assessment sessions, 12 weekly therapy sessions (with occasional gaps for holidays or childcare reasons) and then 4 follow up sessions which were approximately monthly. The sequencing of interventions is outlined below.

Psycho-education

Firstly, brief psycho-education about PTSD and depression was covered. In some ways this did not seem so pressing as the symptoms had already reduced and Sam had already covered sufficient psycho-education in his individual CBT. However, it was important to recap on some of the information about PTSD symptoms and these being a normal reaction to extreme events, mainly for Jane's benefit. She was already aware of flashbacks and nightmares being distressing symptoms, but it was helpful to ensure she was aware that irritability and anger could also be sequelae of trauma.

Managing conflict and high affect

Ensuring that both were confident in techniques for reducing conflict and managing high affect. Again, this did not need to be the main focus of treatment as there had clearly been considerable progress in this area. How-ever, it was important to consolidate these skills before embarking on more intense topics in later therapy sessions. The couple had not really needed to work on these skills earlier in their relationship as both tended to avoid conflict and favoured respectful and constructive problem solving instead; but the period of high stress in the first year post trauma had severely tested them. Some time was spent in the very early sessions clarifying that they both knew what to do to manage their own affect, to relax, self-soothe and to agree a 'time-out' if it was needed. This way we could be sure that conflict would not escalate to the level they had experienced a year ago prior to treatment.

For example, as Sam was still prone to irritability after periods of pro-longed tension it was agreed that he could signal a need for some time-out of a family situation and take himself away for 5 minutes to calm down, by using breathing exercises and grounding techniques learned in individual therapy.

THERAPIST: Sam, how could you signal to Jane that you need to do this?

SAM: Well, I don't think I should say too much if the kids are there and I can't say 'time-out' as to them that means the naughty step. I could say that I need to go to the toilet or that I just need a few minutes.

THERAPIST: Jane, how would that feel for you? If Sam said something like that, to let you know that he is feeling tense and needs some time out?

JANE: I think it's best not to say that you need the toilet as the kids might get curious or start copying you to leave the dinner table and go to the toilet. But if you said something like "I need a few minutes" that would be ok. I'd much rather you take the time-out than end up getting irritable with us.

Communication skills training

'Sharing thoughts and feelings' conversations were the main focus of 6–8 sessions of therapy. Initially the skills were discussed, briefly role played and practised, with some reading on this topic for homework. The couple were well able to use this method with low affect topics as both were socially skilled, had respect for each other and were able to take another person's perspective. The challenge was in putting the techniques into practice with 'hotter' topics. It was very important to practice the sharing of thoughts and feelings about 'medium intensity' topics in sessions, to give the couple an experience of being able to express their feelings in a context that felt safe and contained and for them to see that this did not lead to unmanageable conflict or uncontrollable affect. Where hostility and criticism occasionally flared up they were encouraged to use the conflict management and de-escalation techniques mentioned above. This communication was initially only practised in sessions and then later done as a homework practice (along with other simpler strategies for relationship enhancement such as spending time together relaxing or doing enjoyable activities). Problem solving communication techniques were not emphasised so much with this couple as this was an area of strength and of less relevance to the PTSD.

Talking about the impact of the trauma/expressing vulnerability

Next the couple were encouraged to use the same communication techniques for discussion of topics at a higher level of intensity and more closely related to the trauma. This was important in order to tackle some of the more distressing difficulties they were reporting in their relationship but also important in relation to the PTSD. For clients with PTSD the experience of taking 'risks' in expressing vulnerable feelings and opening up emotions which feel difficult to control can be very challenging, as PTSD often leaves sufferers feeling that their emotions are unmanageable and unacceptable and therefore need to be kept bottled up. This 'opening up' also relates to the theme of trust, mentioned later. However, it is important to mention that in these discussions there was no systematic exposure to trauma memories and that this is not part of the protocol for couple treatment of PTSD. In Sam's case he had already done some re-living work in his individual therapy but even if he had not done so it would not have been the intention in couple sessions. There was some discussion about the PTSD symptoms and Sam's response to the trauma, which to an extent involves some gentle 'exposure', but no explicit re-living of the events themselves.

Sam was encouraged to share his feelings in this way in one of the early therapy sessions:

THERAPIST: Sam, can you say a little bit to Jane about the fear that you've felt – but without getting into the details of the event itself.
SAM: I felt terrified, like I might die, and kind of like a child on the ground. And that's how I still feel sometimes.

Jane was then encouraged to reflect back what she had heard, using the guidelines for sharing thoughts and feelings:

JANE: So you sometimes feel terrified, like a child, even now?
SAM: Not as often as before, but sometimes, yes.
JANE: Oh sweetheart – that's awful.

Although in CBCT for PTSD we would not want to conduct prolonged exposure to trauma memories in the sessions it was important for Jane to hear from Sam about his frightened feelings. This provoked a compassionate response from Jane, much more so than when he expressed irritation and anger.

Addressing significant underlying beliefs

For this later stage in couple therapy some of the 'UNSTUCK' (U – united and curious, N – notice the way you are thinking, S – (brain) storm alternative thoughts, T – test them, U – use the most balanced, C – changes in emotion and behaviours, K – keep practising) method advocated by Monson and Fredman was used. This method was used for homework exercises and in session discussions to encourage both partners to identify their own cognitions and to consider alternatives. Monson and Fredman's (2012) workbook for PTSD couple work includes an 'Unstuck' worksheet for work on trust specifically, which was useful for this couple. Sam was encouraged to break down the concept of trust and to consider trust on a continuum in relation to a variety of people (a friend, Jane, the perpetrators of the trauma) and in relation to different attributes and areas of life (e.g. trust not to harm you, trust to tell the truth, trust to manage finances). It worked well to use this workbook method for homework as it gave Sam space to consider the concepts privately in addition to the in-session discussions, making it less likely that he would take a defensive position. He concluded that not everyone would exploit your weaknesses and use them against you, and that Jane could be trusted to treat his feelings with respect (as evidenced in their sharing thoughts and feelings conversations), and although she could not entirely be trusted to manage their finances as efficiently as he would like (by her own admission being much more casual about expenditure and record keeping) he could trust her not to spend money behind his back or to deliberately mislead him about their financial situation.

Reflective tasks planned as homework helped Sam to acknowledge that he could trust Jane to not use personal information against him in the way that the bullies had. He quite readily acknowledged that in many ways he could trust Jane; to not be manipulative, to be honest and to be on his side. However he continued to feel some reservations about disclosing information to Jane which showed his vulnerability, and this needed exploring further in a session:

THERAPIST: So Sam, you talked last time about how since you were bullied and hurt as a child you've believed that other people can't be trusted and in particular that if people know about your 'weaknesses' they will use this against you. We then talked about how some people are more trustworthy than others and you were sure that Jane is definitely at the more trustworthy end of this continuum. I asked you to think about the ways in which you can trust Jane. Can you tell us a bit about this?

SAM: Well, obviously I know rationally that Jane isn't going to use my weaknesses against me in a cruel way. She is a kind person and she isn't going to deliberately manipulate me.

THERAPIST: And can she be trusted not to be unkind when you show vulnerability?

SAM: Yes she can. And I know that she is on my side. But it's like a gut feeling that when I feel weak and scared I need to hide this. I need to stay strong and to cope.

THERAPIST: And that was difficult to sustain last year?

SAM: Yes, very difficult. Impossible a lot of the time.

THERAPIST: And what effect do you think that had? Trying to hide how you felt?

SAM: I had to kind of hide myself. I had to literally keep away from Jane and the children sometimes.

THERAPIST: To hide how you were feeling?

SAM: Yes. And then sometimes we'd need to all be together, like in the car or at dinnertime – and I'd have to work so hard to hold it all together that sometimes I'd explode.

THERAPIST: And what about now?

SAM: Now it's a bit easier to keep up a front, as I feel less anxious, and I'm not getting the full-on flashbacks anymore.

THERAPIST: And do you feel that with Jane, when the children are not around, you can let that front down? That you can let Jane know when you feel anxious or uneasy?

SAM: I've done that here in our conversations, haven't I?

THERAPIST: Yes – you've taken some important steps in the conversations here. How does that feel now?

SAM: That feels ok, now that I've got used to it.

THERAPIST: And did you feel safe, that you could trust Jane with this information about yourself?

SAM: Yes, of course.

THERAPIST: And what about outside of these sessions?

SAM: Mmm…. I don't know why, but that feels much harder …. It's silly but it feels kind of risky, like it could all go wrong if I try to say some of this stuff at home. Like I could get hurt. I don't know why though.

THERAPIST: It's understandable, given the beliefs you developed as a child, about not letting anyone see you be vulnerable. This is a change for you.

SAM: Yes, maybe.

THERAPIST: And intellectually – you said that you think that you can trust Jane not to use this information against you and not to be unkind.

SAM: Yes, of course. This is stupid. It's like a gut feeling. I don't want to show it and I shut down.

THERAPIST: As you described before, this is what you had to do when you were a child – you had to shut down a bit to cope and to go to school as normal. But do you think that you could try out sharing more with Jane at home, outside of these sessions?

SAM: Umm…. Maybe.

THERAPIST: Is there anything you need from Jane, in order for that to feel possible to try?

SAM: Urr... I don't know. Maybe not to make too big a deal of it. Not to make me feel weak. Not that I'm suggesting she'd do anything deliberately to make me feel weak, but...

THERAPIST: So, you'd need Jane to not make a big deal of it, if you do tell her that you're feeling anxious or scared?

SAM: Yes, maybe not to focus on it too much.

THERAPIST: So would you want to just tell her briefly and not focus on talking about it for too long?

SAM: Yes – just as long as I know that she's understood what I've said and that she doesn't think I'm crazy.

THERAPIST: What do you think Jane?

JANE: Yes I can do that. I want you to be able to let me know when you feel anxious. I'd far rather know what's brewing – much better than you holding it all in and then biting my head off.

Here Jane's response is not as warm and compassionate as I had hoped for, but Sam seemed to find her pragmatic tone helpful. He had felt able to speak about his fear without feeling 'weak' or 'crazy'. He was then able to test out this kind of communication without therapist support, outside of the sessions by briefly 'flagging' to Jane that he was starting to feel anxious and uneasy, with reduced concerns about the negative consequences of revealing his vulnerability. Meanwhile Jane fed back that it was helpful for her to feel more informed about how Sam was feeling and through this she felt closer to him again.

This work exploring the multi-dimensional nature of trustworthiness and it being on a spectrum or continuum was a significant process over a number of sessions and homework tasks, and continued to be a work in progress as therapy came to an end. Sam could cite many experiences from his past traumas which indicated that others could be untrustworthy, and the shift in perspective to considering the exceptions to this belief required much repetition and reinforcement.

Jane's beliefs were also examined, more briefly. She expressed a binary view of distress and conflict; stating that her role since the trauma tended to be to placate and soothe Sam, suppress conflict and not express her own feelings. Sam's angry reactions during the worst period of PTSD symptoms reinforced this view that she needed to focus on managing Sam's affect. She began to consider an alternative view; that perhaps she could sometimes express distress to Sam without him erupting in anger or tears, and that perhaps he could sometimes support her emotionally now. The conversations during the sharing thoughts and feelings exercises illustrated this for her, as did further behavioural experiments (such as trying out confiding feelings in Sam, and directly asking Sam how he would prefer her to interact with him). This synthesis was achieved mainly through a 3-way conversation in therapy, where the therapist asked Jane explicitly about whether there was any evidence against her belief that she had to always take care of Sam and could not express her distress to him. She tentatively suggested that there had been times in the past (pre-PTSD) when she had been sad or stressed and had been able to rely on Sam and when he had not crumpled in the face of her distress. She was then encouraged to test out in-session how it felt to express distress to Sam now and this was built on in homework conversations.

Achievements in Therapy

At the end of couple therapy there were improvements in relationship satisfaction rated on the CSI-32 (Funk and Rogge 2007) for Jane and Sam and there was some improvement in mood on standardised measures.

In addition, there were important behavioural changes; enhancement of skills for managing conflict, reduced withdrawal, more mutual support, more frequent constructive sharing thoughts and feelings conversations at home, more joint and individual relaxation and engagement in enjoyable activities. There were also modifications of significant beliefs about trust and about sharing distress. The work on beliefs was very much a work in progress and it was crucial that there was an extended follow up period in which this work could be consolidated and reinforced. If therapy had ended abruptly at 12 sessions this progress *may* have been too fragile to be maintained. For example, in relation to trust there was still some wariness from Sam and at times he reported defaulting back to his position of suspicion and hostility. It was helpful to reflect on this in follow up sessions and to encourage him to continue to test out his newer more multi-dimensional and continuum-based view of trustworthiness with more behavioural experiments.

Challenges and issues for consideration in this work

As a therapist it can be difficult to manage a situation where one partner expresses considerable resentment about the past behaviour of the other partner. The therapist needs to make a decision about how much time to allow for expression of this resentment. Some expression may be vital for emotional processing and 'moving on', but on the other hand if too much session time is spent on this ventilation it can become aversive for the other partner who is being criticised. With Jane and Sam some expression was needed but I also had to stay mindful of the fact that Sam's previous irritability, whilst distressing for Jane to manage was also a symptom of his PTSD. Too much time spent recalling the impact of his behaviour would be likely to elicit feelings of shame and to lower his mood. I decided that it was best to be quite explicit about this process and the need for balance; stating directly to the couple that it was understandable that Sam had become irritable but also understandable that Jane felt some resentment about this and needed to speak about how she felt. I suggested that we spent some time on this (making sure to include psycho-education about PTSD) but not dwell on it for too many of their sessions.

There can be a tendency in CBCT where one partner clearly has and is still suffering with a mental health disorder, to focus more on this partner and potentially to overly pathologise them. It is particularly easy to fall in to this 'trap' with couples who are already engaging in this pathologising. This was to some extent the case with Sam and Jane, where Jane was viewing Sam as the emotionally fragile or volatile one and believing that she needed to shield him and keep her own feelings hidden. Therefore, it was important to remain aware of this dynamic and as a therapist remember to encourage Jane to express her own feelings. This was helpful in countering the view of Sam as the unwell one with urgent needs and overlooking Jane's needs, and it was also helpful in rebuilding their intimacy.

It was also important to achieve the right balance in understanding and making sense of Sam's previous anger and irritability. Whilst it was useful to help Jane to understand this as a symptom of PTSD it is also important not to advocate a relationship dynamic where one person needs to spend the rest of their life treading carefully around the other person and always prioritising their needs, and it is certainly not acceptable to appear to condone a level of verbal aggression that could start to feel emotionally abusive. Therefore the therapist needs to achieve a balance between communicating acceptance and understanding but also encouraging self-control and behavioural change where needed. In the case of Sam and Jane this balance was relatively easy to achieve as some improvements had already been made before starting CBCT, but with some couples the verbal aggression is still present and needs to be addressed very directly whilst also acknowledging it as a response to trauma. There is an increased risk of intimate partner violence amongst PTSD survivors and it is therefore very important to ensure safety and to beware of colluding with even subtle levels of abusive behaviour. Risk of physical aggression was not a concern with this particular couple but it is important to assess for this and for factors (such as alcohol use) which could increase the likelihood of aggressive outbursts. It appears that sometimes couple therapy can increase risk of verbal aggression (as Johnson 2002 found with emotion focused couple therapy).

As explained in Chapter 5 on interpersonal violence, there are some situations where aggression means that it is not safe to proceed with couple therapy or at all; for example, where there is severe violence and/or coercive control. Even where couple therapy seems appropriate, if there is any physical aggression it is crucial that the therapist addresses safety first and helps the couple to reduce conflict and aversive interactions as soon as possible. It can be important with some couples where there is aggressive behaviour that the emotional intensity is lowered through the therapy discussions. With Sam and Jane, although there was some irritability and verbal aggression, this seemed to be a consequence of Sam's impossible attempts to stifle his anxiety, so for this couple it was important to facilitate more expression of primary emotions such as fear rather than lowering the emotional intensity. However, it was still necessary in the 'heat of the moment' for Sam to be able to de-escalate his mounting irritability and to find ways to interrupt an interaction and take himself away for some self-soothing in private.

With this couple we did not focus explicitly on post traumatic growth as the cognitive work needed a considerable amount of time both within and between sessions, but this is a part of the Monson CBCT approach to trauma and ideally should have been included.

Implications for future treatment

I found myself wondering whether it would have felt acceptable to offer CBCT according to the Monson and Fredman model as an entire treatment for PTSD, as it does not include any re-living or formal reprocessing of trauma memories. With Sam this couple approach (without reliving) felt appropriate as he had already processed his trauma memories in individual therapy, but I would have felt a little unsure of offering CBCT as his only psychological treatment. However, it is worth remembering that the Monson and Fredman (2012) model has achieved improvements in PTSD symptoms without exposure or re-living (Schumm, Fredman, Monson and Chard 2012 and Pukay-Martin, Macdonald, Fredman and Monson 2016).

In the UK the NICE guidelines for PTSD (2018) do not recommend CBCT as a treatment for PTSD, though they do emphasise the importance of paying attention to the support needs for the family of the person with PTSD and considering the impact of the PTSD on significant others. Therefore, in the UK it remains an additional option in some NHS services and in fact is not routinely offered even in veterans organisations.

It is worth considering CBCT for PTSD as an 'add on' to NICE recommended individual PTSD treatments to enhance the couple relationship and reduce risk of relapse. Or, as Pukay-Martin and colleagues (2016) suggest it is possible to cover some of the elements of the CBCT programme prior to embarking on an individual treatment. They recommend working with the couple on psychoeducation, developing a shared understanding of PTSD, reducing conflict and eliminating therapy interfering behaviours before moving on to individual treatment for PTSD.

There is a need for fuller evaluation of CBCT for PTSD, as published studies to date mainly compare the intervention to waiting list controls rather than to evidence-based individual treatments. It would be interesting to see how CBCT compares to trauma-focused CBT. This could be helpful information clinically, as there may be some clients where it would be difficult to undertake individual treatment without also addressing relationship factors, or where the client might not engage in individual trauma focused treatment without support from their partner in doing so.

There is also a need for evaluation of CBCT across more diverse patient groups, aside from US veterans. How do US army veterans and UK-based non-military patients with PTSD compare, and are different treatments more attractive to and even more effective for different patient groups? Is it that attending as a couple or family is more palatable to veterans (with individual therapy perhaps feeling more threatening or stigmatising) and therefore offering CBCT improves their access to therapy?

It is also worth considering how CBCT treatment for PTSD could be adapted for couples where the trauma happened to both partners. In these circumstances, it likely that each individual has their own idiosyncratic interpretation of events, but offering at least some of their PTSD treatment jointly could help to accelerate treatment, enhance understanding of each other and reduce relationship distress. This could be relevant to situations where couples jointly witness a traumatic event or go through a similar experience, such as the traumatic loss of a loved one. This could be an approach to consider in the aftermath of COVID-19; with the increase in clients presenting with traumatic bereavements it could be efficient to treat couples together where appropriate. However, there are many potential complications to consider when embarking on this work; for example, where a couple have ostensibly had the same experience but reacted very differently to it. It would be helpful to investigate how successful a CBCT approach would be where the trauma is shared but only one partner has PTSD, as proposed by Brown-Bowers, Fredman, Wanklyn & Monson's (2012) model. In theory a couple approach could be more time efficient for shared traumas but there are many variations in experience to consider which would require adaptation and flexibility on the part of the therapist and of the service in which they work.

Therapist tips

- Think very carefully about the sequencing of interventions; for example, not embarking on a whole course of CBCT when the partner suffering from PTSD is feeling overwhelmed by the most disruptive trauma sequelae.
- The primary intervention could be an individual evidence-based treatment for PTSD with some supplementary couple sessions to address the impact of the PTSD on the relationship and to enable the partner to assist recovery.
- Whilst some gentle exposure to discussion of the trauma or related stimuli can be helpful, be careful not to accidentally move into reliving or re-experiencing.

Suggestions for further Reading

Zayfert, C. and DeViva, J. C. (2011). *When someone you love suffers from posttraumatic stress – what to expect and what you can do.* New York: Guildford.

References

Brown-Bowers, A., Fredman, S. J., Wanklyn, S. G. and Monson, C. M. (2012). Cognitive Behavioural Conjoint Therapy for Posttraumatic Stress Disorder: Application to a Couple's Shared Traumatic Experience. *Journal of Clinical Psychology*, 68 (5): 536–547.

Baucom, D. H., Fischer, M. S., Corrie, S., Worrell, M. and Boeding, S. E. (2020). *Treating relationship Distress and Psychopathology in Couples – A Cognitive Behavioural Approach.* London: Routledge.

Fredman, S. J., Macdonald, A., Monson, C. M., Dondanville, K. A., Blount, T. H., Hall-Clark, B. N., Fine, B. A., Mintz, J., Litz, B. T., Young-McCaughan, S., Hancock, A. K., Rhoades, G. K., Yarvis, J. S., Resick. P. A., Roache, J. D., Le, Y., Wachen, J. S., Niles, B. L. and Peterson, A. L. (2019). Intensive Multi-Couple Group Therapy for PTSD: A Nonrandomised Pilot Study with military and Veteran Dyads. *Behaviour Therapy.* doi:10.1016/j.beth.2019.10.003.

Johnson, S. M. (2002). *Emotionally focused couple therapy with trauma survivors: strengthening attachment bonds.* New York: Guilford.

Kulka, R. A., Schlenger, W. E., Fairbank, J. A., Hough, R. L., Jordan, B. K., Marmar, C. R.*et al.* (1990). *Trauma and the Vietnam War Generation: report of findings from the National Vietnam Veterans Readjustment Study.* New York: Brunner/Mazel.

Monson C. M. and Fredman, S. J. (2012). *Cognitive Behavioural Conjoint Couple Therapy for PTSD – Harnessing the Healing Power of Relationships.* New York: Guilford.

Monson, C. M., Fredman, S. J., Macdonald, A., Pukay-Martin, N. D., Resick, P. A. and Schurr, P. P. (2012). Effect of Cognitive Behavioural Couple Therapy for PTSD – A Randomised Controlled Trial. *JAMA*, 308(7): 700–709. doi:10.1001/jama.2012.9307.

Monson, C. M., Macdonald, A. and Brown-Bowers, A. (2012) Couple / family therapy for post traumatic stress disorder: review to facilitate interpretation of VA / DID Clinical Practice Guideline. *Journal of Rehabilitation Research and Development.* doi:10.1682/jrrd.2011.09.0166.

Monson, C. M., Stevens, S. P. and Schnurr, P. P. (2005). Cognitive-Behavioral Couple's Treatment for Posttraumatic Stress Disorder. In T. A. Corales (Ed.), *Focus on posttraumatic stress disorder research* (pp. 245–274). Nova Science Publishers.

Pukay-Martin, N. D., Macdonald, A., Fredman, S. J. and Monson, C. M. (2016). Couple Therapy for PTSD. *Current Treatment Options in Psychiatry*, 3: 37–47.

NICE (National Institute for Health and Care Excellence). (2018). *NICE guidance [NG116] for management of post-traumatic stress disorder in children, young people and adults.* www.nice.org.uk/guidance.

Schumm, J. A., Fredman, S. J., Monson, C. M. and Chard, K. M. (2012). Cognitive behavioural conjoint therapy for PTSD: initial findings for Operations Enduring and Iraqi Freedom Male combat veterans and their partners. *American Journal of Family Therapy*, 41(4): 277–287. doi:10.1080/01926187.2012.701592.

Suomi, A., Evans, L., Rodgers, B., Taplin, S., and Cowlishaw, S. (2019). Couple and family therapies for post-traumatic stress disorder (PTSD). Cochrane Database of Systematic Reviews 2019, *Issue* 12. Art. No.: CD011257. doi:10.1002/14651858. CD011257.pub2.

Whisman, M. A., Sheldon, C. T. and Goering, P. (2000). Psychiatric disorders and dissatisfaction with social relationships: does type of relationship matter? *Journal of Abnormal Psychology*, 109: 803–808.

Funk, J. L. and Rogge, R. D. (2007). Testing the ruler with item response theory: increasing precision of measurement for relationship satisfaction with the Couples Satisfaction Index. *Journal of Family Psychology*, 21(4): 572–583.

Zayfert, C. and DeViva, J. C. (2011). *When someone you love suffers from posttraumatic stress – what to expect and what you can do.* New York: Guildford.

Chapter 14

Infidelity

Dan Kolubinski

Infidelity refers to the act of being unfaithful or breaking the trust within a committed relationship, particularly in terms of engaging in romantic or sexual interactions with someone outside of the established relationship boundaries. It involves a breach of the agreed-upon or assumed physical or emotional exclusivity between partners and often leads to emotional distress, hurt, and a breakdown of trust within the relationship. Infidelity can take various forms, including physical affairs, emotional affairs, or engaging in secretive communication or interactions with someone else in a way that undermines the commitment to the primary relationship (Perel, 2017).

Interpersonal betrayal, on the other hand, encompasses a broader range of actions beyond just infidelity, but carries the same violation of trust, loyalty, or confidence that one person has placed in another. It involves acts or behaviours that undermine the perceived or agreed-upon mutual expectations, leading to a sense of betrayal, hurt, and emotional damage. For example, if an individual discovers that a partner has hid a substantial debt from them or engaged in secretive behaviours that they had denied doing (drinking, gambling, smoking, etc.). Like an affair, the secretive nature of these behaviours strikes at the heart of the individual's understanding of their partner and their relationship. This chapter will focus on a couple dealing with the fallout of a sexual affair, but the model could also be applied to many couples where trust has been violated.

The presenting couple: Josh and Sue

Josh and Sue have been together for 19 years and married for 12. They were childhood friends, who started dating in secondary school and still live in the town where they grew up. They have three boys (9, 7 and 4) and Sue is at home with them full-time. Josh runs his own business in the construction industry, which he took over from his father 6 years ago after he retired.

One day, Sue found a suggestive text on Josh's phone from her best friend, Lisa. When she looked through the message history, she found that there were no other messages from Lisa apart from this one. When Sue confronted

DOI: 10.4324/9781003024439-16

Josh about the suggestive text, he went quiet at first, refusing to talk about it, which put Sue in a state of panic. Eventually, after 2 days of prodding by Sue, Josh admitted that he and Lisa had 'sexted' back and forth for three months and that he usually deleted the messages after reading them. On this last occasion, he had forgotten to do so.

Sue spent the following two months feeling like "*my world had been turned upside down*". She cried daily and refused to speak with Lisa. For the sake of the children, however, she did not tell anyone else about what had happened, and eventually decided to 'put it behind' her.

About six months later, however, Sue borrowed Josh's car when hers was in for repairs. Whilst getting the family groceries with her mother, Sue found a pair of women's underwear in the boot of the car. They were not hers. Sue described this moment as the "*single worst moment of my life*," but has difficulty recalling any details aside from breaking down in the car park and screaming at her mum that "*THAT BASTARD LIED TO ME!*" When Sue got home, Josh was there. She ran up to him screaming and started hitting him in the chest. Josh and Sue's mother were able to restrain her, and the rage eventually subsided. What followed was a very long conversation between Sue and Josh, during which Josh admitted that he and Lisa had been having a sexual relationship for approximately 5 years. Josh felt very emotional during the conversation and stated that most of the sex took place at Lisa's house when her husband was at work, but there were occasional times when Josh also had Lisa over at their house for sex. There were at least three occasions when Josh and Lisa went away together for several days.

Sue felt her world collapse when she heard this. It was doubly painful, because she had already come to terms with Josh and Lisa's behaviour, but that was under false pretences. She immediately cut Lisa out of her life, but sent a text message to Lisa's husband, Dave, telling him about what she and Josh had been doing behind their backs. She considered it her 'revenge' after being hurt so badly. After convincing herself that she was going to leave the marriage straightaway, Sue decided to give Josh another chance. However, she expected him to find a therapist for them, and Josh soon after contacted me for couple therapy.

Theoretical framework

Healing after infidelity is a gradual process that requires commitment and effort from both partners. Baucom and colleagues (2011) have developed a trauma-based treatment model that integrates strategies from cognitive-behavioural couple therapy, trauma interventions, forgiveness interventions, and insight-oriented couple therapy. Trauma theory focuses on understanding the psychological and emotional responses to distressing events. The betrayal, breach of trust, and emotional upheaval associated with infidelity can lead to feelings of shock, disbelief, anger, depression, and anxiety.

These reactions mirror many of the responses observed in individuals who have experienced traumatic events (Baucom et al., 2006).

By incorporating trauma theory principles into their treatment model, Baucom and colleagues (2011) provide couples with a framework that acknowledges the emotional trauma of infidelity and offers a path toward healing. This approach helps partners navigate the complex emotional landscape that follows infidelity, empowering them to gradually process their emotions, rebuild trust, and work together to create a stronger and more resilient relationship.

Course of therapy

Following the initial assessment, the course of therapy consists of three primary stages. It is important to note, however, that despite the logical progression from Stage 1 to Stage 3, progress is not always linear and sometimes it is necessary to return to previous material. The first stage is the *Impact Stage*. When a couple presents for therapy following an affair, and the injured partner is often experiencing the symptoms of trauma discussed above, the first aim is to provide a foundation from which they can experience their distress whilst still maintaining a sense of routine or normality.

The second stage is the *Meaning Stage*. This entails developing a full understanding of the factors involved in the participating partner's decision to engage with the affair. In many cases, it can be a challenge for the injured partner to be able to move forward from the affair without a clear understanding of why it happened. This stage comprises a significant number of the treatment sessions and involves exploring four themes: i) relationship factors, such as the level or quality of communication or intimacy; ii) environmental factors, such as stressors or availability of the affair partner; iii) factors related to the participating partner, including characteristics, beliefs, and past experiences; iv) factors related to the behaviour of the injured partner.

The third stage is the *Moving-on Stage*. Up until this point, it is recommended that both the participating partner and the injured partner postpone any final decisions about the future of the relationship. Once there is a clearer understanding of the contributing factors that led to the decision of the affair, both individuals are encouraged to make an informed choice about whether to commit to moving forward together or deciding to end the relationship. This stage focuses on that decision, its implications, and concepts like trust and forgiveness, which help to facilitate that decision.

Assessment

There are a few points to consider when conducting the assessment. In addition to the standard questions about the relationship history and current functioning, special attention should be paid to the events and experiences that led to the affair; whether or not the affair has ended; if not, why not; what the injured partner knows about the affair; the nature of the disclosure of the affair; and who else in the couple's support network knows about the affair. Each of these key points will be addressed in the treatment plan, generally in one of the first two stages.

Additionally, the individual sessions that are commonplace in the assessment stage of CBCT are also very valuable when dealing with infidelity. However, the secrets policy should be very clear at the start. Some clinicians will take an 'all or nothing' approach to secrets, where the couple is told that everything that is disclosed in the individual sessions will be shared with the other person or that nothing will. Both have their pros and cons regarding security and transparency; however, I think it is important to balance them by stating that disclosures are at my discretion based on what I think is clinically best for the relationship.

When arranging the individual sessions following the first appointment, I informed Josh and Sue that anything that was said during the individual appointments might come up in further sessions but doing so would be at my discretion. I needed to make sure that Sue was aware that I would not collude with Josh if he told me that the affair with Lisa was ongoing. At the same time, Josh needed reassurance that I would not disclose to Lisa everything that he might say in our individual session. Maintaining the balance between being transparent and offering a safe space to share initial thoughts and feelings is a challenge for any couple, but this is compounded by the secret nature of the affair.

Stage 1: Impact stage

The *Impact Stage* focuses on the immediate fallout of the affair. In many cases, these early days require more attention from the therapist than most couples, including increased frequency of sessions or phone calls in the opening weeks. At the start of treatment, Sue was experiencing all the hallmarks of the traumatic response. She was spending many of her waking hours ruminating about Josh and Lisa, often focusing on the specific sexual acts in which they had engaged. She was consistently looking out for signs of further betrayal and was heavily emotionally dysregulated. We held all three assessment sessions in the first week and I spoke with her on the phone twice in between sessions. These calls took place when she was feeling highly distressed and had a strong impulse for revenge, where we would discuss other alternatives for her to self-soothe. If offering this as an option to couples at the start of treatment, it is important to be boundaried, and ensure that either partner do not use these calls in between sessions to complain about the other person or disclose secrets (Baucom et al., 2011).

Damage control

The purpose of the first treatment sessions can be summed up by the motto, *"Do no further harm."* Before any sense could be made of how they ended up where they were, they first needed to cope with the fallout and prevent things from getting worse. When feeling angry about Josh's affair, Sue acknowledged that she wanted to *"make him pay for what he did",* which is why she had messaged Lisa's husband, Dave. Our opening sessions focused on setting boundaries. For Sue, that meant limiting her desire for revenge, including wanting to share with others the details of what Josh had done beyond those who already knew. At this point, most of Sue's family were already aware of the affair.

Josh had pleaded with Sue not to tell his family, which was very hard for her. At one point she stated, *"I just want his mother to know what her good little boy has been up to."* We discussed the common notions of *restitution, retribution* and *retreat* (D. H. Baucom, personal communication, May 15, 2014). Due to the high level of perceived injustice, it is common for the injured partner to view the affair like debt, requiring some sort of payback to move forward. Restitution occurs when the injured partner says, *"you have done me bad and now you owe me good".* Retribution, on the other hand, is when the injured partner says, *"you have done me bad and now I owe you bad."* The problem with either approach, of course, is that it is very difficult to quantify the 'debt', which makes it impossible to know when it is paid off in either direction.

Closely linked to the punishing aspect of retribution, but also including a self-protection element, the injured partner may *retreat* from the relationship. In addition to wanting to punish Josh, Sue no longer felt emotionally safe around him and had withdrawn emotionally. We discussed the potential short and long-term consequences and highlighted the need to interrupt that reflex, to keep her from pulling away from the relationship before the necessary work could be done. This required her to communicate with him in as civilised a way as possible and to reframe some of her hard emotions (e.g., anger, etc.) in softer terms (e.g., sadness, hurt, etc.). I also provided Sue with a list of common questions that she may wish to ask Josh, including *"When did the affair start?", "Who is this other person?", "Why do you think you did it?",* and *"Where does this leave us?"* Many of these questions would be answered more directly in later sessions but having these to hand in the early stages gave Sue some control over her ability to understand what had happened and why. The main rule, however, was to prevent any discussion about the explicit sexual acts performed during the affair. Having a clear picture of those details can make the situation worse rather than better, as it gives the injured partner a specific image on which to ruminate.

Restoring equilibrium and order

The next step is to restore the day-to-day functioning for the couple. Due to the traumatic nature of infidelity, the regular routines of the family tend to get thrown into disarray. It is important to work towards building back a sense of normality with respect to the functional aspects of the relationship, or what I like to refer to as the 'business-side'. This can include day-to-day functioning, such as the logistics of school runs and meal-planning. It can also include deciding who is going to sleep where during this time, as the injured partner may not feel comfortable sharing a bed or a bedroom with the participating partner, and what the expected boundaries are with respect to the affair partner. This last part was relatively easy for Josh and Sue, as they were able to sever ties with their friends. However, this can be more complicated for couples where the affair partner is a co-worker of the participating partner, or family member of the injured partner, where couples may not be able to sever ties so easily.

At this point, I reminded Sue of the main symptoms of trauma and we discussed her recent intrusive thoughts. She acknowledged several episodes over the week where something had triggered a reminder about the affair, and she had started to dwell on what Josh and Lisa had done together. Some of these triggers seemed innocuous, such as listening to a song about sex or driving past the pub where the two couples used to hang out together. I informed Sue that we refer to these experiences as *flashbacks* and that they were very common. I asked her how she tended to act towards Josh during those times and she acknowledged that she usually got irritable or angry and would often lash out or yell at him.

We then discussed the strategies that are useful to deal with flashback experiences.

THERAPIST: So, Sue, let's delve into the strategies regarding dealing with flashback experiences. Remember, the first step is awareness. When you find yourself experiencing those flashbacks triggered by environmental cues, like the song or passing by a particular place, try to recognise that moment.

SUE: Okay, I'll try to be more aware when those moments happen.

THERAPIST: Great. And when you feel upset or angry, it's crucial to pause and ask yourself whether it's because of something Josh is doing in the present moment or if it's connected to the past. Anger is a valid emotion, especially if something in the present triggers it. However, sometimes those feelings might stem from memories of past events.

SUE: That makes sense. But it's tough to separate them at times. It's like I react instantly, and it's hard to distinguish where the feelings are coming from.

THERAPIST: That's completely understandable. It takes time and practice to recognise those triggers and separate the past from the present. Remember, Josh's current actions might not necessarily be linked to what happened before. It's important to avoid punishing him in the present for past mistakes. Does that make sense to you?

SUE: Yeah, it does. I know it doesn't help if I unfairly blame him for something he isn't doing right now.

THERAPIST: Exactly. We'll work together to help you manage these emotions and responses. The goal is to support both of you in fostering a healthier and more balanced dynamic. If you find it challenging, we can explore more strategies to assist you in this process.

Sue learned strategies to deal with those moments when she realised she was responding to Josh's past behaviour, rather than his present behaviour. It is useful in those moments, first of all, to acknowledge one's own hurt and pain and to inform the participating partner of those softer feelings, linking it to the memory of the affair. The aim is not to 'keep bringing it up', but rather for people to come to terms with the emotional consequences of the behaviour without trying to suppress them. The next step is for the injured partner to be clear about what they need in that moment. A hug? Reassurance? Space to be alone? During this exchange, the participating partner is asked to meet that immediate need. The injured partner, though, is also encouraged to reflect on their own options for self-care, to take responsibility for their own feelings and behaviour and to rely less on the participating partner when a flashback occurs.

On some occasions, it can be helpful for the participating partner to distinguish between feelings of guilt and feelings of shame that emerge when the injured partner experiences a flashback. Guilt is the feeling that we have when we acknowledge that we have done something to hurt someone else. It is meant to serve as a motivator to check our behaviour and repair our relationships. However, shame is the feeling attached to thoughts that we are bad or 'less than' as a result of our behaviour (Brown, 2006). I cautioned Josh that feeling guilty when Sue acknowledged a flashback is perfectly normal, but that it can be very challenging if he starts to question his own self-worth and feels shameful as a result. At times, being reminded of the affair sent Josh on a negative spiral of self-deprecation and hopelessness, making it difficult for him to hear Sue when she was feeling triggered.

Understanding and validating each other's experiences

Couples often require skills-based training in communication to shift from a position of 'listening to respond' to one of listening in order to understand. As we will see in Stage Two, there are many factors that can increase the risk of a partner choosing to have an affair, and it is paramount that the couple can hear one another properly before those factors are explored. Furthermore, communication skills are also necessary to regain a sense of order and routine in the day-to-day functioning of the relationship. Much as we would do for any couple in distress, Josh and Sue were taught the skills for having conversations about thoughts and feelings and conversations for problem-solving (See Chapter 2 for details).

Additionally, when conversations escalate quickly, particularly due to intense emotions, it can be useful for the injured partner to write down their thoughts and feelings for the participating partner to read. I encouraged Sue early in our sessions to spend time alone writing out her experiences over the recent months, highlighting what she needed Josh to hear. However, I asked her to write two letters initially. The first was focused on 'venting' her hurt and frustrations with as much hurtful language as she could muster. Name-calling, swearing, threats and punishments were all allowed in this first letter. However, there was one very important rule and that was she was *not* to share it with Josh.

Once it was finished, she was instructed to destroy it and to start again. This second letter focused, instead, on the softer feelings of hurt and pain and she was to reflect on the key messages that she needed Josh to hear. In the letter, it was also necessary for her to acknowledge that her thoughts and feelings were from her own perspective and that she also knew that Josh might see things differently, as hard as it was for her to admit that.

Letter-writing can help the injured partner wrap their heads around what is important to them and why in order to help facilitate better conversations. It also helps with compartmentalising the uncomfortable thoughts and feelings so that behaviour in any given moment is not reactive. I often tell couples that I think that one of the keys to life is to feel comfortable with feeling uncomfortable, and processing thoughts and feelings in a letter can help build that distress tolerance.

Potential pitfalls

There are a few aspects of this stage of treatment that the therapist must bear in mind. Firstly, as we will see in the second stage, the decision to have an affair is a complex one and it is imperative that the therapist not take sides with the injured partner or judge the participating partner. This is particularly true if you can relate to the injured partner from your own experience. Secondly, it is difficult to underestimate just how emotionally dysregulated some injured partners will be at the start of treatment. As such, it can feel overwhelming to the therapist, who can get lost in the chaos. A clear sense of direction, the ability to contain the couple, and tolerance of uncomfortable emotions are crucial. Lastly, because of the emotional dysregulation, the injured partner may be at increased risk of self-harm or suicidality, harm to the participating partner or to the affair partner. As such, it can be challenging to distinguish normative distress from danger.

THERAPIST: It is crucial that we address the heightened emotions and potential risks involved in this situation. Sue, I understand how over-whelming it can feel, and I'm here to support you. It's essential to dif-ferentiate between understandable distress and potential danger. Your emotions are valid, but if you ever feel at risk of harming yourself or others, it's vital to seek immediate help. Safety is our priority here. Josh, I want you to understand the severity of this situation. While Sue navigates her emotions, your support and understanding are crucial. We'll work together to ensure everyone's safety and well-being.

Stage 2: Meaning

Once there is a foundation of routine, communication and emotional regulation, the couple can start to explore the factors involved in the participating partner's decision to have an affair. As we saw in the first session, couples engage in therapy with complicated emotions following an affair, many of which stem for the moral assumption that having an affair is wrong. Injured partners may seek restitution or retribution for the wrong that has been done to them. Participating partners may feel shame for having violated their own moral code. However, the factors involved in the decision to have an affair tend to be numerous and complicated and it is imperative not to impose a moral stance of goodness or badness on behaviour.

Nonetheless, we are not saying that all behaviour is value-neutral, or that partners can engage in any behaviour they wish. Instead, I like to make a distinction between *excusing* behaviour and *explaining* behaviour. What I aim to do is highlight the various factors that contributed to the participating partner's decision-making process. At no point will either partner be able to view the decision as inevitable or condone it as the *correct* decision; however, that does not mean that we must view it as being bad or wrong either.

Based on the first stage of treatment, the participating partner will be aware of the impact their behaviour had on the injured partner. Often, that traumatic outcome is not a result of having a physical or emotional connection with someone else but is instead the result of the violation of their 'contract', implicit or explicit, with the participating partner. In a monogamous relationship, that contract suggests full physical and emotional exclusivity. In a consensual non-monogamous relationship, however, partners may engage physically or emotionally with other people, yet it is still possible to violate the contract and call it an affair. The aim here is to explain what contributed to the decision to violate a contract. Doing this reduces the risk of making the same decision in the future. This also leads to greater predictability in the relationship, helps both partners to understand each other, their own perspectives and contributions to the relationship better, and highlights aspects of the relationship, environmental circumstances or individual perspectives/behaviours that may need to change to move forward.

The foundation for these conversations starts in the assessment, where the therapist can ask targeted questions about what was going on inside and outside the relationship. The therapist guides the couple through guided discovery, open to exploration and at times unsure of the destination. There are some topics, though, that are best avoided, including the explicit details of any sexual acts or the aspects of the affair partner that the injured partner lacks. In either case, this can inhibit the injured partner's ability to heal emotionally.

Providing the rationale for this stage to Sue was a challenge. She had a difficult time distinguishing between explanations and excuses and would often make comments about Josh trying to 'logic' his way out of taking responsibility for his actions. Comments like these served as signals to me to make sure that we had covered the necessary ground in Stage 1.

Relationship Factors

The first set of factors we explored centred around the relationship between Josh and Sue. They were able to identify that they had both struggled with the shift to parenthood when their eldest was born. Prior to becoming parents, the two of them used to 'party hard'. They, along with Lisa and her husband, Dave, used to be the central figures in their social circle, always going out on weekends. Josh highlighted that after they started dating in adolescence, they had transitioned into adulthood whilst keeping their wild routine with the same group of friends. By the time they became parents, they had been together for about 10 years and were forced to unlearn habits and routines. Josh admitted that he struggled with this more than Sue did. They both identified that Sue was very maternal, but that Josh struggled to redefine himself as a *"dad"* instead of a *"lad"*.

Sue also identified that she had pushed for a third child, being one of three herself, but then had difficulty conceiving. This meant that sex between them became 'work' for over a year, and they struggled to regain a satisfying sexual relationship after she gave birth. Where for years they used to have passionate sex two to three times per week, their physical relationship had become mechanical and 'soulless'. Sue found this very difficult to accept, because she realised part way through the session that Josh and Lisa's sexual relationship had started while they were trying to conceive their youngest.

Environmental Factors

Environmental factors can include external circumstances, such as stressors, or the influence of other people, such as a willing affair partner or friends who encourage the behaviour. Josh and Sue both acknowledged that Lisa's willingness to engage in the affair was a contributing factor, though Josh was never clear as to who made the first advance. Additionally, Josh acknowledged that he experienced a great deal of stress when he took over his father's business six years ago and the affair was his way of managing that stress. Sue asked whether taking over the business provided Josh with the freedom and flexibility to be able to leave for a couple of hours to visit Lisa, which Josh acknowledged was true.

Participating Partner Factors

These factors involve aspects of the participating partner's background, personality and characteristics that contribute to them choosing to have an affair. There can be overlap between individual and relationship factors, but it is important to distinguish between them to get a fuller understanding of why things developed as they did, and also to be clear about what might need to change or be acknowledged in order to prevent similar choices in future. These factors can include affirmations of worth, poor boundary setting, the need for escapism, the tendency to view short-term gain over long-term gain, or the normalising of affairs from different role models.

Josh had acknowledged that he struggled with the transition to parenthood and the impact that it had on their relationship, and when discussing this I asked him to elaborate on his experience of the shift from *"lad"* to *"dad"*. We discussed how his identity had been based around his friends and their weekend trips to the pub for all his adult life. Since he and Sue were the first of their friends to have a child, he developed a heightened fear of missing out when they first became parents. He also acknowledged that he mourned the loss of his carefree attitude to life, because *"we became responsible for keeping this human alive and the pressure was unbearable"*. He acknowledged that his affair was partly an attempt to relive his 'wild days'.

We also explored some of the relationships that Josh viewed when he was growing up. His dad worked late hours, often travelling to tradeshows and this had a significant toll on his parents' relationship. They fought often, had poor communication, but still stayed together through it all. Over a couple of sessions, we explored the impact that his parents' experiences had on Josh's view of relationships. He was able to identify that he had developed a belief over the years that relationships endure during the hardest times and partners stay together. Rather than addressing the difficulties in his relationship, he acknowledged that he didn't bother trying to fix things, because *"that's just how relationships are sometimes."* In retrospect, he was able to see how this attitude moved him further away from Sue and had a significant impact on his decision to have an affair.

Injured Partner Factors

We also explore how Sue may have indirectly and unintentionally contributed to Josh's decision through her own behaviour. It is important to highlight, though, that this does not impart responsibility for an affair on the injured partner. Whilst it can be an uncomfortable discussion to shine the attention in this way, there can be something empowering about the process if the injured partner recognises that having an impact on the decision to have an affair may also mean that there are aspects of this situation that fall within their control going forward.

Common factors here might include difficulties in meeting the needs of the participating partner, having too high expectations of him or her, or difficulty confronting the participating partner about challenges in the relationship. Each of these factors could lead to decrease in the level of satisfaction for either partner, feeding into some of the relationship factors described earlier. Other factors might include lack of awareness around potential warning signs about the affair or a tendency to overlook poor boundaries with others, in general, or with the affair partner, specifically.

In Sue's case, she was able to acknowledge that she had been aware of Josh's difficulties transitioning to parenthood and tended to minimise or dismiss his concerns, calling him *"childish"* or *"selfish."* She identified that by ignoring the issues, they hadn't gone away, as she had expected, but ended up making him feel ignored. When Lisa expressed concern about how he was feeling, that helped to strengthen their connection and weakened his connection with Sue. As we probed deeper into her reaction during that transition, she said that parenthood was just *"something to get on with."* She noted that her parents had largely focused on the functioning of their relationship, whilst giving little care to their friendship. They were still together, but she was able to acknowledge that there was little love between the two of them in their retirement. Lastly, Sue also admitted that, in hindsight, she had wondered why Josh was so keen to spend their holidays with Lisa and her husband Dave in recent years. Although the two couples had been close for many years, she had noticed that their involvement in each other's lives had increased significantly since the birth of their youngest child.

Generating a Formulation

Once the four sets of factors have been explored, it is useful to consolidate these conversations by bringing the factors into a unified understanding of the participating partner's decision to have an affair. However, it is important to emphasise that as these decisions are highly complicated one may never get to a perfect understanding. The formulation is generally developed by asking the couple to write down how the various factors may have contributed to the initiation, maintenance and, where applicable, termination of the affair. The process, however, may be different for each couple, depending on how willing or able they are to discuss the topic constructively and work together as a team. The therapist may wish to consider whether this is an activity that can be done in the session with the therapist or something for the couple to do as homework between sessions.

When we finished exploring the various factors across about three sessions, I felt comfortable with Josh's forthrightness and willingness to take responsibility, and Sue's ability to emotionally self-regulate during the difficult discussions. I suggested that they take an evening or two during the week to review the various factors and to work together to generate the consolidated

list, highlighting how the affair with Lisa started and the factors that contributed to it lasting for as long as it did. In the following session, I asked
Josh to recount the reflection so that Sue could hear him acknowledge the
various factors. In their case, I thought this would help reassure her that,
should they stay together, Josh would be aware of the factors involved in his
decision so that we could move into conversations about what could be different. In some cases, though, I have asked the injured partner to recount the
factors instead if I think that doing so will help them in their journey of
healing.

Stage 3: Moving-on

Once they have generated their formulation of the affair, the focus starts to
turn toward the third and final stage of treatment. If the first stage focuses
on the present and the second stage focuses on the past, the third treatment
stage shifts the focus to the future. The aims of this stage are to define what
forgiveness means and how to implement it, to make an informed decision
about the future of the relationship, namely whether the two partners wish to
stay together or not, the rebuilding of trust, if applicable, and to discuss the
implications and obstacles related to their decisions.

Forgiveness

As mentioned above, over the course of Stage 2, the injured partner learns
the distinction between excusing behaviour and explaining behaviour. This
distinction is key for the injured partner to understand the factors involved
in the decision to have an affair and a clear distinction is made between
understanding and *condoning*. Forgiveness requires a similar distinction, and
many injured partners have a difficulty with the concept of forgiving the
participating partner, because they fear that doing so will mean that the
participating partner will 'get away with what they have done'. I start this
conversation with a clear description of what forgiveness is and what it is
not, and I start with the latter. First of all, forgiveness is not about condoning behaviour. Nor is it about reconciling or saving the relationship. Lastly,
forgiveness does not mean having to pretend that the event or action did not
happen. Holding any of these beliefs about forgiveness will make it very hard
for the injured partner to consider forgiving the participating partner.

Instead, forgiveness is about acknowledging what has happened without
being dominated by negative emotions. It is about accepting that the past
cannot be controlled, but through exploring the factors discussed in Stage 2,
it can be understood and put into a wider context. Most importantly,
though, it is about choosing to forfeit the right to punish the participating
partner for their actions going forward. Fundamentally, forgiveness is not
something that the injured partner does to or for the participating partner. It

is a gift that one bestows to oneself so as not to be controlled by the negative thoughts and feelings. Some of this work is done in Stage 1 when discussing the difference between restitution and retribution, but it is worth defining it very explicitly once these factors are better understood.

Sue had a particularly difficult time with the concept of forgiveness, and we had to revisit the concept over several sessions. I had to emphasise that forgiveness is not about condoning, it does not mean that she is committing at this point to stay in the relationship, and it does not mean she needs to forget about what happen. I operate on the principle of 'forgive, but don't forget'. The affair is now a part of their story, and they cannot pretend it didn't happen. I asked Sue what she thought the consequences for her would be of holding on to the pain and being ready to hold the affair over Josh's head whenever they had a disagreement in the future. She identified that holding on to the negative feelings could allow these to grow in time, making her even more bitter and angry. She also acknowledged that whilst she liked the idea of having the power to *"play the affair card"* in future arguments, she could see that by doing this it would not be possible for her to ever speak to Josh as an equal partner in the long-term.

THERAPIST: Sue, let's revisit the topic of forgiveness. I understand it's been a challenging concept for you. Forgiveness doesn't mean you're excusing what happened or committing to staying in the relationship. It's about finding peace for yourself and moving forward without holding onto the pain.

SUE: It's hard to let go of what he did. I don't want to act like it's okay, because it's not.

THERAPIST: Absolutely, your feelings are valid. Forgiveness isn't about pretending the affair didn't happen. It's acknowledging that it's a part of your story without letting it define your future. What are your thoughts on holding onto the pain and using the affair as a card that you can play in future disagreements so that you always win?

SUE: I've been thinking about that a lot. Holding onto this pain will only make me more bitter, and I don't want that. But it's tough to let go of the anger. I like the idea of having that power to remind him of his mistake, but I see now it'll damage our future.

THERAPIST: You're recognising the consequences of holding onto the pain. How do you envision your future conversations with Josh?

SUE: I want to move towards a place where we can talk as equals, not where I feel like I'm always holding this over him. I want a partnership where we can both grow without this shadow always looming over us.

Decisions about the future

Up to this point, we have not spoken about what will happen to the relationship after therapy ends. This is largely because it is helpful for the injured partner to go through the processes of understanding the factors involved in the decision to have an affair, as well as the process of forgiving the injured partner, regardless of whether the couple will stay together in the end. Even if the ultimate decision is to separate, this process will allow the injured partner to understand factors that may be relevant in future relationships and minimise the amount of emotional baggage they might bring into that relationship.

However, once these steps have been taken, I then ask the couple to reflect on what they would like to do going forward. Do they want to stay with their current partner and discuss moving forward together or would they prefer to shift the focus of dissolving the relationship? Of course, it takes two people to agree to stay together and only one to decide to leave. The injured partner must ask themselves whether they think that the participating partner has been remorseful about the pain caused by the affair and whether he or she understands enough about the risk factors to not fall back into old patterns of behaviour. If so, we can then discuss what it means to rebuild trust as a crucial step. The participating partner may wish to reflect on whether the affair reflected a need that was unmet by the relationship with the injured partner, whether the relationship could be changed to meet that need, and, if not, would the relationship with the injured partner be worth closing the door on that need? In essence, both partners are evaluating each other, themselves, the relationship, and their environment to make a decision about whether to progress forward together or separately.

Sue and Josh were both clear that they wanted to move forward together. However, it is worth mentioning that staying together should not be the aim of this process and the criteria for considering therapy to be successful. If either partner decides to leave the relationship at this point, but they do so with a better understanding of why things developed as they did and are not ruled by the negative emotions that were present at intake, then I would consider that a success.

The injured partner may decide to end the relationship for many reasons, even after deciding to forgive the participating partner. Remember, forgiveness does not mean committing to stay in the relationship. *It is a gift to oneself.* Despite forgiving the participating partner, he or she may not have shown enough remorse or insight into the various risk factors. These can serve as a signal to the injured partner that the risk level for engaging in another affair is too high. In other circumstances, the injured partner might decide that his or her understanding of the participating partner or of their relationship has been irreparably altered by the affair. Building a relationship based on this new understanding might not be appealing and he or she may decide that being single or finding another partner is a more attractive option. Again, if this decision is not made out of spite or fuelled by negative emotions, I would still see this as a successful outcome.

The participating partner may also decide to leave the relationship at this point, which could be a challenge if the injured partner has decided to stay.

This can, at times, provoke a sense of rejection and/or injustice in the injured partner and could potentially be retraumatising. However, it may be that the participating partner has decided that the affair was able to meet an important need that could not be met in the relationship, or, upon reflection, the affair was a symptom of greater issues in the relationship and he or she would rather leave.

Rebuilding trust

Trust is something that we often take for granted when relationships are going well. One of the biggest predictors of the success of a relationship is how someone answers the question, *"Do I think my partner has my back"*? (Gottman & Silver, 2012). Even when there is distress and miscommunication in a relationship, trust can still be high. Many injured partners will start the therapy process with some version of the phrase, *"I knew we had issues, but I never thought that he/she was capable of doing something like this"*. That the behaviour goes against the injured partner's understanding of the participating partner's character is what makes an affair so challenging to understand. The secretive nature of affairs, then, significantly impacts the level of trust between them, and if a couple has decided to stay together, it will be important for them to reestablish that trust between themselves.

Trust is the mechanism that allows us to cope with uncertainty. We might not always know what our partner is doing when we are not around and if we had the certainty that this knowledge would bring, we would never need to trust (D. Baucom, personal communication, 16 May, 2014).

Building trust has two separate components to it. First, one must put themselves in a place where one *could* be hurt. This involves taking a risk that will often put the injured partner outside of their comfort zone. The second component requires time, where that risk pays off consistently and the hurt never comes. It is not uncommon for the injured partner to be hesitant about taking such a chance, either because it could lead to them being hurt again or might seem as though the participating partner is getting off without any consequences.

THERAPIST: Sue, rebuilding trust after an affair is undoubtedly challenging. If we could guarantee that Josh always acted perfectly, trust wouldn't be necessary. But the reality is, trust is about navigating uncertainty. We can't always know what happens when we're not present.

SUE: I get it, but I'm scared. Trusting Josh again feels like I'm setting myself up to get hurt or letting him off the hook without consequences.

THERAPIST: Your concerns are understandable, Sue. Trust involves taking a chance despite the fear of potential hurt or lack of consequences, and like we talked about regarding forgiveness, holding this over him will lead you further from the relationship that you want to have. It's a risk you are considering and remember that there isn't anything that Josh could do where you would think that his debt has been paid in full.

SUE: It's tough to take that risk.

THERAPIST: It is. But remember, it's possible that both outcomes could happen. However, if the relationship you want with Josh involves rebuilding trust, it's essential to take that leap. Trust is a necessary part of creating the relationship you desire.

SUE: I guess I need to try, even if it's scary.

THERAPIST: Absolutely. It's a process, and it will take time. By taking this step, you're investing in the possibility of rebuilding a relationship based on trust and mutual understanding. It's a chance to move forward towards the relationship you would like to see.

Forging a new relationship

As the therapy drew to a close, we revisited the formulation again to discuss what Josh and Sue would need to consider when moving forward together. It was clear to both that the transition into parenthood had been hard on their relationship and that they needed to explore new ways to connect. For some couples, revisiting activities that they did in their early days as a couple can be a useful way of rebuilding connection. That is not possible, however, when those activities are no longer conducive to the life that they are living. Josh and Sue discussed new ways of spending time together, such as quiz nights at the pub, going to the cinema and joining a gym together.

Josh also identified the need for him to have healthy outlets where he could have fun and de-stress, so that being responsible and having fun could co-exist. He could be the 'lad' *and* the 'dad', within limits. He also acknowledged that he wanted to have a better relationship with Sue than the one his parents had with each other, which meant showing up and putting in an effort to connect with her regularly.

THERAPIST REFLECTION: Working with Josh and Sue was challenging for several reasons. Firstly, Sue exhibited immense emotional distress at the start of therapy, which was understandable given the intensity of the affair, Josh's choice of affair partner, and the disclosure over multiple occasions ('the fake-truth' and 'the truth-truth'). Initially the therapy sessions focused on enabling a semblance of open communication, allowing Sue to express her emotions in a way that didn't threaten the relationship. Secondly, Josh felt significant levels of guilt and shame and the shame was a significant barrier to his ability to hear how hurt Sue was. In early sessions, he would often try to change the subject when she mentioned how he had hurt her. By facing the hurt that he caused without it translating into his own self-criticism, he was able to sit with her in her pain and disclose the context of his affair with Lisa. Being able to hear Sue and talk about the factors underneath his decision to have an affair indicated a willingness from Josh to engage in the therapeutic process.

Therapist tips

- Don't judge! Affairs are rarely simple and there are usually many different factors that contribute to someone's decision to have one. It is very tempting to blame the participating partner for doing "the bad thing", but as you can hopefully see from this chapter, there is a context behind that decision, and in many cases, the participating partner will often be critical of themselves already.
- Affairs are rarely just about sex. For the participating partner, they are about developing a connection with someone, often when the connection is poor with their partner. For the injured partner, it's the secrecy of it that tends to hurt the most.

Suggestions for further Reading

Baucom, D. H., Snyder, D. K., & Gordon, K. C. (2011). *Helping couples get past the affair: A clinician's guide.* New York: Guilford.

References

Baucom, D. H., Snyder, D. K., & Gordon, K. C. (2011). *Helping couples get past the affair: A clinician's guide.* New York: Guilford.

Baucom, D. H., Gordon, K. C., Snyder, D. K., Atkins, D. C., & Christensen, A. (2006). Treating affair couples: Clinical considerations and initial findings. *Journal of Cognitive Psychotherapy*, 20(4), 375–392.

Brown, B. (2006). Shame resilience theory: A grounded theory study on women and shame. *Families in Society*, 87(1), 43–52.

Gottman, J., & Silver, N. (2012). *What makes love last? How to build trust and avoid betrayal.* Simon and Schuster.

Perel, E. (2017). *The state of affairs: Rethinking infidelity.* London: Hachette.

Chapter 15

Neurodiversity

Natasha Liu-Thwaites

Simon was referred for psychological therapy after struggling with 'melt-downs' which were impacting on his day-to-day life and his relationship with his partner Lucy. He had diagnoses of Autism Spectrum Disorder (ASD) and Attention Deficit Hyperactivity Disorder (ADHD) made in adulthood.

In his first assessment appointment, Simon presented as a highly intelligent man, who was articulate in explaining his difficulties. He worked part-time in an academic role at a university. However, his wife reported that he struggled with managing day-to-day life in the home, such as helping with household chores like laundry and cooking. He would very easily get overwhelmed by such tasks or forget to do things. He also preferred things to be done in a certain way, and if things were moved or done differently in the house, he was quick to lose his temper, and he would feel very guilty about this afterwards. He tended to put off admin tasks like completing forms, and this procrastination led to frustrations in the couple relationship, with his wife feeling like she was having to act 'like his mother' at times, despite him being so intelligent. The couple had talked about having children but could not see how they could manage this in their current situation, as it felt like an 'unequal' relationship.

Introduction

Autism Spectrum Disorder (ASD) is a neurodevelopmental condition char-acterized by life-long, persistent differences with social communication, social interaction and relationships, restricted, repetitive activities and interests, and sometimes sensory differences. It is a common condition with an increasing estimated prevalence of 1.1% in the UK (NICE, 2020). Males tend to be diagnosed more than females, with a ratio of approximately 3:1 (Loomes and Hull, 2017). There has been a lot of terminology used to describe ASD over the years (including Autism Spectrum Condition, Autism, Asperger's Syndrome, 'on the spectrum', Atypical Autism, and Pervasive Developmental Disorder). For the purposes of this chapter, we will use ASD.

Attention Deficit Hyperactivity Disorder (ADHD) is characterised by life-long difficulties with inappropriate levels of inattention, hyperactivity and

DOI: 10.4324/9781003024439-17

impulsivity. There are three main diagnostic subtypes: ADHD – combined presentation (where symptoms of both inattention and hyperactivity/impulsivity are present above the cut-off scores for diagnosis); ADHD – predominantly inattentive presentation (where symptoms of inattention predominantly are present above the cut-off scores); and ADHD – predominantly hyperactive/impulsive presentation (where symptoms of hyperactivity and impulsivity predominantly are present above the cut-off scores). It is also a common neurodevelopmental condition, which is estimated to affect about 3–4% of the adult population, and to have a male to female ratio of 3:1. (NICE, 2023).

The reasons for the differences in gender ratios are not fully understood, but it is thought that females may present differently in both conditions, and more research is needed in this area.

People can be diagnosed with ASD or ADHD, or with both conditions as in Simon's case. Some individuals with ASD or ADHD present as being very high functioning while others are more affected by their symptoms and the challenges these present.

Common themes in couples where there is a neurodevelopmental condition present in one or both partners

ASD difficulties affecting relationships can include:

Difficulties with socialising

Difficulties with socialising can create conflict if one of the partners is more sociable than the other. For those with ASD, socialising may be very difficult due to anxiety or sensory sensitivities in social situations, having differences in reading social cues and navigating social interactions, and generally preferring to do things on their own.

Special interests

Getting absorbed in special interests could lead to a number of problems, including not spending enough time with a partner in favour of engaging in the special interest, talking obsessively about special interests over other things, and lack of interest in their partner's interests or viewpoints.

Cognitive rigidity

This can make it difficult for individuals if things are not done in certain ways, or according to the person's routines. Similarly, sudden, or unexpected changes to routine can also be very difficult to deal with, and can lead to increased anxiety, and/or sudden loss of temper, which could be characterised as an 'autistic meltdown' (further described below).

Autistic meltdowns

An autistic meltdown can occur in a number of situations but can be understood as 'an intense response to an overwhelming situation.' It happens when someone becomes completely overwhelmed by their current situation and temporarily loses control of their behaviour. The loss of control can be expressed in many different ways, including verbally (such as shouting, screaming, and crying) and physically (such as 'lashing out', throwing things, hitting, kicking, and biting).

This can be very hard for a neurotypical partner to understand, as they may be likely to take it personally, see it as a 'temper tantrum', or, indeed, there may be instances where they are at risk of harm. It likely results from the person's condition meaning they find it difficult to express how they are feeling in another way.

There are also a number of other ways in which an autistic person may express themselves when they are overwhelmed, such as refusing to interact, withdrawing from situations they find challenging, or avoiding difficult situations completely (NAS website, 2020).

Alexithymia and perceived empathy issues

Some autistic people may suffer from alexithymia, and have significant difficulty with identifying, expressing, and describing their emotions. This can be problematic in a couple relationship if it appears that the person lacks empathy, is not able to pick up on their partner's emotions, or is not able to offer comfort in the conventional way. To some partners, the autistic person can come across as 'cold'. In fact, it is often not that the person is not experiencing emotions, and many can actually be very sensitive to different emotional energies. However, their means of expressing and describing these in conventional ways may differ.

Sensory differences

These can potentially cause difficulties in the living environment and outside environment and can be the cause of 'meltdowns' at times. Sensory differences can also sometimes contribute to lack of intimacy for example if a person is uncomfortable with touch, and even affectionate gestures, such as hugging, can feel awkward for an individual at times.

ADHD difficulties affecting relationships can include:

Organisation difficulties

Executive function difficulties can pose challenges for organisation. This can cause problems in the home environment as it can be hard for an individual with ADHD to be organised when it comes to household chores and administration. They may have a tendency to be messy, forget things, find it difficult to plan, procrastinate, or not complete tasks. They can find it hard to remember dates, such as birthdays, and this can cause issues in a couple relationship too. These organisational difficulties can also cause problems with an individual's employment, which can put extra pressure on a partnership.

Not listening/distractibility

Those with ADHD may tend to 'zone out' or 'drift off' in conversation, which can cause a partner to feel they are not being listened to and can also affect wider friendships. This can be due to difficulty concentrating on conversations, or difficulty following conversations due to getting distracted easily by external stimuli, or by their own thoughts.

Restlessness

A need to be 'on the go' all the time can be problematic in a couple relationship in several ways. It can be difficult if the person with ADHD is not able to sit and relax with their partner, for example, not being able to sit and watch a film together or go out for dinner together. The person may tend to fidget with something, always be moving their leg, and not being able to sit still, which can be irritating for a partner.

Being a 'chatterbox'

This can be an attractive quality, and those with ADHD tend to be charismatic, funny, and likeable. However, a tendency to talk all the time can also be tiring or irritating for partners, as can a tendency to interrupt them, or blurt out inappropriate things.

Impulsive behaviours

Impulsive behaviours can present in many different ways and can cause a number of problems in relationships. As above, saying things impulsively, 'without a filter', can be perceived as rude, thoughtless, or embarrassing. Those with ADHD can be 'quick to temper' and get into impulsive arguments about small things. This can even add an element of excitement to the relationship for some. Impulsive spending can lead to debt. Impulsivity in driving can lead to risk issues if there is a tendency to speed or get into 'road rage'. Impulsivity can also lead to substance misuse issues in some individuals.

Getting bored easily

Some individuals with ADHD will describe getting very easily bored in relationships. Coupled with impulsivity, this may lead to an increased tendency to being unfaithful or promiscuous.

Common themes in both ASD and ADHD

For both ASD and ADHD, self-esteem issues can be a problem if the individual has had difficult lifetime experiences related to their neurodivergence, such as being told they were lazy from childhood, or being rejected by others because they were perceived as being annoying or 'weird'. Some describe experiencing *Rejection Sensitive Dysphoria*, which is characterised by having intense emotional experiences related to being inordinately sensitive to rejection. Although this has not been fully researched or understood, it may develop as a result of a combination of emotional dysregulation and having a number of difficult life experiences. Individuals with Rejection Sensitive Dysphoria are more likely to experience stress at work and at home.

It is important to note that some of the above features can potentially be strengths and work well in a relationship, and so do not always cause problems. For example, if partners have a shared special interest, this may not cause a difficulty at all, or if neither are particularly extrovert people, socialising may not be an issue either.

Theoretical framework

Therapy was approached using a Cognitive Behavioural Couples framework (Epstein and Baucom, 2002; see Chapter 2), with some adaptations in the context of Simon's ASD and ADHD. It is worth noting that the neurodiversity movement has grown significantly over recent years, allowing people to think differently about conditions such as ASD and ADHD, both within and outside of contexts of disability and mental health. Clinicians working in the field of neurodiversity draw from the literature that is available (for example, the suggestions for further reading at the end of this chapter). However, there are also a wide variety of ideas around neurodiversity found in online forums, magazines, message boards and social media platforms, encompassing many different themes, such as identity, and experiences potentially unique to neurodiverse conditions, like 'autistic meltdowns' and 'Rejection Sensitivity Dysphoria'. As well as being popular with neurodivergent individuals themselves, these platforms are used by people working with neurodiversity to share ideas around their clinical experiences, and better understand what their clients are experiencing. The work carried out with this couple used a CBCT approach with some adaptations to take neurodiversity into account.

The presenting couple: Simon and Lucy

Simon and Lucy met at university. They had initially been attracted to each other due to their shared interest in academia, with both going on to work on PhDs in archaeology.

Lucy noted that she had found Simon funny and 'quirky' when she first met him, and different from the other boyfriends she had had. She felt she was able to have intellectual and interesting conversations with him, and she described him as a very kind and honest person, whom she trusted fully, and whom she felt was *"never trying to take advantage"*.

They married not long after completing their studies, and this was the first time they lived together too. They generally managed this well at the beginning, with both being busy at work but having shared interests like hiking and going to art galleries.

A few years into their marriage, Simon took on an academic role at a local university. This involved teaching, and he started to find this very stressful due to the need to interact with people on a daily basis. He also struggled to socialise with colleagues, stating he just didn't enjoy this, and that he thought they may dislike him as a result. In addition, he struggled to organise his work, finding it difficult to prioritise the planning of his lessons, particularly those he was not as interested in. Around this time, Simon looked into being assessed for ASD and ADHD, after this was mentioned by his employers. He was diagnosed with ASD, and the inattentive predominant presentation of ADHD.

Lucy had always led on household chores, and initially she had not minded this. However, as her own job as a teacher became increasingly demanding, she had less patience for Simon's difficulties with helping around the home. At one point he forgot their anniversary, and this led to a big argument. Not long after this, Simon started to get increasingly overwhelmed by stressful situations, having 'meltdown' experiences where he would become extremely anxious, and suddenly 'lose it', leading to him crying, shouting, pounding his chest, and throwing things. He had caused damage to the walls in their house during these meltdowns, and Simon was very upset to note that Lucy had been scared by him one day, although he had never hurt her directly. One meltdown had happened while they were out in public. Simon had been feeling stressed due to work and he became overwhelmed by the crowds. During this episode, someone called the police, and this was a very harrowing experience for Simon, which filled him with shame. Following this he became fearful that he might be arrested or hurt someone, and this heightened his agitation and levels of anxiety, with him becoming quite depressed.

Simon was referred for cognitive behaviour therapy (CBT) to help with the management of his meltdowns. Over the course of therapy, difficulties in the couple relationship were identified, which were contributing to his unhappiness. He reported that he often felt to blame when things went wrong, and it was also noted that Lucy seemed anxious to know what was happening in his individual therapy. This led to them being offered a course of couple therapy.

THERAPIST REFLECTION: I felt quite anxious when I first started the therapy sessions with Simon and Lucy because they seemed to be placing a lot of expectation on the couple therapy as an intervention. This felt positive, as they both seemed very engaged with the process, but I also worried that they were expecting a 'magic wand' process in which they would not take a shared responsibility for the difficulties. I was also concerned that the meltdown experiences that Simon had been having would end up dominating the sessions, although of course addressing these would be an important part of the therapy.

Formulation

The couple's difficulties were conceptualised using a Cognitive Behavioural Couples framework, paying particular attention to the interaction between Simon's ASD and ADHD, his mood and anxiety, and the relationship functioning. It was clear from the start that Simon and Lucy shared common interests and values and had a genuine fondness for each other. Simon had not been diagnosed with ASD and ADHD when they first met, and it appears that he started to struggle more with these conditions in the context of experiencing increased demands from his work and his marriage, and this precipitated the relationship difficulties. Increased stress led to Simon having meltdowns, which then really heightened Simon's issues with shame and low self-esteem. He had always struggled to express his emotions to Lucy, but communication around emotions became increasingly difficult, and Lucy felt she had lost any sense of connection with him. This led to her feeling anxious and frustrated with Simon. They had discussed the possibility of having children but were both worried this would add another layer of stress to their lives.

Aims of the intervention

Simon and Lucy wanted to be able to understand each other's difficulties better, learn to communicate with each other better, and 'learn to live in harmony' with each other again. Simon also wanted to be able to reduce the frequency of his meltdowns.

Course of therapy

Prior to the couple-based intervention, Simon had some individual therapy focused on managing meltdowns. In this therapy, he and his therapist had mapped out a 'meltdown thermometer' to help him recognise when he might be heading for a meltdown, and what to do at different stages of his stress levels. This was based on the idea of using a 'feelings thermometer' to help recognize different mood states (Attwood & Garnett, 2016). He felt his meltdowns had reduced, but he still had an ongoing fear that they would happen, and that he might hurt or upset Lucy in the process.

Simon's individual therapist reported that he had responded well to therapy, often taking things on in a very intellectual way, but also making definite changes and shifts once he understood the concepts.

Simon and Lucy attended 20 treatment sessions together. The following interventions and techniques were used to address their goals and concerns.

Focus on strengths and positives

Initial discussions focused on identifying and reconnecting with strengths and positive aspects of both individuals and the relationship. For example, discussions were facilitated about how Simon and Lucy had met, and what they had liked about each other, and what continued to work well in the relationship. Both partners were easily able to identify positive attributes in the other person, and this helped to build motivation and engage them in working together as a couple.

THERAPIST REFLECTION: At this point in the therapy, I felt very hopeful, as Simon and Lucy seemed to get real pleasure from discussing how they had met, and the positive qualities and strengths they saw in each other. They both identified these easily, and left the session discussing strengths and positives looking a lot happier.

Psychoeducation about ASD and ADHD

This was an important part of the therapy for both Simon and Lucy. Tony Attwood and Carol Gray have written an article looking at ASD from a strength-based perspective (Attwood and Gray, 2013), and it was useful to offer this as reading to both the partners, and for them to make notes on this for further discussion. This offered more understanding to both of them about ASD, but also boosted Simon's self-esteem. Similarly, they were given some reading resources about ADHD, and Lucy felt this gave her a better understanding that Simon's executive function and processing issues were not always about him being lazy or thoughtless.

Addressing 'meltdowns'

This was an important part of the therapy and was one of Simon's goals. The meltdown thermometer that Simon had worked on in his individual therapy sessions was shared more explicitly with Lucy, and was used to help them both understand what his triggers for meltdowns might be, how to recognise when they might be coming on, and what he could do to bring down his stress levels and prevent a meltdown from happening. As well as this, both partners were encouraged to see that although they may not be able to prevent meltdowns completely in the future, they could work together to reduce their frequency, severity, and impact. As Simon also reported feeling very fearful about what might happen during a meltdown following the episode during which the police were called, a pie chart was used to explore the probability of different outcomes.

Simon was encouraged to share with Lucy what a meltdown was like for him to help her to understand and empathise with his experience.

THERAPIST: Simon, would you be able to talk through what it is like when you have a meltdown? Can you explain to Lucy how it actually is for you?

SIMON: (looking down, with head in hands): Well, it's hard... I think others look at it like... Like I'm having a tantrum maybe. Like I am like some 2-year-old losing control of myself. And that is embarrassing, as I'm obviously not 2 years old.

THERAPIST: It sounds very upsetting for you when you have a meltdown?

SIMON: Yes, it is...

THERAPIST: Can you maybe start by just explaining what happens? When was the most recent time it happened?

(Pause)

SIMON: It was probably a couple of weeks ago. Lucy had asked me to unload and hang the laundry before I went to work, as I was going in later in the afternoon. However, I completely forgot... I just had so much to organise that day. I had a seminar that I needed to be prepared for, and I was highly anxious about it. One of the other tutors had said they may come in to observe me for part of it, and I was really dreading that. Also, I had been watching Question Time the night before, and that had really wound me up. I find it very hard to watch Question Time without getting really cross with the things people are saying. When she had got home, Lucy had found the laundry in the washing machine, and went mad at me when I then got home. And then the meltdown came on, I guess...

THERAPIST: I see.... So, it sounds like there was a lot going on that day... Is that usually a trigger for meltdowns?

SIMON: Yes, definitely. Anxiety about work and social things is a huge thing for me, and it felt like that was dominating me somehow. And when I forget things that Lucy has asked me to do.... It really upsets me... I don't like to upset her, and.... well, let her down, I suppose. I see it as letting her down. And Question Time... Yes, watching anything like that, where there are strong opinions about things, and sometimes really stupid opinions, well that makes me very, very tense. That was one of the things we specifically put on my meltdown thermometer in my individual therapy.

THERAPIST: That is interesting to hear. I know you have a copy of your meltdown thermometer. Maybe we could have a look at it together...

(Therapist and couple look over Simon's meltdown thermometer.)

THERAPIST: So, what I am noticing is that there were about 3, maybe 4 triggers there for you that day – the anxiety about the group setting of the seminar, and being observed, the difficulty with planning the seminar, forgetting to do something for Lucy, and feeling tense because of having watched Question Time...

SIMON: Yes, looking at the thermometer, I can see more clearly that there were a lot of triggers that day.

THERAPIST: And so, what happened?

SIMON: Well, I started to feel even more anxious when Lucy was shouting at me, and I was very sweaty and stressed, and I was pacing up and down the living room, and trying to explain, but it was all coming out wrong. Before I knew it, I was throwing the wet laundry across the room and punching at my chest, and I.... I felt like crying, like screaming. I nearly did both. It becomes a bit of a blur at the time.

THERAPIST: That sounds very distressing for you.

SIMON: Yes, and then afterwards, well, that is always a terrible time, as I just felt dreadful, like killing myself really, as I am such a horrible person.... And Lucy was even crosser with me, as I had thrown the clothes, and they were clean and everything. Oh, it was just awful....

THERAPIST: Okay, so Lucy, I wondered if you would be able to summarise what you have just heard from Simon?

LUCY: Well, it is actually really upsetting to hear him talk about it, and to hear how distressing it is for him... I hate that it is that way for him. In these sorts of situations, I often can't help but feel that I have been the one who 'tipped him over the edge' by nagging him, but then I feel cross, as I think, is it such a lot to ask from your husband? But hearing Simon talk... I have more understanding that it is the build-up of lots of things that ends up overwhelming him. Understanding both ADHD and ASD more now, I do see that it is really difficult for Simon to remember things in the same way as other people, particularly when he has other things going on, or if he is anxious about other things. I am trying to be more understanding about that, but there are times when it does still get to me, when I have had a bad day, or if I am tired, etc. Simon has shown me the meltdown thermometer before, but hearing him talk now makes me get it more. And I hadn't quite appreciated that disappointing me is a really big trigger for Simon.... I'm sorry that causes you such stress. I'm now looking at this thermometer and thinking there could have been things we both did earlier to stop it getting to the point it did....

THERAPIST: That's really insightful of you to notice, Lucy. Can you say more about that, about what you think would have been helpful to do earlier?

LUCY: Well, I knew Simon had the seminar and was anxious about it, and so perhaps on days like that we both need to be aware that other tasks will be harder? But I would like Simon to be more upfront with me about it really. To tell me that this is going to be a bad day, so other things are more challenging, and maybe say if he feels he can't do it. Sometimes I don't think he is aware of it himself though, and that can be frustrating...

THERAPIST: What do you think of that, Simon?

SIMON: I think Lucy is right. I seem to find it hard to know when I am heading towards a meltdown sometimes. If I had looked at this diagram, I would have seen there were lots of triggers, and that I was beginning to feel worked up. And I think it was a mistake that I watched Question Time the night before. I wouldn't do that again, and maybe I should have had an early night, and just done something a bit more calming... And maybe I would say to Lucy that it was going to be a bad day for me, so I may be more forgetful, and not able to do household chores as easily...

THERAPIST: That sounds sensible, and like it would really have helped. Would anything have made it easier for you to tell Lucy?

SIMON: Well, I suppose I'm worried she will be cross, so I avoid saying anything at these times.

LUCY: But I would prefer you did, Simon. I will end up being more cross if I have no clue what is going on....!

SIMON: I understand that, yes.... I think the awareness issue is a problem. Sometimes I forget about this meltdown thermometer, although it has really helped me understand myself better.

THERAPIST: Do you think you could put it somewhere more prominent, so you can view it more regularly. Maybe somewhere both of you can see it even?

LUCY: Yes, I think that would be a great idea! Maybe on the fridge, what do you think, Simon? I would be happy with that....

SIMON: If you don't mind that, I would be happy to. I think I need the visual prompt to help me, so I think that is a good idea....

THERAPIST REFLECTION: I felt the couple worked really well together on Simon's meltdowns, which led to me feeling more positive about their understanding and management of these in the future. The meltdowns didn't end up dominating the sessions, as I had been concerned about, and I think it helped that Simon had already discussed these in his individual therapy. Sharing the strategies he had learned in individual therapy with Lucy in more depth proved to be really useful, and I felt this was a turning point in the couple therapy, where I could see it could be really practically helpful for the couple going forwards, and which they seemed to see as well.

Activity scheduling

Activity scheduling was used to try and reinstate shared activities that Simon and Lucy had always previously enjoyed with each other. The concept of 'energy accounting' was also introduced (Attwood and Garnett, 2016), as it was acknowledged that there were some activities which Lucy liked that were 'energy withdrawing' for Simon, such as large social gatherings, and so they tried to find activities that were 'energy depositing' for them both, whilst allowing times in their schedules for doing their own individual activities. For example, Simon liked having some time on his own after work so he could restore some of his energy levels, and Lucy arranged to do more social activities with some of her friends at that time to meet her needs for social interaction.

THERAPIST: Simon, so, we've been talking about this idea of activities which might actually drain you of energy, rather than be enjoyable and restore your energy. And that Lucy may have different activities that drain and restore her energy levels. What sorts of activities do you think are energy withdrawing for you?

SIMON: Well, definitely socialising for a start, which I know can be really difficult for Lucy, as she likes to do things with groups of friends sometimes, like when we are invited to dinner parties or something. I also find it energy withdrawing when I make a mistake. I think that's why I find it so hard when I do something wrong in the home. Coping with anxiety and crowds also drain me of energy.

THERAPIST: Okay, and what about energy depositing activities for you?

SIMON: I love walks in nature. It's why I enjoy hiking so much. I don't have to talk to people that much, and can just enjoy the scenery, and the peace and quiet away from any crowds. Really, being on my own and solitude is my best energy deposit activity. I don't want that to sound bad for Lucy. I enjoy spending time with her, but I also restore my energy levels being on my own, I think.

THERAPIST: Yes, that makes sense. And Lucy, what about your energy withdrawal activities?

LUCY: Well, I think I have fewer activities which drain me of energy, but I suppose doing things which I find boring, like household tasks, can be quite energy draining for me. Things which are not very stimulating, or mundane things. I like to be intellectually challenged. Simon is right, I do like going to gatherings with friends. I think it is lovely to go for dinner with friends, and we have had a few weddings this year, which I think are really good fun. But I wouldn't say I have to be socialising all the time, and sometimes I like some quiet time as well, and I also find crowds quite draining.

THERAPIST: That is really useful to hear. And what about energy depositing activities for you?

LUCY: I would say I also really like hiking in nature, and find that very restorative. I like doing that in hiking groups, which we have both joined before, or just with Simon too. As I said, some social activities are fun for me. I have a few close friends from uni, and we sometimes do things on our own too, which I enjoy, like going for coffee together or going to the cinema. I also love going to the theatre and art galleries.

THERAPIST: That sounds good. So, thinking about what you have both said, do you think there is an activity that would be a good one to schedule together over the next week?

LUCY: Well, I think hiking seems to be the more obvious one. We haven't been on a hike for a while, and it would be nice to do that this weekend.

THERAPIST: What do you think, Simon?

SIMON: I would like to go for a hike again. I... I suppose I did want to say that although I don't mind the hiking groups sometimes, I prefer just hiking with Lucy on my own, so that would be good, yes.

THERAPIST: That sounds an important point to make, Simon. Were you aware of that, Lucy?

LUCY: I don't think I realised it was that stressful for Simon going with the groups.

SIMON: (interrupting) Well, not exactly stressful. I just prefer that quieter time with us two. It is more energy depositing for me.

LUCY: Okay, I understand that... It makes sense given what you've said. I think it would be nice to plan a hike this weekend then. And I suppose some of these other activities we enjoy, we don't always have to do together.

SIMON: Yes, that's right.

Work on communicating emotions

Working with emotions was an important part of the therapy, particularly developing skills for communicating emotions. It needed to be acknowledged that this was more difficult for Simon than for Lucy, as he had a tendency to alexithymia and expressing emotions had never been easy for him. He also struggled to make eye contact at times, which could make Lucy feel he was not listening to her properly. The couple needed to develop a shared language for discussing thoughts and feelings. The sharing thoughts and feelings guidelines (see Chapter 2) were used, and an emotions wheel was used to help explore this shared language (Willcox, 1981). The meltdown thermometer was also incorporated into this work, for example when they practised conversations around how Simon could let Lucy know that he was beginning to feel overwhelmed, and perhaps 'heading for a meltdown'. Video clips of individuals and couples talking about emotions were used to support this work and Simon and Lucy did some role plays based on these to develop a shared way of communicating about emotions that worked for them.

THERAPIST: So, we've talked a bit about sharing thoughts and feelings, and I wondered if we might practise that, thinking about a similar situation to the one you described where you had that meltdown before, Simon. We have talked about this situation a few times now, and how you had lots of triggers happening at once. You have been able to say you felt anxious and 'wound up' the day before, but you didn't communicate the full extent of that to Lucy at the time, which would have been helpful. Do you think you could practise trying to say how you felt at the time using the guidelines we have discussed?

SIMON: Okay, it is difficult, but I'll try... When.... When I have seminars where I am being observed, I feel bad.... anxious, and when I have lots of other triggers building up as well...

THERAPIST: Like what triggers...?

SIMON: When I have lots of other triggers like having to plan out the seminar, and doing things like watching Question Time, and needing to help with household chores, I feel .... I don't know how to say it....

THERAPIST: Remember when we were looking together at the emotions wheel? Can you think back to that, and what language we thought might help you to describe your feelings? What would you pick out on the emotions wheel in this situation?

SIMON: Yes.... So.... When I have seminars where I am being observed, I feel more anxious than usual, and when I have lots of other triggers on top, like having to plan out the seminar, and doing things like watching Question Time, and needing to help with household chores, I feel very tense and overwhelmed.

THERAPIST: And can you communicate what consequences that might lead to?

SIMON: Because of this, I might be more likely to forget things and have a meltdown.

THERAPIST: Okay. And Lucy, are you able to summarise what Simon has said?

LUCY: I hear that you are feeling more anxious, tense and overwhelmed at the moment, as you are anxious about the seminar, both planning it and doing it, as well as other triggers. I understand that this may mean you are more likely to forget things and have a meltdown, so maybe we need to make a plan for that. I am feeling glad that you've told me about it.

THERAPIST: That was great, Lucy. And Simon, what do you think of what Lucy has said?

SIMON: I feel better in a way, and calmer, as she understands the situation I am in at the moment, and we might be able to make a plan to prevent things getting worse.

THERAPIST REFLECTION: At some points in the therapy, I found myself feeling a little bit stuck. In particular, I felt some frustration in trying to help Simon with sharing thoughts and feelings, as he had a tendency to intellectualise things, rather than truly seeming able to identify and describe his emotions. I found myself aligning with Lucy's feelings of annoyance and exasperation at these times, but I had to remind myself that this was not entirely Simon's fault, and that his neurodivergent difficulties with alexithymia were likely contributing to this. He needed a lot of coaching during exercises and discussions around sharing emotions, and Lucy was much better at picking this skill up. There were times when I was not sure he would get very far with this, but once he had learned more of a format for doing this, he seemed to manage it better. Although he was still struggling with spontaneous identification and expression of his emotions towards the end of therapy, this intervention did seem helpful for specific situations, such as talking about potential upcoming meltdowns, which was an important part of the therapy for both Simon and Lucy.

Problem solving and decision-making conversations

Problem solving and decision-making guidelines were introduced and practised around specific issues that could come up around the home, such as household chores needing to be done, or dates being forgotten. Simon and Lucy were encouraged to use this more structured decision-making process when dealing with more complex or challenging issues, and to take their time to gain a good understanding of each other's priorities and needs before moving on to the 'solution' part of the conversation.

Discussion and chapter reflections

In summary, due to the differences in relating to others that neurodivergence can present, relationship difficulties are not uncommon. Most important to take away is whether you can help the couple to develop a shared understanding and language for the difficulties they have, and a focus on neurodivergent strengths.

Initially, the couple were not easy to work with, as Lucy had a tendency to blame Simon for all their difficulties. However, as both of their understandings of neurodivergence grew, they were able to find ways to live with these conditions that worked better for them both, and the outcome was very good. Simon's meltdowns did reduce, in particular as he became less fearful about having them, especially when he knew that Lucy had a better understanding of them. The couple were having more shared positive experiences with each other again by the end of the therapy and had enjoyed and valued the conversations about how they had met, and being able to reflect on the positive qualities each of them had. Although they had needed quite a lot of therapist support and scaffolding around communication to start with, they were able to discuss difficult topics more easily and had developed a better shared language for talking about emotions and thoughts. They had also been able to have further conversations about having children and decided that ultimately they did not wish to do this as it was not right for them.

THERAPIST REFLECTION: At the end of the therapy, I felt hopeful for Simon and Lucy going forwards. The therapy was not going to take away Simon's neurodiversity, but I felt satisfied that the couple had achieved their goals of understanding each other's difficulties and perspectives better, learning to communicate with each other better, and better understanding and managing Simon's meltdowns. They had also ended up having important discussions about their future plans together, which I felt was a real bonus. They left the therapy feeling happier in their couple relationship, yet still holding onto their own 'quirks' and qualities, and that was rewarding to see.

Therapist tips

- Developing a shared formulation is essential.
- Familiarise yourself with the conditions of ASD and ADHD and liaise with specialists in neurodevelopmental conditions if needed.
- Ask the patient and partner about their beliefs about ASD and ADHD. A focus on strengths and positives can be really useful, as outlined above.
- Some individual work may need to be done first to address some specific problems, e.g., autistic 'meltdowns' in this case.
- Communication may need special attention in the case of ASD, for example, avoiding metaphors that may not make sense to someone with ASD who may have a tendency to take things literally.
- Sessions may need to be shorter with regular breaks for those with ADHD who struggle to concentrate or sit still for long periods.
- Interventions such as communicating emotions and activity scheduling may look slightly different when adapted for those with ASD/ADHD, due to specific difficulties, such as alexithymia, issues with eye contact, and individuals finding certain activities challenging rather than enjoyable.
- As with all couple therapy, it is important to stay objective, and avoid colluding with either partner's unhelpful beliefs.

Suggestions for further Reading

Aston, M. (2014). *The Other Half of Asperger Syndrome (Autism Spectrum Disorder): A Guide to Living in an Intimate Relationship with a Partner Who is on the Autism Spectrum.* London: Jessica Kingsley Publishers.

Attwood, T., and Garnett, M. (2016). *Exploring Depression and Beating the Blues: A CBT Self-Help Guide to Understanding and Coping with Depression in Asperger's Syndrome [ASD-Level 1].* Jessica Kingsley Publishers.

Gaus, V.L. (2011). *Living Well on the Spectrum – How to use your Strengths to Meet the Challenges of Asperger Syndrome/High Functioning Autism.* Guilford Press.

Gaus, V.L. (2019). *Cognitive-Behavioral Therapy for Adults with Autism Spectrum Disorder.* Guilford Press.

Orlov, M., and Kohlenberger, N. (2014). *The Couple's Guide to Thriving with ADHD.* USA: Specialty Press.

Safren, S.A., Sprich, S.E., Perlman, C.A., and Otto, M.W. (2017). *Mastering Your Adult ADHD: A Cognitive-Behavioral Treatment Program, Therapist Guide* (2nd ed.). Oxford: Oxford University Press.

Young, S., and Bramham, J. (2012). *Cognitive Behavioural Therapy for ADHD in Adolescents and Adults: A Psychological Guide to Practice.* London: Wiley-Blackwell.

References

Attwood, T., and Garnett, M. (2016). *Exploring Depression and Beating the Blues: A CBT Self-Help Guide to Understanding and Coping with Depression in Asperger's Syndrome [ASD-Level 1].* London: Jessica Kingsley Publishers.

Attwood, T., and Gray, C. (2013). The Discovery of Aspie (Autism). In: Attwood, T., and Garnett, M. (2016). *Exploring Depression and Beating the Blues: A CBT Self-Help Guide to Understanding and Coping with Depression in Asperger's Syndrome [ASD-Level 1].* London: Jessica Kingsley Publishers, pp. 87–90.

Epstein, N.B., and Baucom, D.H. (2002). *Enhanced cognitive-behavioral therapy for couples: A contextual approach.* American Psychological Association.

Loomes, R., Hull, L., and Mandy, W.P.L. (2017). What is the male-to-female ratio in autism spectrum disorder? A systematic review and meta-analysis. *J Ame Acad Child Adolesc Psychiatry*, 56: 466–474.

National Autistic Society (NAS) (2020). *Meltdowns – a guide for all audiences.*

National Institute for Health and Care Excellence (NICE) (2020). *Autism in adults.*

National Institute for Health and Care Excellence (NICE) (2023). *Attention deficit hyperactivity disorder: How common is it?*

Willcox, G. (1982). The Feeling Wheel: A tool for expanding awareness of emotions and increasing spontaneity and intimacy. *Transactional Analysis Journal*, 12 (4): 274–276.

Chapter 16

Substance Misuse and Addictions

Andre Geel

I work as a Consultant Clinical Psychologist in a large mental health trust in London specialising in addictions. Over the years I have come across and used a variety of psychological therapies in my practice. One such approach is that of two American Psychologists Tim O'Farrell and William Fals-Stewart called Behavioural Couples Therapy (BCT) and designed specifically to treat alcohol and drug problems. It was introduced into the UK in about 2007 when it was included in the National Institute for Health and Care Excellence Guidelines (NICE, 2007) as an evidence-based treatment for alcohol problems even though, up until then, it was relatively unknown in the country although it had been extensively researched in the United States.

Unlike CBCT and IBCT that are principle based, BCT for substance misuse is a manualised form of behaviour therapy designed to be used by a couple to help the individual patient maintain abstinence. It differs from some other forms of behavioural couples therapy which tend to focus more on how the couple can address and reduce their broader distress (often as a means to also improve a range of individual psychopathologies) as well as improve the relationship and communication within it. Those approaches appear more like traditional 'couples therapy', whereas this approach is more like individual therapy with the partner playing a helpful, collaborative role alongside (what in CBCT would be regarded as a partner-assisted intervention or a disorder specific intervention (see Baucom et al., 2020). It's highly manualised approach means that the couple are given specific exercises and between session practice tasks to complete under the guidance of the therapist, who tends to lead the sessions, rather than taking a more client-centred or client-led approach.

This more practical and hands-on approach means that one focuses on behaviour change and not on cognitive or emotional change, insight or understanding of the problem, although these may all result from effective behavioural change. I often describe it to my patients as 'Nike Therapy', as it is a "*Just do it*" approach, where the couple are given exercises to practice between sessions and then report back to the therapist the following week. The emphasis is on *action* not *reflection*, on *doing* rather than *thinking*. The

DOI: 10.4324/9781003024439-18

therapist is seen as more of a director and behavioural coach for the couple in teaching them skills to manage the problem – teaching them new and better behaviours and getting them to practice these on a weekly basis and refining them from week to week. BCT has two primary areas of focus – teaching skills at maintaining abstinence and working on communication skills for the couple.

The beginning

I first met John at the drug and alcohol clinic I was working at. He had been referred to me by his recovery worker to see if I could assist him with his alcohol and cocaine problem. Usually patients are referred to me if my colleagues feel that an additional treatment such as cognitive behaviour therapy would help in their recovery. As the psychologist in the service, I tend to provide a more specialist type of psychotherapeutic intervention in addition to the counselling, advice and support that the drug and alcohol workers offer.

John had been referred to the service at the insistence of his wife who was increasingly concerned about his alcohol and cocaine use. She had effectively provided him with an ultimatum that it was either *"me or the alcohol and drugs"*. He needed to get help fast before she terminated the marriage! His rather sheepish and nonchalant presentation was typical of a large proportion of clients – usually men – referred to the service by their long-suffering partners to get help in reversing the effects of progressive drug and alcohol use that had developed into misuse and dependence. As a couple they had probably both started out using alcohol and drugs recreationally, but over time their individual patterns had changed with one of them slowly reducing their consumption and the other increasing theirs. The reasons for this are numerous and usually complex, but interestingly and incidentally it is possible to address them with much of the BCT package as we will see in the coming sections.

Rationale and formulation

My first consultation with John involved confirming his substance use history – already taken by the recovery worker during his initial appointment at the clinic some weeks before. That comprehensive assessment included a bio-psycho-social overview and medical examination. This confirmed that John had recently developed a dependent pattern of consumption, where he was now drinking almost daily in order to *"steady my nerves"*, experiencing the withdrawal symptoms of physical agitation, anxiety, mood swings, and feeling "nervous, depressed, irritable, and tired." This had made it increasingly difficult for him to work at his usual fast-paced and energetic manner as an electrical engineer at a local, newly-developed electric car factory.

On top of his now fairly regular drinking pattern – mostly spent in the evenings at the local pub with *"old drinking buddies from college"* and some of his younger workmates – he would also indulge in occasional cocaine use later in the evening as the alcohol had made him more disinhibited, with a smaller group of friends encouraging him to *"make a bigger night of it"*. Recently this was occurring once or twice a week, when he would then stay out until the early hours of the morning before returning home to his part-ner, invariably inebriated. Going out once a week *"with mates for a drink"* had not been a problem for the couple and they had followed this routine for most of the 10 years they had been together, quite often as a couple too in the early years. This had not initially been a problem but the frequency of these 'binges' in recent years and increasing problems with "communication and misunderstandings" had led to a more conflicted relationship. *"She just doesn't listen to me anymore"* John said at our first meeting, *"and blames me for being a bad father and husband."* John and Sarah had two daughters aged 6 and 3.

Engagement and exploring Motivation

"Would Sarah be prepared to be part of the treatment sessions and would you find this supportive?" I asked as my way of introducing BCT into the con-versation. Usually, patients are somewhat ambivalent or reluctant at this point, as they have probably been chided into attending therapy by their partner in the first place and therefore are suspicious of their partners' motives going forward. There is also the fear of them losing control in sub-sequent sessions and not feeling that the sessions are for them, but rather for their partner, with the inevitable sense of coercion that goes with that.

BCT as an intervention

I am usually the one who suggests couples therapy rather than the patient requesting it, but I don't introduce it as 'couples therapy' – rather as a way that both parties can learn to manage the problems that drugs and alcohol cause for them and how to control that problem itself. As with a strategic therapy approach (Haley, 1973), I maintain focus on the 'index patient' and on 'the problem' being the drug/alcohol, thus externalising the focus and keeping it on an objective and concrete target. I do not suggest that this is a form of couples therapy or that the problem has anything to do with the interpersonal dynamics of the couple or is 'caused' by any psychological deficiency in either individual. My own view is that the approach I adopt above creates a non-blaming, reassuring, supportive framework, introducing the learning theory approach to the couple as a way of helping them build practical skills that they can use together to overcome the challenges pro-duced by the problematic consumption of these substances. There is a definite intention on my part as a strategic therapist to present the intervention in a disarming and neutral manner, although throughout the therapy itself I maintain a positive, hopeful, and optimistic position. This is very much in line with the way the BCT manual is written.

Resistance

John was initially unsure and possibly taken aback by my suggestion to include Sarah in the treatment, as he might have been expecting the more traditional approach of the psychologist 'doing CBT on him' and us embarking on an individual relapse prevention programme. I had however taken note of the fact that his wife had "referred" him to the service and therefore was clearly invested in his recovery or in some kind of change. As suggested by Paul Watzlawick (1978) or Alex Copello and colleagues (2009), including 'interested parties' in the therapy itself can have a very powerful effect on change as well as prevent any sabotage of the process as the patient begins to make noticeable advances. I said to John that we could approach Sarah and see if a three-way meeting would allow us to proceed with behavioural couples therapy, and if not, he and I would proceed with individual therapy anyway. John appeared open to this idea and said that he would approach Sarah during the week, and if she agreed they would both attend the following appointment.

On some occasions I would take the above approach but for others I would get the client to contact their partner in the session – usually by phone – or indeed I would call the partner myself if that appeared to be the most appropriate way forward. My rationale at this initial stage is to get the couple into the consulting room with me to judge whether there is enough goodwill and a mutually constructive attitude to agree a workable arrangement to proceed. The first session in BCT is very much set up in this way as it presents the structure and options and necessary and sufficient conditions for BCT to work to the couple and then allows for some discussion on if and how the couple could sign up to the therapy package. This first session is key in getting an idea as to how the couple problem-solve together, how they work collaboratively, how much they 'buy into' the therapy, how realistic and achievable their goals are, their motivation, commitment and any sabotage potential that might exist. One is looking for a couple who are willing to practically problem-solve by engaging in a series of behavioural exercises over the course of the treatment package – usually 8 to 12 weeks. As the title Behavioural Couples Therapy suggests one is doing *behaviour therapy* with a couple not couples therapy with behavioural exercises. But more about this later.

Starting therapy

John and Sarah arrived the following week for the agreed session. They had both taken time off work – Sarah working as an accountant in a local firm –

to attend the early afternoon appointment that I had set aside. I reassured Sarah that, although I had met with John first and that he was 'my patient', I would approach them as equal partners in this problem-solving exercise and that the three of us would work together towards the common goal of John's continuing and sustained abstinence. The first session would be an introduction to the program to see if it would be appropriate for them.

I clarified that it was an abstinence-orientated approach and designed to help the patient, in conjunction with their partner, to maintain abstinence throughout the therapy and beyond. I confirmed that it was an 'evidence-based' psychological treatment approved by NICE and answered questions they had about this. This was explicitly done to reassure them that this was a proper, reliable and genuine psychological treatment.

After this brief preamble, and checking if they would still like to continue with the therapy, I introduced John and Sarah to the first session, which is presented as a series of handouts covering such topics as confidentiality, rationale for BCT, the session structure and content, what would be needed from the couple to make the therapy work, and the therapy contract. The session ends with homework exercises and activities (described in detail later) to do between sessions and to be reported on in the next session. This is very much like the traditional CBT session structure.

All handouts are given to the couple in the session, and the therapist reads, role-plays and demonstrates the exercises to ensure all parties are aware of and understand the content. I often make the (amusing/ironic?) observation that even I, as therapist, need to read the script and the material in order to make sure we follow the manual properly! I do this for two reasons. The first one is practical, in that BCT is a manualised therapy which has a detailed and comprehensive manual (436 pages!), which needs to be followed closely to achieve the outcomes intended. Secondly, doing so provides the opportunity to model for the couple how they would follow the manual in doing the exercises themselves in session and at home. This modelling follows basic learning theory principles. Indeed, BCT is so manualised that there is even a script for the therapist to follow to ensure that the couple get precise information to match the handouts they are given. Again, I make some fun of this with the couple, as I do read the script verbatim and then explain and elaborate on it. It also needs some 'translation' from 'American' into British English which again enhances the collaborative approach highlighted in traditional CBT, as I discuss with the couple the best wording to use. This is again part of my strategy to engage the couple in the treatment and to get them involved in a collaborative, joint problem-solving exercise.

Specific Interventions

I proceed in the first session by reading the first part of the script, which is on the topic of confidentiality. The overall purpose is to cover confidentiality and safeguarding, ensuring that the couple feel safe in the sessions to discuss any relevant issues, as well as to advise them on when you as therapist would need to breach confidentiality. As many of our clients are on court orders and/or have children living at home with them while continuing to use substances and engage in risky behaviour, this is an ongoing and consistent consideration for our service as we try to conduct effective psychotherapy with this complex client group. It is another way of setting boundaries as well as preparing the couple for the therapy contract that follows in the session.

Both John and Sarah agreed to the confidentiality principles and so I moved on to the first handout and proper introduction to BCT. This is a handout called "Why BCT?", which very intelligently and presciently lists many of the problems that the couple may have experienced or may experience in the future, and lists the ways in which BCT would address these issues session by session. This is another unique aspect of the BCT approach in that it preempts many of the issues that the couple are likely to bring up and provides a future plan to address them – another way in which the therapy gets 'buy-in' from the couple at an early stage – which gives them hope for future sessions as well as helps navigate challenging stages in the therapy process later on.

The first session of BCT is quite therapist heavy and one needs to be familiar with the (numerous) handouts and be prepared to talk through them in an engaging and entertaining manner. Most of the session is psycho-educational, but one needs to keep a close eye on how both clients are engaging with the process and make sure they are involved in the dialogue.

Sarah commented that the material was particularly useful and relevant as she had found there were now more arguments regarding John's drinking and late nights, and that they had been spending less quality time together as a couple than before. The BCT handout explicitly states that there will be exercises to reduce conflict, improve positive time together and develop better communication skills. We had a brief conversation around this in the session at that point to emphasise that we all looked forward to the point at which we could address these issues.

Keeping therapy on course

As the session progressed, I noticed there was more eye contact between John and Sarah and what appeared to be a more collaborative feel to the session and the material. I could see that Sarah was beginning to become invested in John's recovery. This was a good sign at this point as it is important to get the partners' 'buy-in' at an early stage in the treatment. In this particular case it was Sarah's first session and she was in some ways the 'odd one out' and needed to be brought in as an equal partner in this exercise. However, I reminded myself to make sure I kept the involvement and contribution of each person equally balanced so that they felt they were both usefully contributing to the process. This was particularly important as it was possible later in the therapy that Sarah might start to occupy a more dominant position as she became more competent with the therapy exercises. My hypothesis here was twofold. Firstly, and obviously, Sarah did not have the drug or alcohol problem and therefore the exercises would be less challenging for her. Secondly, it was likely that the dynamics between the couple might have taken on that of a Parent-Child relationship, which is often seen in couples where one has an addiction problem and the other is sober. (Hadži-Pešić et al., 2014). This might unconsciously result in Sarah leading the sessions and John following. Also, the next exercise would likely be a particularly challenging one for Sarah, so I wanted to get her on my side before attempting this.

The next exercise is called "Promises", and I usually translate this title into a more British-consistent, toned-down version of what Carl Rogers would have called "the necessary and sufficient conditions" for therapy to work. It is a list of 4 agreed behaviours that appear in the contract the couple will later sign and (generally!) abide by throughout the 12 sessions of treatment. These 4 conditions are: no threats of divorce or separation, no violence or threats of violence, focus on the present and future (and avoid negative arguments about the past), and attend sessions and actively participate.

Both Sarah and John found these conditions helpful but for different reasons. Sarah said they helped to create a safe environment and she looked forward to John in future continuing to maintain his abstinence. For his part, John said it was helpful not to focus on the past and the mistakes he had made, and the conditions helped create a 'clean slate' to work from. Sarah countered that there were a number of things John had done wrong in the past and that it was too soon to 'forgive and forget' or 'brush them under the carpet'. I intervened at this point and reassured both of them that we would deal with these issues in future sessions in a constructive way and teach them skills to address them constructively.

The therapist's role

The strategy at this point was to create a safe and neutral ground to allow the three of us to establish rules of engagement and a style of conversation that was not too 'emotion-laden' or cathartic and did not dwell too much on their old issues. I wanted to model a new type of conversation where we could create space to think about an alternative future without those past expectations entering the frame. There was also some modelling of distress tolerance and delayed gratification in what is often a volatile, reactive and impulsive relationship.

Once John and Sarah had agreed to these principles (and I had made a mental note to bear in mind that they could break them in the coming sessions, and that much of the ongoing therapy is an exercise in gradually shoring up these more adaptive behaviours in collaboration with the couple), we moved on to the next exercise called the "Trust Discussion". This is a brief role play of a ritual where the couple spend a minute each day reaffirming their commitment to each other and the abstinence and recovery process. Again, there is a script to follow, but I often adapt the words (and language if English is not the couple's home language) to suit their particular circumstances. Some time could be spent in discussion with the couple deciding on the words, but this is all part of the process of collaborative problem-solving which runs throughout the therapy. As with every exercise, I demonstrate and role play it myself and, when I am the only therapist, I rehearse it with each partner individually and then ask them as a couple to practice it in front of me. Once they have demonstrated the conversation fairly fluidly then they are instructed to practice it at home daily from then on. If I am working with a co-therapist then we would role-play the script as a couple and ask the clients to repeat what they had seen. We would coach them if the script was particularly stilted, but otherwise leave it to the couple to practice daily and then review it weekly in the therapy sessions, where we would ask the couple to demonstrate how they did it at home.

Both John and Sarah found the exercise amusing and said they would not usually use this language at home, but were happy to 'play' this ritual out – almost to humour the therapist.

"*I have been drug and alcohol free for the last 24 hours and plan to remain drug and alcohol free for the next 24 hours*" said John, smiling with a rather sheepish grin, "*and thank you for listening and being supportive of my effort to be drug and alcohol free.*" Concealing some obvious disbelief, Sarah replied: "*Thank you for staying drug and alcohol free for the last 24 hours. I appreciate the effort you are making to stay clean and sober.*" She seemed to hold back a laugh at this point and both of them looked at me in what could best be described as puzzled, curious scepticism.

"Now *the therapy begins*", I thought to myself. "*Right, that was good, but do it again and mean it this time*", I said to them, feeling like I was directing a play.

Using interventions skilfully and strategically

Sometimes couples will take the direction and repeat the exercise and at other times will say something like: "*This is not real, I'm sure he won't stop drinking and even if he does, it won't be for long*". Sarah and John were prepared to play along. They repeated the script and this time it seemed a little more earnest and serious, and like they were actors taking the role play to heart. "*Great, that's better.*" I said "*Practice that at home each day until our next session. Just like you've done it here.*"

For couples that initially 'resist' this instruction and intervention, I emphasise the behavioural nature of the therapy and ask that they "*just do it"* – as the advert says – rather than think about it. This is where the principles of behaviour therapy and behaviour change come into play, in that this exercise is not about 'thinking' rather it is about 'doing'. The behavioural principle is that if you change behaviour, and continue to behave in that new way, others then respond to that observed behaviour, changing their responses accordingly complement that new behaviour, and a virtuous circle develops, with a consequent change in beliefs and interpretations. This is the essence of assertiveness training, where when you 'act' (fake-it) as if you are confident, others respond to that behaviour, providing positive feedback and reinforcing the beliefs (cognitions) that go with it.

This is only a 15–30 second script and yet I think it is the most important exercise in the entire therapy package and is possibly one of the key factors that determines a successful outcome to the intervention. It is the point at which the couple engage in the behaviour change process, possibly suspending their assumption about the intractability of their problem, and join the therapist in a new way of behaving. The success of this depends upon the alliance the therapist has built with both parties, the trust all have in the process, the constructive working relationship that is being built, the credibility and authority of the therapist and the mutual respect that exists for all parties.

It is also the template for the way in which all future exercises are modelled and conducted and therefore is a litmus test as to how the couple and the therapist will work together on subsequent tasks.

Having overcome that potential hurdle in the session, I proceeded to present the contract (two paper copies – one for the couple and one for me) to John and Sarah and read through it with them. It is effectively a summary of what had gone before, binding them to abide by their agreements to attend sessions, do the tasks and homework, follow the promises, engage in any other activities that were part of John's recovery such as attendance at the local clinic for check-ups, key work sessions and medication (Naltrexone as anti-craving for alcohol) and participating in the local AA and NA groups. We signed the copies and kept a copy each.

"That covers the main work of today's session and we have really done well to get off to such a good start," I said. *"There are just two more things to do before we finish."* And with that I introduced them to the final exercise and task for the week, and exercise called *"Catch your partner doing something nice"*. This is a common exercise in couples therapy and is used widely even outside of cognitive and behavioural therapies, and was probably an exercise that predated both. The couple are asked to note down each day one thing that they noticed their partner doing that was good, kind, thoughtful, positive or helpful that day. They are not to tell the partner what it was, but are invited to bring this list to the next session. They are given a handout of examples as well as a blank record sheet for the task. Another fun exercise to shift the focus of attention in the relationship and identify strengths.

"The very last thing I would like you both to do is keep a daily record of the things we have agreed to do, so that we can review each week accurately and make adjustments as necessary, as well as remembering to do the exercises on the days agreed so we don't miss any". I gave them a printed blank weekly record sheet for this exercise. *"It might be useful to keep these in a file or folder as I will give you new ones every week and they will soon mount up,"* I said. *"I have a ring binder we can use,"* said Sarah, and I thanked her as we concluded the meeting and agreed to meet next week.

THERAPIST REFLECTIONS: I sat back and reflected on what had been an incredibly busy and intense session – particularly for the therapist – in having to lead and direct, and yet ensuring that the couple stayed engaged and feeling like they were participating too. I knew that future sessions would be less intense for me as the couple engaged with more exercises and I played the role of supervisor or coach.

The course of therapy

I have included the first session in detail as I feel it gives the best idea of how the therapy works, the relationship between therapist and couple and how a delicate balance between psycho-education and integration of the material is key to moving forwards. Each session has a feel like this.

I had got off to a good start with John and Sarah but this was no guarantee of future success.

The next three sessions focused on building up the positives in the relationship: having them continue noticing good things about each other, practicing feeding this back, organising fun things to do as a couple and building this in as a routine – all the while using the material as scaffolding and adding to it with new exercises.

"I had forgotten about the good things that brought us together in the first place and the things about John that I do appreciate, but seem hidden with all these problems," said Sarah during the second session. *"These exercises force us to take the time to listen to each other as well as to look for the good stuff that is there".*

"Yes, it's nice to have a structure and a special time to look at all of this, and I don't feel blamed either, so it's easier for us to talk more and discuss more things without arguing," replied John. *" It's also nice to have you tell us we have to meet, otherwise we might not."*

"Yes, and also good to have to report back to you each week, which keeps us on our toes," said Sarah.

There was a relapse early on – as there often is when couples begin to notice change – and in that instance we spent some time in the session problem solving, looking at triggers and coping styles and what could be different next time, and then repeating the trust discussion role-play to ensure both Sarah and John would be reminding themselves of their intentions to stay focused on their goals each day.

"*I knew this was going to happen,*" said Sarah at the beginning of the session when they were reviewing the previous week. "*It was just a matter of time, and it's just like John – he's so unreliable and has really let us both down here.*"

I stepped in quickly "*Yes, you're absolutely right to be disappointed, angry and feel let down, and we have to see what we can do to turn that around. Although we don't talk much about lapses here, they can occur, and indeed could be seen as part of the persons' recovery in that they are learning new behaviours, but will slip up now and then on that road to abstinence. John, can you tell us more about what happened so that we can review it in more detail and see what we all need to do differently next time similar conditions arise?*"

The middle section of the package – about 5 sessions in all – teaches communication skills, how to be assertive, how to manage conflict and leads into a recovery plan and how the couple will continue after the therapy concludes. As with every session, the therapist role-plays and demonstrates for the couple and then coaches them on the new behaviour which they practice at home and report back on at the next session.

"*This feels so artificial and fake,*" said Sarah as they were practicing an assertive communication and listening exercise in front of me.

"*It is,*" I said, "*and it's supposed to feel unfamiliar and in some way you are 'faking it until you make it', but this is exactly how it feels when one does something for the first time. It is only with practice that it becomes comfortable and a habit. Remember that some of your old habits are part of the problem, and therefore we want to introduce new skills to replace those old habits – and being able to have better conversations is one of those new skills. Shall we try that conversation again here in the session? And this time pretend that you mean it!*" I said with a smile to both of them.

I had purposely used the "*pretend that you mean it*" instruction as this allows them not to take it too seriously at first whilst still being able to practice the whole exercise, but not feeling responsible for the outcome. It allows us all to have fun with it whilst allowing some time for the couple to begin to observe the effects of the exercise without judging them. It also avoids a "battle of wills" (resistance) between the couple and the therapist.

During the course of treatment with John and Sarah, John had two further lapses and the couple had three arguments that had resulted in one or the other partner leaving the house on that occasion and only returning the following day. However, all instances were worked through as learning examples in subsequent sessions with their mutual respect and commitment to treatment still intact.

"It's amazing how you both are sticking with the programme in spite of the challenges that have faced you both recently. This is just the type of commitment to each other and to the programme that is needed to make it work. We are absolutely on the right track here," I said, reinforcing their commitment to the programme and adherence to the contract they had signed.

We parted with John and Sarah thanking me for introducing them to *"such useful techniques and skills"*. They reported a major improvement in their relationship and in conflict management as well as the children being easier to manage, although there were still the occasional 'lapses' when John would have a difficult day or week at the office or when his friends persuaded him to come out for the evening. However, these were significantly less frequent and often led to him and Sarah refocusing on the need to 'do the homework properly' the following day.

Discussion and reflection

The aim of this approach, in my view, is not to achieve a perfect relationship, but to provide the couple with skills they can use to establish a 'good enough' way of getting along in spite of the challenges they have faced up until this point and the reason they came into therapy in the first place.

I have two key reflections at the end of this chapter, both of which I have learned through actually *doing* behavioural couples therapy rather than thinking too much about it. The first is that it is very challenging as a therapist, in these times where there are so many competing models of couples therapy, to be a good 'behaviour therapist' and stick to training people in useful skills without appearing too 'psychological' about it. The second is coming to the realisation that many people either do not possess the social and communication skills to make for positive, effective and satisfying relationships, or have these skills but are not using them effectively for one reason or another. In these contexts, structured exercises to improve communication can be very beneficial. People do not want to suffer; they suffer because they do not know of or cannot see an alternative to what they are doing.

Therapist tips

•   Stick to the manual!
•   Focus on ensuring a good therapeutic relationship with each partner – use lots of positive reinforcement.

- Be clear that this work is focused on supporting abstinence rather than working on all aspects of the relationship, and particularly those aspects that are not related in some fashion to the substance misuse issue.
- Most couples struggle to complete homework, be gently persistent with this.
- What happens between sessions is more important than what happens during sessions.
- BCT, in its manualised version, is a 'doing' therapy more than just a 'talking' therapy – be clear on what skills you are helping the couple learn and by what criteria you can assess their adoption and maintenance of these skills.

Suggestions for further Reading

O'Farrell, T. J. & Fals-Stewart, W. (2006). *Behavioral Couples Therapy for Alcoholism and Drug Abuse*. New York: Guilford.

References

Baucom, D. H., Fischer, M. S., Corrie, S., Worrell, M., & Boeding, S. (2020). *Treating relationship distress and psychopathology in couples: a cognitive behavioural approach*. London: Routledge.

Copello, A., Orford, J., Hodgson, R., & Tober, G. (2009). *Social Behaviour and Network Therapy for Alcohol Problems*. London: Routledge.

Haley, J. (1973). *Uncommon therapy: The psychiatric techniques of Milton H. Erickson, M.D.* W. W. Norton.

Hadži-Pešić, M., Mitrovic, M., Brajovic Car, K., & Stojanovic, D. (2014). Personality of alcohol addict according to the theory of transactional analysis. *Procedia – Social and Behavioral Sciences*, 127, 230–234.

National Institute for Health and Care Excellence. (2007). *Drug misuse in over 16s: psychosocial interventions*. Clinical Guideline No. 51 [CG51]. https://www.nice.org.uk/guidance/cg51.

O'Farrell, T. J. & Fals-Stewart, W. (2006). *Behavioral Couples Therapy for Alcoholism and Drug Abuse*. New York: Guilford.

Watzlawick, P. (1978). *The language of change: Elements of therapeutic communication*. New York: Norton & Co.

Chapter 17

Endings and Separations

Michael Worrell

James and Rachel sit slouched on opposite ends of the large couch in my con-sulting room, squeezed into its outer edges, as if looking for loose change. I feel there is a danger that one of both will end up on the floor. They look exhaus-ted, defeated, as I fear I may be as well. James looks me straight in the eye and suddenly rightens his posture:

"Michael... isn't there a point at which we just have to say it's just too damn hard?... it's too much?... isn't there a point at which it's just better for everyone to stop trying?"

I felt completely silenced by this statement and aware of a heaviness in my chest and that I was barely breathing. Both their eyes were fixed on me now. Should I not be saying something helpful? Something that offers hope? A new technique we haven't tried? Some brilliant new insight about what is going on that somehow has escaped my mind and is hiding behind the couch?

Couple therapy and Separation therapy

Most versions of couple therapy are careful to maintain that the goal of therapy is never to keep a couple together 'come what may'. Indeed, it is well recognised that many couples may enter therapy with at least one partner considering separation. Additionally, some couples may enter therapy with one partner carrying the agenda of stating their desire to separate during a therapy session and leaving their partner in the care of the therapist (Lebow, 2019). In cognitive behavioural couple therapy (CBCT), the overarching goal is to help a couple make the best decisions possible about their relationship. This can include the decision to separate. At the same time, it is probably true that most therapists go into couple work with the hope of supporting relationships rather than facilitating separations. Furthermore, therapists have their own schemas about relationships that can often make working with separating couples a challenge. A couple deciding to separate can, despite the stated philosophy, feel like a failure. Frequently, where a couple decides to separate, or when one partner does despite the wishes of the other, they are not 'feeling good' at the end of therapy. Services that evaluate the

DOI: 10.4324/9781003024439-19

value of an intervention in terms of mood scales are likely to agree that such interventions represent failure. This does not seem 'true to life'. The partners may well be feeling worse than when they started as the hope for improvement has been lost, and yet this may well be the best outcome in the circumstances.

As Lebow (2023) has noted, the professional literature that focusses on separation is surprisingly sparse. Lebow (2023), in a review of the available literature, also suggests that there are 'better' and 'worse' ways of separating. A separation process appears to go best when the separating partners have opportunities to communicate and where there is a sense of being given an opportunity to work through the impact of the separation. Additionally, separations go better when infidelity or intimate partner violence is not part of the context and when children are not drawn into triangulated relationships. This suggests that many of the interventions and principles of CBCT and IBCT may be of assistance in managing a 'good enough' separation even where this is also a distressing and difficult process. Key principles, drawn from both these models of couple therapy, would suggest that therapy can assist couples in reaching the decision to separate, even when this decision may not be a mutual one. They can also support each partner to express and manage the strong feelings that usually accompany such a life transition, as well as providing space to allow each partner to describe what the relationship has meant to them (and avoiding a redescription of the entire relationship as a mistake or a failure) and supporting a whole range of decisions that may be needed such as those around finances, children and possessions. Here, there is a fuzzy boundary between the activity of couple therapy focused upon assisting partners to separate in the least damaging way possible, and the activity of mediation, which is more devoted to achieving compromise and agreement but where little attention may be paid to processing the strong feelings of hurt, sadness and loss that may be involved.

Lebow (2019) draws upon the research of Ahrons (1994) to describe a 'taxonomy' of separating couples. This includes five types of potential post-separation relationships: 'Dissolved Duos', 'Fiery Foes', 'Angry Associates', 'Cooperative Colleagues' and 'Perfect Pals'. Dissolved Duos are characterised by a great deal of distance and where there is little communication, Fiery Foes maintain ongoing acrimonious conflict and communication and are locked in a deep unresolved hostility. Angry Associates are less furious with each other and can manage some communication and coordination of post separation decisions. Cooperative Colleagues and Perfect Pals have in some way managed a separation process that allows ongoing contact and joint decision making about issues such as childcare with the Perfect Pals type being somewhat bewildering to their wider field of family and friends due to their apparent ability to get on so well after a separation. Fiery Foes and Angry Associates are more likely to show up in a therapist's office experiencing a 'difficult' separation process.

This chapter is a story about once such attempt at initially supporting the possibility of an improved relationship followed by an attempt at a 'good enough' separation, initially in the form of a goal of becoming Perfect Pals with a more realistic compromise of somewhere between Angry Associates and Cooperative Colleagues being the (at the time the therapy ended) apparent result.

James and Rachel – 'The Manager' and 'The Bear'

James and Rachel were referred to me by a colleague, a psychotherapist with a long experience working with addictions. Rachel had been seeing my colleague for individual therapy for a period of three years and for many months their work had focussed on the stress and dissatisfaction that Rachel experienced in her relationship with James. Following the general principles and processes of CBCT (Baucom et al, 2020), I saw them initially for a couple session followed by two individual assessment sessions. As I saw them in a private practice setting, I was free to adopt my preferred approach of avoiding the initial use of psychometric measures or formal observations of communication styles, unless these seem appropriate after the initial meetings. My preferred therapeutic style is to adopt as little structure as is necessary and to allow the couple to unfold their story in their own way and in their own time. Initial sessions are primarily aimed at creating a 'safe enough' space to explore the relationship and to form a therapeutic alliance with each partner as an individual. Thus, the following emerged slowly both during the initial assessment sessions and during subsequent treatment sessions (the distinction between the two being arbitrary).

In our first session James and Rachel presented very much as a "last chance couple" (Fraenkel, 2023). They entered the therapy room bringing with them an atmosphere of mutual accusation, desperation and bewilderment. Rachel, a slightly built woman dressed in 'executive' style business clothes and jewellery and French manicured fingernails, sat on the very edge of the couch fidgeting nervously with her hair and looking quickly and frequently between myself and James. James on the other hand presented as somewhat deliberately and overly relaxed, wearing sports clothes and long greying hair and a 'hipster' beard, with one arm revealing multiple detailed tattoo art of a variety of mythical creatures. While James spoke in a dramatic and expressive style, frequently raising his voice to make a point and employing large bodily gestures, Rachel spoke quietly and deliberately, seemingly attempting to think through her statements and edit them before saying them out loud and watching intently for their impact.

"*So, what brings you to couple therapy?*" I asked, interested in who would pick up the baton first and how long they would attempt to run with it. James spoke first, and in some detail.

JAMES: We just are stuck really. We can't seem to get along. We have so much potential, such good energy and passion between us. We always have had. But we can't get along day to day. We bicker and fight and snipe at each other. I know... I know (looking quickly at Rachel)...I am just as bad as Rachel is... I have a mouth on me and once I get going, I can get pretty nasty and sometimes I can be abusive...I know it's not ok... I really need to take responsibility for my stuff and stop putting my stuff onto the relationship. I project all over the place and Rachel just gets triggered and then runs away from me... as though I'm the big bad bear which I'm not. I can't stand being made to feel like I'm the toxic male who is angry all the time. I do feel angry though. I mean we could be so good together. We really want to have a child together. We have the dog... the new house... I am just hoping we can get rid of the toxic stuff between us and learn how to be together...

Rachel takes a deep breath in, takes a pause, and then speaks quietly. Looking only at me and avoiding any eye contact with James:

RACHEL: It really isn't OK what happens between us... We do shout and we do call each other such horrible names. How can we be a couple if we speak to each other like this? It's like we hate each other and yes, I do feel triggered and frightened. I know you have never raised a hand or threatened anything physical. Well... You have thrown a few plates... not at me... but I find that just too scary and triggering. And why can't we seem to get anywhere? I'm such a good planner and organiser. You know I am... you call me 'The manager'!... but you block and disrupt any plans we make to go forward... even planning a night out just the two of us becomes a drama...it gets cancelled, or you claim to forget. You don't seem to try much, and I feel you just find me irritating... it's like you just want to be in your man cave...listen to old David Bowie records and drink that fucking ginger tea...sorry! Sorry... I didn't mean to swear.

Despite their obvious sense of desperation and distress, my initial reaction to them both is one of hopefulness and interest. They both seem open to thinking about themselves and their relationship and very much wanting to improve things. There are references to 'we' in their talk as well as the expected pattern of blaming and pathologizing the other. They describe many patterns of interaction and behavioural processes that fit well within a CBCT 'lens'. They describe having difficulties communicating their emotions and concerns with each other, both acknowledging that they find it hard to listen well when their emotions are aroused. They also describe significant difficulties making decisions about how they want to advance their relationship and how they want to coordinate their careers and manage their finances. Additionally, as they go on to explain when asked, they show a marked 'approach-avoid' pattern where Rachel, typically, approaches James in the hope of engaging him in decision making or to share her concerns, and James shuts down and avoids engaging. Once Rachel continues to press for contact, James starts raising his voice, claiming that her sense of timing and priorities doesn't make sense to him. Rachel then finally withdraws from these conversations *"triggered"* and feeling hopeless and *"without a voice in this relationship"*.

In our initial session I ask them to talk me through how their relationship began, what initially attracted them to each other and how things progressed over time. I am interested in how key events were experienced and how they made decisions about moving from dating to being a couple. The mood substantially lightens and there are smiles and eye contact as they both eagerly describe the beginnings of their relationship. Rachel seems now more relaxed and finally allows herself to sit back into the couch. They explain that they had been a couple for approximately 6 years at the time they started sessions with me. They described how their relationship had initially been something of an exciting secret as they had met in a 'sex and love addiction' support group where part of the rules for joining the group was the agreement to avoid forming any romantic relationship with any other member of the group. They both agreed that they did not fully identify with the label 'sex or love addict' but had joined this group as an additional form of support due to their mutual history of problems with alcohol and how alcohol had affected previous relationships. Once their relationship had been 'outed' by another member of the group who had seen them in the car park, they left never to return. Both had also attended many years of individual psychotherapy of various sorts but neither had ever attended a couple-based therapy before. They stated that had both been sober for over 10 years with no relapses.

James stated that he was very attracted to Rachel physically from the beginning, she seemed always *"poised and in contact with something deep"*. He soon also liked her way of being highly organised and planful, paying attention to detail in a way that he found remarkable. He described feeling almost immediately that Rachel was *"my soul mate"* and someone that he could finally imagine building a home and a life with. Despite their current conflicts and difficulties, James believed these positive aspects were still very much present in Rachel and that when they were relaxed and had a sense of connection with one another he felt the relationship helped him to calm down and to modulate his usually racing mind that *"jumps from project to project and problem to problem"*.

Rachel described being immediately attracted to James' highly relaxed and easy-going style. He seemed at home in his body and could engage anyone in conversation in a way that she admired and somewhat envied, as this contrasted with her own socially anxious and quiet way of being. Rachel loved that James was a committed Jazz saxophonist as well as running his own second hand bookstore that he had inherited from his mother. She found him to be *"eccentric, authentic, and alive!"*. Rachel stated that she felt sure that she and James could start a family together, that the time was right for her, and that there was little time remaining to act on this possibility. She acknowledged that many of the things that attracted her to James also currently *"drive me crazy – I mean does he have ADHD? He can't settle down to solve any problem we have and can't make decisions!"*.

Individual sessions

Consistent with general practice in CBCT, I opt to see each person individually after the first couple session. I make it clear that the content of these sessions remains confidential (over time I have found that detailed conversations and explanations about the grey areas and exceptions to confidentiality are unnecessary and distracting, revealing more about the therapist's anxiety than facilitating engagement). In these sessions I invite each partner to talk more freely about their current concerns before asking them to describe aspects of their history, to the extent that they feel these may be relevant, such as their family of origin, their experience of their parents' relationship as well as their own relationship history. I explain my interest in these areas as arising from the notion that we all 'carry forward' experiences, concerns, and dilemmas, based upon these past relationships and that there may be both things that they are seeking to avoid, to overcome or correct, or indeed to maintain and develop in the current relationship. Again, I avoid over structuring this, preferring instead an open conversational process rather than a formalised assessment. I prefer to take the risk of overlooking a domain of functioning in favour of avoiding the interaction being experienced as a 'top down', regimented assessment interview.

Rachel attends the first individual session and begins by again describing her experience of feeling *"triggered"* by James's behaviour. Noting this use of therapeutic language, I ask her to describe what she means by this term. This allows Rachel to describe her history of being in what can only be described as an abusive relationship with an ex-partner. This relationship ended three years prior to her meeting James and had lasted a period of about two years. This ex-partner, Robert, had been physically violent to Rachel on several occasions, resulting in at least one visit to hospital plus a visit from the police to their flat due to a neighbour's complaint about shouting late at night. Robert had been a heavy binge drinker with periods of abstinence lasting several weeks. Rachel found it extremely difficult to leave this relationship despite the support and encouragement of her friends, fearing that her leaving would precipitate Robert becoming suicidal and possibly also aggressive and violent to her.

Rachel clarified that James is aware of this past relationship and has been very compassionate towards her, vowing to never behave towards her as

Robert had done. Rachel also informs me of a very difficult relationship with her mother whom she describes as *"definitely a raving narcissist"*. She describes a childhood in which she experienced very frequent criticism and hostility from her mother about all aspects of her appearance and behaviour. She felt that her mother clearly favoured her elder sister and considered Rachel to be *"the runt of the litter"*. Rachel has spent many years in therapy dealing with her relationship with her mother and has found that in recent years her best solution has been to maintain as much geographical distance and infrequent contact as possible. Her mother, now in her mid 70s, sends occasional text messages accusing Rachel of abandoning her. Despite these challenges, Rachel has managed to carve out a highly successful career within publishing and describes being well liked and respected at her work, which has remained stable and a source of pride and positive identity for her. Since stopping all use of alcohol, she has also become a committed practitioner of Yoga and adopted a vegan lifestyle, despite James's frequent challenges to this.

James is relieved to hear that the content of our individual session will remain confidential. He is highly engaging in the individual session, as he was in the couple session and I find him easy to like. However, he is a challenge to listen to at times, as he jumps from topic to topic but not to the degree that his narrative does not hold together. James describes feeling very ambivalent about his relationship with Rachel, and in fact he states he is ambivalent about the very notion of a long term committed monogamous relationship. *"I'm not sure I can do it… I mean, I want to… I think. But maybe I'm just not suited to it…perhaps I just want to live a lifestyle of long walks along the beach, playing saxophone in pubs, reading sci fi and having the occasional brief affair?"* *"Perhaps you do!"* I challenge. *"Yes, but I also want this relationship with Rachel…she is my soul mate and helps ground me and I really want to try. After my last relationship I really want to try"*.

James then tells me about his previous relationship with Sharon, a woman who was divorced and with two young children. He feels that somehow, he was too anxious and ambivalent to commit to that relationship (*"I just could not consider being a stepdad!"*) and that he had let something potentially very good pass him by. He thinks about her often with a sense of regret and sadness that maybe she could have been *"the one"*. He also explains, checking again with me about my commitment to confidentiality, that the physical relationship he experienced with Sharon was the most intense and satisfying that he had ever experienced. *"It was total dynamite… I could not believe it. Never before and never since and unfortunately not with Rachel either. I haven't told her this of course. I love her and don't want to hurt her. But I have these memories of my time with Sharon… and I just don't know what that means for the future."*

James describes what he regards as a *"brilliant"* childhood with parents who were *"original hopeless hippies"*, who took him on long road trips through Europe in a VW camper van often missing school. He was an only child and had little contact with any other relatives. He states that his parents split up when he was 13, seemingly without any ill feeling (apparently Perfect Pals) and that he remained with his mother, hearing very little from his father till the present day. He studied music at university, but did not complete his Degree, taking over the management of the bookshop from his mother upon her retirement, with the aim of establishing himself as a professional Jazz saxophonist.

I found Rachel and James highly engaging and easy to like. They were both open about their vulnerabilities and desire to improve their relationship. At the same time, I found myself at times irritated by the 'therapeutic language' both employed such as *"triggered" "my stuff and your stuff" "projecting" "showing up and taking responsibility"* etc., that seemed to conceal far more than it revealed about their actual experience. I also noted early on that in addition to liking and feeling engaged by each of them as individuals, I liked the *relationship* between them, its energy and how they could at times spark off each other's differences in a positive way. I hoped that this relationship could indeed be supported via CBCT.

Formulation

Many of the chapters in this book have demonstrated various ways a therapist can bring together information gained at assessment and link this with theory to derive a formulation. In my own practice I tend to avoid the use of diagrams, preferring instead a process of summarising key domains of concern and conflict with an open invitation to discuss and modify this preliminary description. Often, the formulation will initially focus on the extent to which the couple's difficulties represent what can be considered a form of secondary distress (Baucom et al, 2020). That is, the arguments, resentments, and distress that have arisen as a consequence of the couple's best efforts to resolve their dilemmas and differences. This secondary distress and the patterns of miscommunication and avoidance associated with it block efforts at clarifying and resolving areas of primary distress which typically relate to each individual's core needs and values that are being frustrated.

This description then leads on to a broad discussion of goals for the work. I prefer to avoid over-specifying these as they frequently evolve over time and in my view a too quick specification of behaviourally defined targets can promote a more superficial process. Consistent with CBCT however, I try to include a description of processes and factors at the level of each individual, the couple as a unit, and the environment that they live in.

Regarding each of them as individuals, they were both 'therapy veterans' and had read a range of literature related to couple therapy. They both spoke about themselves as 'anxious-avoidant' types and stated that they wanted to promote a 'secure base' between them. While I disagree with the reductionistic aspects of attachment theory, this nevertheless seemed to capture some aspects of their experience. Early on, James shared the hypothesis *"I wonder if we spend so much time arguing and fighting, and struggle to stop because actually what we are both terrified of is actually being intimate and vulnerable with each other?"*

For Rachel, we highlighted the impact of her previous abusive relationship and that she had experienced a great deal of anxiety and distress due to this. She readily identified beliefs such as *"I don't have a voice; my needs are not important and if I speak up, I will get punished"*. Additionally, she described coping strategies such as *"keeping myself quiet and avoiding conflict and working very hard to be perfect and manage everything."* She quickly linked this with her childhood experience, noting that keeping herself small and quiet and developing a finely tuned radar for her mother's rapidly changing moods was an adaptive strategy that had unfortunate side effects in her later romantic relationships.

James readily identified a need for autonomy as a basic personality characteristic that he valued and felt *"I should not have to apologise for"*. Additionally, he identified some downsides to this in terms of beliefs such as *"I should not let others try to control or limit what I do."* He related this directly to his upbringing and the modelling he received from his parents regarding the virtues of *"going with the flow"*. James also acknowledged that he sometimes experienced difficulties with his emotions especially when anxious or angry. He found that he took a long time to calm down and sometimes used abusive or derogatory language as a way of creating distance. James was aware that some people, friends and even professionals such as his GP, had suggested he may have a diagnosis of attention deficit disorder. He had never had this assessed and stated that he did not believe this was necessary as when he was interested in something his attention levels were just fine. Nevertheless, he did acknowledge that relative to Rachel, he was much lower on conscientiousness and planfulness, and higher in distractibility and impulsivity.

Our discussions of the formulation also included a description of the typical processes of demand-withdraw that characterised their relationship. While James was often in the role of withdrawing and avoiding, he could be in the approach role when his emotions were aroused, and when he felt a degree of self-righteousness and anger towards Rachel, whom he would often challenge with the statement *"why can't you just show up and be vulnerable?… we have to talk about the deep stuff instead of the details!"* In response to this Rachel would typically shut down and withdraw, experiencing James as *"bullying and overbearing…like a big grey bear!"* From a simple behavioural perspective, they also presented with a high degree of negatives and a low frequency of positives. There were many arguments and disagreements, difficulties making decisions and no regular pattern of protected time for them to enjoy each other's company.

Key to their environment was their engagement in their work lives. Rachel deeply valued her high-pressure demanding role in publishing and worked a great deal. She was on the cusp of significant career advancement. At the same time, she stated, *"my biological clock is ticking very loudly and we need to make a decision soon – are we going to have a family or not?"* For James on the other hand there were significant career difficulties. His bookshop was losing money and he experienced real difficulties managing the financial aspects of the business. He refused Rachel's offers of help with this, feeling, 'managed', insulted, and belittled. He lamented the setbacks he had experienced in establishing himself as a professional musician, and his occasional gigs also functioned to prevent any regular couple time as Rachel disliked the crowded noisy environments plus the presence of alcohol.

Initial goals

Rachel and James readily stated that their goals included significantly reducing the intensity and frequency of their arguments, as well as finding new ways to approach each other in a positive fashion. They wanted to learn ways to *"soothe each other and ourselves"* as they could see how much their arguments resulted in physiological stress as well as poor sleep. Their main goal, stated in the first session, was a desire to learn how to communicate well with each other and to find ways of connecting and experiencing greater intimacy. Finally, they hoped to be able to make some significant decisions about their relationship and whether to progress towards the possibility of starting a family. This entailed making a range of other decisions, such as whether to move to another part of the country and whether the bookshop should be closed and sold off.

Early sessions – reducing negatives

Our early sessions took an explicit behavioural focus. Rachel and James agreed to monitor their pattern of using abusive or pejorative language with each other and to engage in response prevention. I also asked them to try to be aware of how they experienced the attempt to do so. Both acknowledged that while on the one hand this simple and direct intervention did result in an overall improvement in the atmosphere between them, they also at times felt frustrated as these negative patterns of communication at least functioned to allow them to *"get out what we are feeling rather than sitting on it."* The attempt to introduce more regular patterns of relating positively (such as 'date night'), however, met with much less success, as while they both agreed that they wanted this, they experienced difficulties making and keeping to decisions as to what they might do. This then led us to focus more directly on communication.

Sharing thoughts and feelings and problem solving

As was described in Chapter 2, work around communication skills is a central feature of CBCT. For James and Rachel, it did not appear to me that these skills for listening and speaking clearly and directly were absent, rather it was the degree of emotional distress that they experienced that blocked their ability to use them. Nevertheless, they showed great initial enthusiasm when presented with the communication guidelines as offering the potential for creating the *"safe space"* between them that they both stated they deeply desired but despaired of ever experiencing. Very quickly however, I found our sessions together to be very challenging. While my sense of liking and hope for them as a couple did not diminish, I too started to gain a direct sense of the frustration they both experienced with each other as communication work was frequently and rapidly derailed in session after session. The below was not an untypical series of interactions between the three of us:

THERAPIST: Rachel, I wonder if you would be willing to take the speaker role first today?

RACHEL: Yes ok…but I'm not at all sure he's willing to listen… he says he is, and it seems to me that he almost acts as if he is when he's here in the session, like he's on his best behaviour and wants to show you that he's such a good listener. But at home, if I approach him… even if we had agreed when and where we would practice this…he just shuts me down with an imperious wave of his bear paw!

JAMES: (raising his voice and looking at the sky) Oh come on Rachel… will you just for once step up to this? Why can't you be willing to show up?… have some courage and share how you're feeling for once rather than just picking at me with little barbs. What's the point Rachel? What is it?

THERAPIST: Ok, can we pause? Can I ask you both to pause? Maybe breathe a bit and sit back in the couch. Just take a second.

(In a session previous to this I had introduced them both to a practice of mindful breathing, which we had practiced in session and which they both found helpful, Rachel linking it to her years of practicing yoga.)

THERAPIST: Rachel – you got a pretty sharp and hard response there from James… any sense of how that might have happened?

RACHEL: Yes Ok… again I called him a big angry bear. I'm just feeling defensive, I guess.

JAMES: As usual!

THERAPIST: Ok…well let's start again. Give yourself a chance Rachel to get to what's important for you. Try and present it in a way that's more likely to be something James can hear. And James… keep breathing! You say you want Rachel to talk more openly…try and show her…with your body language and eye contact…that you are willing to listen and that its safe for her to speak to you.

JAMES: (raising his voice again) But it is safe! How can I make it safer when its already as safe as it gets? And anyway, what does it mean to be safe?

Why must we feel safe? How can we get to anything deep and important if at the same time we have to feel safe? What if it's not actually safe? Can't we just get to something important and deal with it?

THERAPIST: (Leaning forward and addressing James directly while trying to also relax my own breathing). Of course, that's important James. It is important that you two get to talk about what is most central. We are working to try and make that possible. But what's your sense now James? What's your best guess about what the impact of your statement just now has been on Rachel?

JAMES: (more quietly now) Well I think she will just shut down and stop. We are stuck again aren't we? I'm sorry... I just get frustrated. I want to get somewhere in our session that's all. I'm sorry Rachel. Please do speak. I'll do my best to listen.

RACHEL: (with tears starting to show and looking down) I just feel I have no voice. I have no voice in this relationship. I can't be in a relationship in which I don't have a voice! Anything I bring to you just gets this reaction, I just get shut down...

THERAPIST: Rachel... it's true that you often feel shut down and without a voice. We are working to change that experience. Give yourself a minute just to get in touch with something you would like to address with James. Have a look at him now. Look at his face. He seems to be willing to hear from you and has said that he will do his best to listen. If you have a look, do you think it could be worth the risk of trying?

RACHEL: (looks at James for a good 30 seconds while trying to slow her breathing). Ok...Ok...so I will go for something specific. I mean yesterday is just a clear example. I tried to talk to you James... you say you also want a baby... you say we are a great couple and that we will move ahead. But you won't even talk to me about it... I came to your office... knocked on the door and even before I can sit down you are throwing a book at the wall and stamping your feet!

JAMES: (again raising his voice) Oh come on! That isn't fair! That's not legitimate at all Rachel. For a start I didn't throw a book or stamp my feet. I was deep into the financial mess that I'm in...deep into trying to sort things out so we can move ahead, and you approach me with a look that says I'm about to tell you that you have cancer! Then you leave without a word and slam my door on your way out!

THERAPIST: Ok let's pause again! Take a breath!

Working with central themes

Sessions with Rachel and James progressed in a one step forward two steps back fashion. The sessions often felt dramatic, draining, and also engaging and hopeful. I found that I often needed to use more structure and to intervene more frequently that I typically like to do. I worried that I was adopting too much of a teaching, paternal role. This was made even more explicit when during one heated session James took a pause and stated to me *"well I can really see we benefit when there is one adult in the room..."* This feeling of taking on too much of a parental role was reinforced in supervision, with my supervisor challenging me as to why I seemed to be working so hard, harder at times than the couple appeared to be. This was a challenge to think about. However, both in my practice as a couple therapist, and as a supervisor of couple therapists, I have found it invaluable to reflect upon the possibility that the therapist's schemas are implicated in whatever impasse or dilemma is being encountered.

Nevertheless, mostly ignoring this good supervisory advice and giving my own schemas a pat on the head to calm down, I persisted, and slowly, the sessions which focussed on the most recent incident of upset or conflict evolved into discussions of more central, cross situational themes. There was a gradual reduction in the frequency of arguments and pejorative language although this could still be set off very rapidly should a suitable trigger be experienced. With some humour, Rachel and James acknowledged a sense that there was something more familiar and somehow reassuring about engaging in a familiar pattern of fighting, like watching a re-run of a favourite sitcom. We gave a name to these interactions *"The manager and the bear"*. More unfamiliar and challenging, was maintaining a relationship of intimacy and calmness.

Their efforts at decision making regarding the future of the bookshop and plans towards having a child remained a consistent block for the work. Each time these themes were addressed a pattern of approach-avoid, negative reciprocity, and avoid-avoid resulted. Most often, James felt these conversations did not work as he felt controlled and cornered, his need for autonomy, difference and space threatened in an unwelcome fashion. For Rachel, these conversations served to raise her anxiety and increase her sense of hopelessness, as her need for certainty, planning and security was consistently frustrated. Feeling this frustration, Rachel started to talk of the possibility of separating, expressing that it was somehow impossible to go forward, at which James would become highly anxious, accusing her of inauthenticity and cowardice while at the same time asking her to stay and keep fighting for the relationship. *"You ask me to stay and fight and yet when I approach you give me your bear growl and all I can do is run. How can we live like this?"* We seemed to reach a point of stalemate during sessions and no amount of psychoeducation, empathic joining, structuring, homework setting, sharing thoughts and feelings, or even the infrequent feeble attempts at semi-psychodynamic interpreting got us unstuck. As James remarked, these sessions could feel *"just too damn hard!"*.

Crisis

A break in our weekly sessions occurred after session 25, with James going away to a book fair. Rachel, in a state of anxiety, took this opportunity to look through James' office and to her horror and deep distress she discovered that James was very seriously in debt to a level he had not previously disclosed. Additionally, she discovered via her IT skills that he had been texting with Sharon (his ex-partner) and had met her on at least one occasion. These messages appeared flirtatious and indicated that James had mentioned ongoing problems in his relationship to Rachel. Rachel was devastated and furious. Upon his return Rachel confronted James with her 'evidence'. James pleaded with her to listen, insisting that he had not had an affair with Sharon, that it was *"just talking"* and that he was working as hard as he could to solve the financial situation. In our sessions, Rachel came to believe that James was stating the truth about his communication with Sharon, but she could not accept the level of secrecy surrounding the financial debt. For my part I remained sceptical about the contact with Sharon. James seemed to plead with us both to accept this as just a minor blip *"come on! It isn't a South American soap opera! Nothing has really happened. We can deal with it!"*

Break up

While the initial shock of Rachel's discovery soon dissipated, the frequency of the couple's arguments and their use of pejorative contemptuous language returned to previous levels. Rachel requested a two week break from sessions as well as from contact with James. Upon her return, Rachel announced, in the session, that she had decided she needed to end the relationship.

RACHEL: I just can't do this James... I just feel so unsafe and insecure all the time with you. And I can't seem to get over the money thing. I just don't see you actually trying to resolve it and you won't let me help you with it at all, so I still don't know what's really happening. I can't live this way. I'm too old for this really.

JAMES: (angrily) Well that's just cowardice isn't it! Why after all this work would you walk away now? We have been working so hard to fix things and have learnt a lot. We communicate much better than we did. It's getting better not worse, isn't it?

RACHEL: No, it's not getting better. I just feel for me what's happened over time is that I see more and more clearly what happens between us. I know it's not the same as it was with Robert. I know you are not an abusive man. But what happens is still not healthy and I don't want to live in this sort of stress.

JAMES: But...

THERAPIST: (interrupting) James can I ask you to slow down just a bit? I just want to make sure you are listening to what Rachel is saying before you respond. As you just said, you have worked a lot on communication here, can you use that now?

JAMES: (sighing heavily) Yes ok… Rachel you are saying you can't take this relationship anymore, you don't have the heart… the strength …for it. It feels too toxic, and you want out.

RACHEL: (also sighing) Well I did not use any of those words… it's not about strength or heart… well…It is about heart, I guess. My heart can't take this. I want…I need to separate.

THERAPIST: Rachel, it seems that you waited for the session to say this. I am wondering, does this statement mainly reflect the frustration and distress you are having right now? As in, is this mostly a reflection of how hard it feels at the moment, or is this a decision you have made and that seems correct to you… even if you feel ambivalent?

RACHEL: (stating firmly) This is a decision… I have taken time to think… I have spoken to friends who have for months and months urged me to leave… I haven't told them everything of course but I have listened to them as they say I have been looking terrible…lost weight, tired and haggard all the time. No – this is not just an emotional reaction. I need to do this for me, for my sanity's sake.

This session proved to be a painful one. James remained angry and hurt at Rachel's statements and disbelieving that she was serious. Rachel suggested that perhaps now was the time to end our sessions and James furiously agreed, stating *"well yes… what's the point if you are no longer willing to work, no longer willing to fight for this relationship?"* Towards the end of the session, I made the case for continuing, even if this meant our goal was now one of working with a separation process.

THERAPIST: I would like you both to really consider returning for a few more sessions. As we discussed right at the beginning of our work together, our goal has primarily been one of helping you both to arrive at the best possible decisions about your relationship. That's true even if you both make different decisions. I think there can be substantial benefit to coming back to talk through the impact of this on you both and what this relationship has meant to you both.

JAMES: But why? If she just wants to leave, she should leave. I don't really want that, but I know I can survive that and be ok… we should just cut and run now… it's over.

THERAPIST: Yes, you could do that… and often when a relationship ends people tell themselves a new story about the relationship. Usually, a highly negative one in which the whole thing was just a mistake, and their partner was crazy or bad. This in one way can help the separation as it gives some fuel to anger and contempt. But it doesn't do any justice to what the relationship has actually meant to you both. What the loss means and how you are actually experiencing that. James, you often speak about the need for courage and to show up. I am asking if you are willing to show up and have a separation process that does the least damage possible to you both. Are you both willing to do that?

Separation Therapy

James and Rachel agreed to attend three further sessions to see how this might be of help to them. In these sessions I asked them to stay with the communication guidelines that they had worked with in order to listen to each other as deeply as possible. I asked them to talk to each other about what this relationship has meant, what it means for them to separate and what they are losing. These sessions were difficult, with frequent need for me to interrupt and provide structure. They could easily slide into rehashing the argument from a day or two ago, however with support they were able at times to talk more openly and with some vulnerability.

RACHEL: James... we have argued and fought and tried really hard to fix things between us. I know you have really tried. I can't stay in this relationship. I know that a lot of that is to do with me. It's to do with my past relationships and just how scared I get. We tried to make things feel safer and more secure. But they don't feel secure for me.

THERAPIST: James can you let Rachel know what you heard? I know this is really tough...I know it's not what you want...but can you let her know you have understood her?

JAMES: (looking deflated) Actually I am exhausted too... and I think you are right. It's just been so hard and yes we have tried. You are saying that it's too hard, that I make you too anxious and afraid and you can't get over it. You want to feel better, safer, and not to have to worry so much.

THERAPIST: Rachel can you say more? Can you say what this means to you? This relationship ending?

RACHEL: Yes... (now with tears but still maintaining eye contact) James you are a lovely man. You can be gentle and kind and I still love your go with the flow easy style. You can light up a room and just be so much fun to be with. I am losing that and I am losing the hope of us having a child together. That is so so hard to walk away from. I am getting older, and I may not get another chance. I am losing the future we talked about and that I had planned out in my head in so much detail. I have no idea now what I am walking towards.

THERAPIST: James what is Rachel telling you?

JAMES: (also with tears) That's she still thinks I'm a lovely man... not just a big angry bear... That she is losing the future she hoped for with me. That it's awful but she doesn't know what else to do and has to leave...I just don't agree...

THERAPIST: James, can you also tell Rachel what this means to you, how this is for you to separate?

JAMES: Yes. This feels like I lose my best friend. And my last hope to have a good relationship. My last hope to change how I am. I'm losing the fun and passion we had, the chance to be a father and to have something more grounded and settled. In part it's also a relief… I'm tired of fighting and I feel defeated. I just want to rest now as well.

Rachel and James attended three sessions devoted to exploring the meaning of separation for them and how they were experiencing this. To some extent they managed to validate each other's experience, and this seemed to help them regulate the deep feelings of hurt they both felt. There was little to do in terms of practical decision making as they had not yet entwined their finances and possessions, a fact that they had previously referred to as an expression of their mutual avoidance of the relationship. I asked each of them how it was for them to come back for these three sessions, focussed as they were on separation:

JAMES: Well its terrible. Awful and painful. And also somehow its very different from what I would usually do. I would usually just end the relationship as quick as possible and probably have a tantrum and just decide the whole thing was a mistake. Somehow this was at least something that meant we separated with some grace…we honoured the relationship rather than trashing it. That's new. Maybe I can take some of what we did into the future somehow…but definitely not now. I want to just walk along the beach now.

RACHEL: Its definitely terrible. But it also helped me. I would have left scared and worried about James and how he might react even though I don't think he would do anything as such. But I would be scared. I felt he heard me and respected my decision and could still see the good things in our relationship. This was new for me also.

Conclusions

Can there be such a thing as a 'good enough separation'? Working with Rachel and James felt to me highly engaging, and also frustrating, bewildering, and confusing at times. Despite the stated goal of helping a couple make the best decisions possible about their relationship, which includes the possibility of deciding to separate, I was, throughout, working hard to improve things. I felt committed to the project of improving the relationship and believed that this could be achieved. I liked them both and the energy in their relationship, and hoped that things could be improved to the point where their relationship did indeed feel like a safe space. This hope was not realised, and this felt like a loss and a failure for me as well. I was aware that I did not feel convinced that separating was "*the best decision*". It's not up to me, I reminded myself. I admired their courage to come back for those three separation sessions and to sit with and explore the impact and meaning of that. My supervisor was correct of course, that I worked a bit too hard and took a bit too much responsibility in this work, reflected in subsequent supervision sessions where I attempted to locate the various 'mistakes' I had made and possibilities for intervention that I could have, should have tried. For example, this couple very much fit the description of a "High Conflict Couple" (Fruzzetti, 2006) and while I did include some practice of body focussed mindfulness strategies to increase distress tolerance, more could have been done to emphasise distress tolerance and there could have been a greater focus on the experience of validation in the communication work. These reflections can of course be carried forward into future relationships with challenging couples.

Therapist Tips

- Be aware that while a stated goal of couple therapy may be to improve or save a relationship, one or both parties may have seriously considered separation.
- While separation may result in some severe negative reactions from couples, such a decision and outcome is not necessarily a failure.
- Couple therapy need not end at the point at which the decision to separate has been reached. Many of the interventions used in CBCT and IBCT can assist a couple in managing the emotional fallout from the decision, regulate their distress, explore the meaning of the relationship and its ending, and make needed decisions about a whole range of issues that arise such as finances, belongings, and parenting.
- Good supervision is essential when working with such couples as it can be demanding work and the therapist's own schemas, beliefs and emotions regarding relationships may be implicated and challenged.

Suggestions for further Reading

Lebow, J. L. (2019). *Treating the Difficult Divorce: A practical guide for psychotherapists.* Washington, DC: American Psychological Association.

References

Ahrons, C. R. (1994). *The good divorce: Keeping your family together when your marriage falls apart.* New York: Harper Collins.
Baucom, D. H., Fischer, M. S., Corrie, S., Worrell, M., & Boeding, S. (2020). *Treating relationship distress and psychopathology in couples: a cognitive behavioural approach.* London: Routledge.

Fraenkel, P. (2023). *Last Chance Couple Therapy: bringing relationships back from the brink*. New York: W W Norton.

Fruzzetti, A. E. (2006). *The High Conflict Couple: a dialectical behavior therapy guide to finding peace, intimacy, and validation*. Oakland: New Harbinger.

Lebow, J. L. (2019). *Treating the Difficult Divorce: A practical guide for psychotherapists*. Washington DC: American Psychological Association.

Lebow, J. L. (2023). Divorce Issues in Couple Therapy. In J. L. Lebow & D. K. Snyder (Eds.). *Clinical Handbook of Couple Therapy*. 6th Edition. New York: Guilford Press.

Part Three

Concluding Comments

Chapter 18

The Challenges, Dilemmas, and Rewards of CBT Couple Therapy

Michael Worrell and Marion Cuddy

As we hope has been apparent throughout the chapters of this book, working with couples can be challenging! At the same time, we believe this book has provided ample illustration that the broad field of CBT approaches provides the therapist with a wealth of perspectives, possible interventions, and ways of making sense of couple difficulties. Working with couples from a CBT perspective can be highly engaging for those who venture into the field. It can be a richly rewarding aspect of a wider clinical case load, even where the therapist does not wish to present themselves as a 'couples expert'. In addition, our own experience is that working with couples, and learning to think more relationally within a CBT frame, also changes the way one works with individuals, families, and groups, one's approach to supervision, and has an impact on one's own interpersonal relationships. In this final chapter, we the editors reflect on our experience of working with couples, plus what we feel has emerged from reading the many varied clinical stories presented in this book and working with our contributors in the creation of their chapters.

Challenges

What makes working with couples so challenging, demanding, and at times frustrating, alarming and infuriating (as well as rewarding)? As many of the preceding chapters have shown, a good deal of the challenge arises from having two people in the room, plus the relationship between them, and the therapist's own position as a 'third' in the relationship. This creates a challenge in terms of complexity.

Complexity

The CBT couple therapist needs to process a great deal of information, in any particular session, and at the same time relate this information to key aspects of theory and empirically based research findings, and decide how to intervene. When formulating and planning treatment they need to consider

DOI: 10.4324/9781003024439-21

both partners as individuals, including the contribution of their individual personalities, preferences and physical and mental health concerns, as well as the couple relationship and the context in which they exist. Furthermore, they often need to do this while at the same time managing the couple's difficult interaction and preventing it from escalating.

Most of the approaches to CBT couple therapy described in this book, with the exception of Chapter 16 on BCT for substance misuse by Andre Geel, emphasise that the approach is *principle based* rather than protocol driven. As such, the therapist needs to rely on their ability to flexibly draw upon key principles, in order to select and employ an intervention strategy in a manner that is appropriate for the specific couple at that specific point in the therapy. CBT couple therapy would therefore seem, for the most part, to be appropriate for therapists who both enjoy and have a capacity to process complex information quickly, as well as a tolerance for a degree of 'not knowing' what the direction of a particular therapy session or a therapy as a whole may be.

The therapeutic relationship

A second challenge arises from the 'expanded' therapeutic relationship in couple therapy (Sprenkle et al., 2009). The therapist's needs to form an alliance with the partners both individually and as a couple, and there needs to be a 'good enough' working alliance between the partners in order for therapy to succeed. Ruptures can occur in any of these alliances, for example if the partners are not in agreement about the goals for therapy, if they have a weak *collaborative set* (see Chapter 3), or if one sees the therapist as siding with the other partner. The couple therapist needs to come across as credible and a 'safe pair of hands' in order to engage the couple and instil hope and motivation for change (Cuddy, 2018). An ability to work with an appropriate degree of flexibility, keeping participation of both partners balanced, and to adopt a more directive approach where needed are all important.

One issue that arises in the therapeutic alliance, and that is reflected in some of the chapters of this book, involves the therapist's own reactions to the two individuals or the couple. In other models of therapy this might be understood in terms of the therapist's counter-transference. While the term counter-transference is not quite at home in the CBT lexicon, it is well recognised that competent CBT therapists are able to become aware of and to work with their own personal reactions in therapy, and that doing so can at times be of great benefit to the clients (Moorey and Lavender, 2018). Authors such as Leahy (2015) have advanced CBT consistent models and perspectives on the nature of the phenomena captured by the terms transference and counter transference, and have pointed to the central role of what has been termed 'therapist schemas' in understanding this. This can include schemas that a therapist hold in regards to their understanding of self-as-therapist as well as broader schemas relating to self-other and self-world.

Therapist beliefs

Our experience is that working with couples can often lead to therapists becoming aware of, and needing to reflect upon, a range of couple and relationship related schemas that may not be active in quite the same way in individual therapy. Most often these schemas are revealed in supervision sessions where a therapist has had an uncharacteristically strong emotional reaction in response to a couple or one of the individuals that make up that couple. In supervision focused on individual therapy, it is not uncommon to find that an apparent impasse in therapy is in some fashion related to the supervisee's schemas around perfectionism or the need to be of help to all clients. While such schemas certainly show up in couple therapy focused supervision, schemas and beliefs related to *"this is not how a couple relationship should be"* or *"this is not how one should interact with in-laws/children/others"* or *"this is not how power and control should work in a relationship"* also tend to be activated.

One of us, (MW) recently taught a class of advanced doctoral level trainees in clinical psychology on the topic of couple therapy. During a video demonstration focusing on the strategy of guided behaviour change, one trainee became very angry at what was perceived to be the sexist attitudes of the male partner, who had (tentatively and anxiously) expressed a previously unsaid desire for his partner to dress *"a little sexier"*. The reaction was understandable and potentially could lead to a fruitful discussion of the history of feminist challenges to models of couple therapy and how the issues of power can be addressed. In order to do so however, trainees would need to be supported to become aware of both their own reactions and the requirement to remain focused on the needs of the individual and couple, even when these are inconsistent with or a challenge to their own attitudes and beliefs.

The practice of CBT couple therapy is likely to expose trainees to wide range of relationship behaviours and beliefs that are different to their own. One of our hopes in creating this book was that authors may choose to show a little more of their own experiences of working with couples so that readers could get more of a 'lived sense' of what this work is like. This we hoped would include times of confusion, frustration, annoyance, excitement, and satisfaction that we both know can be encountered. On the whole, our authors have chosen to be mostly discreet in a British fashion and to emphasise how their personal reactions are managed by reference to theory and supervision. This is of course entirely appropriate. We hope that nevertheless readers have managed to gain a helpful glimpse, even if brief and somewhat 'neatened up' of the therapist's experience through these tales of couple therapy.

Therapist stance

The couple therapist needs to be adept at simultaneously managing the session structure, their interaction with each individual, and the interaction between the partners. Most forms of couple therapy, both within and outside of a CBT perspective, advance a relatively more active and directive therapeutic stance compared to individually focused therapy. Here 'directive' can be understood in terms of *process* directive rather than *content* directive. That is, the therapist needs to be able at times to interrupt the couple or an individual, such as when they are engaging in negative reciprocity, and to redirect them onto processes that may have a greater chance of assisting them to achieve their stated goals.

Both of us are heavily engaged with the training of individual CBT therapists as well as CBT couple therapists. For the most part, people complete their individual CBT training and become adept and confident in this work prior to taking on CBT Couple therapy training as a new modality to extend their clinical practice. One of the most commonly encountered early challenges for such well-trained individual therapists, is that of taking on this more active and directive therapeutic style. In most cases, the training they have received favours a highly collaborative and receptive stance and they have worked very hard to become highly Socratic in their approach. Many new CBT couple therapy trainees report that learning to interrupt a couple or individual "*just feels rude!*" However, the direct contingencies of working with couples in distress will generally shape their subsequent behaviour in the direction of greater process directiveness. That is, therapists quickly realise that although it can be a helpful part of the assessment to observe a couple's negative pattern of interaction 'live', allowing arguments to escalate during therapy sessions tends not to be constructive.

A somewhat related issue is the need for CBT couple therapists to become comfortable and adept in dealing with couples' emotional experience in a more direct way than may be the case in individual therapy. They may need to deal with high levels of expressed emotion, minimised emotional expression, or differences between partners in their emotional experience that lead to conflict and distress. Both of us have had the repeated experience of CBT couple therapists in training saying to us something like "*wow, this is really challenging, in our individual CBT training we were not really taught to work with emotions like this… it feels a bit scary!*" This may reflect a deficit in this aspect of individual CBT training, but more likely, it results from the reality that due to the nature of couple work, therapists need to be comfortable in containing and responding to higher levels of dysregulated emotions as well as the very broad range of emotional experience that shows up when dealing with one of the most meaningful domains in many people's lives- their most intimate and close personal relationships.

Access to training and supervision

CBCT is a relatively new field in the UK, and as outlined above, working with couples can initially feel very different and even deskilling to therapists who are trained to work with individuals. The need for high quality specialist supervision is therefore paramount. Whilst this supervision is usually provided to therapists while they are completing a couple therapy training programme, many struggle to access ongoing supervision and additional training once they have qualified. This means that therapists can find it difficult to consolidate their skills and grow in confidence, and in some cases newly qualified therapists have ceased to work with couples because they did not feel supported to do so in their workplace. Organisations such as the Couples Special Interest Group of the British Association for Behavioural and Cognitive Psychotherapies (BABCP) are working to develop supervision networks, organise training events, and promote interest in CBCT in the UK, but more of this is needed to allow the discipline to flourish across the country and develop a community of CBT couple therapists.

Outcome measurement

Another challenge in couple therapy relates to what constitutes a good outcome. In many individual therapies, and certainly in individual CBT, outcome tends to be measured by the extent to which the person has *recovered*, or at least *reliably improved* according to validated measures of the problem being treated. Certainly, most couple therapists feel that their work is more rewarding when a course of therapy leads to improvements in the relationship and on measures of relationship satisfaction and psychopathology. However, is this the only good outcome for therapy? We would argue not. For example, a therapist may work effectively with a couple and achieve some improvement in their relationship functioning as a result, but ultimately one or both partners may decide that they wish or need to end the relationship. At this point, if the clinician were to administer any of the commonly used scales to assess depression or anxiety, the results may seem to indicate a 'failed' intervention. In reality, the meaning of such a result may be far more ambiguous and may change over time. An increase in these symptoms might be experienced, understandably, during the acute phase of the separation, followed by a gradual reduction as the individuals adjust to their new life circumstances. As described in Chapter 17, sometimes in spite of the pain and upheaval a separation causes, it is ultimately the best long term decision for the partners' wellbeing or even safety.

There is a story (of uncertain origins) about a Chinese diplomat being asked by a European counterpart what their opinion was of the French revolution, or more specifically *"do you think this was a good thing?"* The response was apparently *"It's too early to tell."* Many outcomes of couple therapy may not be well captured by simplistic use of outcome measures.

The challenge of defining and measuring outcome in couple therapy poses problems for research evaluating the effectiveness of interventions and also in the commissioning of services, both of which rely heavily on quantitative measures of symptoms improvement over relatively short periods of time. Although these measures are important and useful, they do not capture the whole picture and the additional inclusion of both qualitative methods of evaluation and service user involvement and feedback can be hugely beneficial.

Culture and Diversity

Culture and diversity offer both challenges and rewards to the couple therapist. As described in Chapter 9, culture has a significant impact on a person's approach to and expectation of their interpersonal relationships, and also of therapy. There are a number of other diversity considerations that need to be held in mind, including sexual identity and orientation, racial identity, neurodiversity, disability and age. The therapist needs to be curious about both partners' attitudes and beliefs, their similarities and differences, the impact of these and also consider the context in which they occur. There needs to be agreement about the tasks and goals for therapy, which can be tricky even without a cultural barrier or diversity considerations, and the therapist needs to ensure that these are consistent with the values and beliefs held by both partners, even if they hold different values themselves.

As therapists who are not British ourselves but who practice in central London, we find that culture and diversity can be immensely rewarding for relationships and for the therapist. It is not unusual to see a couple who are both from different cultural backgrounds, neither of which is the same as ours. Therefore, the therapist needs to be aware of three sets of cultural beliefs, or possibly four if neither partner is from the UK. There are additional issues to consider if one or both partners are second generation migrants to this country. This may sound like a headache to some, but it allows for fascinating conversations exploring, understanding and normalising differences, and can feel like a very enriching experience for the therapist. For some individuals and their partners, it can feel more acceptable to explain their temperament or their difficulties in cultural terms such as being a *"loud Greek person"* or an *"Irish guy who doesn't do feelings"*, and if this helps to reduce blame and accusation and engage clients in constructive conversations about their differences it can provide a first step towards empathic joining.

Dilemmas

Different perspectives

One of the interesting dilemmas we faced when editing this book was how to respond when we had different perspectives from the author, or even from each other. To some extent this is a normal dilemma in edited texts, which occurs on a continuum ranging from "*I would have used a different word here*" to "*I frankly disagree with what was said and think it is wrong/bad practice*". As editors, we had to hold the dialectic of wanting to preserve the authors voice and style, particularly since we had encouraged this expression and it was very much the ethos of the book, and feeling responsible for presenting what we considered to be helpful, sound and where possible empirically supported information to readers.

On the whole, we were hugely impressed by the quality of the chapters we received and feel that we have learned a lot from reading them. Nevertheless, it is quite interesting to reflect on the range of cognitive and emotional reactions we had to the chapters, at times feeling 'bowled over' by the clarity or richness of the information, excited about the contribution we think it will make to the field of couple therapy and development of future therapists, and of course at times anxious about whether and how we should reframe a passage we did not agree with. This was also the case when we wrote together or provided feedback on each other's chapters, and helped us to reflect on our own styles as both therapists and authors and note the similarities and differences. We believe that the differences are complimentary and that we have struck a good balance of acceptance and change in our role as editors, in line with the principles we hope to illustrate.

What have we missed?

Another dilemma we encountered in the preparation of this book concerned what to include and what could be left out. As mentioned in Chapter 1, the field of cognitive behavioural couple therapy is broad and there are exciting new developments occurring in a number of areas. Indeed, in the time it has taken us to put this book together there have been significant advances and changes. One that seems important to mention is the increased acceptability of delivering couple therapy remotely through video appointments, which many therapists would have been reluctant to do prior to the Covid 19 pandemic.

None of the chapters in this book have explicitly addressed the experience of challenges of remote couple therapy, and there are other important areas that we have not included. We have not described the challenges of offering couple therapy through an interpreter. Although there are chapters on couple-based interventions for several forms of psychopathology, we have not described couple-based interventions for disorders such as anorexia nervosa, obsessive-compulsive disorder, and bipolar affective disorder, although such interventions have been developed and show promising results. We have not mentioned working with couples where there is intellectual disability or a neurodegenerative condition. We have not presented the challenges of working with couples who have 'blended' families, or even the normal garden variety challenges of couple therapy in the context of multiple normal competing demands such as having to juggle teenage children, ageing and increasingly dependent parents and stressful jobs.

In spite of these gaps, we believe we have put together a rich and varied collection of case studies that therapist can learn from and note principles and techniques that can be generalised to other settings. We did not set out to provide an exhaustive list of couple presentations. This would simply be impossible, and actually every couple presents with a unique set of challenges, so that two couples with the same primary problem such as depression could have very little in common and require substantially different courses of therapy. As has been mentioned several times already, the approach we take is principle based, and we hope the key principles of CBT couple therapy and how they can be adapted and applied to different couples and situations have been well illustrated throughout this book.

Underrepresented client groups

Most couple therapy research across all orientations has focused on white, heterosexual, and largely married couple, often in university towns. Clearly this is not representative of all the couples that become distressed or could benefit from a couple-based intervention.

Some attempts have been made to develop more responsive ways of working with the specific needs of a range of individuals and couples, such as those with low incomes, same sex, non-cisgendered couples as couples from non-Western cultures, but more attention needs to be paid to these under-represented groups. Significant advances have and continue to be made in research that explores the issues of difference, diversity and intersectionality. In this book, Chapter 7 on sexual minority clients, Chapter 9 on the complexities of language and culture, and Chapter 15 on neurodiversity are significant contributions to this and in our view demonstrate that CBCT and IBCT contain within them the theoretical and practical resources to assist therapists in effectively challenging and developing their competence in these areas.

Rewards

One of the most rewarding aspects of couple therapy, particularly when it goes well, is that it offers the therapist the opportunity to witness change occurring *in the therapy room*. Individual therapies rely largely on clients' self-reported improvements in symptoms or functioning. In contrast, the couple therapist is able to observe changes in the couple's interaction during sessions. It can be immensely validating as a therapist to see partners who previously presented as hostile or guarded towards each other *soften* in their interactions, or notice that they are smiling at each other or holding hands when entering the therapy room.

Having the 'problem' *in the room* also offers opportunities for active, in session interventions. It can be more challenging to treat individual problems, for example, when they only occur in certain contexts, such a person with OCD who only engages in checking rituals at home and late at night. This limits the opportunities for in-session change methods such as behavioural experiments. With couples, where the focus is at least partly on the relationship, there are ample opportunities to use active interventions in every appointment.

As mentioned at the start of this chapter, working with couples can help a therapist to become more relational in their thinking no only when delivering therapy, but also in the context of supervision, organisational management and in their own interpersonal relationships. Couple therapists will say this relational understanding can help them become more appreciative of their own partner, offer more compassionate leadership in their managerial roles, and add another dimension to their supervision practice.

Furthermore, our experience has been that one of the benefits of working with couples is that it sensitises the therapist to the relational dimension of seemingly individual problems. As many chapters in this book have shown, issues such as depression (Chapter 10), post traumatic stress disorder (Chapter 13) and personality disorders (Chapter 12) all have a relational element and relational consequences that may remain invisible and unaddressed by therapists who only see the individual with the diagnosis. This is in no way a criticism or a challenge to the effectiveness of individual treatments for these clinical presentations, but rather points to the possibilities that might be realised by taking a wider relational lens and more formally involving partners in treatment when appropriate.

We hope that the chapters in this book have inspired readers who have not yet added couple therapy to their repertoire to obtain training to do so, as well as giving food for thought and offering new ideas and possibilities to those already practising couple therapy as a regular and valued part of their day-to-day work.

References

Cuddy, M. (2018). Couples. In Moorey, S. & Lavender, A. (Eds.), *The Therapeutic Relationship in Cognitive Behaviour Therapy* (pp. 243–253). London: Sage Publications.

Leahy, R. L. (2015). *Emotional schema therapy.* New York: Guilford.

Moorey, S. & Lavender, A. (2018). (Eds.) *The Therapeutic Relationship in Cognitive Behaviour Therapy.* London: Sage.

Sprenkle, D. H., Davis, S. D., & Lebow, J. (2009). *Common factors in couple and family therapy: The overlooked foundation for effective practice.* New York: Guilford.

Index

macro level themes 28, 29
maladaptive communication 6
maladaptive strategies 19, 38, 174
marginalisation 110
marriage 3, 4, 108,
marriage counselling 4
Martell, C. 155
meaning stage 228, 234–238
measures 7, 27, 299–300
mechanisms of change 7
medical interventions 90
medication 90, 147
meltdowns 245, 246, 248, 251–255
meltdown thermometer 251, 253, 254
mental illness, cross cultural perceptions, and its treatment 141–142
metaphors 27, 32, 54, 64, 259
microaggressions 109, 118
micro level factors, 29
mindfulness 32, 44, 197, 198; skills 206; strategies 203, 205
minority stress 109, 110, 121
minority stressors 107, 113, 114
Minority Stress Theory 107, 111, 118
monogamy 110
Monson, C. M. 210, 217, 222, 223
Moore, T. M. 73
Moorey, S. 127
motivation 19, 29, 41, 43, 60, 95, 251; exploring 263
motives 19, 20, 24, 33, 263
moving-on stage 228, 238–243
mutual attack 42, 197, 203, 206
mutual trap 39, 41

National Institute for Health and Care Excellence 8, 261
needs 18, 19, 22, 24, 30, 33, 34, 37, 41, 47, 60, 65, 76, 83, 118, 145, 178, 196, 237, 302; core 24; for intimacy 23
negative: attributions, re-evaluating 82–83; automatic thoughts 25, 32; behaviour 17, 22–23, 29, 33, 47, 75, 146, 152; beliefs 117; emotions 26, 185, 238; reciprocity 23, 199, 204, 286, 298
neurodevelopmental conditions 245–248
neurodiversity 244–260, 300, 302; focus on strengths and positives 251; meltdowns 251–255; work on communicating emotions 256–258
neuroticism 19

Newman, C. 85
no-aggression contract 78, 79, 85
non cisgender couples 21, 302
non-monogamous relationships 114
Nordsletten, A.E., 175

obsessive compulsive disorder (OCD) 8, 174–175, 301, 303
O'Farrell, T. 261
operant conditioning 6
organisation difficulties 246–247
orientations 23, 26, 106, 300
outcome 7, 8, 17, 35, 107, 166, 234, 240, 252; measurement 299–300; treatment 7

Padesky, C. 155
pain 43, 90, 126, 131, 138, 203
Paprocki, C. 174
parenthood, transition to 71–87; couples and 73–74; couple therapy to support 75–76
parenting 41, 73–74, 76, 113–114
participating partner factors 236
partner aggression, couple therapy for 74–75, **75**
partner-partner transference 4
passive-aggressive communication style 120
patient-therapist transference 4
pattern of interaction 20, 38, 40–41, 43, 135, 196, 203, 298
Pentel, K. Z. 111
perfectionism 115, 117, 119
personality 18, 19, 37, 40, 54, 148, 150, 152; differences 22; factors 19, 33
personality disorder 191–207, 303; Double Chain Analysis 206; emotional regulation difficulties and couple therapy 191; treatment 197–205
physical aggression 72, 79, 221
physical environment 19
physical health (see also long term conditions) 8, 29, 72, 110, 125
physical relationship, working with 96–97
physical violence 73, 205
planning treatment 27–29, 33, 49, 153, 295
polarisation 39, 41, 42, 103, 129, 160
polarities 104